BIG BAD WOLVES

Masculinity in
the American Film

By the same author

THE BATTLE OF ALGIERS

MARILYN MONROE

WOMEN AND THEIR SEXUALITY IN THE NEW FILM

VOICES FROM THE JAPANESE CINEMA

THE WAVES AT GENJI'S DOOR: JAPAN THROUGH
  ITS CINEMA

BIG BAD WOLVES

MASCULINITY IN THE AMERICAN FILM

BY
JOAN MELLEN

PANTHEON BOOKS, NEW YORK

Library of Congress Cataloging in Publication Data

Mellen, Joan.
Big Bad Wolves.

Includes index.
1. Men in motion pictures.   2. Masculinity (Psycho-
logy)   3. Moving-pictures—United States—History.
I. Title.
PN1995.9.M46M4 1977   791.43'0909'352   77-5189
ISBN 0-394-49800-3

Grateful acknowledgment is made to the following for permission to reprint
previously published material:

M. Evans & Co., Inc.: Selections from
Additional Dialogue: Letters of Dalton Trumbo,
1942–1962, edited by Helen Manfull. Copyright ©
1972 by Dalton Trumbo. Reprinted by permission
of the publishers, M. Evans & Co., Inc., New York,
NY 10017.

FOR ELEANOR PERRY

"The Walls of Jericho will protect you from the big bad wolf."
Clark Gable to Claudette Colbert in
It Happened One Night (1934)

"Everybody knows nobody ever stood in the street and let the heavy draw first. It's me or him. To me that's practical, and that's where I disagree with the Wayne concept.... I do all the stuff Wayne would never do. I play bigger-than-life characters, but I'll shoot a guy in the back. I go by the expediency of the moment."
Clint Eastwood

"Screen characters seem more like young ladies than real men, and it's time to re-establish the balance."
Sylvester Stallone

Acknowledgments

I would like to thank the National Endowment for the Humanities for a grant which enabled me to complete this project.

For their help and encouragement, I would particularly like to thank Julie and Phyllis Jacobson for generously lending me rare documents from their private library and for many fine insights about the filmmakers of the forties and fifties.

Many people have discussed with me our culture's notions of what it means to be a man, but I would like especially to thank Jim Garrison and Donald Richie, who provided original ideas regarding the male perspective.

Charles Silver, head of the Film Study Center of the Museum of Modern Art, shared with me his considerable knowledge of the American cinema. I am also grateful to Stephen Harvey and Emily Sieger for working with me on the American silent film. Seth Willenson of Films Incorporated arranged private screenings of *The Crowd*, *Wings*, and *Cimarron*, for which I thank him. Films Images (Radim Films) generously made available their William S. Hart and Tom Mix Collection.

Jim Peck has been a discerning editor whose probing questions made this a better book.

Finally, I would like to thank Ralph Schoenman for reading this manuscript with rare intelligence and perception, and for bringing to our relationship the sensitivity of the liberated man.

CONTENTS

Illustrations

BIG BAD WOLVES

Masculinity in the American Film

Clint Eastwood: The ideal man of our films is a violent one. To be sexual he has had to be not only tall and strong but frequently brutal.

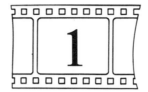

Introduction

This book is about the fabrication in American films of a male superior to women, defiant, assertive, and utterly fearless. Repeatedly through the decades, Hollywood has demanded that we admire and imitate males who dominate others, leaders whom the weak are expected to follow. The ideal man of our films is a violent one. To be sexual he has had to be not only tall and strong but frequently brutal, promising to overwhelm a woman by physical force that was at once firm and tender. Male stars are people manufactured from the raw material of humanity to appear as supermen overcoming women and lesser men by sheer determination and will, involving, in varying permutations, competence, experience, rationality—and charm.

Real men rarely exist who look strong and unflawed enough to portray such an ideal. As they could not be found, they were fabricated. Papier-mâché human beings were created to conceal real-life vulnerabilities in the male no less than in the female star. If Marilyn Monroe was a manufactured human being, a concoction of plastic surgery and hair dyes, so the males whom Hollywood has exalted as "stars" have been patched up to convey unrelenting, if pre-bionic, masculinity. Clark Gable had his ears pinned back and from a very early age wore false teeth. The false teeth of James Dean were also acquired young. And Gable shaved his chest and underarms in keeping with the pristine standard of the day, although that Fairbanks-style moustache was grown to convince us of his virility. Alan Ladd, a short man, stood on boxes to make him seem as tall as the women in his films. Errol Flynn had his nose bobbed. Douglas Fairbanks himself, originally named Julius Ulman, had to change his name to one sufficiently

Anglo-Saxon to impress women and enemies alike. As the most virile men were believed to come from the West, Tom Mix, born in Pennsylvania, a state presumably full of weak "Eastern" men, changed his state of origin to conform to the legends of masculinity and myths surrounding the conquest of the frontier.

A name like Marion Michael Morrison was thought far too effeminate, which induced its owner to become "John Wayne." Crowned "The Duke," Wayne could parade as the undisputed possessor of greater sexuality and power than were found in other men, even though in later years, like Henry Fonda, he would don a toupee. Fonda himself would undergo a face-lift. George Raft put on elevator shoes, and Marlon Brando, corsets to conceal his bulk. (Although in *The Missouri Breaks*, a film he made when he was already past fifty, Brando, weighing more than two hundred and fifty pounds, would defy the macho norm by concealing his bulk this time with a dress!) And Humphrey Bogart, who was born on January 23, 1899, had his birthdate changed on publicity releases to Christmas Day, 1900, in order to epitomize the energy of a new century.

Masculinity in American films has constantly been allied to both patriotism and Christianity. Rarely does a hero appear who is not Anglo-Saxon in origin, much less non-Caucasian. Exceptions like John Garfield, Kirk Douglas, or Paul Muni have changed their names, Garfield from Julius Garfinkle and Douglas from Issur Danielovitch Demsky; Paul Muni was originally Muni Weisenfreund. Latin lovers like Rudolph Valentino were a special, slightly suspect breed: a bit wild, mad, and not truly wholesome. We have become accustomed to deploring the falsity of the woman star with her silicone breasts, nose-jobs, and face-lifts. But no less than women have men been snipped and chiseled, remade according to an image Hollywood as an industry has found it desirable to invent.

The Big Bad Wolves of our movies are those male stars who have consciously and stridently demonstrated on screen what it means to be a man. Among them have been stars who appealed most to women, like Rudolph Valentino and Robert Redford, those who were men's men intended for a male audience, like John Wayne and Clint Eastwood, and those who offered material for fantasy in which both men and women could indulge, from Clark Gable to Humphrey Bogart.

The indomitable male has populated our films since the last shot of *The Great Train Robbery*, made in 1903, when a sinister-looking gentleman with a fierce handlebar moustache pointed his gun and fired at the audience. To this tradition belong the male stars who are meant to fulfill our purported need for heroes: men who protect the weak, serve justice, defeat evil, and relieve us, men and women alike, of any need to take responsibility for doing those defiant things in our own lives. The Big Bad Wolves include all those "strong," dominant screen males such as William S. Hart, Tom Mix, Douglas Fairbanks, Sr., Gary Cooper, Errol Flynn,

Henry Fonda, Alan Ladd, Marlon Brando, Kirk Douglas, Rock Hudson, Paul Newman, Charles Bronson, Steve McQueen, and Clint Eastwood. But they do not include those heroes of comedy who share with us our human vulnerability: Charlie Chaplin, Stan Laurel and Oliver Hardy, Buster Keaton, and even the Marx Brothers, powerless despite the havoc they wreak. Those heroes of the musical who dance and sing away our pain without overcoming it, led by Fred Astaire and Gene Kelly, are equally not among the Big Bad Wolves, for they fall outside the stereotype of the self-controlled, invulnerable, stoical hero who justifies the image of unfeeling masculinity as a means of winning in a world that pounces on any sign of weakness. The comedians treat as absurd and the musical stars as unreal the harsh world in which male heroes pontificate platitudes such as that invoked by an elderly John Wayne in *The Shootist:* "I won't be wronged, I won't be insulted, I won't be laid a hand on. I don't do these things to others, and I require the same of them."

Hollywood knows well that men cannot live by the models of masculinity it proffers. Never intending that men actually attempt to model themselves on such heroes, who would sacrifice every comfort and security for the sake of their beliefs (how dangerous to the social order!), it offers fulfillment to the audience through figures capable of feats of power and control inaccessible to mere mortals. Such heroic images afford men and women vicarious release while rendering them small and timid by comparison. They wish they could *know* such men; they have no illusions about resembling them. An abiding malaise results in the male, victimized by this comparison between himself and the physical splendor of the hero with whom he has so passionately identified. The vicarious discharge in the dark of his daily frustrations carries with it an unavowed threat of emasculation because he must re-enter the world feeling even less adequate—the opposite of what the movies seem to promise. Frustrated women, observing these same screen males, are equally released and frustrated again. When we leave the theater, catharsis behind us, we are left with nothing so much as an overwhelming sense of our own inadequacy. In seeming to entertain us, movies in a very real sense have exacerbated our pain.

American films have not only sought to render men powerless by projecting male images of fearsome strength and competence. They have also proposed consistently over the years that the real man is not a rebel but a conformist who supports God and country, right or wrong. The heroes who exhibit the most power stand for the status quo, even as they suggest that physical action unencumbered by effeminate introspection is what characterizes the real man; thus, in the most profound sense, the bold exterior of these men on screen conceals the fact that the films actually foster a sense of passivity by suggesting that such men are never rebels but can always be trusted to acquiesce in the established order.

A cacophony of whispering voices from television commercials, athletic coaches, and the backs of cereal boxes have urged the boys who have become our filmmakers (it is still overwhelmingly men who make movies) to offer us this image of manhood through characters modeled as closely upon John Wayne as possible. The authoritarian male who would be a strong and comforting father to us all resembles the patriarchal god of the Old Testament, just as the suspicion of women as dangerous to the sexuality of men is enshrined in the oldest male-recorded documents of our civilization. As the Book of Proverbs cautions, "Give not thy strength unto women" (31:3).

The immigrants who became studio moguls breathed in this ideology even as they brought to it remnants of feudal values of their own, perceiving them as the means of becoming successful in America. Reflecting existing values and emphasizing those which both satisfy and protect the corporations like Gulf & Western, Kinney, and RCA which have become the financiers of film, an image of men exercising raw authority, at once fearing and punishing women, has increasingly become the norm in American cinema.

This is the prevailing male image approved by writers, directors, and producers, and no less by the actors themselves who play such roles and then assume the posture in their own lives. Having grown up in a culture that punishes men for being nonphysical, actors have altered their lines and been willing to purge all psychological nuance from their roles in order to appear as unqualifiedly dominant males, at once reflecting and perpetuating entrenched values of male prowess and superiority. No matter that among such peoples as the gentle Arapesh of the South Seas, as pointed out by Margaret Mead, a man who is aggressive is shunned by all as disturbed and deviant. In our society, such is the power of the taboo surrounding the world of moviemaking that the actors themselves refuse roles which allow even a hint of male vulnerability. In *Polly of the Circus* Clark Gable balked at playing a priest, a man who could not exercise his virility in sexual relations; the role was changed to that of "preacher," the evangelist male exuding raw sensuality. Gable enjoyed *The Call of the Wild*, where he could exert his male power over nature, and *Test Pilot*, in which he could command the outer atmosphere. He did not consider Fletcher Christian in *Mutiny on the Bounty* a suitable role, fearing he would appear unmanly in knickers and pigtail. Another project was rejected by Gable because in the script the heroine hesitated too long before choosing him over Errol Flynn. He adamantly refused to affect a Southern accent for *Gone with the Wind* because he considered it effeminate, and battled for some time with his friend, the blatantly macho director Victor Fleming, over Fleming's insistence that he shed tears in the scene in which Scarlett O'Hara miscarries.

But it is not only Gable who has seen his role in movies as one of perpetuating the image of male power. Robert Redford brings to the screen the same sensibility. A real man, according to Redford the real-life person, acts and does not indulge in sissified thinking, always the sure sign of an inadequate male: "People who sit around analyzing all the time drive me crazy," Redford has declared. "They don't do anything, they don't go anywhere. They've never gone to the playground." The infantile image of the schoolyard reveals a profound fear for the safety of male sexuality, so deep that a sufficiently powerful threat would return men to being boys. On the set of *The Way We Were*, Redford insisted upon changes for the scene in which he is in bed with Barbra Streisand but, being under the influence of alcohol, fails to make love successfully. The script called for him to apologize and to promise, "Next time, it'll be better." Had it remained in the film, this line would have afforded us a rare moment of male sensitivity on screen. But Redford would not speak such words; he could not even admit that the character he was playing could ever fail to perform sexually on demand.

Similar anxiety was revealed, appropriately enough, by Redford's screen partner in *The Sting* and *Butch Cassidy and the Sundance Kid.* In 1976 Paul Newman considered playing a homosexual coach in a film called *The Front Runner*, a project he buried because, unlike Al Pacino in *Dog Day Afternoon*, he feared that portraying a homosexual would undermine both his screen and his real-life image, notwithstanding his fifties role as Biff in *Cat on a Hot Tin Roof.* Newman rationalized rather thinly: "I worried that the screenplay would be sensationalized, that the homosexual aspect would override the respect for individual differences ... loyalty, humor, generosity, talent, gentleness; these are traits I see as much more relevant than someone's sexuality." Actors, directors, producers, and writers alike censor themselves on behalf of highly restrictive mores, producing time and again in our films the myth of the heroic individual who tames the world through solitary personal effort.

As every culture has norms and dominant values defining what is "masculine" and "feminine," our films have been made in the service of quite specific images and ideals of manliness. The more a man possesses those qualities deemed feminine—such as intuition, tenderness, and affection for children—the less secure our films make him feel about his identity as a male. There have always been rumblings of discontent from men unwilling to harden themselves to conform to the standards approved by football coaches and army recruiters. But one overriding reason why change in our assumptions about the identity of "real" men has been so long in appearing in our culture is that the popular arts have been single-minded in their repeated demand that males in America conform to a cave-man model of masculinity. The question remains: what

Robert Redford: The script called for him to apologize and to promise,
"Next time, it'll be better."

stereotypes are promoted in our mass media and why? Who benefits from the dominance of certain values, and what are the consequences for people who are shaped by them?

Men and Violence

Film after film has insisted that the masculine male is he who acts—and kills—without a moment's thought. To think is to be a sissy, a bumbling eunuch of a man. At worst, the male in American movies has brutalized women, his violence incomplete unless it is reflected in his sexuality. It is as if masculinity would vanish were the male prerogatives of assertiveness and domination over others relinquished. Men with despised "female" traits, which may mean nothing more than gentleness and compassion for the weak, are scorned as unworthy of their sex. Our films are the products of a culture that is the opposite of those described by Margaret Mead in which men were *not* taught as boys to hate, despise, and fear women. Competitiveness under the guise of silence, solitariness, and freedom from domestic commitments defines the style of the violent hero.

And things have gotten worse. In the sixties director Sam Peckinpah came to the financial fore, asserting in his films that men are biologically aggressive and sadistic, while women are instinctual teases longing to be mastered by force. His males are most themselves when they can send geysers of blood into the air, and it would be repellent to Peckinpah that a society could exist where the rape of a woman by a man would be unthinkable.

When that rarest of images, that of the humanized male, appears, as in Al Pacino's performance in *Dog Day Afternoon,* the stereotype is abandoned in many of its vital aspects. Suddenly the hero is small and dark. He can overpower no one. He is not Anglo-Saxon—Pacino, an Italian, plays a Pole. And he is homosexual, having chosen that mode, not out of fear of or contempt for women, but because it genuinely pleases him. Yet Pacino's homosexual is at once more masculine and more at ease with his body than the rigid Eastwood or Bronson hero because, unlike them, he is relaxed about his sexual preference. He need prove his masculinity to no one; he need not hate his wife, although he has chosen another, nor be ashamed of Leon, his male lover. But this is one of the few positive portrayals of male homosexuality in the history of the American film.

Instead, most movies portray men in competition with each other, for women, money, status, and power, with the best man, the male hero played by Cary Grant or Gary Cooper or Clark Gable, winning. Individual initiative and the pleasure of competition are values approved by our

Al Pacino in *Dog Day Afternoon:* Pacino's homosexual is at once more masculine and more at ease with his body than the rigid Eastwood or Bronson hero because he is relaxed about his sexual preference. He need prove his masculinity to no one.

economy, and the male star demonstrates their virtue. Thus Clark Gable played a gambler in many of his films. To display weakness before another man would grant one's opponent an "edge," as the old Indian warns Clint Eastwood in *The Outlaw Josey Wales* (something Indians, who never had the edge, would know). Such values lead men to mistrust each other and hence to emotional impoverishment. Whether or not competition in fact still exists in an age of conglomerates does not matter: the value remains useful, if only to keep people at each other's throats in competing for work. This distortion, in life as in films, prevents many men from having male friends. The "Catch 22" applies again, as men, responding to the culture's demand that they not be vulnerable to each other—which has deprived them of open and feeling male friendships—use this deprivation as a reason to scorn women. This has resulted in the appearance in the late sixties and seventies of the "buddy film," in which a man, not out of unalloyed homosexual impulse but from the desire for male friendship, chooses one man to whom he can bare his soul.

The tradition of male violence in the American film derives from the Western's justification of the settling of the frontier by means of conquest. Countless Westerns celebrate this genocide and enshrine the violence essential to it in the figure of the silent, solitary hero devoted to justice in a community where the law either has yet to arrive or is already too corrupt to serve the needs of the people. From its beginnings the American film has maintained that only force enables a beleaguered community to survive, the family to continue, and the hero, victor in any competition with his adversaries, to remain alive. The Indians have usually been converted into vicious, marauding savages—not real men no matter how violent they appear—and the conquerors have become virtuous victims acting in self-defense. In chronicling our unavowed guilt and fears, our films have rewritten history.

In a primitive, ritualistic manner movies have defined manliness in terms of getting the "enemy" before he gets you. It is a set of values designed to nurture suspicion, fear of one another, and the need to rely on authority, as well as to exorcise through images of male prowess the sense of helplessness that life in America really induces in us. And this violence also expresses and releases the rage twentieth-century men feel over the diminution of masculinity that they suffer in their present-day lives, a masculinity that seems to have flourished on the open plains. As cowboy, cavalry man, gangster, private eye, or cop, the male hero has been created on the model of the frontiersman. To this primal experience American films repeatedly return, enabling audience men and women to escape from the impotence of white- or blue-collar life in which no wilderness remains. Movies reflect and create the need for a world where physical strength counts for everything, the opposite of the automatized society where violence is most often directed against ourselves.

Providing the most imaginative and attractive arena for escape, our films have fostered the need for heroes, men larger than life who derive from the legends of America's youth, the Mike Finks and Davy Crocketts who exorcised pioneer men and women's fear of the unknown and dangerous wilderness by exaggerating men's physical capacities. From this primitive desire for individual power over an alien environment, movies have drawn their men.

Because their circumstances are so fraught with peril, these heroes are depicted in films as loners, or they are accompanied by one male buddy, with whom they explore virgin territory, as Wayne and Walter Brennan do in *Red River,* one of the finest American Westerns. The hero drawn from pioneer legend is invariably undomesticated, enlisting his physical strength and skill in violence for the survival of a community of women, children, and weaker men, as Henry Fonda demonstrates playing Wyatt Earp in *My Darling Clementine* and as Alan Ladd does in *Shane*.

But the heroes of earlier films were violent only when necessary. As our social order has deteriorated, the image of maleness in American films has evolved to the point where violence is always necessary, and if a male begins as physically incapable of defending home and hearth, as Dustin Hoffman does in *Straw Dogs*, he learns soon enough that a man is not a real man unless he is also a competent killer. The male hero must always succeed alone. And this image of the loner who is indomitable enforces the notion that men must compete with each other in distrust and not get together for common ends. Atomizing men, paradoxically, keeps them weak, not strong, and by indirection keeps those in power strong and unthreatened, an insight that rarely surfaces in the American cinema.

The most dominant male image of all shows the hero as unburdened by family life, the plot sometimes compliantly freeing him from domestic commitments through accidental tragedy. John Wayne often played such a male, as do Dustin Hoffman and Robert Redford in *All the President's Men* as they delve into the mysteries of Watergate free of all those family responsibilities, mortgages, dental bills, school fees, and summer-camp selections which tie down nominally less masculine men, obligations which in our films are rendered the subject of comedy.

In the seventies the male hero is more violent than ever before, as if we in the audience, men and women, were more alienated from and discontented with our lives than were people in the past. The violence of the hero, instead of being projected into an obsolete frontier community, is now seen as the necessary weapon of the male citizen attempting to survive in the cities. The victims of poverty, slum dwellers, have become the new Indians, presumably to be dealt with as were the originals. Implicit is a racism as virulent as that directed toward the American Indian in early Westerns.

Violence in the Westerns was usually presented as necessary because the system of justice, the judges and the juries, the lawyers and the law, had been appropriated by evil, greedy men, and this was supposedly possible only because the community was not yet civilized. Today the hero takes the law into his own hands because the community is *too* civilized, the law too compassionate and understanding of the criminal. The hero can protect not just individuals but Western civilization itself only by restoring individual vigilante violence. With the cities disintegrating, police forces are not enough to keep order. Screen males, led by Clint Eastwood's Dirty Harry Callahan in three films, are urged to "supplement" the police against the mugging poor.

When a frustrated community seeks recourse in violence, the hero becomes a veritable dervish of violence himself, routing the unruly with his superior strength. The audience, although they resemble the victims rather than the hero, respond with approval because the film appeals to the very need of control over their own lives which, poverty aside, leads them to discontent. Played by Eastwood, Bronson, or one of their imitators, the hero of these vigilante films of the seventies trusts almost no one. Any stranger may turn out to be one of those disgruntled malcontents, and compassion itself might undermine his strength. It might damage as well his willingness to wreak the enormities of violence required to protect the social order from its multiple, nameless victims and hence enemies. The more violent the male in our films, the less likely he is to have a permanent woman in his life. The early gangsters had few; the vigilante of the seventies has none.

Dirty Harry is a man of very few words indeed. And the silence of the male hero in American films dates from *The Virginian*—ironically enough, from the beginnings of the sound film itself. Its origin was the frontier code in accordance with which companions on a cattle drive would not ask too many questions or inquire into each other's past. This was considered prying into a man's own business and likely to reveal instances of wrongdoing best left concealed. On the cattle runs the true cowboy was supposed to eschew complaining, bragging, and lying. He was judged by how silently he could endure the rigors of his life. His solace had to come, not from what were considered weak-minded confessions of uncertainty, regret, or fear, but from inner strength, self-confidence, and pride in tasks well done. To talk too much would violate this code and demean his mission. And complaining of the demanding conditions of his existence was not to be tolerated precisely because these were harsh and inescapable. If a man was a valuable person, others would soon enough discover it for themselves. But the reason for the equally tight-lipped posture of the ideal male of the seventies, with his impassiveness and brooding silence, is another matter entirely.

Although the Virginian, as befitted his profession of cowboy, spoke little—Gary Cooper was to remain taciturn in all his films—the early gangster movies were peopled by very talkative men. Little Caesar seems rarely to have been silent. When temporarily baffled, he could always produce his favorite put-down of a gangland rival: "He can dish it out, but he can't take it." But as the decades have passed, the silence of the cattle drive has been resurrected more and more as a model for all twentieth-century men, for cops like Dirty Harry as well as for those cowboys played by Henry Fonda, Gary Cooper, and Glenn Ford.

To be silent best befits a man of action who scorns analysis, has few thoughts, and feels little need for the irrelevance of explanations; our heroes have never been intellectuals. Bogart, of course, who often portrayed a man of clever mind if never an intellectual, talked a great deal, and so did Gable. But in the seventies, male silence has been sanctified with almost religious fervor. The Magnum pistol is to say it all. The more silent the hero, the greater his nobility and the more, illogically, we are urged to trust him. We are asked, in fact, to surrender ourselves to men about whom the film deliberately tells us little, as if in our real lives we were being prepared to grant power on faith alone to a leader about whom we actually know next to nothing.

Ours is an epoch of films glorifying the ideal of an elite of such leaders, who insist that only they are able to solve our social problems. At its close *The Towering Inferno* outlines this program. Fire chief Steve McQueen has barely spoken throughout the film. Now that the fire—a disaster parallel to that of the sniper on the loose in *Dirty Harry*—is under control, he makes his one significant speech. He pointedly informs the architect, played by Paul Newman, that if Newman wishes to prevent such disasters in the future, he must come and see him. McQueen is the leader better aware than the rest of blundering mankind, particularly its soft intelligentsia, of how to survive. He has proven this in action and not with words, which are appropriate only to babbling women and homo-sexual males. We, who are daily besieged by disaster, need now more than ever a strong man to take matters into his own hands.

The seventies epic thus brings us only a mini-step away from fascism. It is also significant that fireman McQueen, who has no involvement with women in the course of the film, is presented as infinitely more virile than Newman, who is engaged in a torrid love affair with Faye Dunaway. This assertion that the paternal, protecting, powerful male is the man most sexually alive prefigures the way that fascist values insinuate themselves into democratic communities by reviving the myth of the superman.

So universal has the image of the silent leader become that the actors who play these heroes must prove they are as silent in their personal lives as they are on screen. To grant their roles authenticity, actors personally become caricatures of their screen personae. "It's just that I don't like to talk very much," Charles Bronson has said. "Steve dislikes open emo-tions," McQueen's former wife has explained. "He believes that the true nature of a man is how much he can feel without showing it." The world of the seventies is perceived by filmmakers as so frightening and hostile to the male that for him to speak at all is to risk exposure of self and hence rejection, failure, and a kind of death—which may be no more than the collapse of the male façade.

Men and Men

When men in American movies are heterosexual and share their lives with a woman, they are generally deprived or incapable of friendships with men. From Brando in *On the Waterfront* to Bogart in *To Have and*

Have Not, The Big Sleep, and *The African Queen,* the model of masculinity in films is presented with an implicit choice: if he would link up with a woman, he has disqualified himself from enjoying male friendships.

Alternatively, adult male friendships, when they do occur, are preceded by the exclusion of women from the lives of the men. These quasi-homosexual friendships, such as that between Newman and Redford in their films, proceed only when women have been eliminated, as is Katharine Ross as Redford's woman in *Butch Cassidy and the Sundance Kid* when she realizes that her presence is superfluous. Conceding defeat, she leaves the two men to spend their final days alone together.

The male bonding in American films in which two men travel together, epitomized by the cowboy with his sidekick—Hopalong Cassidy and Roy Rogers with Gabby Hayes, the Lone Ranger with Tonto, John Wayne with Walter Brennan or Victor McLaglen—resembles the preadolescent bonding of young males who temporarily fear women and prefer each other's company, yet indulge in excessive displays of machismo to convince everyone that despite their exclusively male grouping they are really heterosexual. These schoolboy relationships are meant to give way in maturity to heterosexual ones. But in the American film we repeatedly find adult men whose fear and distrust of predatory women lead them to form obsessive male friendships essentially homosexual in character yet sexually chaste.

These are not depictions of homosexuality as a conscious choice, like that portrayed sympathetically in *Dog Day Afternoon,* but rather of unavowed homosexual emotion. That at some deep level the men are aware of how closely their feelings approach the homosexual leads them to engage, like their preadolescent counterparts, in displays of male bravado such as the dangerous trip down the rapids in *Deliverance.* Because these relationships involve so much sexual repression, the men become mindlessly violent.

At times the director is aware of this correlation, as William Wellman demonstrates in *The Ox-Bow Incident,* when the major who is so concerned about the manliness of his supposedly effeminate son is the one who leads the lynching. In the films of Howard Hawks the conflict is presented without much awareness on the part of the director. All that is implied, Hawks insists in *Red River,* is that John Wayne would have been incapable of building his magnificent ranch and forging the Chisholm Trail to make the first cattle run had there been a woman in his life who feared for his personal safety and thus undermined his masculine resolve. The violence of the all-male group which treats women only as objects and with scorn appears over and over in the Sam Peckinpah films, but particularly in *The Wild Bunch.*

In real life, men long for the openness of male friendships and seek to overcome the fear that closeness to another man may be homosexual in character. On screen the taboo against male intimacy is treated more seriously than in life. Only in a culture which was not as hostile to women as is ours could male friendship develop without the suggestion that it was homosexual and hence forbidden. And only in such a culture could homosexuality be depicted without trauma as a conscious choice open to men. Such a portrayal was attempted in *Dog Day Afternoon,* where Al Pacino as Sonny chooses his lover, Leon, and his male friend, Sal, without hating women, and a weakness of that film is that Sonny's wife and mother are made physically unattractive. In spite of this miscasting the film is not undermined, because Sonny repeatedly insists and in fact demonstrates that he loves his wife; it is only that his first choice is now homosexual.

In the seventies, when women are no longer acquiescent in their humiliation off screen, the male seems capable of loving and trusting only other men, although he must do so without violating the taboo against homosexuality. Yet he would rather live an asexual life than have anything to do with women, so great is the strain of confronting awakened women in the society and still remaining unable to surrender to the "effeminate" consequences of loving only other men.

The full dehumanization of women in our films began in the 1950s when women were encouraged to abandon the workplaces they had entered during the war and return to the home. Career women played by Rosalind Russell, Bette Davis, Joan Crawford, and Katharine Hepburn were replaced by women as pure objects of sex like Marilyn Monroe. But this demeaning of women in film was accompanied by a liberation of the male personality quite remote from the distortions of the seventies.

If in the fifties women were robbed of their identity and intelligence on film, we were still offered images of men with a multifarious range of emotion and an unprecedented degree of sensitivity as they looked inward during the McCarthy period's taboo on social concerns. These were often heterosexual men who found comfort and pleasure in the presence of women. It never occurred to them that to be masculine they would have to banish women from their lives; in these films the women were played, not by Marilyn Monroe or Jayne Mansfield, but by more interesting actresses like Eva Marie Saint or Eleanor Parker. Their heroes would have found it preposterous to view women as a *threat* to their sexuality.

In the real world of the seventies, women are feared with unparalleled hysteria as competition in the labor force. The pressure of the women's liberation movement for equal jobs, equal standing, and equal power, despite its failure to close the gap in earnings between men and women, has disturbed the financiers of film, who are nearly always male and often corporation directors. They respond to the pressure of women for employment—and equal wages—with a venom that leads them to create and finance projects which are hostile to women in general. When women demand to be portrayed on screen with as much courage, intelligence, and personal strength as men, Hollywood reacts by presenting the most satisfying erotic relationship as that between two men, even if it is not based on avowed or natural homosexual inclination.

The male film personality in the seventies has been created partially in response to what is perceived as the economic threat posed by working women. It is as if the enemy once personified by evil kings in historical romances, or by hired killers in so many Westerns, were now no longer corrupt other men waiting to be conquered and subdued, but the entire opposite sex. Without declaring himself homosexual, the male makes a point of not needing women at all, one step removed from the posture of heroes like the Lone Ranger or Hopalong Cassidy, to whom the prospect of linking up with a woman simply did not occur. If Hoppy and the Lone Ranger were like prepubescent boys excluding "girls," the seventies film males are emotionally postadolescent in the sense that they actively hate women. These Western figures of schoolboy appeal feared women and the emasculating consequences of domesticity, but they were not actively hostile. An almost ritual renunciation of female company occurs in *Midnight Cowboy*, where the provincial hero, Jon Voigt, whose plan had been to hustle women in New York as a male prostitute, abandons the enterprise because the psychic effort is too enervating. Women prove themselves to be castrating bitches at heart, and a man is finally happiest in the presence of a male companion. The relationship between hero Stallone and Talia Shire in *Rocky* (1977), a film otherwise pervaded by the macho stereotype, is a notable exception.

There is also an intensified sexual fear apparent in the disappearance of women from the lives of screen heroes of the seventies, from Burt Reynolds to Clint Eastwood. Male sexuality, it is feared, might shrivel away to nothing were there a strong instead of a passive and morally inferior female partner on the scene. (And here, of course, *Rocky* is no exception whatsoever.) The belief that an active, spirited, and autonomous female sexual partner would destroy the virility of the male is an absurdity that is contradicted by many films of the thirties and forties, including those with Bogart and Bacall, Hepburn and Tracy. Nevertheless, actors today are not merely concerned with preserving their "masculine" screen image, but express the same psychic preference for male companionship over female in their real lives. Joanne Woodward as Mrs. Paul Newman has complained, only partly in jest, about the real-life relationship between those male buddies of *Butch Cassidy and the Sundance Kid* and *The Sting:*

> When those men get together, forget opening your mouth if you happen to be female. Bob [Robert Redford] and Paul really do have a chemistry. Someday, Paul and Bob will run off together. And I'll be left behind with Lola Redford.

If even stars participate in Hollywood's current distaste for women, younger, more impressionable audience males may be expected to model themselves accordingly. And unless this pattern is broken, films will lose their female audiences, who are tired of being offered Robert Redford as a sex object only to observe his marked preference for the company of other men. Women overwhelmingly preferred Redford in *The Way We Were* to Redford in *Butch Cassidy* or *The Sting* precisely because he played a male whose impulses were directed toward women. Young men are damaged by being offered so one-sided a view of eroticism, and so are women, whose value as human beings is denied in such films in a manner unknown to earlier screen heroes—to, for example, Clark Gable, whose fantasies in *It Happened One Night* include both a desert island *and* Claudette Colbert.

There is another important difference between the buddy films of the seventies and those of earlier decades. Previously the buddy relationship was handled lightly and with humor, expressing the pleasure of a tender intimacy with a male friend—a closeness like that shared by Laurel and Hardy. It was unburdened by any idea that it would be perceived as a flight from the imminent destruction awaiting all men who take up with women. In *Rio Bravo* John Wayne kisses buddy Walter Brennan on the top of his head and calls him his "treasure." Pleased, shy, and rendered ill-at-ease by this unusual demonstration of feeling which he has purposely elicited from Wayne, Brennan affectionately applies a broom to Wayne's backside. By the seventies, the love between men is pursued without humor and in dead earnest.

Males now bond and travel almost exclusively in pairs, not because they enjoy erotic play with each other, but because male bonding is seen as necessary for survival in a hostile environment where women pose a danger and a threat to one's manhood. Some of the early bonding films like *The Great Escape* were placed in settings where the absence of women is natural—the field of battle, for example. Today, with the era of the anti-Nazi film in the past, the open enemy is often woman, challenging the decree that she remain forever subservient.

Screenwriter John Milius, whose credits include *Magnum Force,* has said that he would people the screen with American "samurai," those warriors of medieval Japan who also bonded together in a code of loyalty and willingness to face death for what they believed. Milius has also spoken of his fondness for the "bitter, lonely hero." On screen this male becomes one who would extinguish the world in a holocaust rather than permit change, and who has nothing whatever to do with women.

It is from such imitators of Peckinpah, preposterously still claiming that men are wiser, better, and more clever than women simply because they are men, that the male image now issues. But this image can be sustained only by allowing the men no sexuality at all, and by fixing them in claustrophobic relationships with other men equally in flight from the dangers of what Milius has called "the new order."

Men and Women

Male bonding has not always provided the primary emotional pattern for the screen hero. Since the beginnings of the American film, male stars have sought and been gratified by relationships with women.

In films of the twenties and thirties, images appear of the male as a friend to women and children, as nurturer and partner. We find Tom Mix giving a little girl a piggyback ride and a little boy his castor oil. His sexuality was not diminished by this game, or by his open fondness for children. Gable in *Gone with the Wind* was a doting father, delighting in his daughter. Spencer Tracy could be a man and yet be *Father of the Bride* and—horror of horrors—a grandfather (*Father's Little Dividend*). Even in the mid-fifties Paul Newman as Rocky Graziano in *Somebody Up There Likes Me* could enjoy fatherhood. But can anyone imagine James Bond or Dirty Harry Callahan as a father surrounded by toddlers? Today the male's distress over his loss of control over the fate of the community where he resides is reflected in our films in the absence of emotional space for fatherhood. In *The Way We Were* Redford has broken up with Streisand before the birth of their child, and we are spared the sight of Redford, the eternally virile, youthful American male, as the nurturer of a weaker creature. Manhood has become irreconcilable not only with fatherhood but with heterosexual love, with the nurturing relationship between man and woman.

The less violent a male has been required to be in our films, the greater has been his interest in heterosexual love. Unburdened by the need to sublimate his sexuality in sadistic acts of violence, the hero in earlier films could express it naturally, and women were essential to his happiness. Male personalities like Tracy, Barrymore, and Fairbanks who transcended the "buddy" pattern were also capable of a far wider range of emotion, from tears and sorrow to laughter and joy, than those solitary figures whose manhood is so dependent upon not being subjected by women to discipline and "civilization." One might contrast the wit and vivacity of Tracy, Bogart, and Gable with the somber, vacuous facial expressions of Eastwood and Bronson. Up to and through the fifties the hero was often sufficiently confident in his manhood to laugh at himself and to accept his human vulnerability, as does Brando. As a natural consequence of their psychic health, these male figures could allow women to enter their lives. Despite the sexual permissiveness of the late sixties and seventies, most film heroes today behave as if they would feel sullied by physical contact with women. There was far more erotic pleasure between men and women in the days when people kept their clothes on, because Fairbanks, Gable, Tracy, and even Tom Mix genuinely liked women.

Since the sexual revolution, women have been encouraged to find pleasure in sex. And men, as if fearing that their sexual capacities will for the first time be evaluated according to how well they satisfy not only themselves but their partners, have begun on screen to treat sexual intercourse as a distasteful power struggle, or as a mechanical act to be terminated as quickly as possible. James Bond's careless philandering was viewed as "cool" by some young men of the sixties because his partners, unlike theirs, were always so grateful for his favors, so easily satisfied, and content even to be left for another when the exigencies of the adventure required the hero's departure. Bond vicariously relieved men of their anxieties by offering the fantasy of the continuously potent male rewarded with an endless variety of grateful and unquestioning women.

In other films the always latent hostility toward women in American culture has surfaced in the characterization of the independent woman as a demonic castrator, a device used in an attempt to keep women in their old inferior social place. In *The Graduate* Dustin Hoffman finds that lovemaking with an aggressive woman who likes sex holds no pleasure for the male. He must struggle so hard to please the insatiable Mrs. Robinson that he never gets a moment of enjoyment himself. Meanwhile, his relationship with her daughter Elaine, a woman who would not make impossible sexual or emotional demands, flourishes.

Clint Eastwood, a pathologically isolated figure, is too "masculine" even to hook up with a male buddy in his films. But neither does he often have the time or the inclination to sleep with a woman. When he does, as in *Coogan's Bluff,* he selects a filthy, unattractive hippie solely to gain information on the whereabouts of one of the criminal lowlives he so relentlessly pursues. Or he chooses a crude stereotype such as the "submissive Oriental woman" in *Magnum Force,* whom he abandons for his work but who is waiting for him in his bed when he returns. With the attractive policewoman in *Coogan's Bluff* even his dinner, let alone potential sex, is interrupted by calls to duty—the macho counterpart of the "headache." And Eastwood informs the policewoman in *The Enforcer* that he does not "get friendly" with his partners, male or female. The male in the American film has always placed work above sex, but in the seventies and particularly in the cop-glory films, work has become all-consuming, leaving no room for relationships with women.

When it does occur—for nature will out—the sex between men and women is photographed as unappealingly as possible. The man's real partner is himself, the only person he can trust. Often he seems entirely unaware of the woman's presence. Jack Nicholson seems to be thinking about something else, using sex only as something he has to do, not only in *Carnal Knowledge,* which purports to be critical of the macho hero, but in *Five Easy Pieces, Chinatown,* and *One Flew over the Cuckoo's Nest.* In *Carnal Knowledge* we watch him virtually relieve himself with Candice Bergen without an ounce of feeling. She waits for the act to conclude, interchangeable with any pretty woman he might have chosen to be his "first." Their lovemaking is filmed like the rape of *Last Summer,* where the male pounds to completion, his eyes focused somewhere away from his terrified victim until he is finished. The myth that one of the casualties of the sexual revolution is male potency is openly accepted and bemoaned in *Carnal Knowledge* as Nicholson, grotesquely lifelike, reaches manhood in the mid-twentieth century with a primitive dread of women. By the end he has labeled them all—including his little daughter—as "ball-busters," a philosophy reinforced and encouraged precisely by such films which basically share the attitudes they pretend to scrutinize.

By the seventies the social emasculation of men is taken for granted. Sex that would be accompanied by an emotional commitment to a woman now seems frightening because were a man to lose control of the sexual side of his life, he would be left with no power at all. Domestic entanglements had best be avoided. If a man is married, he had better treat his wife brutally, since according to so many American films this is what arouses women. Thus Dustin Hoffman in *Straw Dogs* becomes a killer to satisfy his sexually greedy wife. For his own protection, a man must offer virtuoso performances of sex without love, as Jack Nicholson does in *Five Easy Pieces.* Were a man to show tenderness, he would become vulnerable to an emasculating put-down like that delivered to Donald Sutherland in *Klute* after he makes energetic if gentle love to an independent woman (Jane Fonda), translated here as a call girl; she rewards him with a devastating rebuff: "I never come with a John."

With so narrow a range of feeling allowed him, the male loses much of the erotic resonance he once enjoyed in the American film. In *Rebel Without a Cause* James Dean was pleased to be the protector and surrogate brother of younger, weaker Sal Mineo. His paternal feelings found an outlet in open affection for another male. At the same time the film allowed Dean strong heterosexual feelings toward a girl his own age, played by Natalie Wood, feelings he also showed toward Julie Harris in *East of Eden.* When Mineo was killed, implicitly because his feelings for Dean were too expressly homosexual and therefore, in keeping with the taboo, he had to be eliminated from the film, Dean still retained his loving relationship with Wood. Throughout he was portrayed as a young man with a varied and complete sensual nature, capable of accepting his own vulnerability and more emotionally complex than any screen male of the seventies.

Men and Work

When they have been employed at all, the work ethic has consumed the heroes of our films as they struggle for success, recognition, and supremacy. Rarely, of course, have they been engaged in the type of work most people do. Valentino and Fairbanks seldom worked in their films, and Tom Mix too seemed idle enough so that when a call to right wrongs was sounded, he was ready and available to answer it. By 1930 inspiration was provided by the pluckiness of Little Caesar, who starts from the bottom and works his way to the top of gangland, proving that hard work is all. In such early gangster films, made at the time of the Depression, when social outlets seemed few, the gangster exhibited the ferocity and inner reserves of stamina and drive which real-life men were expected to apply to lawful enterprises. The hero who rebelled was shown to be only a gangster who wound up dead in the streets. Never did the hero see either his work or his avocation as that of rooting out inequity or corruption at its source.

The masculine male in the American film does his work within the established order. By 1929, Tom Mix, with his carefree ways, had been replaced by foreman Gary Cooper as the Virginian, who, in the service of the cattle owners of the area, mounts a posse and hangs his best friend because he has become one of the rustlers. At the moment of his rise to the ranks of the dominant male personalities of the American film, Cooper commits a moral act unthinkable to Douglas Fairbanks, Sr. And the more seriously the hero takes his work, the more domineering he becomes toward both women and weaker men.

While the male in American films has always been smarter, wittier, and more powerful than any woman, the degree of his brutalization has altered with historical changes in the society. The carefree twenties produced men who had no trouble earning a living, the great comic heroes forming a major exception because they served to distract audience men and women by appealing to their sense of helplessness for release in laughter. Boom times in which the audience participated allowed people on and off screen a measure of relaxation.

The strains of the thirties produced a hard-boiled, no-nonsense male in the gangster film, while the screwball comedies depicted a world of inherited wealth as an avenue of escape for the Depression audience. For only by ignoring or denying that earning a living was a critical issue, as it is in real life, could these films plausibly urge upon men the role of the individualistic hero who, acting alone, can right all wrongs and whom the foundering group would do well to follow. The Gable films sought to demonstrate through the charisma of their hero that, notwithstanding the Depression, men could still flourish as free spirits and defiant individualists; they did not need to band together in groups or organize to make society more hospitable. The fear of mass action has resulted in the depiction in the American film of those solitary heroes who solve all problems for themselves; and, typically, they roam the wild West more frequently than they toil on the assembly line.

In the thirties also the issue of work was posed almost exclusively in terms of those who had no trouble earning a living. Jimmy Stewart as a senator in Washington, demanding that the system purge itself of corruption, is never personally concerned with how to make ends meet. Gary Cooper's Mr. Deeds is an eccentric individual who inherits a fortune, an event designed to prove that upward mobility was ever possible in America; it is money that he does not need. With his new-found wealth, Deeds offers poor farmers a stake so that they may make it on their own. Frank Capra's lone-individual heroes argue by their actions that social welfare programs and a government which grants concessions to the needs of the people are infinitely preferable to more dramatic types of struggle.

During World War II the issue of employment was resolved for male heroes because films defined masculinity in terms of patriotic fervor and doing battle for the country. It would be left to the more interesting postwar films to raise the questions of work and the dependence of men presumed autonomous on the pleasure of others, matters left dangling or deliberately ignored during the Depression. The hero who returned from the war painfully felt his way among suddenly corrupt social institutions. His fight for justice overseas had, paradoxically, brought him alienation on return, a renewed sense of helplessness, and the posture of the disillusioned anti-hero. All the forced patriotic optimism of the war was dissipated in shock and despair when society after the war proved as exploitative as before. His maleness, epitomized by John Garfield's tortured screen souls, could now be expressed only through the negative action of giving up his claims to success as a means of protesting against widespread social venality.

Rarely in the fifties did the hero's work reflect the repressiveness of the postwar period or the issues posed by the attacks on "internal subversion." The heroic again required escape to the Western past, where Alan Ladd as Shane could pause in his solitary wandering to chop wood for his keep while ridding the community of predatory bullies. Men became more sensitive and thoughtful in fifties films than they had ever been before, ironically at the very time that society denied them the right to challenge official repression and the violation of basic freedoms. In less tyrannical historical moments, introspection was as unnecessary a pastime for the vital male as it was deemed unmanly. In the fifties, it was the only arena left open. And the working reality of men did surface on screen; Brando could play a longshoreman or a factory worker; Ernest Borgnine, a butcher. But that the hero could no more safely be a rebel on screen in the fifties than at any other time is reflected in Brando's longshoreman, who does battle with corrupt union officials by telling a government investigating committee what he knows. The male proves himself heroic by demonstrating that it is right and good to inform!

Realistic occupations became fewer in the films of the sixties; the male hero was often a secret agent, a caricature of a human being, but reflecting nonetheless Hollywood's distaste for the civil rights and antiwar movements, uniformly parodied as counterculture psychopathy. Dissent and nonconformity were portrayed in the late sixties as threats to the community's safety and sanity.

Sean Connery's James Bond, touted as an ideal man, actually enjoyed little autonomy in the pursuit of his profession; whatever his physical prowess and courage, he was never man enough to question, let alone to disobey, the orders of his superiors. Film after film busied Bond with demonstrating the technological triumphs accessible to that dashing figure of the cold-war period, the secret agent, soon in the seventies to be exposed as either an assassin or a whining Watergate burglar.

There is invariably a cultural lag between the historical time of an event and its screen appearance. Therefore it was not until the 1970s, when the student movement had already dissipated, that the counterculture protester began to make his appearance in the American film. When he did, he appeared as a maniac, screaming and thrashing about, a psychotic committing vicious acts everywhere. He was permitted neither principles nor ideas; even a sympathetic young man like Dustin Hoffman in *The Graduate* never once mentions the Vietnam War or any other aspect of American life that might be assumed to distress him or at least to register with him. Hoffman's protest is presented as one more adolescent rebellion soon to be replaced by mature conformity.

By the late sixties and seventies the job of the screen male who would be "masculine" and "strong" becomes the overt protection of a social order in danger of collapse. In an era of deteriorating cities, unemployment, and escalating violence, the hero is not the underdog but the cop, the more brutal the better. An astonishing number of television series and films are devoted to glorifying the policeman in and out of uniform. His enemies are represented as deranged anarchic forces striking out at society solely because they have become sour, having failed to measure up to its standards for success.

The more devoted he is to "justice," the more willing and eager is the cop to violate the law on behalf of what he deems right—and the more masculine he appears. It is as much with a lackadaisical and cowardly police force, caving in to craven liberal politicians, that Dirty Harry must do battle as it is with the lurking counterculture and ghetto monsters who slip through the fingers of flabby authorities with their insidious invocations of the Bill of Rights. That document has, in the seventies film, become a Satan's manual of the maniac. In other films the hero is an architect or a taxi driver, a vigilante civilian who assumes the role of cop because the real police are so ineffective. The wilderness of earlier American films is no longer used to camouflage the society of the present. Frequently the setting is now explicitly the filthy and decaying cities, the cowboy a cop. The male pursues justice not merely on behalf of the law but in spite of it because its very rules prevent wiping people out with impunity as the vigilante and the Eastwood-style cop desire. To defeat the new enemies of order the hero must use far greater violence than did even John Wayne when he killed anyone seeking to wrest his illegally gained property from him in *Red River* or when he shot down Liberty Valance.

By the seventies, the unbending male who pursues his job unhampered by ambiguity, moral or otherwise, is the sexual ideal, however infrequently he chooses to engage in the act of love. His impassivity is presented, not as the reflection of a stunted emotional life, but simply as what is required to accomplish his ends. His quick-on-the-trigger violence is applauded as effective. Having always been dedicated to protecting the status quo in the America of the time in which a film was made, Hollywood has given us the male ideal of the seventies in Clint Eastwood's increasingly successful films about Inspector Dirty Harry Callahan.

The harsh struggle for economic survival on the part of most people, coupled with this culture's insistence that a genuine male achieve financial success, continues to influence the image of men in films. The struggle for profit expresses itself in the advocacy of traits in men that are required to sustain competition. Aggressiveness is viewed in films as sexually appealing, not because men are biologically born aggressive, but because the way people must earn their living depends upon fierce competition, particularly among working people who scramble for employment in a shrinking job market. To survive in such a community indeed requires dehumanization, the cultivation of hard qualities which are made palatable on the screen by being portrayed as the traits of men who lived in earlier epochs where individual aggressiveness actually succeeded in its end. Residing in a world where success and manliness have been made synonymous, and often failing to achieve any success at all, the man in the audience is comforted by seeing those unrelenting qualities of male strength displayed by men in an environment where they are able to win out over the forces lined up against them.

Men today remain alienated in workplaces that are hierarchically structured, with one person always superior and hence more "masculine" than another. Frequently they lack any connection with the goals of their work. The decisions involving that work are made by others. It is no wonder that they look backward with longing to times when men belonged to themselves. But, too unsure and too fearful of the consequences often to rebel against dehumanizing conditions, males of our time may feel relieved to find that filmmakers still have no intention of suggesting that rebellion against the powers that be defines the masculine male. Films that place the burden of men's impotence on castrating women must offer a comfortable point of view to many.

The mood of disenchantment that came with the failure of protest in the sixties to effect meaningful social change, the post-Watergate moral malaise, have inspired nothing so much as the demand for a hero who at least is not a whiner, who does not demand the impossible. As a man who can take disappointment as it comes, who leanly endures the kind of barbarisms we ourselves daily face, the cop hero of the seventies meets the needs of an audience amply disappointed in the quality of its life, but with no faith in its personal or collective power to change it.

Refusing to challenge the injustices of a world where rebels meet the unhappiest of fates, we seek comfort anew in screen males, past and present, who had a chance against evil, from Alan Ladd's Shane and Gary Cooper's sheriff in *High Noon* to Clint Eastwood's nine-lived Josey Wales. "I've got the world by the tail with a downhill pull," boasted Davy Crockett, a forerunner of the impish Douglas Fairbanks, Sr., and the spunky Dustin Hoffman. We long for the self-confidence of Crockett and content ourselves with its expression in our films, if not in our lives.

Fearing that we can never be adequate men or women, we satisfy ourselves by applauding screen heroes like Bronson and Eastwood and so conspire in our own impotence. We people our films with men as unreal as Davy Crockett and place them in an America of legend. We take comfort in John Wayne, who is at least what we are not, a man whom no one walks all over and lives to tell the tale.

Wayne keeps alive our ideal image of ourselves by being uncompromising in his refusal to allow anyone to "make small" of him, the humiliation that drove Erich von Stroheim's McTeague to his wildest displays of violence. Women who protest their image in film might well argue that not only have they been denied the portrayal of themselves as they are, but they have even been deprived of the "true grit" of a John Wayne and the cool impassivity of a Clint Eastwood, so competent and sure of themselves that no one would dare put them down—or refer to their real or imagined inadequacies.

The nostalgia that colors so many films of the seventies is appropriate to our sorrow that our lives do not permit us to stand as tall as Wayne. Our tragedy may well be our false belief that it is only in our films—and in films set in the past—that such a man can still exist. For at the same time, we are admitting that we have given up on ourselves. We must, in fact, look back to the 1920s to find male heroes capable of joy and abandon and to discover a diversity of male types, each with his own unique set of qualities but all defying the later standard to be set by Wayne, Cooper, and Eastwood.

From the Beginnings Through the Twenties

A plenitude of male images graced the twenties screen, from comic stars like Buster Keaton and Charlie Chaplin to dashing figures like Douglas Fairbanks, from romantic sex objects like Rudolph Valentino to strong, patriarchal heroes like William S. Hart and Tom Mix, and including sensitive and delicate yet no less desirable men like Richard Barthelmess. The very youthfulness of film as an industry, as an entertainment medium, and as an art form encouraged the emergence of a variety of images. Each was tested for audience approval; each offered its own special appeal; each was welcomed and accepted for its unique charm. Filmmakers recognized then a truth which seems since to have been lost: audiences can be pleased by a multiplicity of male types. And Hollywood recognized that films could successfully be made for special audiences. If Tom Mix and Douglas Fairbanks might appeal more to men, Valentino and John Barrymore and Wallace Reid particularly delighted women; and Chaplin, of course, belonged to everyone.

Unthreatened by audience defection to any competing entertainment form like television, heartened by the enthusiastic welcome movies received from the population, filmmakers were free to experiment and to explore. The twenties, the "jazz age," were in general a decade of experimentation in life-styles, and films echoed the public's thirst for liberation from repressive sexual norms.

Indeed, such experimentation was part and parcel of the political repression which had reared its head in America during the early 1920s, one more reason why films devoted themselves to an exploration of the male personality: his psyche, his every gesture, his personal style. Safe from the upholders of political orthodoxy so long as screen males were not presented as in conflict with the America of their time, movies could gratify an audience engaged in the process of self-discovery. People were eager to forget World War I, and just as eager to respond to the influence of Freud in valuing the individual personality for its own sake. Sensitive, adventurous, exotic, tender, haplessly endearing—so long as he was devoted to exploring the delightful byways of his personality, a male type could find space on screen. Carefully avoiding the harsh realities of American life, film as a fledgling art, aware of its potential influence on audiences, conceived of itself primarily as a form of entertainment. In that quest to divert and to please, in this male-dominated culture the male much more than the female image could flourish in all its diversity. Only one image was taboo and would remain rare on the silver screen through the decades: that of the average man, whether factory or office worker, for whom the myth of rugged individualism represented but a bitter irony.

The frontiersman of legend, an independent, supremely virile male, was now gone, replaced by the little man reduced to a dreary life behind a desk, nondescript, frightened, and boring. He followed routine rather than his own instincts. "As a group," wrote C. Wright Mills of the increasing numbers of American men who had become white-collar workers, "they do not threaten anyone; as individuals, they do not practice an independent way of life." If the legendary individualists of the nineteenth century were portrayed as working for nobody but themselves, the male of the century when the American film began was often a city-dweller who worked for someone else, whether in a factory or in an office. Rarely could he be the hero of a cinema which would reach back into myth, the exotic, and a legendary past for its ideal of the masculine male.

I

In the silent era King Vidor's *The Crowd* (1928) stands out as one of the few films to examine the real life of most men of the 1920s. Defying Hollywood's prescription that the screen male must be a superman, it offers as its hero little Johnny Sims (James Murray). Vidor intends Johnny to stand for the male of our century; he is born in 1900. "There's a little man the world is going to hear from all right," says his father on the day of his birth. An ironic title informs us that Johnny begins with the early advantages of a Washington or a Lincoln (implying, incredibly, that Washington had a no more privileged background than Lincoln) and is surely destined for "something big."

Social reality soon destroys such illusions. Most men do not become Washingtons or Lincolns, as Vidor shows in one of the few painfully honest films about the American male's real opportunities for success and heroism. Johnny is lucky to have a job as one more faceless bureaucrat working in an insurance company, hidden amidst a sea of endless desks. They stretch beyond the vision of the camera as Vidor's visuals embody his theme: Johnny is a cog in an impersonal machine, undifferentiated from other men. All are automatons, mouthing the same bland words, moving identically as the clock pushes toward five o'clock. Survival for the real American male depends upon conformity.

Vidor finds no heroic opportunities for men to distinguish themselves, no calls upon their physical strength by which they might demonstrate their "manliness," a term equated by all, including Johnny, with personal accomplishment. Johnny longs for success. As a passive member of a crowd of men like himself, his chances are slim. Vidor has given us a film about the fate of the male in a bureaucratized, industrialized society where real decisions are made outside his knowledge and control. His hero seems so small because he is life-sized.

The one area for romance in American films set in the present has often been the choice of a marriage partner. Love at least still belongs to the individual. And Johnny Sims does marry for love. But romance cannot survive within an otherwise unheroic life. Johnny and his wife, Mary (Eleanor Boardman), are reduced to a shabby tenement apartment where the bathroom door is always popping open and the toilet is on the blink. Beset by tragedy, they lose most of their feeling for each other. They have a family, but their youngest child dies in an automobile accident. Later American films might allow the hero to transcend the pain of personal loss, but this would require abandoning any semblance of look-ing at people's real lives. In the seventies the outlaw Josey Wales becomes a hardened avenger after his child is burned to death and his wife is raped and murdered, but little Johnny Sims is no Clint Eastwood, no superman of the gun-toting West. He falls apart. Grief-stricken, he quits his job. Having always wanted to be "different," he winds up with a job where, disguised as a clown, he juggles balls in the street to lure passers-by to a local restaurant. Love recedes as Mary declares she would rather see Johnny dead than idle and out of work. A man who is not a success loses his manliness. Our Johnny is even too cowardly for suicide.

When Johnny and Mary remain together at the end, imprisoned in their slum dwelling, it is not because, despite a dreary existence, they have at least retained a passion for each other. Rather, it is because Johnny in his pathetic indolence has become dependent upon his wife, and she pities him too much to leave. The office and hospital sets emphasize the small-ness of this twentieth-century man who, unable to find the room of his wife, panics in the gigantic hospital corridor. He is ridiculed by a doctor who sneeringly remarks, "We've never lost a husband yet."

The man who works for a giant corporation is a lonely man, like Johnny pathetically playing his ukelele on the beach and singing, "All alone, I'm so all alone." In the midst of crowds or even among loved ones, he is nobody. Defeat and failure stalk him; energy, ambition, and a pleasant personality are shown to count for nothing. Hence we can perceive the importance of the Western myth in American films with its nostalgia for an indomitable male. For just as the American film came into its own, the American individualist myth seemed exhausted. Crowds of men like Johnny Sims competed without success for the very few promotions allocated for those working their way up through the ranks. Upward mobility was a chimera.

The last scene of *The Crowd* finds Johnny Sims, reconciled with his tired wife, enjoying a rare evening at the theater. His seat neighbor nudges him, pointing with delight to a witty advertisement for "Sleight-o-Hand, The Magic Cleaner," which Johnny had once written and which offered him his one moment of triumph in the course of the film. Johnny beams. Then the camera pulls away to reveal him seated once again among the many, a faceless man whose one claim to accomplishment is ironic because it is so paltry. Yet such moments provide the only "success" attainable by most men in twentieth-century America.

Precisely because Vidor's male image was so true and yet so intolerable, many more American filmmakers perceived the purpose of cinema to be one of palliation, to soften discontent and to entertain by distracting men from the inadequacy of their lives. People would be offered instead a vicarious entrance into a far more fulfilling, if distorted, emotional reality on screen. One result of the escapist films of the twenties was that the Johnny Simses of the audience could regain their self-respect by identifying with screen idols for whom the staking of claims was still possible, the frontier still open.

With few exceptions the screen male of the twenties lived in the past. From the sands of the Sahara to sunny Spain, he dwelled most often in remote places. He fought in the Russian Revolution—almost always, of course, on the side of the Czar—or he gained his manhood in the French Foreign Legion. Rarely did he pursue an urban—or a suburban—style of life in the actual America of the twenties. Though as frequently gentle as violent in this film period, he rarely lived at home.

The Western proved to be so resilient a genre because the legendary past provided a superb setting for the free, sexually ideal hero. His time and energy were at his own disposal. Competition could offer him self-realization because the illusion of individual autonomy was still credible. There were no conglomerates to squeeze out the little man. The environment allowed him to feel large. And when things went wrong, he had the power to make them right, as William S. Hart and Tom Mix consistently demonstrated.

For the male hero in films of the twenties there was rarely even the concept of "work," a term which at once suggests boredom and alienation. What a man did was to express himself, and by so doing he happened to earn a living. His choice of work was likely to be related to his sense of justice. Tom Mix takes job after job in his films in order to right wrongs, not because he is in search of wealth, let alone the means of survival. Because the audience was so preoccupied with the issues of wages or salary, these terms are absent from the concerns of the twenties film hero. He roams wide-open spaces where neither unemployment, hierarchy, nor competition for status exists.

II

The association of maleness with violence makes its appearance in the earliest American films. Edwin S. Porter's *The Great Train Robbery* (1903), our first true Western, already has males in physical conflict with each other. The thieves, crude villains, are clad in black shirts, the association of blackness and evil being conscious and soon to become standard. They board a train, kill a crewman, and blow up the safe. The body of one of the trainmen is thrown from the moving train. When a passenger about to be robbed protests, he is instantly shot and killed.

Meanwhile, the "good people" of the town are enjoying themselves at a square dance. They rally for a confrontation against those who would disturb their tranquil life. *The Great Train Robbery* ends on a rare close shot. Staring straight into the camera is a character (played by George Barnes) whom we have not met in the film. Tough, with a handlebar moustache, he looks like the fiercest of the desperadoes. As he fires his gun directly at the audience, he grimaces, dark and glowering. So strongly does this one close-up contrast with the rest of the film that he might be villain or hero, ravager or protector. Whatever his moral posture, his prowess suggests that only comparable brutality will be sufficient to best him. Above all, there can be no doubt about his maleness. Overpowering, intensely physical, and unrelenting, he is the prototype of the strong male hero in the American film leading to John Wayne and Charles Bronson. He projects a code of masculinity which transcends even the side it represents. Good or evil, maleness is associated with ruthless power.

Porter further developed models of male behavior in *The Life of an American Fireman* (1903) and *Rescued from an Eagle's Nest* (1907). Porter's heroic firefighters never hesitate a second as they break down doors and windows, intent upon rescuing weaker members of the species. A woman lies helpless in her bed, lacking the will and competence to save herself. Threatened by smoke and flames, she remains passive, awaiting a man who will take her fate in his hands. And a fireman does carry her out of the burning house, as the hero in American films would so often manifest his virility by lifting the heroine, contrasting his physical strength with her emotional and physical weakness. Such masculine strength also protects women, as does the protagonist of *Rescued from an Eagle's Nest.* An eagle seizes a baby from its mother, and our hero must descend a steep incline to a ledge on the side of a mountain. There he does battle with his mighty feathered adversary. The baby is rescued, the eagle defeated in nothing less than hand-to-beak combat. Spent and collapsing with fatigue, the male model of Porter's little sketch is rewarded with a kiss.

With Cecil B. De Mille's *Male and Female* (1919), the issue of male sexuality was out in the open in the American film. In this adaptation of J. M. Barrie's *The Admirable Crichton,* strength, capability, courage, and leadership belong to the male in pointed contrast to the female, regardless of social class. The butler, William Crichton, tall, handsome, wavy-haired, and noble in demeanor, possesses all the ingredients for power and success save those of birth. The rich young ladies of the English household he serves are languid, passive, and idle. They are Crichton's moral inferiors, and his intellectual inferiors as well, for he reads poetry in his spare time. (Even when he plays a domestic servant, the male in the American film is the intellectual superior of any woman, including those who enjoy greater advantages.)

The egalitarian, democratic spirit of the American film emerges in De Mille's characterization of lower-class man as possessing far greater virility and sexuality than the young ladies' foppish male counterparts. Chauffeurs and butlers are physically alive; the rich dandies, effete European aristocrats, are effeminate, intellectual, and helpless.

All come together on a remote desert island where the rich and pampered are stranded together with their servants. Crichton alone is clever enough to teach the rest how to survive. Outside of a hierarchical, industrial world, an unjust class society, Crichton can become a veritable "King of Babylon," about whom he has so avidly read. His mistress Mary, whom he carries onto the island limp and lifeless, will be his slave.

What is truly male, De Mille tells us, transcends social class or wealth. It emerges from innate physical as well as intellectual superiority, a quality lost to the self-indulgent rich who have forgotten how to do things for themselves. A head taller and twice as brawny as his wealthy male antagonists, Crichton assumes power on the island. It is the butler and not the timid Oxford graduate who knows how to keep a starving woman warm. And the women respond sexually to this self-sufficient, dominant male, admiring a man who self-confidently orders others to do his bidding. In our culture male power and sexuality come allied; the concept has so penetrated the consciousness of us all that these women *automatically* respond to a Tarzan-like Crichton dressed in leopard skins and exuding that air of inaccessibility which makes him all but irresistible to the women upon whom he once waited.

De Mille has, of course, returned us to what he presents as the blessed state of nature, where men are in command and women happiest when they can serve a strong, superior male. Civilization, says De Mille, has alienated us from our true natures. With regret, his heroine Mary endures the rescue which will reduce the supermale Crichton once more to serving her drinks on a tray.

Yet, like John Ford decades later in *The Man Who Shot Liberty Valance* (1962), De Mille acknowledges that there is no turning back from civilization and "progress." No revolutionary, he does not advocate an overturning of class distinctions that would permit a relationship between Mary and Crichton. Mary's friend Ellen, by contrast, marries her chauffeur only to find herself cast out by her family and saddled with an employable husband. Their marriage, we are meant to suppose, will resemble that later irritable union between Mary and Johnny Sims.

Instead, Crichton must marry the scullery maid, Tweeny. The two migrate to America, where class distinctions do not prevent a man from forging an independent existence. The American De Mille plays upon national memories of escape through immigration from European class society. He contrasts the unjust English setting of the present with a romantic, mythological America of the frontier past, which offered a man an arena for his masculinity. Effete English society deprived males of the opportunity to be "men," as the world of the present deprives them of meaningful outlets for their natural physical selves.

The Western became so rich a genre because it provided male heroes with that precivilized environment in which they could exercise potency free of emasculating restrictions, those imposed by class, law, and education. Wealth, too, was a danger eluded in the Western since it might lead a man to physical softness and the erosion of his animal masculinity.

Yet even though we are often told that physical prowess leads to power, in actuality those who have ruled have usually been the physically soft, those effete types so scorned in our films for not being "real men." But, our movies console us, their riches make them poor; their effete society makes them impotent. Thus the poor and the less privileged in Hollywood's fantasy world become the truly manly rather than the "happy few" on top.

An early film like *The Deserter* (1916) indicates why the Western developed so compelling a capacity to restore male pride and self-esteem. The hero is Lieutenant Parker (Charles Ray), an impetuous young man in whom "the blood of youth runs hotly." Parker is in the army, a situation which on film invariably provides men with countless opportunities to distinguish themselves. In the cavalry, as in combat, a superior ethic of manhood prevails. But Parker has a hot temper, and only extreme fortitude and devotion to his duty will later provide him with the means of redemption.

Brooding over the loss of the woman he loves to a captain (as early American films freely admitted that some class distinctions haunt us all), Parker joins a gang of rowdies and "sinners" at cards. Drawn into one of their brawls, he is arrested and court-martialed. With public disgrace and a dishonorable discharge near, he escapes onto the open frontier, intending to begin anew as a pioneer attached to a wagon train. But the Sioux are on the warpath. Their hostility provides the film's justification for the view that true masculinity is found, not in pursuing domestic alliances, but in devotion to the all-male society of the army, which protects and paves the way for civilian life. And the women who appreciate real men are seduced, not by rank, but by physical courage and its display.

Thus, although a wanted man, Parker, a true male, elects to return to the fort to obtain help for the settlers besieged by hostile Indians. Dressed in fringed buckskins, he becomes even more manly than when garbed in the cavalry uniform which subjected him to emasculating rules and restrictions. Although army combat is the arena for manliness, masculinity blossoms most fully in freely chosen acts of heroism unavailable within the rigid circumstances of the fort.

Parker arrives with his message only to expire, the victim of encounters with hostile Indians which he survived solely by that extreme act of will which is always a mark of the authentic male in the American film. *The Deserter* is climaxed by Parker's long ceremonial funeral, which marks him as the best of cavalry men. That he could express his courage and determination only outside its gates is a telling irony which seems to have escaped the filmmaker.

The real man is thus defined by superhuman physical strength and endurance. Placed in the service of justice, defined as the established order symbolized by the army, the true male can demonstrate his manhood. Death becomes a small enough price to pay, since the unmanly life is not worth living.

III

The first great male hero of the American film was the originator of the authentic Western film, William S. Hart. Hart created the masculine model later imitated by Gary Cooper, for Cooper's silence derived from a rationale expressed by Hart in his autobiography, *My Life East and West:*

"The bigness of the West makes men quiet; they seldom talk unless they have something to say. The altitude clarifies their brains and gives them nerves of steel."

Hart grew up in the West and spoke Sioux as a boy. Spending many years in New York only reinforced the images of his youth and led him to create the stereotype of the strong, silent Westerner, honest, simple, and straight. Not surprisingly, given the emphasis on the rigors of physical endurance as a standard of maleness, Hart's first ambition in life had been to attend West Point. Lacking the necessary formal education, he chose instead the stage and then the film. In the Western, a form he loved and forged, he attempted to create as realistically as possible the world he knew as a boy, the world of his "iron-hearted, loving father" whom fighting men (the only real men) had always admired.

The West, Hart later wrote, was a place where "there were only kind-hearted, friendly things; those that would fight to the death in battle, but in peace would shrink from inflicting pain." The morality of the Hart Western derives from his admiration of the West as a place where "none are stoned for adultery of mind or body, because there is no adultery of mind or body." In Hart's films, many of which he directed himself, we encounter a vision of the West of the last half of the nineteenth century, at the moment of the closing of the frontier, an event portrayed with considerable pathos in Hart's last film, *Tumbleweeds* (1925).

To Hollywood, Hart brought the frontiersman. He persisted until he was allowed to make Western pictures in his own image. "I would go through hell on three pints of water before I would acknowledge defeat," Hart said later, speaking for the male hero of countless films to come. He adhered always to the code of the cowboy, for whom physical and moral courage were wholly natural. Hart's credo would be emulated by male stars from then on.

> One of the most dangerous things in life is to lose your courage. If you can keep your fighting spirit, you always have a chance. The very fact of keeping an undaunted front may cause the other side to weaken. If your courage goes, you are whipped—your enemy and the world soon know it.

The Hart hero is already "the best" at whatever he does; his Keno Bates is predictably described as "the best shot in Arizona." The fiercest male imaginable, he is always stoical, forever immune to the fear of danger. Hart was physically tall, muscular, and straight-backed. Hawk-nosed, thin-lipped, and rarely smiling, he projected an image of male power.

But the Hart films were no simple parables in which the "good" hero defeats the "bad" villain. Foremost in Hart's mind was a "faithful" portrayal of the Old West, and with authenticity, ambiguity inevitably appears. "Good" and "evil" were not absolutes in the Hart film. Unlike Cooper and Wayne, he frequently played a villain, albeit a villain who

William S. Hart in *The Toll Gate:* "I would go through hell on three pints of water before I would acknowledge defeat." The fiercest male imaginable, he is always stoical, forever immune to the fear of danger.

could be reformed by love and tenderness. The West was an ideal place for Hart precisely because it provided so fluid a world in which a man gone wrong could reverse himself and pursue a course directly opposed to what he had previously sought. He could experiment with morality freely, as any man should have a right to do. A strong male could even make up for past transgressions, a choice which in itself embraced the boldness allowing masculinity to flourish.

In *The Toll Gate* (1920) Hart plays the outlaw Black Deering, dressed villain-fashion entirely in black, from neckerchief to vest and pants. His humane side asserting itself, he decides to reform. Rendered masculine by his previous amoral violence, which established his credentials of manliness, the hero can safely pursue a moral course. But Hart does not make this action simple. His fellow gang members refuse to part with Black Deering, forcing him to join them in another raid where he is shot and captured.

As he escapes from the pursuing posse, Black Deering's horse breaks a leg. To spare the animal further suffering, he takes the time to shoot it, an act of kindness which informs the posse of his whereabouts. The plot of a Hart film never proceeds in a straight line. By the end of *The Toll Gate* Black Deering has fallen in love with a woman who has shielded him. But it is too late for happiness. Survival is now possible for him only below the Mexican border. He abandons this woman who loves him and whom he loves because life with him would bring her only further suffering. Women were not superfluous to the Hart hero, as they would ultimately be for Butch Cassidy and the Sundance Kid in George Roy Hill's 1969 paean. Black Deering goes off alone because a real man is selfless and protects the weak even at the expense of his own happiness.

Violence is thus not central to the Hart hero, although he is capable of it on occasion, as in *The Taking of Luke McVane* (1915) when, without a flicker of hesitation, he shoots down a man who cheats him in a card game. Nor is invulnerability, although in *Keno Bates, Liar* (1915) a serious gunshot wound fails to elicit from him the slightest expression of pain, and Black Deering emerges unscathed despite having flung himself from a moving train with his feet and hands tied together.

Instead, we remember his many moral and emotional transformations. The solitary individualism of the Hart male in the precivilized West allows him to choose freely an integrity which for Hart was the mark of a real man. In the Hart ethic, a man is a man only when he is true to himself; the obligation to do what in *The Toll Gate* is revealingly called the "white" thing becomes binding. The Hart outlaw can become a marshal, as in *The Return of Draw Egan* (1916). Or like Luke McVane, he can nurse back to health the pursuing sheriff whom he has shot, wiping his brow and fussing over him with real concern, because the male hero is incapable of leaving any wounded man to perish alone in the desert.

Sometimes a "good woman," a stereotype frequent in the Hart Western, inspires the Hart rowdy to become a valuable man. In one of his best films, *Hell's Hinges* (1916), Hart plays Blaze Tracey, a tough hombre in a wild gold town. The respectable people have sent for a churchman, and a preacher has recently arrived in town, but order is required before they can be assured safe, civilized lives. Blaze Tracey, a title informs us, is an "embodiment of the best and worst of the Early West." A "man-killer," his motto is "shoot first and do your disputin' afterward"—an early Little Caesar. Hunching his shoulders, he draws two blazing guns, firing them simultaneously. Laughing and twirling his pistols, Blaze arrives in Hell's Hinges on Fritz, his dappled horse; he is in full agreement with the drunks and gamblers that "neither Law nor Religion shall ever come to Hell's

Hinges." A cigarette dangles casually from his lips, an explicit symbol of male virility from the origins of the American film through Humphrey Bogart to the present.

Yet once Blaze meets the preacher's virtuous, beautiful sister, he does a complete about-face. The example of goodness can be inspiring, especially to "one who is evil . . . looking for the first time on that which is good." Blaze Tracey removes his hat. He leans against the barn that is now a makeshift church. He is disturbed. He succumbs. When the Sunday church service is broken up by bullies, and two roustabouts accost the preacher's sister, demanding that she dance with them, Blaze announces, "There'll be no more dancing in here." Blaze joins the parishioners, admitting to the preacher's sister, "When I look at you, I feel I've been ridin' the wrong trail." She kneels and prays, and so does he. If her example provides him with moral purpose, his male strength is needed to enact it.

Hart's Westerns were too realistic to idealize weak women, since those who pioneered the wilderness had to be physically and emotionally robust. The preacher's sister is a strong woman, unlike her namby-pamby brother who, seduced by a dance-hall floozy, sets his own church on fire in a drunken orgy.

At the close of *Hell's Hinges*, Hart singlehandedly rids the town of its evil inhabitants. Like a scourge, the screen now tinted red, he chases them out of town, a noble figure outlined by fire in godlike splendor. A gun in each hand, he burns down the saloon as the bad people scatter.

The preacher dies. In a blue-tinted scene Hart and his woman bury her weakling brother and set off together, though not before he prays to God that she will be happy. A title informs us that "whatever the future [it is] theirs to share together." Throughout this last scene Hart is gentle and affectionate, putting his strong arms around his woman and stroking her face.

Though a double standard prevails in the Hart films and women are treated like another species, they are also approached with a gentleness revealing masculine confidence, in contrast to the behavior of later screen males whose brutality toward women more often than not conceals a core of sexual doubt on the part of character and filmmaker alike. With Hart the male ideal is a man who is unequivocally heterosexual. He has no sidekick or male comrade with whom alone he can be himself. Violence is separate from his sexuality and is directed only toward evident evil. Despite his stoicism and refusal to express many of his feelings openly, the Hart hero is psychologically far more integrated than those later males who appear in Westerns which exclude women as threats to masculinity, superfluous, dangerous, and to be denigrated and scrupulously avoided.

The saddest of the Hart films is *Tumbleweeds*. It chronicles not only the demise of the open frontier but that of the rootless, free cowboy hero who had always been able, like a "tumbleweed," to pull up stakes and move westward. With the West gone, the Hart male, unlike Blaze Tracey in *Hell's Hinges,* for whom it was a matter of choice, is now forced to settle down. The once footloose male is now descending toward the restrictions of marriage and a homestead. The only other opportunity open to him is that of moving to Latin America, an alien dead end for the Western hero, which Hart rejects, and which Butch Cassidy and the Sundance Kid accepted with fatal consequences.

In an early scene in *Tumbleweeds,* Hart as cowboy Don Carver rescues a litter of wolf puppies. He is always capable of tenderness because he has no need to prove his fully apparent manhood. It is not that he eschews violence, just that "it's not my day for killing varmints." The eyes of Don Carver narrow and slant as he watches the endless stream of wagons moving into the open country and the great herds driven out to make room for them. Five cowboys, Carver among them, sit quietly on horseback and observe. Carver takes off his hat in homage to a freedom about to be lost forever. "Boys—it's the last of the West," he murmurs. Then the others remove their hats. A very slow fade leaves them blackened silhouettes against the sky. The domesticated homesteaders keep coming and a town grows up before their eyes.

Tumbleweeds culminates in the settlers' mad stampede, like domestic cattle abruptly startled out onto the open strip, each out to stake a claim to the best land. The villains show greed. Carver himself decides reluctantly to claim the Box K ranch for himself and the girl he has chosen. This man of free spirit, who had vowed that the only land on which he would settle down "will be under a tombstone," goes "courtin'," sheepishly sneaking a bouquet of flowers out of his saddlebag for his Molly. He then hides them under his vest so he will not appear "soft." He is endearing in his simplicity; when his cowlick stands up and won't flatten down, like the free male symbol Hart's uncontrollable hair had become, he cuts it off. He's "housebroke," although it doesn't make him any less a man, because he retains his sense of self. Nor does his use of force to aid the weak lessen his masculinity, as when he helps two old folks stake their claim. If the ending of the frontier confines him, he has not yet surrendered to it.

Nor does the Hart hero have to demonstrate his masculinity by slaying treacherous Indians. In *Tumbleweeds* Hart represented the Indians as reasonable, loyal, and good, as he remembered them from his boyhood. In this film Hart's depiction differs markedly from the frequent portrayal of the Indians as irrational savages constantly plotting murder and mayhem out of no motive other than their own innate brutality. Such a characterization appears in *The Taking of Luke McVane,* an early film directed by Hart that is less careful in its formulations than his later work.

A band of maniacal Apaches circle and finally kill the Hart hero without cause. Depriving the Indian both of an intellect and of any humane emotions would remain the rule for the American Western; like a mountain bobcat or a deadly rattlesnake, the Indian was to be killed and preferably exterminated. The Indian was rarely represented as a free, sensual and physically powerful male, in part because most Westerns have been devoted to justifying the racist massacre of the native peoples of America and championing the settling and political appropriation of this continent by Europeans. Hart did not personally direct *Tumbleweeds;* but he remains its *auteur,* and, particularly in its careful and sympathetic depiction of the Indian, it bears his personal stamp.

When Don Carver is accused in *Tumbleweeds* of being a "Sooner," a person who runs out onto the strip to stake his claim before the appropriate moment, the Indians come to his aid ("If you say, we fight"). This moral endorsement of the Indians marks the Hart hero as a real man, as does his lack of greed. He could never succumb to the hysteria of the land rush because he is unresolvedly ambivalent about its desirability.

A real man, above all, never defends himself against a false charge with words. When Molly mistakenly accuses him of stealing her brother's claim, Carver replies, "Do you believe that?" and then rides off to prove otherwise. Words alone are useless, and a man does not waste them. "Women ain't reliable, cows are," he concludes, anticipating what will soon become received wisdom in the Western. He decides to go to South America after all.

But by the end the villains have been safely lassoed and Don Carver has cleared himself. His honor is such that his assurance alone is sufficient to convince the sheriff: "I give you my word I'm innocent, but if you say so, I'll climb back in the bull pen [jail]." The psychological strain, however, has been great even for so stoical a man, and Hart puts his hand over his eyes, crying with relief now that the conflict is over. He will build a life with his Molly. All the Hart heroes finally endorse the value of home and hearth.

Even a Westerner knows the value of building a family. And the man best equipped to accomplish this is the noble frontiersman Hart embodied: violent only when necessary, physically strong, and possessed of the dignity of a man who always knew who and what he was and how to handle himself in the most precarious of circumstances.

IV

Other films of the twenties—Westerns like *The Iron Horse* (1924) and *Three Bad Men* (1926) of John Ford, and Raoul Walsh's fine *What Price Glory* (1926), the most important war film of the decade—presented men of action whose rough masculinity provided early models for later male images. In these films a theme first emerged which was to culminate in the seventies—male bonding, men who frequently traveled together as buddies, excluding meaningful relations with women from their lives.

As John Wayne would later become the central male in the Ford pantheon, the Ford heroes of the twenties paved the way in moral rectitude and the physical ability to make good their ethical claims in action. Davy, the hero of *The Iron Horse*, played by George O'Brien, has a tough, determined father, a surveyor, whose dream is to "reclaim the wilderness." He sports a handlebar moustache and smokes a pipe, emblems of the masculinity he would pass on to his son. Ford's glorification of the push westward is in opposition to Hart's despair over the same event. It is expressed through this rough, bearded visionary whose dream of participating in the taming of the American wilderness will be fulfilled by his son.

Davy watches his brave father murdered and scalped by an Indian. In order to sustain the myth of the nobility of taming the West, Ford, no less than his artistic inferiors, found it necessary to dehumanize the Indians. In *The Iron Horse* they are forever attempting to sabotage the building of the first transcontinental railroad eulogized in the film's title. Work on this project separates the authentic men from the weak; for Ford the Protestant work ethic marks the real man. Physical prowess is a must; toughness, allied to the pioneer spirit, makes life worth living. If Hart mourned the passing of the frontier of which the railroad was a primary cause, and if Vidor revealed the real nature of the industrial order in America, Ford sought to attach the male values of the frontier to the railroad which rendered these values obsolete. In assigning to the present the imagined heroics of the past, Ford makes a further descent into unreality as the male prowess of the cowboy increasingly masks the powerlessness afflicting all in the age of bigness and impersonal corporate life which the gaiety of the twenties sought so desperately to conceal.

Davy begins to wear a fringed Buffalo Bill jacket—later to be satirized in Robert Altman's *Buffalo Bill and the Indians* as fraudulent dressing up, demonstrating nothing more than male egotism and the spuriousness of our heroes' claims to greatness. But Ford in 1924 is in dead earnest as he adds a quasi-religious note to the project of building the first railroad linking the east and west coasts of America. "Foreigners" are unwilling to work on the railroad because of the inhuman working conditions, but Ford's beloved Irish, the best and most patriotic men and hence the most masculine, convince them of their duty. There are even "good" Indians, Pawnees who help the whites by turning on their own people and who, like a surrogate cavalry, come to the rescue at the appropriate moment. In the end Davy, the Ford hero, receives the ultimate honor expressed by physical action: "With his own hand. . . . [he has] driven the last spike."

In *Three Bad Men* Ford again focuses on immigrants seeking "happiness in America." But here the masculinity of George O'Brien as immigrant Dan O'Malley is cast in doubt. He is compared with the three "bad men" of the title, led by Bull (Farrell MacDonald), the fiercest of all. To be "bad" is to be a "real" man, a desperado most comfortable with male companions and tough enough to stand up to the most corrupt of rural sheriffs. In contrast, Dan O'Malley plays a harmonica and moves West for lack of anything better to do. Already in Ford films the marriage-bound male is ineffectual. Where Dan is unaggressive, too slow even to kiss an impatient heroine, Bull is always effective, the predator with a heart of gold who alone is able to protect hero and heroine alike. "I must be goin' blind," says one of the bad men; "fired three shots and only got two of them." Killing comes naturally to the real man, as does aiding the weak. The sentimentalism of such seeming kindness flows from the fact that it is gratuitous, allowable to brutal people as a form of display, a way of asking for acceptance of their infantile savagery.

Tall, tough, and grizzled, Bull is presented as being too much a man for marriage and civilization. At the end, having settled hero and heroine down to marriage, he dies fending off the evil sheriff. It is Bull who brings the woman, Lee, and O'Malley together, having first rejected a local dandy who announces that he's just "reached manhood." "Then you'd better reach again," replies one of the "bad men." "Not so bad," is the verdict of one, regarding O'Malley. "Not so good," is his crony's and Ford's reply. The girl makes the decision: "He'll do," invoking the exact words Howard Hawks would later have John Wayne utter in accepting Montgomery Clift as his surrogate son in *Red River*.

Strong and free, Bull and his friends are a different breed of man from the settlers. Once civilization takes over, they are superfluous. Unlike the reluctant William S. Hart in *Tumbleweeds*, who becomes a rancher if only with the greatest misgivings, they will not sully their honor by taking part in the great land rush. Any kind of permanent settling down would be alien to their natures. Each of the buddies chooses to die for the others in a finale which exudes male love. The baby later born to Lee and Dan O'Malley is named "Bull." Mischievously playing with a loaded gun, he is watched over by three silhouetted figures on the romantic Ford horizon, his three dead godfathers who join hands for a moment in the next world before they ride off forever.

A similar glorification of male bonding is at the heart of *What Price Glory*. The heroes are Quirt (Edmund Lowe) and Flagg (Victor McLaglen), professional soldiers called to the front as part of a company of marines in World War I. Their monosyllabic tough-guy names, like those of schoolboys, express the same pubescent male code. Comrades on the field of battle, they are friendly rivals over women, although it is clear that no woman can vie with the camaraderie experienced by these men when they are alone together. Their comradeship is especially intensified because the war itself is presented in this pacifist film as cruel and inhuman, chaotic and full of danger, with no redeeming principle behind the senseless killing.

Yet *What Price Glory* insists that men do their duty and fight unquestioningly despite the absurdity of war. Real men obey orders, and although Flagg will weep at the loss of one of his boys, he orders the rest not to let up until they stop a bullet. A real man proves his toughness by never weakening before an order; nothing will cause him to rebel. The best man proves himself by being the first to expose himself to the enemy's artillery. But the men who survive are the most masculine of all. A "mother's boy," who worries about losing his identification tag lest his mother not know what happened to him, is portrayed as a weakling and, of course, perishes. Real men are certain to endure, another aspect of the film which undercuts its nominal pacifist content.

Quirt the lady-killer and Flagg the good-natured buffoon seem to be sworn enemies as each desires the lovely Charmaine (Dolores del Rio). But it is their rivalry over her that allows the relationship between the two of them to flourish. They enjoy each other vicariously in apparent quest of the same woman. Real men must prove their masculinity by an obligatory pursuit of any pretty woman on the scene, but neither Flagg nor Quirt is emotionally committed to Charmaine. If the film is unconscious of the emotional ramifications of this rivalry, it remains apparent that the eros coloring their feelings for each other is stoked by their rivalry over the incidental object, who happens to be female.

Several instances of their deeper involvement make this apparent. Flagg only pretends to hate Quirt. He declares of Quirt with pride and admiration, "There isn't a smarter marine ashore or afloat." War and duty —which allow men to be alone with each other—come first. In a brilliant set piece Flagg, who has been cooking dinner for Charmaine while wearing an apron, immediately pulls off the unlikely garment with no small measure of relief upon receiving his long-awaited orders to proceed to the front. As in *Three Bad Men,* the chains of domesticity cut into a man's masculinity.

Luckily, war permits the debilitating reign of women over men to be brief. Trumpets sound. The call of the "glory racket" finds the two old marines "always faithful." Honorably fulfilling one's duty among male comrades is an infinitely more attractive style of life than that binding a man to a woman. Even the inhumanity of war, which *What Price Glory* records, is less evocative than the masculine ideal which finds in war an arena where real men can prove themselves.

The last moments find Quirt and Flagg reunited in an atmosphere heavy with the implication that this time they may not return from the front. "Hey, Flagg!" calls Quirt. "Wait for baby!" Quirt puts out his hand to Flagg. Flagg supports the limping Quirt by putting his arms around him. No injury can prevent Quirt from joining his buddies and seeing action once more. His war wound serves to permit this touching between the two men, to render it credible and untinged by homosexual feeling, despite the emotion trembling between them throughout the film. If it takes wounds to make men feel free to express physical affection for each other, wounds they shall have. If Walsh quite rightly recognizes the utterly natural need of men to express intense feeling for each other without being labeled something less than men, he has to disguise it by the contrivance of violent injury. Off go Quirt and Flagg, two buddies, to die, we may be certain, in each other's arms. No consummation can be more transcendent, suggests this film, than that experienced side by side with a male friend. In the process, women are reduced to largely passive, weak, usually emotional creatures with little depth or character, mere foils for setting off the more intense affective bonds whose repressed form is enshrined in the indomitable male. Paradoxically, it is the very dread of being unmasculine which causes the suppressed affection of men for each other to be so powerfully homosexual in character. By rejecting women and settling for sublimated emotional relations exclusively with other men, while all the time having to deny that emotional bond, the hero in the American film often is, in fact, choosing asexuality. Were masculinity not confused with the suppression of feeling, women would not, in this curious inversion of the masculine ethos, be a threat to male sufficiency.

V

Far more than the Western or the war film, it was the romance in the twenties in which the masculinity of the hero was paraded before audience men and women. Whether in the France of 1432 or the Russia of 1917, heroes like Douglas Fairbanks, Rudolph Valentino, John Barrymore, and Ronald Colman could demonstrate what it was like to be a real man. Not for them the middle-class world, let alone the monotony of the assembly line. They operated in romantic and faraway places.

The opposite of conforming "organization men" or regimented workers, they were free-wheeling, passionate, committed to action on behalf of their sense of justice, and responsible only to themselves. When and if they chose, they could be great lovers. Success for these men was never defined as obedience to the demands of a group or institution; their code was fidelity to their own intensely individualistic natures. Never consumers, members of the middle class, or factory workers, they most often portrayed either peasants or aristocrats. Yet unconsciously the great romances of the twenties like *Don Juan* (1926), *The Sheik* (1921) and its sequel, *Son of the Sheik* (1926), *The Thief of Bagdad* (1926), and *Beau Geste* (1926) reveal a pre-Depression malaise. The very escapist environment in which the hero is placed reveals a disaffection from American social reality. The real and equally dramatic events of their own time, such as the Palmer raids and the trial of Sacco and Vanzetti, are disregarded as the romances spirit the audience away from any conflicts in their own era which challenged the established order.

Valentino, Fairbanks, and Barrymore played men whose boundless energy expressed itself physically in the service of a simple code of good and evil. Explicit conformity to the status quo was not at stake because the terms of their rebellion were ultimately personal. The choice that would permit their passionate natures free rein was unburdened by ambiguity. Never men of ideas—a persona difficult to characterize in the silent era anyway—their imaginations were directed toward the instant realization of simple goals; their objectives were seen as obviously true and just. The romantic, unreal settings of many of these films freed the hero from significant social choice. His individuality was never threatened by pressure to be like other people: who would suggest to a sheik that he conform? It was beneath such supermen to resemble anyone but themselves, let alone feel obliged to be like others. Neither Valentino nor Barrymore subordinated his boundless ego or postponed for long the fulfillment of his desires. They were self-oriented. They lived exclusively by the light of their passions, and the concerns of others not attached to them never ruptured the cocoon of their self-centered splendor.

The exaltation of male camaraderie in *What Price Glory* found its way into the adventure tale *Beau Geste*, a romance of the love between men. The opening title promises the male viewer a more perfect love than that found between men and women: "Love of man for woman waxes and wanes. Love of brother for brother is steadfast as the stars." *Beau Geste* then follows the pattern of the romance, showing that such feeling is possible, not in modern-day England where the heroes grow up, but in the Foreign Legion on the sands of the Sahara. Only far from the claims of the twentieth century can men be themselves. In the Foreign Legion the three Geste brothers eagerly face death because their love for each other is stronger than fear.

The definition of manhood is woven into the fabric of their earliest education as boys. As children they play war games, citing each other for bravery. Having taught them that they are most masculine when engaged in combat, the film has the Gestes grow into "splendid manhood."

The leader of the three is Beau (Ronald Colman), small, dark, dashing, slim, and elegant. No John Wayne, he is one model of the man's man of the twenties, sporting a small black moustache, a symbol of heroic virility in this decade of Barrymore and Fairbanks. Warm and natural physical embraces are frequent between the three brothers who so love each other. The plot takes them all to the Sahara in self-exile and adventure centering on loyalty and the pursuit of honor.

As in *What Price Glory*, no matter the injustices perpetrated, masculinity is impossible without patriotism. The Gestes remain loyal to the French flag, refusing to join in mutiny against their evil commander, Lejaune. Defeat is not wholly undesirable because it permits an intensity of communion between Beau and his brother John that might not have been possible had their lives been less precarious, had they either feared danger or shielded themselves from personal risk. The two drink a last cup of wine together, in actual communion, and smoke the last of their cigarettes. Up to the moment of his death Beau, as the ideal, retains a cool rationality and self-possession.

As children the brothers had promised to give each other Vikings' funerals by fire. The love of the three is raised to ritual as the third brother, Digby, fulfills the promise of their boyhood and sets the corpse of Beau alight. The corpse of the evil commander will provide the "dog at his feet" required for the ritual funeral of the true Viking. The cremation of Beau is the emotional high point of the film, the ultimate and near-erotic expression of the love of one brother for another. Dig plays taps for Beau softly, a tear running down his cheek, for these were times when a film male could still freely cry. He lights the fire, and the body of his beloved Beau goes up in flames. He and the newly arrived John salute as the smoke billows. Later Dig will sacrifice his life that John may survive.

Barrymore and Valentino played men accessible to women, and this partly explains why audience women much more than men responded to these male stars. In two typical Barrymore films, *Beloved Rogue* (1926) and *The Tempest* (1928), the hero divides his loyalties neatly in half, balancing his life as a man and as a lover. The "beloved rogue" is the French poet and adventurer François Villon, a commoner in sympathy with the downtrodden and an impudent challenger of tyrannical authority. He is also a madcap and a great lover of women. This wide a range of male activity was especially appropriate to Barrymore, whose trademark was the ease with which he donned many masks in a variety of personae. Nowhere did he invoke this talent more strikingly than in *Dr. Jekyll and Mr. Hyde* (1920).

The multiplicity of personalities accessible to Barrymore allowed him to offer a large and unrestricted definition of masculinity. His characterizations had a far greater range than those which would be found in the American film after 1929 when the hero was frequently reduced to a rigid, single personality and often, as in the case of Clint Eastwood, confined to but one facial expression. Barrymore's real man could be alternately clown or Robin Hood, lover or avenger of the weak. The Barrymore performances exhibited his many facial and emotional transformations, unmaskings which in the silent film allowed him the appropriate transition from one state of mind to another. In *Beloved Rogue*, upon learning that he has been exiled from Paris, Villon wipes off the clown make-up in which he had been entertaining his cronies to become —himself.

Unlike the many-faceted, emotionally rich heroes of the twenties films, the women were invariably reduced to stick figures, doll-like objects like the aristocratic woman of Villon's heart. Charlotte of Vauxcelles is a prototype, hopelessly passive and a political pawn of her relatives. Forced into an engagement to the wicked Thiboult, she must await Villon's rescue and remain chaste. When she coyly accuses Villon of infidelity, a charge which is accurate, her words are said merely to strike a pose. She knows, as do we, that a real man must bring sexual experience to a woman, who serves him by remaining a waiting vessel, pure and chaste. In these romances the male rewards his woman with marriage for her compliance with the double standard. She remains one-dimensional. He, exuding bravado, durability, and poetic genius, has always many sides to his life. "Every man has two souls," Villon declaims, "one for the world and one for the woman he loves." The ideal male of the twenties was too large a figure to be encompassed by a single relationship. If he did admit women into his life, he always remained two separate people.

Barrymore's Villon is most himself in the world where he engages in those athletic feats which symbolized male potency for the twenties hero. Gaiety was a common complement to acrobatic skill and physical variety. Wielding a gigantic slingshot, Villon rains confiscated delicacies upon the poor people of Paris. His *joie de vivre* is inexhaustible; he remains a charming man who will not be thwarted. And his imagination is feverishly active; as an admirer notes, "God might send bread, but only Villon would think of brandy."

Above all, in Barrymore as in all the great male stars of the twenties, sexual doubt and an ensuing hostility toward women were unthinkable. For Villon there is no conflict between the demands of masculinity and love for his mother, whom in several scenes he kisses passionately on the lips. Villon neither worries about his sexuality nor dreads the consequences of his irreverence for authority. He outmaneuvers the king with wit, thereby saving his own life and winning the woman destined to be his. And yet, if Barrymore was not hostile to women, this may well have been because the women he pursued, as in *Beloved Rogue*, were so often passive, one-dimensional recipients of his charm. His range of emotions did not include a relationship with a woman who was his moral and intellectual equal, and with whom he might have to sacrifice some measure of his flamboyant dominance.

Barrymore's trials are far greater in *The Tempest*, where, as Ivan Markov, he must confront both the ruthlessness of the Czarist regime and the brutality of the revolution that replaced it. Ivan stands for justice based upon merit, a code obeyed by neither the old order nor the new. The Barrymore hero stands perplexed between these two worlds, his classic profile highlighted through a predominance of three-quarter shots in close on his face. The dimples in his chin, the furrows in his brow, bespeak his authenticity. He embodies in his person the truth of his insights.

Ivan begins as a poor dragoon who is promoted to the rank of officer in the Cossacks because he is so fine a soldier. Life looks good. In the ranks men enjoy a camaraderie, and the harshness of the discipline is softened by devotion to one's buddy. Ivan's best friend is his pal Bulba; in one scene the men bathe together with much splashing and horseplay. The carefree moments end when Ivan incurs the wrath of the general's snobbish daughter, who calls him a "peasant beast." His attraction to this woman, whose arrogance symbolizes that of the Czarist regime, leads to his long imprisonment.

For despite the woman's open contempt, Ivan falls so in love with her that during a party he finds his drunken way into her room, fondles her photograph, and kisses her pillow. In the twenties a male could be so consumed by love without compromising his masculinity; audiences and filmmakers felt no conflict between maleness and dependent, romantic love. When this woman enters her room, Ivan kisses the hem of her nightgown. It doesn't matter to him that she is utterly unworthy of his devotion; being "a fool for love" in a Barrymore film enhances, rather than diminishes the hero's masculinity. She immediately reports him, and he is sentenced to five years at hard labor.

World War I intervenes. With the passage of time a dramatic transformation occurs in Barrymore, which distinguishes the film. Condemned to darkness in solitary confinement, Ivan observes through his narrow window other prisoners leaving for the front. Anguished, gaunt and hollow-eyed, with huge tears escaping from his eyes, he grows nearly insane with frustration. Superimpositions tell us he is hallucinating as wild and luminous images of soldiers parade before him. He pretends to make ready to join them. His hair falling across his face, he collapses into the arms of Bulba, his rescuer. Imprisonment has wrought a deep psychological change, rendering him pathetic and isolated. The deep shadows under his eyes make him appear twenty years older. But that his mind has been affected by intolerable circumstances does not render him less masculine. Unlike a current male star such as Robert Redford, who lacks any psychological nuance in his films, twenties heroes like Barrymore could suffer and show frailty without being diminished as men.

From the ambitious dragoon who cared only about being promoted, Ivan has become a conscious person. The Barrymore hero exhibits manhood through growth; his mind and ideas alter in keeping with new experiences and a changing world. At first he hopes that the revolution will fulfill his sense of justice. But as a male ideal of the twenties, strong enough not to fear gentleness and compassion when they surface, he cannot accept a system which is shown on the screen as confusing vengeance with justice. Enlisted as a judge of the revolution, he cannot condone the killing of his old friend the general, the father of Tamara, whom he still loves.

Ivan's buddy Bulba, a lesser man, puts out a cigar on a man's neck, the same gesture habitually indulged in by the cruel, monocled Czarist officer of earlier scenes. Barrymore's eyes gleam. Tyranny, even in revenge, is alien to him. Warm and tender while strong and defiant, he cries at the death of the general, whose execution proceeds despite his opposition. Large tears flow from his eyes as he cradles the head of his old friend. This emotional gesture induces the "revolution" to arrest him for treason, his crime being that he wept at the death of an aristocrat.

If *The Tempest* tends to equate the old and new orders, it is not simplistic in its attack on the Russian Revolution. The abolition of class differences permits Barrymore to come together with Tamara as her social equal. "The Tempest," a metaphor for the revolution, permits a free, complex expression of the hero's masculinity. In prison Tamara cries while Ivan taunts her for having revealed herself at last to be "like a human being." But before long he embraces her and kisses her bleeding shoulder. Like Villon, Ivan as a proud, feeling, principled male gives every indication of being an exciting, satisfying lover. With the aid of buddy Bulba, who now recognizes the weaknesses of the new order, Ivan and Tamara escape over the border. As in *Beloved Rogue* the hero expresses his maleness by his passion both for love and for humanitarian ideals. Ivan Markov has twice sacrificed all for these ruling passions: when he entered Tamara's room, and when he abjured the possibilities of power by challenging the injustice of the revolution.

Rudolph Valentino, in film after film, would choose to live solely for love. As a fantasy figure for women in the twenties, Valentino, when faced with a conflict between the two, always chose love over work. Passion for a woman was a sufficient form of self-expression, superseding any occupation, whether that of Cossack, matador, or sheik. The pattern was established in *Blood and Sand* (1922), the first film in which Valentino received star billing. As Juan Gallardo, impoverished boy of the streets turned famous matador, Valentino is ever vulnerable to women. He is deeply involved with his mother, whom he lustily embraces after his first success. His thick, dark eyebrows furrow when Carmen (Lila Lee), his wife-to-be, tosses a flower to him in the ring. And he becomes so obsessed by his passion for the seductress and loose woman Doña Sol (Nita Naldi) that he is ruined as a matador and as a man.

John Barrymore in *The Tempest:* The Barrymore hero expresses his maleness by his passion both for love and for humanitarian ideals.

Valentino did not play the man who succeeded in the world and attracted women through the aphrodisiac of power; he embodied a sex object pursued, wooed, and won by women, a role Robert Redford would assume much later in *The Way We Were*. As a matador dressed in a "suit of lights," his arms muscular and well developed, Valentino was treated by the camera itself as a desirable object. Juan Gallardo is fawned upon and treated like a breakable doll.

Because he was a persona of the twenties, a decade in which the hero had not yet been reduced to an unbending icon of impassive strength, Valentino in films like *Blood and Sand* is a highly vulnerable figure. His passion for the temptress Doña Sol, who woos him away from his wife, totally destroys him. He knows that she is dangerous, and he loves his wife; films of the twenties were sophisticated enough to accept the idea that a man could love more than one woman simultaneously. But he cannot give her up.

Valentino also played an animal-like, fierce male whose sexuality was allied to violent passion, which excited his women. Doña Sol, admiring his muscles "like iron," calls him a "big fine animal." His "strong hands" stir her, and she urges him to bring to their lovemaking the violence with which he attacks bulls in the ring. When, in one scene, he breaks a vase and departs in anger, Doña Sol lies back in ecstasy, deeply aroused by his brutality.

The twenties resisted easy moralizing, allowing an ambiguity in films which would be undermined in the thirties when the Hays Office and the Legion of Decency restricted the depiction of sex. If Juan Gallardo has been ruined as a matador, he is not wholly condemned for succumbing to the aggressive entreaties of the sultry Doña Sol. The film implies that no full-blooded male could resist pursuit by so dynamic a woman; Valentino's masculine image is enhanced by this affair. Only in the last moments of the film does a contrived and halfhearted morality return. Gallardo, grown slack and sullen, is punished for his transgression by being fatally gored by a bull, in marked contrast to the norm of later decades, when it would be the sexually free *woman* who invariably received retribution. Removing a snake ring, a gift from and symbolic of the serpentine Doña Sol, he begs his wife's forgiveness.

Altering Blasco Ibañez's novel, a satiric attack on bullfighting, the screen version revolves around the pitfalls besetting the sexually active male. Buddies are not to be found. If in this film Valentino is ruined because he gives all for love, in his later films the sanctity of his love for women proceeds unhindered by any claims of morality.

Valentino's final films terminated an astonishingly brief career, for he died at thirty-one. Yet so great was his impact that by the time his last two films appeared—*The Eagle* (1925) and *Son of the Sheik*—Valentino was perceived as the quintessential sex object, whose fulfillment derived solely from passionate involvement with a woman. It was this aspect of the Valentino films which caused his extraordinary popularity with audience women, even as it explains his lack of appeal for men, who often accused him of being effeminate. The male in American culture had to prove his masculinity, preferably in the exclusive company of other men. The frontier, the athletic field, the police force, or the wartime front were excellent arenas for such male self-expression. For Valentino, by contrast, physical desire for a woman and the fulfillment of that desire alone attested to his manhood.

Although *The Eagle*, like *The Tempest*, is set in Russia, it takes place exclusively in Czarist times. Barrymore used the Russian setting to define himself by attacking injustice. Valentino too is in the officer corps, but in *The Eagle* the military is seen, not as a hotbed of class snobbery, but solely as a milieu where a man's beauty and bravery are enhanced. Valentino's relations are predominantly with women, rather than with male buddies.

And here the Czar is a buxom Czarina (Louise Dresser), who has designs upon the hero. Pale and slim, with his jet-black hair plastered down until it resembles patent leather, Valentino seems at the beginning of the film to be anticipating an encounter that will kindle his passion. The Czarina chooses him as her object. A woman far more "masculine" than he, she is hardly the appropriate partner, and he refuses her bribe of a promotion to general should he agree to be her lover.

Throughout his encounters with the Czarina, Valentino enacts the role of the passive object, another reason why his demeanor did not appeal to audience males schooled in a Davy Crockett–inspired masculine code. He allows the Czarina to kiss him on the mouth, slipping away only when —with tact—he must finally refuse her offer: "I'm afraid I'm too young to be a general." Precisely because love is his ruling passion, he will yield only to the right woman. For perfect, abiding love he is willing even to risk the Czarina's wrath and a death sentence. He will not give himself for less.

An evil tyrant named Kyrilla has cheated Valentino's family and seized their estate. Valentino assumes a disguise as the "Black Eagle" to lead a band of vigilantes in vengeance against the tyrant. But when he falls in love with Kyrilla's daughter, Mascha (Vilma Banky), he renounces his purpose. When love and social justice prove irreconcilable, Valentino, to whom the righting of wrongs is a less all-encompassing and profound experience, chooses love, to which he devotes himself with such fervor that it absorbs all his psychic force.

In the end, a relenting Czarina, still fond of this unruly Cossack, forges a passport that will permit Valentino a new identity. Dressed now in top hat and waistcoat, he assumes the posture of the fop, as if even a Valentino film cannot help but admit that the violent male is the most masculine.

Coyly he kisses Mascha behind her parasol. He is the single-minded, totally accessible, truly satisfying lover who thinks only of how to arouse and gratify the woman he desires.

If Valentino was allowed to appear effete in moments of *The Eagle*, this was less the case in his last film, *Son of the Sheik*, a sequel far superior to its predecessor. His biceps ripple in muscle-beach fashion, frequently displayed because his costumes are so skimpy. Prominent veins emboss his arms. His appearance offered a defiant challenge to charges like that soon to appear in the *Chicago Tribune* questioning Valentino's masculinity in an editorial entitled "Pink Powder Puffs." The piece appeared during the publicity tour Valentino made for his last film.

In *Son of the Sheik* Valentino is more dominant than in earlier films, more decisive, and consciously less passive. Rape is the central visual metaphor as the hero kidnaps Yasmin, his dancing-girl lover. The milieu is one in which males are totally in control. An evil Moor says of his wife, "When I want her, I whistle"—the antecedent for Lauren Bacall's offer to Bogart in *To Have and Have Not*.

Love is the great theme; the courting of Yasmin proceeds through many stages, offering Valentino the opportunity to be a gentle, tender lover ("Love such as mine can do no harm") as well as a violent one. In the abduction of Yasmin, Valentino throws her over his shoulder and rides off on his horse to a splendid, perfumed tent. The violence, however, is not developed because it is a concomitant of sexuality. Valentino is callous and brutal because he mistakenly believes that Yasmin has betrayed him to her father for ransom money, an entrapment from which he has already extricated himself.

The rape is photographed completely from the viewpoint of the male, not of the female victim. Valentino, decked out in embroidered silks, slowly undresses, his biceps perpetually flexed. It is this strip-tease which entices the audience to become voyeurs. The heroine clings to his knees, begging him to relent. As she pleads, he walks determinedly toward her, and the scene ends with a slow fade, allowing time for the viewer's imagination to sketch in the details of a supreme sexual consummation. Later events in the film suggest it did not really occur, a ploy designed to retain the arousing scene while disclaiming it. But no matter: we perceive the rape as if passionate sexual intercourse were about to take place, the supremely desirable Valentino performing to the woman's total satisfaction.

A flashback to *The Sheik* shows that Valentino has learned his technique from his dominant, strong-willed father, who in his time also refused to take no for an answer. The Sheik pulls Diana, who is to become the son's mother, from her horse with the order, "Lie still, you little fool!" Thus in the Valentino films a real man remains someone before whose superiority women tremble.

In *Son of the Sheik* Valentino is more dominant than in earlier films, more decisive, and consciously less passive. Rape is the central visual metaphor.

In a movie starring Valentino the mood is entirely heterosexual. At the end of *Son of the Sheik,* the son and Yasmin, their lips slowly joined, ride off into the sunset to continue their lovemaking uninterrupted and in dead earnest. Valentino had joined the ranks of the dominant screen males —strong and violent when necessary. Yet to the delight of his female fans, who were tied to men in whose lives they perhaps took second place, he remained committed to his woman, willing to devote all his energy to the act of love.

VI

Rarely in the twenties was that familiar seventies type, the raw, seldom smiling, sullen male, on the screen. The twenties were a time of willed optimism; the hero of the decade, "Lucky Lindy," Charles A. Lindbergh, whose feat endeared him to crowds, was a man who faced danger and the unknown in an act of individual daring, proving himself the supremely masculine male. But just as in the seventies Americans refused to recognize the full implications of the Watergate scandals, so in the twenties the outrageous corruption of the Harding administration failed to move Americans even to repudiate official evil by rejecting the party in power. Harding, at the 1920 Republican convention, had requested "not surgery but serenity" for America, words that presaged the mood of the decade.

The widespread strikes after World War I inspired Attorney-General Alexander Palmer's injunctions against strikers and a ruthless roundup of radicals. The Palmer raids that followed, in which suspected anarchists, socialists, or "Bolsheviks" were hounded and sometimes deported, produced a reign of terror very similar to that which characterized the McCarthyite fifties.

Thus the 1920s were marked by a great but nonetheless revealing paradox—the lawless device of imposing law and order by putting aside the Bill of Rights set the political tone for the decade, yet produced in film many multifaceted, sensitive male portrayals, a phenomenon that would reappear in the fifties. With political freedom under assault, people were encouraged to opt for sexual liberation and more open styles of personal life. The popularity of Freud and the vulgarization of his theories to support the free expression of sex in obedience to the libido spoke to a frustration induced by the fear of being labeled subversive. Fads ruled the day, from Mah-Jongg and crossword puzzles to an intense interest in heavyweight boxing, orchestrated by that new invention, the radio.

Unwilling to challenge the prevailing political mood, which allowed
the breaking of strikes and demanded obeisance to the status quo, film,
as did the culture at large, willfully turned its face away from official
injustice. It created male fantasy figures who could accomplish their
exploits successfully without ever having to deal with the conditions that
led to the Palmer raids or such real-life emasculations as depriving people
of their rights to free speech and freedom of association and the right to
strike. The Western, with its origin in the Wild West show and in frontier
stories from those of Bret Harte to the romances of Zane Grey, presented a ready-made arena where fantasy heroes could realize themselves,
immune to events of the day which so robbed men of their power to
act.

Films like *The Tempest* and *The Eagle* revealed the decade's official
dread of the Russian Revolution, a fear belonging to the business community primarily, which sought to make it a popular concern through
Hollywood. The post–World War I spirit of isolationism led to Congress's refusal to join the League of Nations; the Great War had ended
in revolution after all, a prospect to which America might not be immune.
Thus the desire to avoid any close relationship with Europe, military if
not economic, produced in films the spectacle of Douglas Fairbanks
forever escaping to romantic parts unknown where he need be concerned
only with his own personal happiness.

From its beginnings film was conceived both as entertainment *and* as
a refuge from political reality. And the greater the political repression of
the moment, the more powers were granted the male individual on
screen. The harsh political atmosphere of the twenties led to a characterization of the film hero as so strong that his masculinity was never threatened even by moments of softness and gentleness. Not only Valentino and
Barrymore, but even more frequently Douglas Fairbanks and Tom Mix,
revealed wellsprings of tenderness and compassion which in later films
would become the province solely of women. Gentleness never exposed
Fairbanks and Mix to doubt about their adequacy as men, nor did vulnerability produce that frantic anxiety leading to the repression of open
feelings and the inability to acknowledge weakness and doubt. The world
in which they moved on screen was so amenable to their influence that
Mix and Fairbanks felt un-self-conscious in articulating the impulses of
the good heart. A pristine innocence hovered over their presence like a
halo.

Only in a decade like the twenties could Tom Mix replace William S.
Hart as the most popular Western star. The official carefree mood that
followed World War I required a less monolithic image of manhood than
that offered by the stoical, unsmiling, and often self-righteous Hart.

If Hart shot down his enemies with smoking pistols, the infinitely more
engaging Mix usually relied on the lasso alone to restrain the unruly. The

brute assertiveness with which Edward G. Robinson was to usher in the thirties with his portrayal of the frantic, upward-striving Rico in *Little Caesar* (1930) was also totally inappropriate to the Westerns of Tom Mix, in which "evil" all but willingly yielded before the mere presence of good. The serene world of Mix was not a place where brutality was synonymous with sensuality and ruthlessness the true test of a man. In this difference lies the change in America from a seemingly stable social order to that frightening, disintegrating, chaotic world ushered in by the Great Depression of 1929.

No matter how pervasive the evil he faces, the Mix hero never abandons his good nature. Unlike Hart, he would never play a gangster or an outlaw, nor would he kill his enemies. Even in the darkest of his films, *Riders of the Purple Sage*, Mix permits a man to survive who had kidnapped his sister many years before and ruined her life. The exigencies of their encounter jeopardize the life of a child named Little Fay, to whom Tom has become attached. Rooted in the needs of the moment, Mix lets lapse the abstract demand of revenge. The child is saved, the villain left to go free. As a result of Mix's famous stunts, which he almost always performed himself, his body was riddled with scars. But this physical daring was never characterized by violence.

Like all twenties heroes, and unlike later film cowboys, Tom Mix was unambiguously heterosexual, except for his relationship with Tony, his male horse! At the start of the thirties we would hear Little Caesar taunt his buddy Joe, insisting that men who are tied to women are something less than masculine. "When she's with you," Rico tells Joe, referring to Joe's friend and dancing partner, Olga, "you ain't good for anything." Despite clichés about his horse being the true object of the cowboy's affection, Mix never allowed buddy or horse to stand between him and a woman he loved. Tony the Wonder Horse, intelligent and self-sufficient as he was, may in fact have been Tom Mix's closest buddy—a Sundance Kid to his Butch Cassidy—but if the horse was his trusted companion in heroics, the endings of the Mix films did not present his animal friend as an alternative to the woman in his life. They closed on a threesome: Tom, the heroine, and Tony grouped together in harmonious symbiosis and mutual appreciation. In the last scene of *The Great K. & A. Train Robbery* (1926) Tom, Tony, and Tom's woman retreat to a quiet place. There Tony runs along, free at last of the problems of the K. & A. Railroad. Tom and the heroine sit watching side by side on the rear platform of an unused train.

The engaging quality of the Mix films and the ease with which they approached the whole question of masculinity are typically expressed in *Just Tony* (1922). William S. Hart found it unnecessary for the male star to appear in more than forty percent of the film's footage, unlike later heroes who insisted that their faces appear in virtually every scene. Following Hart's formula, in *Just Tony* the hero is far less Mix himself than his horse.

Tony begins as a wild stallion whose behavior ranges from the mischievous to the sadistic because he "has never known love," a perception about the relationship between unavowed need and violence that applies to many later male heroes but is rarely acknowledged. Mix merely acts as a catalyst. In offering Tony "love and kindness," he restores the animal to his best self. As in so many of his films, Tom Mix subordinates his personality to the exigencies of plot and theme.

Thus if anyone is stridently masculine in the accepted manner, it is Tony himself, wild leader of a herd, capable of planning countless, cunning vendettas against "his enemy, Man." Tom must prove himself humane enough to be worthy of the animal. "I love that horse better than anything in the world," says Tom Mix. His aim: "to make him love me as I know he's going to some day." Tom's woman, Marianne, is part of his life, but in this film it is Tony who allows Mix to express the hidden stores of tender feeling which so seldom surface in the lives of screen males. There is always a vulnerability about Mix's screen characters. He permits himself situations in which he may be rejected, as when he begs Tony to trust him: "I won't hurt you . . . not for the world . . . why, you and I are going to be pals." But the decision is Tony's, for he is capable of crushing Mix as he had earlier injured his trainer. He is physically stronger than Mix, and the action of the film indicates that Tony would be morally justified whatever course of action he chose.

But Tom has proven himself to be a different kind of man from the bullies Tony has known. It is Tom who gave Tony his first caress. Unlike later screen heroines made to desire unfeeling, stoical men, Tony appreciates gentleness. In the last scene Tom, Marianne, and Tony embrace. Tony considers his old freedom, but returns. In exchange, Tom gives him a big hug. Tony puts his head on Tom's shoulder, and Marianne too caresses him. Men and women in the Mix films are equally capable of expressing affection for those who need them, for children and for animals. If *Just Tony* seems like a film for children, it is only because it offers a rare image of a male unashamed of his feelings and capable of expressing them spontaneously.

Dick Turpin (1925) is set in England. Mix, playing a Robin Hood–like highwayman, is equally devoted to his horse, Black Bess. But this is not his only affectionate relationship. He has a male buddy (Alan Hale) to whom he is as devoted as he is to a woman (though, typically, she is forever in need of rescue). His masculinity is also expressed in a traditional manner in the prize-fighting scenes in which Tom impersonates the strongest boxer of the day and wins the purse with ease.

The emotional highpoint, however, comes with the death of Black Bess, worn out after a grueling chase through the English countryside.

In *The Last Trail* Tom Mix's tenderness is directed toward his orphaned namesake, Little Tommy. Tom proceeds to nurture the child, wearing an apron, dispensing castor oil, and uninhibitedly assuming the roles of both father and mother.

"The best friend a man ever had," Tom eulogizes her, declaring, "you deserved a better fate." Crying unashamedly and profusely, he lifts the head of his horse and kisses her goodbye. Then, laying his handkerchief over her face, he proceeds on foot to rescue the heroine. The defining characteristic of Tom Mix was not merely sentimental attachment to his horse but his capacity to express his feelings without reservation or fear. In this he was one of the first and, until the fifties, one of the only gentle yet masculine males in the history of American film.

In *The Last Trail* (1927) Mix's tenderness is directed toward his orphaned namesake, Little Tommy. With the death of Little Tommy's sheriff father, the boy and his buddy dog are placed in Mix's custody. Tom proceeds to nurture the child, holding him in his arms, wearing an apron, dispensing castor oil, and uninhibitedly assuming the roles of both father and mother. When his little Huck Finn strays, Tom uses his temporarily idle lasso to pull him in. There are scenes in which Tom does battle with the local villains, but his strong parental feeling for the boy neither recedes nor takes second place. He winds up with the heroine at the end, only to be teased by his little charge that it is Tom who will now be forced to have the bath with which the woman had repeatedly threatened Little Tommy. The domestic person and the effective male are never irreconcilable in the Mix films.

This is not to say that Tom Mix wasn't "tough." In *Sky High* (1922) he works for a time as a bouncer. In the climactic scene he even descends from an airplane by means of a rope and, singlehanded, defeats the film's small group of villains. But Mix never enjoys violence nor deploys it to establish his manhood. In later films the sight of a man wearing an apron would provoke ridicule and accusations of effeminacy. This was never true for Mix, who lacked the fear characterizing those male stars who would rather be annihilated than acknowledge imperfection. Mix wrote: "How few there are who have courage enough to own their faults, or resolution enough to mend them." His manhood, Tom Mix felt, was *enhanced* by the admission of weakness. His emotional maturity and relaxed warmth set a norm from which future male heroes would wholly degenerate.

Other Westerns of the twenties were equally free of any harsh distortion of the male personality, notably James Cruze's *The Covered Wagon* (1923), the finest single Western film of the decade. The hero, Will Banion, first appears as a man with a scandal in his past arising from his discharge from the army for stealing cattle. In fact, he had commandeered the cattle to save his detachment from starvation. But this does not emerge until late in the film, and throughout the hero assumes a weak and unheroic posture. He is obliged to ride in the rear of the wagon train to round up stray stock, having been denied the rank of captain. Like Tom Mix, Will Banion is a tender companion to children. At the onset of the trip West he helps make a doll for one of the little girls, whose tears he dries with his handkerchief. He is pale and gentle, a far cry from those crude desperadoes who function as masculine ideals in *Three Bad Men*.

The equivalent of Ford's Bull is Will's nemesis, a brute named Sam, Will's rival for the heroine, Molly. Will has many opportunities to kill Sam in a fair fight, but he always refuses to take advantage. Will's buddy, Bill, calls him a "poor, big-hearted worm," an epithet hardly conceivable for the strong, indomitable heroes of later Westerns. At the end it is buddy Bill who kills the evil Sam and so saves Will's life: "Some bacon grease got on my finger and it slipped, though I knew you were set on sparing that critter." Here the hero is a person who firmly shuns violence, even when it is directed against an obvious menace like Sam. And Sam has displayed his villainy by the gratuitous killing of an Indian, perceived as an unspeakable act in a film which, unlike so many earlier and future Westerns, recognizes the Indians' humanity.

At its close *The Covered Wagon* proposes farming as the occupation most befitting a man, instead of gold prospecting or other adventures.

Will, like Valentino at the end of *The Eagle,* has donned a frock coat with a velvet collar. When hero and heroine embrace at the end, *he* buries his head in *her* shoulder. It is the woman who gives solace, comfort, and protection to her man, not the reverse, in this film which consistently advances a set of values alternative to those of most Western films.

The silent era also produced parodies which ridiculed the absurd, aimless violence of the heroes of early Westerns. One of these was Mack Sennett's *His Bitter Pill.* The hero is bald, awkward, "big-hearted" Sheriff Jim, his "mother's pride." His huge moustache contributes nothing to his masculinity. Painfully shy, he chews on his hat as the villain, "Diamond Dan," makes time with Jim's girl.

When the girl chooses Dan, telling Jim she loves him only as a brother, our hero bursts out crying. Wringing his hat like a handkerchief, he flings himself upon his bed, crying and kicking his feet in frustration, incapable at this point of the slightest action. Ma is available and he can cry on her shoulder. Jim is neither physically desirable nor cool and stoical. Yet despite his emotional dependence on women, he gets the girl in the end when Dan proves a scoundrel.

The hero is man as we know him, a vulnerable human being who can be incapacitated by failure, whose "fist may be hard" but whose "heart is soft." The image is both ludicrous and cleansingly antiromantic. The people move in Sennett-like chaos, forever compromising themselves, and are, above all, profoundly human.

VII

It was the most important male star of the decade, Douglas Fairbanks, Sr., who fulfilled the appetite for spectacle and the exotic and also most frequently transcended the culture's rigid definitions of masculinity. The faraway, fairy-tale atmosphere of so many of the Fairbanks films allowed him to develop an image composed simultaneously of adult masculinity and innocence, a combination perhaps rarely met with in the real world, but no less an appealing, romantic ideal. The settings released him from the confinement of life in America, from social and economic limitations. The resulting psychic space allowed Fairbanks to cultivate in his screen personalities those qualities of gentleness, good nature, humility, and fun absent from many later male heroes, who take themselves too seriously because their sense of identity is so much more tenuous. This freedom was seized and exultingly expressed in the bold antics of Fairbanks's heroes. His unparalleled athletic panache, which sent him swinging from ropes, scaling walls, and virtually dancing in choreographed acrobatic splendor, stood for masculinity triumphant and unrestrained.

Douglas Fairbanks, Sr., in *The Black Pirate:* His unparalleled athletic panache, which sent him swinging from ropes, scaling walls, and virtually
dancing in choreographed acrobatic splendor, stood for masculinity triumphant and unrestrained.

Cartoonists Jerry Siegel and Joseph Shuster were inspired to create their thirties comic strip "Superman" by the irrepressible Fairbanks Senior, whose physical magnificence they recalled from the boyhood films that had shaped their sense of maleness. Unlike Superman, however, Fairbanks was no rigid and moralistic protector of the weak; he was a master of the about-face, and from his uninhibited nature joy or sorrow, compassion or determination, love or longing, wistfulness or pleasure might at any moment emerge. The romance and heroics of Fairbanks were as innocently gay and escapist as a children's cartoon. To compare them with the spirit evoked by such figures as Bronson and Eastwood in the seventies is to gauge the degeneration in the culture.

In his pre-twenties films, contemporary with the work of the dour William S. Hart, Fairbanks played anything but a male "faster than a speeding bullet, more powerful than a locomotive, able to leap tall buildings at a single bound." In those early films there is a central notion which serves as a leitmotif throughout Fairbanks's later, better-known work: a man's strength resides in recognition and acceptance of his limitations. His films often imply that manliness itself lies in accepting one's fallibility. He could laugh at himself, alter unpleasant facets of his personality when made aware of them, and accept himself as the limited human being he was.

A typical early film, *Reaching for the Moon* (1917), finds Fairbanks at its conclusion forever cured of an obsessional desire to be as manly as the heroes of old, figures whose personae are invoked by his own name, which reflects his mother's ambitions: Alexis Caesar Napoleon Brown. Alexis is a clerk in a button factory, a timid fellow entirely lacking in the self-confidence of the splendid physical specimen Fairbanks would become in such later films as *The Thief of Bagdad* and *The Black Pirate* (1926). Short and stocky, with thin, pursed lips, a double chin, and rapidly thinning hair, he is the ordinary man, resembling no one so much as King Vidor's Johnny Sims. He lacks that debonair, pencil-thin moustache Fairbanks would sport in the twenties. Alexis is a hero because he learns that the life of an adventurer is less desirable than it might seem.

He dreams that he has become heir to the throne of his homeland, "Vulgaria." The events of his return to this mythical place are fraught with peril. Spies and murderers lurk behind closed doors, their political ambitions demanding his demise. The fantasy affords Fairbanks an opportunity to make full use of his athletic powers as he eludes his enemies. But the moral of the film is that physical supremacy does not make a man. Greater freedom may reside at home, and standing on one's head is an antic best reserved for amusing one's children on a Sunday afternoon. Alexis Caesar Napoleon Brown accepts the fact that he is ordinary; good sense defines him as a man. And being average and entirely undistinguished, lacking both political power and high social status, makes him no less sexual, no less male. *Reaching for the Moon* proposes a non-megalomaniac approach to male sexuality, insisting that every man, regardless of his social importance, can be virile if he sufficiently values himself.

In *When the Clouds Roll By* (1919) Fairbanks again played a male who was not a superman. Again he is the ordinary man, susceptible to unknown forces. His nemesis is a mad scientist named Dr. Ulrich Metz, who decides to experiment on our hapless hero with his own special brand of behavior modification. The doctor plants "psychic germs" of fear, worry, and superstition in the mind of Daniel Boone Brown. Brown does just as he is ordered and even confides in his tormentor. Through most of the film Fairbanks as Brown is hurt, misled, rendered a fool, and betrayed by those he considers his friends. He is dubbed a "dumfuddle" and seems to deserve it. That the male hero must always be stoical and dominant is a notion entirely absent from these early Fairbanks characterizations.

When Daniel Boone Brown's marriage plans fall through, he bursts into tears. Even when he manages finally to assume some control over his life, he never becomes the tight-lipped male of the thirties, forties—or seventies. Nor does he assume the surly, *angst*-ridden demeanor affected by heroes of the fifties. Gaiety remained always accessible to Fairbanks, even in the less interesting films he made in the thirties. In *When the Clouds Roll By,* Fairbanks's reaction, upon realizing the magnitude of his folly, is to burst out laughing.

The transition to the more familiar Fairbanks personality is accomplished on screen in *The Mollycoddle* (1920). Fairbanks begins as a foppish, effeminate man, an expatriate in Europe who has forsaken the male bravado of his cowboy forefathers, but by the end of the film he has returned to the Old West. He wears his familiar moustache, which serves as proof that, as he tells the heroine, he has "the makings of a man."

Yet despite the affirmations of these frontier definitions of maleness, Fairbanks still defies the stereotype by laughing too much. His affable self is amused by the Indians who prefer his cigarette to their peace pipe, an incident that could never occur in a Western where the hero took himself more seriously. As in the Mix films, Fairbanks, our former mollycoddle, defeats through cunning the evil smuggler played by Wallace Beery, but without resort to bloodshed. Fairbanks, in fact, emerges from hand-to-hand combat with Beery requiring no more first aid than that provided by a Band-aid. The battle proves to be as innocent as the evil is amenable to control.

Easy approachability and good-humored benevolence remained aspects of the mature Fairbanks hero throughout the twenties. In *The Mark of Zorro* (1920) Fairbanks, while swashbuckling his way through the film, exhibits an ironic sense of the absurdity of a man's proving his manhood through something as ridiculous as swordplay. In the midst of battle, he takes time out to slash open the ceiling, bursting a pipe for the purpose of creating a delightful waterfall. To dramatize the childish nature of these exploits, he cuts a hole in the seat of an adversary's trousers. Into the eye of another he thrusts hot pepper, even as his Robin Hood will shoot arrows into the hats of friends.

Unburdened by the constant need to prove his masculinity, Fairbanks delighted in such antics and in the playfulness of a boisterous spirit. He always knew who and what he was. In roles like Zorro, Robin Hood, and D'Artagnan, Fairbanks was as involved in righting wrongs and restoring justice as would be future screen males from the Virginian to Shane. But these later heroes would lack the psychic and social capacity for both irreverence and modesty which Fairbanks personified. Later examples of sensitive males like Paddy Chayevsky's Marty could not compete with blatantly virile men and were labeled and perceived as losers. Unlike Marty, whose horizons were so much narrower, Fairbanks could admit to explicit sexual doubt, as in the opening scene of *Robin Hood* when he announces that he is "afeared of women" and prefers wrestling with male companions.

By the end of *Robin Hood*, when the power of Richard the Lion-Hearted is restored, accompanied by the return of justice and order, Fairbanks is permitted precisely that emotional and sexual maturation denied later heroes who are too insecure ever openly to acknowledge anxiety or fear of the opposite sex. Robin has finally married Maid Marian, a far cry from Sean Connery's 1976 Robin who, having abandoned Marian to life in a convent, returns from adventures with his buddies only when he is middle-aged.

On their wedding night, King Richard (Wallace Beery), unable to relinquish the company of the delightful, sensual Robin, knocks on the door of their bridal chamber. Robin is slowly and delicately caressing his wife (Enid Bennett), who sits on the edge of their bed. He ignores the knocking, although he knows full well it comes from the man to whom he has devoted much of his life. Richard persists and is ignored. In the final fade Fairbanks rejects his buddy, enfolding the woman he loves in his arms with genuine tenderness. He is completely absorbed in lovemaking, savoring the pleasure and exuding the simple joy of a man being with a woman that will virtually disappear from films by the 1970s.

This ease with his masculinity and confidence in his maleness continue even in Fairbanks's more "macho" roles in *The Thief of Bagdad, The Black Pirate,* and *The Gaucho* (1927). Never does he adopt the methods of his enemies to defeat them, as will later beleaguered heroes like Dustin Hoffman in *Straw Dogs*. In *The Black Pirate* Fairbanks becomes an outlaw to avenge the death of his father. But he refuses to blow up the passengers of captured vessels in the traditional manner of the pirate. He may join the outlaws temporarily, but he lacks their callousness and disdains their brute violence.

Despite his explicitly masculine behavior and dress, Fairbanks uses humor when dealing with the complex interaction between men and women. In *The Gaucho* his response to the jealousy of his mistress is neither anger nor capitulation but resounding laughter. Patient and affectionate, he is willing to take along on his search for gold not only his tempestuous mistress but the very house he has built for her: ropes are tied around floor and beams, and away they go! By the end of the film his good heart triumphs over baser impulses of greed. The affirmation of good nature and not the defeat of antagonists, as with heroes to come, marks the transcendence of the Fairbanks male.

Fairbanks played men of manifold qualities. He was equally at ease with men, women, and children and, like Mix, with animals. He liked his buddies, as is revealed in the closing image of the Three Musketeers in heaven in *The Iron Mask* (1929), but he nurtured weaker creatures too, as in *Mr. Robinson Crusoe* (1932). His acrobatic virtuosity made him exceptional, but he always personified both the strengths and the weaknesses of the species, displaying a variety of qualities later to be rigidly apportioned between men and women. He persistently was the male human being as he might be were he not so encouraged, both in movies and in life, to repress his impulses and conceal his feelings. Fairbanks conveyed an image of the male in psychic health—and in this sense, alas, he may have been no less a fantasy figure than the stoical, self-contained hero.

VIII

Examples of the fallible hero abound in films of the twenties. Sometimes he was played by the slim and slight Richard Barthelmess, not only as a foil to the girl-heroines of D. W. Griffith but also as the boy-man of an important film like Henry King's *Tol'able David* (1921). The tolerability of David will be determined by whether or not he can measure up to the society's standards of maleness. Boyish, pale, effeminate-looking, and dubbed a "mother's boy," he is the only member of his family who fails to reflect the image of masculinity in our culture. Unlike his physically active father and brother, David is a dreamer who prefers to read books, albeit about muscular Greek heroes whom he knows he will never resemble.

By the end David has become a man by the accepted definition, despite his falling short of the physical ideal. He has delivered the government mail by fending off a pack of local bullies—no matter that, exhausted, he falls prostrate into the arms of his waiting mother, who exclaims, "David must always be my baby." If *Tol'able David* insists that the way to be a man is to be physically powerful, it also affirms that mind and conscience are as much needed as muscle and brawn.

In Griffith's *Broken Blossoms* (1919) Barthelmess plays a pacifist Chinese, a pigtailed racial stereotype, "The Yellow Man," who transcends this cliché through the sincerity of his wish to "take the message of peace to the barbarous Anglo-Saxons, sons of turmoil." Early in the film he shrinks away in horror at the violence of foreign sailors in China and decides to go abroad to offer corrupt Westerners "the lessons of the gentle Buddha."

Sensitive and nonviolent, slim, ascetic, spiritual, and intellectual, Barthelmess projects an image of a compassionate man distressed by the pain wrought by men yet unable to do anything to alleviate the suffering that distresses him. In London he is reduced to becoming a "Chink storekeeper" in the Limehouse ghetto, hardly the setting for a conventional hero. But if he is unable to alter his world, he remains superior to it in his sensitivity. Griffith's sense of values establishes Barthelmess as more admirable than all the strong males in the film, particularly the violent "Battling Burrows," a boxer and his antagonist. "The Battler," a sadist, takes special delight in abusing his adopted child, Lucy (Lillian Gish). The violent male in this film is portrayed, not as the protector of the weak, but as a monster. Men who do not value women are abhorred by Griffith as unspeakable human beings. This sensibility is explicit in the account of a worn-out housewife who advises Lucy never to marry and in the words of a prostitute who warns her against the degradation of her profession.

When the Battler's abuses become more than she can bear, Lucy runs away. The gentle Chinese takes her in, shielding, protecting, and nurturing this frightened child. He offers her the first tenderness she has ever known, and as a result her personality is transformed. She blossoms.

But the Chinese is no match for the Battler, who regains Lucy and beats her to death. Overcome, the once gentle storekeeper shoots the man over and over again. Rescuing the battered body of Lucy, he stabs himself, dying by her side. Out of Griffith's frequent dichotomy between the childlike woman and the rough, violating male emerges an image enacted by Barthelmess which repudiates traditional sex roles. Griffith skirts the issue of miscegenation by making Lucy a mere child and killing off his hero and heroine before their love can mature. But despite this, Barthelmess poses a wholly desirable ideal: the image of a man who would be tender.

The films of the twenties which presented gentle or tender males unafraid to avow normal human fallibility ranged from the melodramatic to the comic, exemplified by a rich range of comic personalities from Keaton and Chaplin to Harold Lloyd and Harry Langdon, who will be discussed later. Among serious films Erich von Stroheim's *Greed*, perhaps the finest American film of the decade, openly attempts to demystify the association of male sexuality with violence. The hero is the McTeague of Frank Norris's naturalist novel, in whose blood flows the potential for brutality inherited from dissipated ancestors.

Like so many women before and after her, Trina, the heroine, is aroused by the brute size and strength of a male whose animal sexuality she feels can overwhelm her. The relationship ends in her murder as von Stroheim deduces the real psychic meaning of associating male prowess with both violence and a concealed disdain for women. McTeague has the capacity to be tender, as he reveals when he rescues a bird put down into the mines to test for the presence of poisonous gases. Von Stroheim contrasts this side of McTeague's nature, the gentleness of a man who can play "Nearer, My God, to Thee" on his concertina while he is courting, with his mad violence.

Economic hardship and Trina's intense greed cause the brutish component of McTeague's psyche to emerge. Its triumph marks a victory for degeneracy, and as it proceeds von Stroheim distances us from the character, denying him sympathy until, at his last moments, dying in Death Valley and chained to the corpse of Marcus, his enemy, McTeague sets free his beloved songbird. According to naturalist theory, McTeague, like us all, had the capacity to be gentle, had heredity and environment not collaborated in his ruin. It is this aspect of his personality which would have made him a worthwhile male.

In many comic films of the twenties the hero lacks by definition the invincible male qualities that are supposed to appeal to women, a problem Buster Keaton attacks in *College* (1927). Keaton plays an intellectual who graduates from high school as "our most brilliant scholar." Unfortunately, his sole admirer is his mother, for in our society the intellectual is presumed to be a protected mama's boy, a failure as a man unless he proves otherwise. Keaton seems unmanly, awkward, and unappealing. The sleeves of his jacket are too short, and the jacket itself is forever popping open during his valedictory address. "Where would I be without my books?" he asks pathetically as the audience doubles up in uproarious laughter.

Arriving at college, Keaton finds that only athletes are popular with girls, even though one of the most favored has taken seven years to graduate. *College*, though it openly ridicules the mindless jocks whose brutish ways have been confused by women with virility, finds no alternative values by which the hero could demonstrate his merit. The hero's fate reproduces that of countless young men befuddled by the insistence that male virility is at war with the concern for ideas and can be demonstrated only on the playing field. Like so many American boys, Keaton feels honor-bound, compelled to prove himself a man through excellence in athletics.

Hopelessly inadequate by the standard that measures men according to their physical attributes, he heroically persists, even reading pamphlets on how to play baseball. But he remains a runt, not to be compared with the "real men," tall and dapper in sweaters on which their athletic letters are displayed. The comedy centers on Keaton's ridiculed efforts, as his glove falls off during a baseball game or as he knocks the hat off the dean's head with a discus. When he begins to fail academically because he must, to no avail, spend all his time on sports, he pleads, "I took up athletics because the girl I love thinks me a weakling."

The male on film must not only be an athlete if he is not to be dubbed a sissy, but he must also win, suggesting that those who have measured up have, in fact, been victors on the playing field. This doubtful premise is insisted upon in movie after movie. Even today in our automated time, films encourage the myth that physical prowess, particularly in sports, is a requisite for power and responsibility. American movies demand that boys, in order to be men, must expend their energies in competitive physical activity. But the reason points more to diverting the athletic hero, and the audience vicariously involved in whether he wins or loses, from seeking positions of social influence or training themselves for such a role.

College ultimately contends that happiness can result only from accepting established norms. The sympathetic dean makes Keaton coxswain of the rowing crew, where he is at first derided by his fellow team members as "Little Lord Fauntleroy." Yet at a crucial moment Keaton finds, through intelligence, a way to compensate for a broken rudder, and his team wins. His athletic triumph may not have derived from physical prowess, but it is triumph enough to give him the physical courage and self-confidence to rescue his girl from an obnoxious athlete who has stolen into her room. Pole-vaulting through the window and displaying all the techniques of the decathlon, he defeats his rival and wins his woman.

If *College* discloses the cruelty of standards that reject men with attributes other than the physical, the sole remedy it proposes is perseverance and finally the total acceptance of such values. Yet if *College* refuses to propose a revolution against this definition of the male, it also brilliantly exposes the problem, admitting that not all men can prove themselves in sports. The ending of *College* might be seen as a wish-fulfilling fantasy of the small male.

A balance sheet for the twenties certainly would contain many characterizations of violent males who would never dream of admitting to vulnerability. But the raw appetite for experience in the twenties led to the predominance of film males who were as often frivolous as they were somber. Because his audience reveled in an atmosphere of economic prosperity, the "real man" was not always obliged to be stern and unrelenting. Often he could laugh at himself, and frequently he would cry. He liked women and, out of genuine regard and pleasure, preferred their company to that of his male friends. (Ford's "three bad men" form an exception to the general heterosexuality of the twenties film hero.) He was not afraid to express weakness or face humiliation. A superhuman invulnerability did not distinguish him from a "weaker" sex.

The silent film was also unique because it so often challenged the crude distinction between the "masculine" and the "feminine." This was true with respect to both quantity and quality. Griffith's *Broken Blossoms* and King's *Tol'able David,* classics of the American cinema, transcended the view that traits associated with power and dominance belong only to men, while sensitivity and gentleness are the province of women alone. And a host of less fine films, like the Mix Westerns, equally refuse to deprive the male of the opportunity to be tender and vulnerable. An overwhelming number of films of the twenties allow their heroes a wide range of responses from the daring to the contemplative, from self-doubt to self-confidence.

This richly varied male image all but disappeared from American films with the Depression. By the time we reach a typical mid-thirties comedy like *It Happened One Night,* director Frank Capra is careful to assign one set of qualities to Gable, the wisecracking, ever-competent journalist, and another to Colbert, his hapless and helpless charge. The male who was both tender and emotionally strong, intellectual and physically active, nonviolent and yet determined, would but rarely reappear in American films.

Crossing into Hard Times

With the Depression came a hardening of the male image. Gone was the hero possessed of an infinite amount of time to explore the byways of his personality, test his strengths, and laugh at his many weaknesses. By the turn of the decade the male hero was becoming fiercely competitive, domineering, and stridently aggressive, as if by his example Americans could be convinced that the individual, through raw nerve and sheer willed determination, could overcome the economic disaster which had befallen the nation.

Sensuality on the screen was at once called into question as a more harshly puritanical morality was imposed upon Hollywood. Movies now suggested that only the absence of a passionate sexual life could make a man fit to endure the Depression. The Hays office and the Legion of Decency played their role in robbing the screen of any thirties Valentinos. Will Hays, a former chairman of the Republican National Committee and postmaster-general under Warren Harding, became the most active censor of the screen male (and female). Hays was un-self-conscious about explaining why:

> No medium has contributed more greatly than the film to the maintenance of the national morale during a period featured by revolution, riot, and political turmoil in other countries. It has been the mission of the screen, without ignoring the serious social problems of the day, to reflect aspiration, optimism, and kindly humor in its entertainment.

As president of the Motion Picture Producers and Distributors of America, Hays took upon himself the task of "cleaning up" movies. Before long he was aided by the Legion of Decency, set up in 1933 by the Catholic Church to agitate against the depiction of sex and crime in films and to boycott movies the Church decided were indecent. Hays was influential in setting up the Production Code Administration to enforce the legion's views, and the resulting Production Code prohibited from the thirties screen homosexuality, miscegenation, abortion, incest, drugs, and profanity. In fact, it was this very profanity which so threatened the industry in the early thirties that would later mark the return to the screen of a believable heterosexual male image. Only in 1938, with the Depression receding from public preoccupation, would Clark Gable as Rhett Butler, by telling Scarlett O'Hara that he doesn't "give a damn" what she will do without him, fully restore to movies the realism that had been so distorted during this decade.

Economic collapse in the society was met in film with a narrowing and desensitizing of the definition of appropriate male behavior. The frivolity of a Fairbanks was out, as were the languid sexual pleasure of a Valentino and the fervent heterosexual passion of a Barrymore. The screen of the early thirties did indeed, contrary to Hays's assertion, "ignore the serious social problems of the day"; but the conception of the hero was deeply influenced by what men like Hays, prominent both in the film industry and in government, decreed was most likely to convince the audience not to look too deeply into the causes of the economic collapse, let alone seek a remedy.

The male image of the early thirties was directly influenced by the fear of the upholders of official morality that sexual license on screen bore some relation to political ferment. The absence of sexual repression was associated with the refusal of the individual to accept a social situation in which a quarter of the population was unemployed. So popular an art as film was to be largely purged of examples of men who were carefree and open in their sexual lives. The frivolity and leisure often inherent in the twenties films were certainly not fully appropriate for Depression audiences, but the basic reasons for the change were much deeper. It was as if the other side of free sensuality was a collective rebellion against a system that was starving its people.

Movies began to talk simultaneously with the Depression, and men like Hays, as well as the Catholic bishops who dreamed up the Legion of Decency, feared that free talk and profanity on screen might inspire free thinking in other areas of life. Hays predicted as late as 1934 that the comedies of the thirties would "laugh the big bad wolf of the Depression out of the public mind." When they were not attempting to distract audiences from their troubles with cathartic laughter, movies were to uphold the myths of the frontier and of individual achievement, despite the message of the Depression that individualism was a devalued commodity in the America of the day.

When actors found their voices, they were forbidden to use the word "sex," just as they were made to believe in Hoover's litany that "conditions" were "fundamentally sound" and that, as his secretary of commerce intoned, there was "nothing to be disturbed about." The song "Happy Days Are Here Again" was copyrighted on November 7, 1929. Popular culture was mobilized to dismiss the implications of the Depression for the ordinary American, at first by stressing how brief hard times would be. Hoover kept insisting that through "rugged individualism" and "self-help" Americans could overcome the effects of the Depression. Hollywood attempted to justify this willed optimism by creating heroes who could personally, and without any need to organize collectively, make the Depression go away like some bad dream.

But movies could invoke the urgency of frontier self-reliance only by imposing a far harsher image of men in film than had appeared in the twenties, when the hero behaved as if the world were unencumbered by social turmoil. The Production Code played its part, attempting to bleach out spontaneity and heterosexuality from the male image, leaving movies free to define the hero solely in terms of his power to endure, to assert himself over others, and to survive through exhibitions of raw courage and nerves of steel. If the Depression questioned the viability of free enterprise in America, Hollywood produced personality types who could make any business work, men appropriate to a thriving system who solved all problems for themselves and overcame adversity through individual perseverance. The economic system, needless to say, was subjected to no critique. Instead, films were populated by heroes who demonstrated that if a man were tough, aggressive, and competitive, all would be his, as if the Depression had not shattered and refuted such a hope.

Thus at the moment of the Depression, movies took as their task the refurbishing of the myths which sanctified big business as a national ideal. Men in films demonstrated that through hard work anyone could go from rags to riches. In contrast to the twenties, alternate images were few and far between. In film after film, including the early gangster films with their perfunctory endings in which, to please Hays and his friends, the hero was punished, the male could be successful if he was sufficiently tough and mean; heroes were individualistic, self-assertive, and aggressive. Rarely did they have any trouble controlling other people or their environment. Women were far less important to the early-thirties screen male than they were to nearly all his twenties equivalents. As opposed to so many films of the twenties, these movies were peopled by men who sought aggressive control over others rather than exhibiting fierceness only when they were forced to respond to trouble. The social antidote to the Depression, as Hollywood usually saw it, required ever greater ruthlessness and unrelenting, determined effort.

I

Victor Fleming's *The Virginian* was released in November 1929, only a month after the crash; yet it already outlined the new male image. Drawing upon the mythic quality of the Western, and based on the 1902 classic by Owen Wister which had already been adapted to the screen, it located its male hero in lawless times, even as the early gangster films would grant freedom from the law to their heroes, if only until final perfunctory sequences in which the law triumphed. *The Virginian* presented an unrelentingly dominant male personality inconceivable in the films of Fairbanks, Mix, or even the no-nonsense William S. Hart. Made as a sound film immediately before the crash, it heralded the very values Hoover would invoke until the end of his presidency.

The Virginian opens within the peaceful world of the cowpuncher. Gary Cooper plays the hero of the title, an innocent singing cowboy who enjoys the comradeship of his best friend, Steve, a drifter unfortunately less morally upright than he. Early in the film the two become rivals for the heroine, Molly, a good woman and schoolteacher from the East who doesn't know a cow from a bull. The cowboys compare her to one of the animals in the herd: "Follow me, ma'am," says one, "and you'll never go astray." The taciturn Cooper soon wins her, an irresistible man of action who, unlike Owen Wister's original character, openly shuns things of the mind: "Would book learning do a cowpoke any good?" Tough with men, around women he behaves like an overgrown little boy full of mischief. Molly attempts to tame and educate him, as women would become the civilizers of rough-hewn men of the trail in countless Western films.

She gives him *Romeo and Juliet* to read. But the Virginian already knows who and what he is, and the invocation of Shakespeare is something he suffers as the price required to obtain his woman. What he likes about Romeo, he says, is that he has the courage to kill his enemies; the Virginian will go him one better by acquiescing in the execution of his best friend, Steve. Direct action and violence have become the sole prerequisites for masculinity. And Fleming clearly admires the Virginian's sturdy common sense. If *he* had been Romeo, says the Virginian, he would have forgone the balcony, marched right through the front door, and confronted Juliet's father. Then he would have grabbed Juliet off the balcony and married her: "Traipsin' up a ladder ain't my idea of a real man." Romeo, he observes, wasted time, causing them both to die.

Hereafter, the male in the American film has neither the time nor the patience for lengthy displays of romance, let alone for magic carpets like that on which Fairbanks spirits away his princess at the close of *The Thief of Bagdad*. The Depression required pragmatic immediacy and effective physical action, granting them both a religious sanction. Having wasted too many words already, the Virginian takes Molly in his arms—"I'll show you what I'd do," he asserts—and kisses her. Men are to rule the world and women to remain dutifully at home: marriage is their true calling. As the conscience of this film, the Virginian remarks, "Being a schoolteacher ain't a real woman's job in life."

After this elaborate demonstration of what is required to be a real man, *The Virginian* swiftly proceeds to its brutal climax. The Virginian's buddy Steve, under the influence of the evil Trampas, has become a cattle rustler. Ever and inexorably upright, our hero joins the posse hunting his best friend, a decision which the film shows us to be at once the touchstone of the man and the reason why women cannot measure up. It alienates the hopelessly soft-hearted Molly. But the Virginian's voice becomes deep. He assumes the role of stern leader whose word is everyone's command, always a mark of manhood after 1929. The hero's achievements must be his alone, never the result of a collective effort, an important ideological aspect of the Depression film. It is the inherent, superior resolve of the few which saves weaker men from their mediocrity. Alone, the Virginian tracks Steve down. If he dislikes tying up his closest friend, duty requires it. The penalty for cattle rustling is death by hanging.

Depression films will endlessly praise ruthlessness. The Virginian is wholeheartedly endorsed by the film in presiding over the execution of the buddy to whom he was devoted and who had responded in kind. The death scene is filmed with pathos. Real men, by the standards of the thirties, do not show feelings—indeed, they root them out as dangerous carriers of weakness. But the fallen man leaves a note in which he admits his love for the friend whose iron dedication to duty has led him to impose the established code without mercy. "Goodbye," Steve has written, "I couldn't have spoke to you without playin' the baby." The Virginian betrays no such emotion and is therefore the stronger and hence the better man. When he later hears a quail call and momentarily mistakes it for the secret whistle with which he and Steve had summoned each other on the open range, he turns his head. For a brief moment he has forgotten that Steve is dead.

The Virginian is thus capable of feeling, and what is crucial about this little vignette is the lesson that a real man never displays such feelings, for they will get in the way of what he must do. The Depression male hero was to be equally undeterred by sentimentality for those who falter in a harsh world. Molly is appalled when she learns that the Virginian has willingly participated in the killing of his best friend. The film presents her objections as mere squeamishness. It remains for the Virginian to instruct her in the code of the West, invoked so blatantly by this film and thoroughly appropriate to official America's approach to the Depression before the New Deal: if reform was not successful in preserving things, then ruthlessness and force were essential. "There ain't no room . . . for weaklings, men or women," says the Virginian.

The film seeks to establish this all the more by revealing how deeply the hero cared for Steve. To reaffirm his love for the friend he has had to destroy, the Virginian redeems himself in our eyes by doing battle with Trampas, the instigator of all the trouble. Only cowardice would account for a man who shrinks from combat and confrontation: "If folks came to think me a coward," says the Virginian, "I couldn't look 'em square in the eye ever again."

Disengaging Molly's arms from his neck, the Virginian goes out to meet his destiny. A close-up reveals the name "Steve" carved on his gun, as he will redeem Steve symbolically by using his friend's own weapon both to serve the law Steve had violated and to avenge him. His loyalty to his dead buddy inspires him to do what a man must, just as killing his buddy fulfilled the same imperative. Lightning-fast, he shoots from the hip, executing Trampas. Having fulfilled the debt which confirms his manhood, Cooper now indulges in one of his rare smiles. In contrast, during his final embrace of Molly, the Virginian's face is expressionless. He assumes the demeanor of the stern avenger, a male who has had the personal resolve to do battle with any enemy, whether social misfortune or personal rival. He, and not that "mangy hombre" Romeo, a weakling, embodies the ideal.

II

In the first half of the Depression decade, the tough, all-conquering male would appear most often as a gangster, not a cowboy. This fascination with gangsters and with the entire genre of crime melodrama bespoke the public's anger and inclination to go outside the norms of property relations. The gangster was both an individualist and an immoral rebel, who was glorified and yet came to a violent end. The gangster hero would demonstrate the same ruthlessness as the Virginian. Even if the hero worked outside the law, the films were designed to suggest by negative example that the same toughness would function better and with more certain rewards within the system if only men could summon the inner strength and disciplined rectitude loyally to wait out the hard times. Only after 1935 was the spunky, individualistic gangster replaced as hero by the G-man, the tough guy of the second half of the decade. The presidency of Roosevelt brought a confidence to American culture that rehabilitated the law and indirectly argued that a man could once more be successful within the system. The secretary of the Motion Picture Producers and Distributors, in the tradition of Will Hays, voiced his approval that the screen could now "reflect and foster a renewed interest in the heroes of the law." From its beginnings insiders in the film industry were well aware that films did not merely reflect feelings prevalent among audiences, but also "fostered" and shaped our definitions of what makes a man a hero.

In the twenties, gangster films offered tough guys whose tenderness and capacity for love were forever peeking through the tough veneer they assumed was appropriate to their station. In *Cradle of Courage* (1920) William S. Hart plays Square Kelley, an ex-gangster returning from World War I. He must decide whether to join his old buddies or go straight. Like all the Hart characters, Kelley is tight-lipped and stoical. He rarely smiles. But there is no romantic and desperate antisocial struggle for wealth, which appears to be unavailable within the system, the touchstone of the gangster films of the early thirties. Kelley is repeatedly shown as a loving and affectionate son, embracing and kissing a mother who repudiates him when he decides to go straight. Square Kelley becomes a cop; in 1920, fearlessness and physical strength were appropriate to patriotic soldiers, Western sheriffs, and the police. The reward for his redemption is reunion with mother and the hand of "Rose"—far from the model of the early-thirties gangsters, who usually avoid permanent attachments to women.

The two best gangster films of the twenties, Joseph von Sternberg's *Underworld* (1927) and *Thunderbolt* (1929), explicitly repudiated the male as brute. Ruthlessness and brutality were still perceived as features of a deranged personality. If Sternberg's films assume the viewpoint of the gangster, they also suggest a man tragically led astray by circumstances. Neither film panders to or glorifies his hard and unrelenting ways.

The hero of *Underworld*, Bull Weed (George Bancroft), is fat, boisterous, and arrogant, but never as ruthless as the Virginian. Jovial in vest, suit, and tie, this image of the gangster is that of the businessman manqué, a theme to be invoked as late as 1971 in *The Godfather*. Unlike the Virginian, the jolly Bull loses his girl, Feathers, to the brainy "Rolls Royce," a down-and-out one-time lawyer whom Bull has made his sidekick. Even if Bull is the male at the center of the film, it does not mean that he wins the woman. Having escaped from prison and intent upon killing "Rolls" for displacing him with Feathers, Bull stops to feed a kitten by letting it lick milk from his finger, which he repeatedly dips into a milk bottle.

The gangster here is no male model, and he merges with his milieu. Huge, lurking shadows pervade the film, and ominous dissolves flow one upon the other, not simply for the purpose of showing the passage of time. In the fine "Armistice Ball" sequence, the dissolves express layers of the unconscious emerging, as the characters recover consciousness after an alcoholic siege. The camera thereby lends a sexual quality to brutality. But male ruthlessness is still seen as a dangerous, violent explosion, like a driver temporarily losing control of a huge truck and crushing innocent passers-by.

At the conclusion of *Underworld* Bull admits he has been wrong about "Rolls Royce" and surrenders. The final image is one of a powerless male, Bull, helpless with his hands up as the police apply their handcuffs. Bull and his arresting officer descend a flight of stairs, the downward movement disclosing the gangster's weakness and defeat, unadulterated by last-minute heroics.

Thunderbolt, with a similar expressionistic use of shadows, presents a repellent, dark inward aspect of man. In a restaurant, Thunderbolt, a tough brute, sprays seltzer on a loud blonde seated at a neighboring table because she is disturbing him. "Ritzie," the woman whom Thunderbolt loses to the gentle Bob, prefers "people who lead decent, normal lives." In no way does the film suggest that the wild, uninhibited gangster life offers an example of approved male behavior.

The most interesting scenes occur on Death Row, where Thunderbolt awaits execution. Slowly the gentle, even tender component of his personality emerges, a process we first detect when a stray dog attaches itself to him and by its barking prevents him from killing Bob, his rival. Thunderbolt takes the dog, who represents his humane impulses, with him to prison. It sits on his cot and presides over the remains of his life. From prison Thunderbolt has managed to engineer a frame-up of Bob, who arrives in the same prison also to await death. Weaker than his antagonist, Bob becomes hysterical as he denounces Thunderbolt: "You framed me. I'm not afraid of you. I'm not afraid to die."

But Thunderbolt, a man larger in spirit if also brutish, grows increasingly calm as the film now proceeds to peel away the layers of his rough façade. This harshest of men conceals a core of soft feeling awaiting release, decent emotions that under normal circumstances would have allowed him to lead a good life. It was his ruthlessness that *prevented* his survival—a pattern which would be completely reversed in the films of the thirties. As a wedding present to Bob and Ritzie, Thunderbolt confesses to having engineered the frame-up. The dog, that expression of Thunderbolt's aspiring decency, contentedly looks on from his vantage point on Thunderbolt's bed.

It is only when he has become, through his violent life, a defeated man that Thunderbolt becomes truly sympathetic. His stature emerges through generosity and good-heartedness, not through a glamorization of his gangster ways. Intending to choke Bob to death at the moment of their final goodbye, Thunderbolt instead puts his hands affectionately on Bob's shoulders. He and his devoted dog then walk together down the final corridor.

Thunderbolt ends with the hero's laughter as he learns that the guard whose name he had tried to guess throughout his imprisonment is called "Aloysius." The tall giant of a man, his shadow trailing behind him, moves chortling to his doom. What is meant to redeem him—and to appeal to us—is that gentler side transcending the ruthless. In the twenties it never occurred to Sternberg to have us identify with Thunderbolt as a tough, brazen bully who forcibly grabs with impunity anything his fancy chooses.

Hollywood's response to the Depression demanded a different reaction. In Mervyn LeRoy's *Little Caesar* (1930) we must approve the viciousness of the gangster because, like the hard-heartedness of the Virginian, it is both successful and an acceptable route to survival. Ironically shrunk in size from the massive George Bancroft, who played both Bull Weed and Thunderbolt, the gangster of the early Depression films was portrayed primarily by small men like Edward G. Robinson *(Little Caesar)*, Jimmy Cagney *(Public Enemy,* 1931), and Paul Muni *(Scarface,* 1932). Their compact bodies closed the distance between them and the little men of the Depression audience, beaten down by a system that angered the many as the government stood by unwilling and unable to redress the growing impoverishment of the majority.

Gangsters became heroes applauded because their daring and brashness showed that survival was a matter of individual effort, even if at present only outside the bounds of official morality. Audience males were encouraged to experience vicarious release by the sight of these violent individuals lusting for money and power—and gaining them. If contrived endings punished the gangster for his lawlessness, his fierce refusal to be beaten in the struggle for material things gave him dignity and status. At the same time, since the male audience could not possibly emulate the brash, brutal gangland leaders, it felt smaller, weaker, and less able to alter its real condition. Thus the fantasy of power was also a means of ensuring the acceptance of impotence.

Yet to a Depression audience these gangsters offered a quite desirable, enviable male image. To their crude bravado was added an intense sensuality, conjoining sexuality and violence, which had been separated during the twenties. The early gangster film thus emasculated the audience in another way. If being brutal was the hallmark of virility, social cooperation and common struggle for a more humane society were to be defined as implicitly unmasculine, sentimental, and effete. Manliness was defined in terms of rebellion and defiance of all moral ties to others. It was the struggle of a drowning man who claws at those going down with him. To the beleaguered Depression viewer the mood was evocative, even if it was also intended to produce the debased panic of "every man for himself."

Instructively, the male image proposed in these films derived from the

same values demanded in official American culture at the height of economic prosperity. Only in his lawlessness did the gangster violate the
male norms conducive to competition within the free-enterprise system,
and this was shown as admirable in spirit if misdirected in practice. The
personal initiative and drive which demand that men define themselves
through being better than others were again proof of masculinity. These
were the very qualities demanded of ordinary men when the economic
system was flourishing. If the opportunity for success was being denied
in reality, the values had long since been internalized and the system itself
absolved of failure. "Do it first, do it yourself, and keep on doing it,"
Scarface intones, his motto the film's intended moral.

Minus the lawlessness, this is but a refurbishing of the old frontier ethic.
The early Depression film willfully denied that this code had proven
itself decidedly inadequate as the sure path to survival in the urban
thirties. As unemployment figures zoomed, the rugged-individualist demeanor was all the more stridently advocated in American films. What
stays with the viewer after these films conclude is not the comeuppance
or death of the hero but the masculine ethos of violent egotism flaunted
by the cocky gangster. However, in case the spirit of the gangster was
not curbed by proper if *pro forma* homilies of morality, the Legion of
Decency, officially formed in 1934, ensured the requisite self-censorship.
Opening titles were attached to films like that added to *Little Caesar:* "All
that take the sword shall perish with the sword" (*sic*).

In *Little Caesar,* the first and best of the three classic gangster films,
Rico (Edward G. Robinson) is presented consistently as a male to be
admired, in contrast to his effeminate buddy, Joe Massara (Douglas Fairbanks, Jr.), whose ambition is to go straight and become a dancer! The
choice is to be either a ruthless man of action or a mincing pansy. Rico
immediately reached out to audience males—an ordinary man and a
provincial who "never got my chance" and who determined to reach the
big city and become "somebody," as did Al Capone, on whom Rico was
modeled. Drawing upon that male credo set forth by William S. Hart in
Hell's Hinges, Rico will "shoot first and argue afterward." Force and
maleness are inextricable. Nor must a man allow himself to be weakened
by the slightest suggestion of "female" traits. "I don't want no dancin',"
Rico tells Joe. "I figure on making other people dance." Rico spoke to
demoralized Depression audiences, warning them that rough, animal-like
behavior is the only solution for men.

Unburdened by scruples or moral compunction, Rico gains a high
place in gangland, not only by his deviousness and willingness to kill but
also by the cunning with which he plots "jobs." The sexual metaphor
invoked to reprimand him for using his gun during a holdup tells us
swiftly that leadership and success are already assured him: "A fine pickle
we're in, you and that rod of yours." Rico, small though he may be, has

proven himself a Caesar—a male, the film suggests, who moves in a mode all real men must follow. Police inspector Flaherty, representing the law, lives pointedly by the same values and suggests the very style of the gangsters. When Rico survives an attempted assassination by a rival mob, Flaherty's gleeful sadism and mobster toughness surface: "If I wasn't on the force, I'd 'a' done the job cheap." In the jungle society of the thirties film, police are indistinguishable in manner and values from those labeled criminals, a point often stressed by the reversion of cop to crook and vice versa. Indeed, gangsters are real men who would do better in uniform. All must embrace the same code and methods in the frantic struggle for survival. Even when Rico guns down Tony, his driver, on the church steps before Tony can confess the holdup to Father McNeil, our sympathy remains with Rico. Tony's loyalty and masculine resolve have been subverted by a whining mother; that the killing is photographed entirely in long shot prevents us from weakening and preserves us from the slightest concern for Rico's hapless victim.

Hard times produced in the thirties, as they would in the seventies, screen males who were wary of females like Tony's mother, women who might emasculate the toughest warrior. Rico's primary emotional attachment remains to his old buddy, Joe. At the banquet honoring him as the new leader of the gang, Rico is the only man present without a "moll," although—lest we doubt his sexual preferences—he loudly declares his pleasure in seeing the other men with women. Men who are but followers may need women, but a leader, if he would retain supremacy, must not become attached to one of these weakening creatures. The central emotional scene for Rico occurs after Joe alerts him to an assassination attempt that he has overheard. Rico chooses this moment for a last-ditch effort to win Joe away from Olga, his dancing partner.

"Dancing," Rico reiterates, "ain't my idea of a man's game." The film supports Rico's view that Joe is therefore a weakling. Rico pleads that he needs somebody he can trust, not a woman, since love, Rico continues, is "soft stuff." "When she's with you," Rico's peroration concludes, "you ain't good for anything." Joe walks out as Rico hurls after him a barrage of infuriated threats, behaving like a jilted lover who has lost out to a rival after he has declared himself.

Lest the film's sympathies move away from the masculine ideal proposed by Rico, his love for Joe, which transcends self-preservation, inspires him to sacrifice all out of loyalty. Olga has called the police, and Joe, weakened by her, has agreed to testify against Rico. But Rico reaches their apartment before the police and has a clear opportunity to save himself by killing his best friend. The camera abruptly becomes one with Rico; his eyes, filled with tears, begin to swim as the camera dollies back and away from Joe. No matter the ruthlessness Rico has flaunted, he cannot kill his buddy.

From this point on Rico loses his capacity to survive. Beset by enormous forces with which he cannot cope, he is now without power. For if his devotion to a friend who betrays him is noble, it is also indecisive and a form of surrender. This moment of weakness sets Rico on the road to ruin and provides Flaherty with the opportunity to hunt him down.

In his very downfall Rico reinforces by negative example his role as an ideal male for the times. His hostility toward women is proven to be justified, for Olga was indeed dangerous. It was she who caused Joe to betray him, forcing Rico to the choice of killing Joe or becoming a fugitive. Unshaven, slovenly, and incoherent, Rico dies beneath a billboard proclaiming Olga and Joe as the new and most successful dance team of the day, the victim both of betrayal and of his own fatal departure from that ruthlessness real men evince and need to survive. If fame and fortune are theirs, it is as the result of this ruthlessness which Rico himself failed to match. Both Rico's ascendance and his decline make the same point: only the strong, unrelenting man who withstands the debilitating corruption of women survives. When Rico dies murmuring, "Mother of mercy, is this the end of Rico?" or when Cagney's Tom Powers gasps, "I ain't so tough," we feel no satisfaction at the just punishment of a lawbreaker. On the contrary, a hero's powers have failed him, and we see he was not relentless enough. Nor do we repudiate the male ideal these men represent. Even as Cagney and Robinson were small men whose tough swagger compensated for their size, so in their demise we mourn the fall of the little guy decimated by the Depression who made a heroic fight to become "somebody." Rico followed the same male code that worked within the law when times were prosperous, and his supreme toughness alone brought him to the top, if briefly, in those hard times.

The psychopathology of the gangster emerges more in *Public Enemy* and *Scarface*. In *Public Enemy* we cannot help but be fascinated by Cagney's vitality, brashness, and pure, uninhibited violence. In both Tom Powers of *Public Enemy* and Tony Camonte of *Scarface*, maleness is defined by violent sexuality. Tommy begins as a virtual sadist, the most vicious boy in town, who progresses from tripping up a girl on roller skates to squashing a grapefruit in a woman's face, the scene which "immortalized" Mae Clarke. He has grown tired of Mae, and her crime has been to complain, accusing him of having found "someone you like better." The audience is meant to respond to the grapefruit scene with as much glee as the scenes it evokes, a pie in the face in the Chaplin or Laurel and Hardy slapstick films contemporary with *Public Enemy*. This violent sexuality is clearly endorsed by the director, for the women in *Public Enemy* are all aroused by Tom Powers, particularly by his brutality. As one declares, "You're so strong, you don't give, you take!" Violence not only enables a man to weather the Depression but also secures him the best-looking women. After he rejects all others, Tommy's moll in *Public Enemy* is Jean Harlow!

Particularly for the gangster whose tenure was in constant jeopardy, women had to be seen consistently as possessions, objects who confirmed a man's power over his surroundings. In *Scarface,* Tony Camonte claims ownership of his sister Cesca and kills his buddy (George Raft) when he discovers the two together. His sister is the truly safe lover and the unchallengeable possession. The masculine ethos which evolved in this obsession with the male as gangster embraced sadism toward women, their fixed role as slavelike possessions, and the eroticism of violent sexuality as essential features of the brutalization of men that marks the gangster genre from the early thirties on.

Edward G. Robinson as Little Caesar: Even as Cagney and Robinson were small men whose tough swagger compensated for their size, so in their demise we mourn the fall of the little guy decimated by the Depression who made a heroic fight to become "somebody."

III

The war film also produced a hardened male. Both William Wellman's *Wings* (1929) and Howard Hawks's *Dawn Patrol* (1930) contend that men best express and fulfill themselves by working together in isolated symbiosis. By the close of the decade, in Hawks's *Only Angels Have Wings* (1939), the pattern of the idealized, exclusively male community which alone fulfills had been elevated to a religious canon. The Depression led to a plethora of films which insisted that only total freedom from women and the restrictions they impose permits a male to be truly masculine. The absence of women preserves a man from that softening of his character which women by their very nature require and instigate. For the ultimate meaning of male superiority is male exclusiveness. The true emotion underlying the insistence upon the priority of male credentials is finally homosexual; the male image so often enshrined in the decade of the thirties is the man who not only is happiest without women but who, in the deepest sense, does not want them.

The films made at the time of the Depression feel as if they were made in wartime, and none more so than *Wings*. The urgencies of combat infuse every sequence, a consequence not only of William Wellman's memories of his own aviation career but of the prescient demand in 1929 for a male who approached life as if he were at the front. Zeal marks Wellman's flyers, who desire nothing so much as to be chosen for patrols against the aces of the German air force. In this late silent film the titles themselves are un-self-conscious, embarrassingly hyperbolic in their full enthusiasm for the enterprise. *Wings* depicts the joys of an exclusively male world in which, once more, two buddies, Jack Powell (Buddy Rogers) and David Armstrong (Richard Arlen), consummate their love for each other in the course of battle.

As *Wings* opens, both young men are in love with a vapid young woman named Sylvia. But as fellow enlistees in aviation school, they soon find that their mutual pursuit of a "path to glory" effaces their sexual rivalry. When that rivalry again surfaces, the consequences are disastrous. Without mutual camaraderie, they cannot survive. The mission which begins without their usual "All set?" and "O.K." proves to be their last. *Wings* instructs us that men must be ever on guard to relegate women to a minor place in their lives, for otherwise the life-sustaining bonds of male friendship themselves could be jeopardized.

A frequent film theme during the Depression will be that poor men are really better off than their rich counterparts since they are physically hardier, less repressed, and more adept at survival. David, who is rich, as he departs kisses his mother full on the lips, pets the dog, and carries away with him the little toy bear of his childhood. He never returns from the war. Jack, a rougher type, is also physically stronger and more virile. In a boxing match, Jack knocks David down with ease, only to admire his sportsmanlike will to continue: "Boy, you're game!" At this the two reconcile their differences and walk off arm in arm, at one in patriotic fervor. Gary Cooper, a fellow flyer, is more gung ho even than David and Jack. He rushes off eagerly to perform a few "figure eights before chow time," always zealous and as dedicated as a boy scout striving for a merit badge. That he does not come back in no way diminishes him.

Buddy Rogers and Richard Arlen (with Clara Bow): *Wings* depicts the joys of an exclusively male world in which two buddies, Jack Powell and David Armstrong, consummate their love for each other in the course of battle.

The world of *Wings* is one of male appreciation that transcends every other value, an ideal shared even by Count von Kellerman of the German air corps. Chivalrously he spares David when David's machine gun jams, because had he fired, it would not have been a fair fight. The aviator is a contemporary knight. When David and Jack are decorated for bravery, their faces are equally impassive. *Wings* prepares and instructs males in adversity as if anticipating the full force of the Depression which, like the calamities of war, they must endure in the service of their country with stoical calm. The discipline of war becomes a training ground for one's male duty in a society expecting stress.

The climax of *Wings* comes when Jack, mistaking David for a German (because, unknown to him, David has stolen a German plane prominently displaying the iron cross), shoots down the person he loves best in the world. The theme of the senseless, insane cruelty of war suited perfectly the mood engendered throughout the decade of the twenties when, with Woodrow Wilson's defeat in the Senate, America had chosen to avoid military entanglements in Europe while concentrating on profits at home.

David, seeing Jack's plane bearing down on him, cries out, "Don't you know me?" Jack, single-minded in deadly combat, can see only an enemy German in his best friend. If combat for one's country is noble and a crucible for male character, there is tragedy in noble warriors, equals in male resolve, killing each other precisely because they share courage in battle and patriotic loyalty.

Before David expires, the two buddies are reunited in one of the most resonant love scenes between two men to appear in the American cinema, surpassing even the conclusion of *Beau Geste*. Jack cradles David's head and their hands touch. Both men cry, able at last to express their concealed emotions now released by the imminence of death. Their arms are entwined as they caress each other gently. Each hungers for the other's consolation and each receives it. "You didn't kill me," says David, "you destroyed a Heinie ship." Jack presses his lips against David's face and allows words to surface which express what all these gestures have meant, what male impassivity struggles to conceal: "There is nothing in the world that means more to me than your friendship."

On this note David dies. Jack bends his head close over David's body and cries, his hand resting on the top of David's head. He lifts David's body in his arms and carries him off, David's arm around his neck. It is the sole love scene in the film. Beside it, Jack's return to Mary (Clara Bow), his home-town sweetheart and the girl he once rejected for Sylvia, pales into insignificance. The remainder of his life will be anticlimactic. Although he is still in his twenties, Jack is now aged and greying at the temples. He has killed the person he loved more deeply and devotedly than any other, a trauma which will remain with him. When Jack for the first time kisses Mary with abandon, we realize that he has become capable of expressing such passion through his relationship with David, which was his real initiation into what it means to love another human being.

But if *Wings* includes a perfunctory female presence in the lives of men whose serious emotions lie in their common purpose, by 1930 the all-male milieu of *Dawn Patrol* is far harsher. There is not a single woman in the film. Set again at the German front during World War I, it re-creates the closed world of men together and the intense feeling vibrating between them. The ever-present threat of extinction that binds these men to each other allows an open expression of that affection which would be rigidly repressed in less extraordinary circumstances. In the early years of the Depression, the war film became enormously popular, appealing openly to that suspicion of women instilled in the culture. The panic accompanying economic collapse caused men to fear inadequacy and failure more than ever, feelings exacerbated by politicians and filmmakers, who invoked self-reliance and the myth that one's personal initiative determined how one fared in the world. Poverty and helplessness were separated from the social conditions that had created them. The all-male films of the Depression spared men the further humiliation of being unable to display male prowess by providing for a dependent weaker sex.

The hero of *Dawn Patrol* is Dick Courtney (Richard Barthelmess), an officer who every day must send neophyte flyers to their doom, hopelessly outclassed by the veteran aviators of the German air force led by the sinister von Richter, whose plane insignia is a skull and crossbones. Barthelmess, now stocky and expressionless, has, like the male presence on film, undergone a physical transformation. It is almost impossible to imagine him a decade earlier as the sweet boy of *Tol'able David* or the gentle Chinese of *Broken Blossoms*. He has deteriorated into a sullen, hostile, tight-lipped, and hard-drinking militarist who represses all gentler feelings. He is renowned for ruthless enactments of harsh military measures, including the dispatch of his closest buddy's young brother to a certain death. This buddy (Scott) is played by Douglas Fairbanks, Jr., and the change in male image from Fairbanks Senior to Junior is another measure of the distance traveled in Hollywood's depiction of men. The action of *Dawn Patrol* duplicates that of *The Virginian* wherein the hero takes part in the killing of his closest friend. *Dawn Patrol* articulates the command of official America during the Depression that people summon their deepest reserves to suffer loyally through what was considered a "temporary" recession.

As in *What Price Glory* and *Wings,* war is called a "slaughterhouse." But as in these other films, antiwar sentiment is rhetorical, for the highest order of male behavior flows from willing sacrifice and group camaraderie, not rebellion. Men not only glory in war but are fulfilled by the discipline, mutual regard, and skill it calls forth. Their initiation as tough, unyielding males proceeds through war, and they measure strength and manliness by the ability to be unquestioningly responsive to orders.

Dawn Patrol evokes an even stronger endorsement of the brave, lonely male whose masculine resolve is heightened when the odds are against him. Because survival is so precarious, the love of officer Courtney for the men he daily sends off to do battle with the invincible Germans is allowable and full of pathos. Courtney mourns the death of each man, but never openly. Ascetic in sensibility, he calls for "another bottle" each time he learns that a flyer's life is in question. "Blubbering can't help matters," a weaker male who has lost his best friend is told, and a drink is forced down the blubberer's throat. With the best of men, this method of inducing the required stoicism generally proves effective.

These films repeatedly and at length depict the physical affection between buddies. When Scott falls asleep at a table over a drink, Courtney hoists him over his shoulder and carries him off to bed. As in *Wings*, verbal communication is kept at a minimum. All they murmur as they are about to go aloft for combat is "Watch yourself!" Courtney becomes annoyed when he is asked routinely if he is carrying papers that might prove useful to the enemy. The truly powerful male wouldn't be so challenged. When Courtney thinks, mistakenly, that Scott has been killed, he drinks and sings, reproving a weaker male appalled by this seeming insensitivity: "Do you think a drink and a song could make me forget?" In a later scene a drunken Barthelmess nestles in Fairbanks's lap as they careen along on a motorcycle, finding in such moments of camaraderie relief from the tension of their daily confrontation with death.

The buddies are estranged temporarily when Courtney sends Donny, Scott's brother and a new recruit, into combat. Donny, although young, is already adept at displaying the appropriate masculine traits. He shows no hesitation and calmly accepts the advice to be a "good loser." "I'm not a bit afraid," he asserts. When Donny dies before Scott's eyes, he can't contain himself and he calls Courtney a "dirty butcher." Alienation from one's buddy is the most painful fate of all, for it is at this moment that Courtney puts his head down on his arms and weeps. He takes quickly and seriously to drink as if he had been cast off by the woman he loves.

Again a final mission reunites the buddies at the moment of death. Courtney elects to bomb the German railhead in Scott's place, first resting his hand briefly on a sleeping Scott's bent head, an act almost of holy communion. Without the love of his comrade, life is not worth living anyway. The Germans are far superior technologically, and the odds are ten to one against him. Yet Courtney manages to kill every pilot pursuing him, including the formidable von Richter. Only one German plane remains, and by this last he is fatally wounded. But in homage to the splendid display of manliness Courtney has exhibited during this "mission impossible," the German pilot salutes him. There is an understanding of the masculine code between all men regardless of nationality and the senseless wars they fight on behalf of their governments.

Scott, waiting below, is heartbroken: "Courtney's out there alone, without me, doing the thing I should have done." In penance, in homage, and out of love, he becomes the new flight commander, dispensing the orders that send young men up to their doom. By his taking Courtney's place and assuming his role, the bond between the two men is sustained even after Courtney's death. *Dawn Patrol* is a paean to the transcendent quality of the love possible between men.

IV

Only Angels Have Wings (1939), one of Hawks's most brilliant films, which closed the decade as his *Dawn Patrol* opened it, poses the question of what happens when a woman enters this homoerotic world of men. The male ideal of *Dawn Patrol* is transplanted to a peacetime setting where, under civilian conditions of equal peril, men living and working together approximate the rarified relationships they shared during wartime. The location is a backwater, a sleepy South American port called Barranca, where Cary Grant runs a tiny aviation company whose task is to deliver mail to remote jungle outposts. It seems as if it rains every day. The company's financial peril parallels the physical danger of extreme conditions of weather.

Grant is the supreme male against whose stoical masculinity all other characters must define themselves. Jean Arthur arrives as a stranded adventuress. Richard Barthelmess comes as a flyer who needs a job because he has been ostracized for committing the unthinkable and cowardly act of bailing out and leaving his copilot to crash to his death alone. Rita Hayworth is an aviation groupie, once rejected by Grant. Determined to have nothing more to do with flyers, she nevertheless has married the aviator Barthelmess; she is an irrational woman symbolic of the entire sex. Thomas Mitchell plays Grant's beloved buddy, "the Kid," the only person capable of sustaining a loving relationship with a man like Grant. He succeeds because he always subordinates his own feelings. If Arthur is to be accepted into his life by Grant, after whom she trails through most of the film like a lovesick puppy, she must learn to imitate the stoical, repressed behavior through which men like the Kid and Grant communicate with each other. *Only Angels Have Wings* reveals how the concept of maleness that arose during the Depression became for decades thereafter the most sacrosanct value in the American film. Long after the

Depression came to a close, the style of maleness enacted by Barthelmess in *Dawn Patrol* and refined by Grant in *Only Angels Have Wings* would be offered to audiences as the quintessential means by which men prove they are masculine.

At first Arthur seems to be a tough woman, undaunted by being stranded in Barranca. But as soon as she meets Grant, she is deflated like a balloon suffering from a slow leak. Alternately called "Jeff," "the Boss," "the Old Master," and "Poppa," Grant, the supreme no-nonsense male, overwhelms her by intimidation. Women, says director Hawks, find men irresistible who, sensibly, have no time for them. Even if a male has more gentle feelings, he must conceal them behind a façade of indifference. When one of his flyers is killed in a reckless attempt to return to Barranca in thick fog and pouring rain simply to keep a date with Arthur, Grant allows his hatred for women to surface.

But first he waits. It is a sacred moment, and he demands quiet. More than anything he hopes the man will make it. Disobeying Grant's order, a command from the patriarch who knows best, the flyer crashes. Arthur is blamed for his death although a man who jeopardizes his life for a woman is no better than a fool: "He wasn't good enough—that's why he died." Jeff's partner, Dutchy, calls him "a hard man—much too hard," but the film tells us that hardness is the true mark of a man. A Hemingwayesque romanticism afflicts Hawks as he proposes, melodramatically, that real men must involve themselves repeatedly in situations where their lives are on the line, proving their maleness with grace under pressure, conveyed here as unrelenting and unalleviated harshness.

Where Dick Courtney sang and danced to contain his feelings, Jeff sits down to eat a steak. He "feels like bawling," but real men never succumb to weakness. He hires the tainted Barthelmess, but even when the aviator redeems himself, completing one dangerous mission after another, "Poppa" still withholds his praise: "What do you want me to do—pat you on the back?"

Hawks concedes that his men maintain a rather tenuous hold on their toughness, but this requires terseness all the more to guard against the slightest lapse. Stoicism is not natural to human beings; hence men like Grant must learn to hate women, whose weakness endangers the precarious hold men keep on their self-control. Admitting to no such weakness, Grant explains that he despises women because they want to "make plans." Commitment forces men into situations where their freedom to live in the midst of danger forever compulsively proving themselves— their freedom to be men—is jeopardized. Why they need repeatedly to prove their manhood goes unexplored; the male psychology in the Hawks film is invariably as pubescent as a Captain Marvel comic book. With so rigid a view of personality, Hawks is reduced to idealizing men who, if they are inwardly unsure of themselves, rise above this "weakness" by refusing to avow its existence. Grant is proud that he would never ask anything of a woman, since to request a woman to stay with him would be to acknowledge need—that dreaded confession of weakness. Why a "real man" cannot admit to being even slightly lacking in self-sufficiency is the question that we must suppress if we are to watch such films at all. The primary import of the Grant style expressed here is to mobilize audience hostility to women, particularly to those who "think they can take it, but they can't."

The Kid must initiate Arthur until she can "take it." Some few women become tough enough to be included in this all-male circle—becoming girl-boys, no longer women at all. Arthur has, after all, placed herself unprotected in this ungodly place. She has traveled around the world on banana boats searching for excitement. She has proven her mettle, and since her mind is a *tabula rasa*, a blank sheet, lacking all beliefs and values, she readily learns to model her behavior on that of the Kid, Grant's male buddy. For most of the film Grant ignores her; it requires no effort at all on his part to resist her charms. A real man in the Hawks universe, which includes his Westerns, can always do without women. Whatever their virtues, they never fail to interfere with those far more important activities which define the hero's manhood.

As long as the Kid remains alive, Arthur cannot find a place in the emotional world of Grant. The male buddy fulfills most of the functions a woman would, and, as a buddy, he knows enough not to make many demands. But as the Kid's eyes begin to fail, foreshadowing his death, he begins to train Arthur in earnest to take his place. She must be prepared to ask nothing for herself, not even Grant's survival. Arthur still calculates and schemes, finally taking a bath in Grant's room in order to attract his attention. Pretending that she is unable to walk, she obliges Grant to lift her up. Even at this moment of "success" she must recite a liturgy of self-denial: she will never attempt to tie him down nor make plans; she will never ask him or bother him for anything. Her life purpose will be to be there for him when he needs her. Such male demands seem eminently reasonable to Hawks because a man is always superior to a woman. Before they even manage a kiss to seal this "bargain," the Kid barges into the room; it is not yet time for him to be supplanted by a woman. Grant is required to go on a mission. Arthur, who has not yet learned to be the partner of a real man, shoots Grant in the shoulder. The Kid takes his place and is fatally wounded in a freak accident.

Soft music plays at the Kid's bedside as Grant comforts him. Light illuminates the Kid's face. Tough to the end, he insists that had a bird not burst through his plane's windshield, "we'd 'a' made it." Since his eyesight is gone, and with it his capacity to fly and hence be a man, there is small point in continued existence. Only his intimate buddy, Grant, is allowed to attend the Kid at his deathbed, and even Grant is not permitted to stay to the end. "So long, Kid," says Jeff. "So long, Jeff," is the sole reply. Words would desecrate a love so profound.

In homage to the Kid, as the ending of *Dawn Patrol* was a hymn to the manhood of Dick Courtney, Grant flies the last mission alone because "the Kid broke his neck trying to make it." Only now does Grant finally cry, an appropriate lapse because he has lost his best male friend. Arthur begs plaintively for commitment: "Do you want me to stay or don't you?" Receiving no answer, she persists: "I'm hard to get. All you have to do is ask me." Grant relents, his weakness a result of the deep emotion summoned up by the death of the Kid. Grant now hands her his coin with two heads, which is pledge enough to convince her to wait for him. Through a rain-splattered window we see her peer ecstatically as Grant's plane moves down the runway.

It is clear what it takes to be a man: his deepest feelings must always be directed toward a male comrade. Outlined as well is the appropriate manner in which a man must treat women. The heroes of both *Dawn Patrol* and *Only Angels Have Wings* are mythic ideals, nonconsumers in a Depression when, in any event, there was no money with which to buy anything. "Poppa" Grant wears the same leather jacket throughout, an outer symbol of his inner fiber. If audience men had difficulty feeding their children, movies in which men had no children could lure them into a few hours' escape from their personal impasse. Romantic violence and danger were close to the hearts of those who faced every day the violence of poverty. The recurrent image of flying during the thirties, also a surrogate mode of sexual release in a world of men, appealed to an audience who wished to abandon the planet itself.

V

The early Depression film narrowly defined the male role. Yet 1930 also saw the release of Lewis Milestone's *All Quiet on the Western Front*, based on the novel by Erich Maria Remarque which had been a best-seller during the "bullish" days of the stock market just prior to the October crash. There have always been films that defied the norms of an era. With its antiwar theme challenging the premise that men prove their masculinity in combat, *All Quiet on the Western Front* was surely an anomaly for 1930. It rejected the entire "grin and bear it" male ethos so prevalent in early-thirties films. Milestone bitterly satirizes a professor who encourages his students to "give every ounce of strength . . . to the Fatherland," to submit unquestioningly to authority. To be acceptable, such dissidence had to be transported to a foreign country, and Milestone chose for his antiwar film a German setting, just as Dorothy Arzner, in her 1933 film *Christopher Strong*, had to exile her liberated heroine, modeled upon Amelia Earhart, by making her an English aristocrat.

At the end of *All Quiet on the Western Front*, humiliated and dehumanized by the miseries of war, as Americans were by the hardships of the Depression, the hero, Paul (Lew Ayres), pleads with a new crop of pupils studying under the same orthodox professor: "You can't live that way and keep anything inside you." In the Hawks films combat was a substitute for what was "inside you." Conformity to external commands, rather than behavior stemming from inner conviction, determined character. Milestone, in contrast, opposes a man's inner core to the brutal physical action which threatens to devour his finer nature and insists that these are antagonists. *Dawn Patrol*, made also in 1930, insists that men are solely what they prove in combat. Milestone shows that it is precisely what happens to a man in combat—the inhuman acts he is required to perform —which corrodes his character. His view of male humanity is dramatically different from that of Hawks, for he proposes that men cultivate and embody feelings of compassion and pity. Repressed and rendered irrelevant by life at the front, such emotions may wither away and a male become incapable of normal human responses, those feelings which Hawks insists emasculate a true male.

Milestone demystifies as well the male camaraderie among men sharing combat. He shows how a life of waiting to die, exemplified in both *All Quiet on the Western Front* and *Dawn Patrol*, breaks people down and turns human beings into barbarians incapable of caring for anyone. War nurtures the sadism that men direct toward their fellows, as in the case of the former mailman, once relaxed and cordial and now a vicious officer. The young recruits begin as raw and friendly. Army life reduces them to the hard-boiled, callous men they must be if they are to accomplish the state's bidding effectively. One goes mad; others are repeatedly tormented by nightmares. Forced to shoot other human beings with a machine gun at point-blank range, one loses all sense of self. War weakens the men in Milestone's film, depriving them of their manhood, which the director perceives as the capacity to live at peace with oneself. In the end Paul, a destroyed man, hurriedly returns to the front, cutting short his leave because he has become incapable of remaining among people who cannot understand what he has endured.

Pacifism and a strong hostility to military engagement were sentiments that echoed throughout the twenties as the continuing response of many not only to World War I but to war in general. These feelings found expression in *All Quiet on the Western Front* and resulted in this film's unique departure from what was becoming the dominant male image of the day. Responding to the theme of the senselessness of war, male and female audiences eagerly accepted a hero who saw the futility and, indeed, the absurdity of defining his masculinity in terms of his capacity to inflict violent acts of aggression upon others. That the powerful sense of distaste for war was one of the healthier currents of social thought of the day is demonstrated in the fact that on screen it led to the depiction of a humane, gentle hero at a time when so many male personalities were being portrayed as ruthless and domineering without the suggestion that these were debilitating and emasculating approaches to experience.

All Quiet on the Western Front does not propose an alternative view of masculinity by defining male excellence in terms of the courage to refuse to fight an unjust and senseless war. But it does challenge the myth of the manliness of the combatant. We see the soldier at the front as a brutalized shell of a human being, a cipher stripped of all desire to continue to live. Paul begs the corpse of a man he has slaughtered to forgive him, so violated is he by the murder he has just performed. He desires to lay his head in his mother's lap and cry, but he is unable to do so, not out of any fear of expressing such needs, but because it would not do any good. Even as he is unable to return to a time when he was cared for and innocent, he is no longer at home in the chauvinistic Germany of his day. In the final shot he reaches out hesitantly for a butterfly, as if he would retrieve his own fleeing, lost soul, now infinitely precious to him. At this point he is gunned down by a sniper. War has deprived him of dignity and human purpose, and hence of manhood itself. Poignant in that it is caused by a wistful, gentle gesture, his death remains anticlimactic, superfluous.

All Quiet on the Western Front was one of the most popular films of 1930, although it shared that acclaim with *Dawn Patrol* and *Little Caesar.* It stands in the tradition of dissident novels of the thirties, books like John Dos Passos' *U.S.A.* trilogy, which also repudiated the conception of masculinity delineated in such works as Hemingway's classic of the twenties, *The Sun Also Rises. All Quiet on the Western Front* stands out as an exception, however, a rare product of the American film industry, which has consistently treated alternative values with scorn and disdain. It inspired no trend, nor was it followed by films with values that might compete with the philosophy of maleness set forth in *The Virginian, Only Angels Have Wings, Dawn Patrol,* or *Little Caesar.* Rather, it must be seen as a special film that stands apart from the aggrandizement of the self-assured male hero which dominated the thirties cinema.

Equally exceptional was the political weakness of the male character, played by Paul Muni, at the center of *I Am a Fugitive from a Chain Gang* (1932), a returned World War I veteran soon to descend into the slough of Depression America. By the end, utterly powerless, out of work, and a fugitive on the run, he captures in his fate that of men in America everywhere. Such an image, of a man persecuted and callously betrayed by courts, media, and politicians, would not be repeated on the thirties screen. For this was to be the decade of Clark Gable, Gary Cooper, and Errol Flynn. And by 1939 John Wayne would offer an image of strident, unrelenting maleness so influential that it would dominate American cinema for the next twenty years.

The Thirties

During the 1930s, eighty-five million people went to the movies every week, but what they saw had as little relation to their lives as the pollyanna books they read. First on the nonfiction list in 1933 and second in 1934 was *Life Begins at Forty,* with its promises of a "second start." A favorite 1937 work was another self-help manual, *How to Win Friends and Influence People,* echoing again Hoover's insistence that through self-reliance alone the individual could overcome the Depression.

A quarter of the population was unemployed, yet movies still insisted that hard work would automatically produce life's benefits for every man. Errol Flynn danced through his films as Clark Gable joked, but all the while the implication remained that it was unmanly to be unable to take care of one's family. Many jobless men had to take over domestic chores and child-rearing; they were early "house-husbands" while their wives, who could get work, became "breadwinners." No film chronicles this role change, even as no film explored the psychology of the hero or exposed the doubt of so many men that they would probably not make it. If a variety of male responses to hard times existed, movies imposed the stereotype of the competent, self-sufficient, and ever successful man.

The "screwball" comedy flourished during the thirties, not only as a mode of escape but as an expression of relief. Films like *It Happened One Night* asserted that people neither desired nor required upheaval, and sought to dissipate energies that might have been directed toward the struggle for social change. The Marx Brothers and W. C. Fields contributed a zany tone to thirties life; they were less male images than explorers of the comic absurdity of social institutions. Groucho and

Fields might be perfunctorily lecherous, but they were not treated as models of male behavior; even when Groucho was involved in a romance, sexuality gave way to satire and the games between men and women became one more object of ridicule.

I

Like Frank Capra's dreamy, tuba-playing Mr. Deeds (Gary Cooper), for whom inheriting a bundle of money was only an irritating annoyance that interrupted his tranquil life, the male in the thirties film was hardly ever short of money. Nor was he unemployed. Often he took pot shots at the idle rich, whom he viewed as effete, bored, and unmanly, allowing Hollywood obliquely to admit the anger of the poor toward the few whom the Depression did not touch. But satire of the privileged was permitted only in comedy; the rich could be ridiculed but not threatened.

Often the male hero of the thirties was rich and privileged, as epitomized by the Robert Montgomery playboy clutching his cocktail shaker. If not, he worked hard. The more trying his circumstances, in fact, the more he believed he could become successful by the sweat of his brow alone. He needed help from no one; else he would not be a real man.

Almost never was a male portrayed on the assembly line—let alone selling apples on street corners, panhandling on Park Avenue, or languishing in a Hooverville. Had the screen hero been of the working class, he would have had to partake of the pain and suffering of the Depression; and given Hollywood's criteria for male sufficiency, manifesting such personal weakness would have cast doubt on his masculinity. Work itself was a forbidden subject, and neither daily life on the factory assembly line nor the routines of office drudgery were accurately depicted on film.

Never, above all, would a thirties screen hero with whom people were meant to identify lose confidence in America. In the nick of time the isolated exemplars of corruption among the powerful would mend their ways. Frank Capra's Mr. Smith is spared having to slink home from Washington in defeat because the bad men realize their errant ways and promise to change. Nor, consequently, need Mr. Smith organize the people to defy established power. The idea of social revolution never enters his head, as it does those of characters in the novels of John Steinbeck, James T. Farrell, or John Dos Passos. Even in the 1939 film version of *The Grapes of Wrath,* Henry Fonda as Tom Joad is left to wait and see; he need not act on behalf of the downtrodden but can bide his time, as a smiling representative of Franklin D. Roosevelt on screen usurps Tom's role as rebel by demonstrating its superfluousness.

Those males in a thirties film who admit the existence of social distress behave as if reform were imminent, having been born with, it seems, or having imbibed with their mothers' milk admiration for both Roosevelt and the New Deal. These heroes are accordingly less defensive, shrill, and hysterical than Little Caesar, Tom Powers, or Scarface. We see the thirties male as a G-man rather than as a gangster because a beneficent system had the right to expect law-abiding behavior from its men. It promised yet again to reward the diligent male for hard work. Cagney and Robinson consistently played G-men as the reformist presence of Roosevelt led film to a rehabilitation not only of the law but of the FBI.

In *G-Men* (1935) and *Bullets or Ballots* (1936) we are explicitly instructed that a lawman can fulfill himself more successfully than could Rico as Little Caesar, boss of a mob, or Tom Powers, weakened by frantic, mindless self-assertion. The G-man became an ideal of moral commitment and dedicated fortitude, usurping the qualities that would have been appropriate to the social rebel of the thirties screen had he been permitted to exist.

The thirties male on screen is permitted few depressing observations. He laughs incessantly—if without adequate cause—as he pours drinks in sophisticated comedies, or he assumes an earnest and gentle demeanor like the hero in Frank Capra's sentimental and populist comedies from *Mr. Deeds Goes to Town* (1936) through *Meet John Doe* (1941). Unlike the savage Rico of *Little Caesar,* he threatens no one. Nor is he self-righteously solemn, like the flyers of *Dawn Patrol.* At the frightening moment when the Depression struck, movies offered an image of a defensive male who attempted through will, bravado, and antisocial violence to overcome his inferior social status. By the mid-thirties, as the New Deal shaped the manly ideal in movies, a less aggressive male could appear; yet despite his personal passivity, he could still defend the system in which the faith of so many had been shaken. His calm was a better antidote to public disaffection than the rage of the gangster sagas. Precisely in order to divert attention from the economic violence in the society, these major male personalities engaged in less physical brutality on screen than did heroes of the early thirties—or than would screen males of the forties, sixties, and seventies. Despite the example of the first gangster films, by 1934 violence was increasingly feared by the authorities as a likely response by those who had suffered without relief since 1929 and 1930. The "Bonus Expeditionary Force" of unemployed veterans and the disaffected camping in Washington had been dispersed in 1932 with tear gas and gunfire by the United States Army, ordered out by President Hoover. One of the goals of the film male of the thirties was to insist that violent action and drastic change were unnecessary because the social structure was basically sound. With the exception of the G-man and the Westerner of the last years of the decade, the male ideal was scarcely violent. After 1933 the figure of Franklin Roosevelt begins to stand in the background of the American film as an implied narrator, proof that injustice could be alleviated from within.

In the major films of Frank Capra, the hero consciously upholds for the audience values associated with "Americanism." He admits occasional corruption—the work of a few individual "Wall Street speculators" selfishly dabbling in foreign speculation and thus alone responsible for the economic disaster at home. The Capra protagonist is rarely domineering or overbearing. A homely, down-to-earth everyman, his appeal is to a down-and-out audience whose faith in America he gently restores without belligerence or hostility. He indicates that individual leaders can right all wrongs. From *It Happened One Night* on, the Capra film argues that whatever the reality, hard work and upward mobility go hand in hand. Untroubled by doubt, the ideal thirties male, including the Capra hero, never indulges in anxious introspection. Those who analyze or provide explanations are held up to ridicule as absent-minded or peculiar, the touchstone of that anti-intellectualism orchestrated particularly in eras, like that of the Depression, when too much thought might lead to grievances surfacing on screen.

The most sexually appealing males of the thirties, Clark Gable and Errol Flynn, are the most successfully immune to the exigencies of the decade. Unlike male images in the films of the early thirties, they are capable of loving relationships with women. More confident in the system's capacity to survive the Depression intact, they represent a softer film image of what it means to be a man than did the early gangsters. The films of Flynn and Gable, however, demand a total escapism, although not always by means of a pirate ship or magic carpet.

Flynn's films were generally set in glorious times past. Gable exhibited, particularly in his films set in the thirties, an ingenuity and resourcefulness so attractive as to imply that if other men had been equally spirited, the Depression itself could never have occurred. The mood was one of willed optimism, not despair. Recovery was assured if only men would summon those qualities of personality, drive, wit, resourcefulness, and good humor so effortlessly expressed by that male ideal of the thirties, Clark Gable.

Gable was an ideal for both men and women, appealing to each. For women his animal power suggested sexuality, dominance, and roughness, a male capable of granting women orgasms every time. In the press he was compared to Valentino: "Clark Gable, Don Juan by popular demand." Men liked the fact that Gable was a he-man and a regular guy, no effete intellectual or rich, effeminate playboy. Uneducated, a member of the lower classes, volatile and tough, he played a man's man. His physical strength and large size were essential to his image, and he portrayed a man who preferred action and could perform any physical task from that of lumberman to oil-rigger to hunter on safari.

In reality, Metro-Goldwyn-Mayer had to arrange for him to hunt and fish in his spare time so that the real man might correspond to the image. Gable began to enjoy pursuits that had never been part of his life prior to his arrival in Hollywood. Men also approved of the fact that a kinship with other males prevented him on screen from pursuing married women; from *Red Dust* to *Mogambo* he sacrifices the woman who is not free in favor of one unattached. And neither men nor women had any trouble admiring a man who was impatient above all with males who were not regular guys like himself.

Fixed and immutable qualities like Gable's, unshakable by turmoil either from within or without, were evident as well even in Cary Grant's films with Mae West. In *She Done Him Wrong* (1933) and *I'm No Angel* (1933), Grant is not merely a passive sexual foil to the independent, spirited West. He is presented as a fully developed, unique, one-dimensional personality, unshakable in his self-confidence. The males of thirties films always know who and what they are, conveying a certainty reassuring in a Depression era of overwhelming uncertainties. Errol Flynn, Clark Gable, and company asked Depression audiences to appreciate them as men in temporary, resolvable conflict with the outside world, as individuals unburdened by internal stress. The model they presented to the unemployed was untouched by irremediable financial difficulties or the slightest sexual self-doubt.

II

The most important film of the mid-thirties was Frank Capra's *It Happened One Night* (1934). Through the person of ace reporter Peter Warne (Clark Gable), it asserted that upward mobility remained an accessible dream in Depression America. The Depression notwithstanding, Peter Warne is the best in his profession, untroubled by the absence of jobs for people of merit; even his editor, for whom Gable's flamboyant style provides many uneasy moments, must admit, "For my dough he's still the best newspaperman in the business." When we meet Warne, he is temporarily out of a job, as a result of the unconventional means he uses to get his stories, but not in a state of chronic, persistent unemployment.

Out of a job or not, Warne's brashness and that fast-talking Gable irreverence are in no way diminished. Quick-thinking, resourceful, and full of initiative and common sense, Warne is the ordinary man with extraordinary resilience. He refuses to be discouraged by temporary setbacks or to lose belief either in himself or in what he does, even as the film maintains faith in an America temporarily beset by hard times.

These qualities enable Warne to hook up with heiress Ellen Andrews

(Claudette Colbert), escaping from her unreasonable father and the prospect of a loveless marriage. A flighty screwball with no ability whatsoever to take care of herself, Colbert needs Gable to see to her needs, even as, the film implies, the rich need the ordinary working man, without whom they too would fall apart. In return, Warne will be lifted, if not by his bootstraps—on which he gaily trips—then through marriage to a rich woman, the reward for his willingness to keep at it. By this obvious ploy worked into the fabric of so entirely engaging a film, Capra manages to reassert his confidence that the poor can still become rich. The erotic qualities of Gable and Colbert are apportioned according to the most sexist criteria. For the male to be a man, the woman must be helpless, passive, and dumb; Colbert acts as a total foil to Gable. Were she bolder and more self-sufficient, he could not serve as her semipaternal protector, guardian, and savior, nor could Capra so easily argue that upward mobility remained possible in the America of the thirties.

The Mae West pictures were among the few exceptions to the unabashedly advocated male supremacy in the thirties film. West may have used her sexuality as a calling card, but her screen image made a mockery of the myth of the superior male. She could think faster and more logically than any male in her films, as witness her crackling wit and triumphs of rationality when she becomes prosecuting attorney at Cary Grant's breach-of-promise trial in *I'm No Angel*. West came to Hollywood as a New York star, and her personal magnetism and immediate appeal at the box office persuaded Paramount to give her, as the scriptwriter for her own films and hence their *auteur*, considerable *carte blanche*, even in matters of production. What emerged were films in which a woman made the decisions that affected her own life, never taking the lead from a man. West scorned marriage as an answer for *this* woman in film after film and was, in short, the true exception, one who did not succumb to the dominance of a powerful male, even in the last five minutes of the film, as so many screen career women would. Needless to say, West never played in a film with Gable.

In Capra's and Robert Riskin's original script for *It Happened One Night*, the Gable character was "a long-haired, flowing-tie, Greenwich Village painter." Frank Capra recounts in his autobiography, *The Name Above the Title*, how this script met with resistance from all quarters until, upon the suggestion of Myles Connolly, Peter Warne was made a guy that "must be one of *us*": "Forget that panty-waist painter. Make him a guy we all know and like. Maybe a tough, crusading reporter at outs with his pigheaded editor." Depression art demanded the traditional view of the virile, competent male. Artists or bohemians were taboo; he had to be one of the boys in a profession where "being hard" counts, as toughness was demanded of faltering American males throughout the thirties.

The erotic undertones which suffuse *It Happened One Night* flow from the coyness of the Gable hero in his persistent refusal to seduce Colbert, although they spend two nights together in motel rooms and one in a deserted field sleeping on a haystack. But Gable is too confident to make advances. His indifferent male manner will be enough to force her to want him. By being so in control and by seeming not to be affected by her—even hanging that legendary blanket dubbed "the Walls of Jericho" across their motel rooms—Gable wins Colbert, just as by not caring about money, status, or position he achieves all three, reaffirming the American myth of upward mobility. Be your self-sufficient self, confidently persist, and the world will be your oyster. Frantic, hysterical struggle will do no good, just as strikes and demonstrations were frowned upon and feared during these trying times. The homily underlying Gable's great success in the film is that everything comes to the man who waits—and who is in fact content to be poor but honest.

In that first and famous motel sequence, it is Gable who is photographed as the sex object. In the manner of Valentino, he slowly strips, removing his shirt to expose a bare chest. A real man does not wear anything so confining and "pansy-like" as an undershirt. He refers to himself as "the big bad wolf," the suggestiveness a result of his withholding himself from sexual overtures, which makes him all the more irresistible. Gable seemed so in control of his sexuality that Capra found it necessary to provide proof of his masculine impulses by having him ask Ellen (Colbert) to remove her underwear—"those things"—from the Walls of Jericho. In the haystack he is about to kiss her, but refrains. His virility is again keyed to the tantalizing reversal of withholding himself sexually. The tearing down of the Walls of Jericho at the conclusion of the film is required not so much to confirm the institution of marriage and reaffirm the staid thirties ban on premarital sex as it is to relieve the overwhelming sexual tension that has been built up throughout the film.

For all his affability, the Gable male exhibits those qualities which would best enable men, according to Hollywood formula, to survive the Depression. The plot consists of a series of proofs that he knows how to do anything better than a woman, excepting, of course, the hitchhiking sequence in which Gable's catalogue of techniques pales before Colbert's effectiveness (she lifts her skirt, thus stopping the first car). "You're as helpless as a baby," he tells her. He must even prevent her from spending their last bit of money on chocolates, so impractical is this heiress who has fallen to his protection and from whom he hopes to get the story that will reinstate him on his newspaper.

When they are compelled to spend the night together, he buys the toothbrushes, has their wrinkled clothes pressed, and cooks breakfast while she sleeps. "Any complaints?" he demands. When they are penniless and hungry and she decides to "gold-dig" a meal, he is tougher than ever: "I'll break your neck!" For all Gable's domestic skills, Capra never allows us to forget that our hero is a real male by cave-man standards. When a blackmailer approaches them demanding some of the reward for the recovery of the heiress, or when a rural lowlife steals Gable's suitcase, Gable reveals how well he can handle himself. "I've a notion to plug you," he tells the blackmailer. Only we know that he is bluffing. To the thief he delivers a black eye and ties him to a tree. In the sequences where he bests lesser, weaker men, Gable is moody, turbulent, and sultry, parallel to the gentle, tender, witty demeanor he assumes when he is alone with Colbert.

The Valentino of the thirties, Gable is tough on the outside, all-knowing, and self-sufficient, but inside he is soft, romantic, and emphatically heterosexual. There isn't a male buddy on the scene. The woman of his ideal, he confides to Colbert during their second motel night together, is "somebody that's real, somebody that's alive. They don't come that way any more." Speaking in lines that might have been borrowed from *True Romances* magazine, he dreams of a deserted island in the Pacific where he would take the woman he loves. She would be a person capable of jumping into the surf with the same abandoned bravado as he. It is a fantasy of a man and woman happy together which utterly transcends those feelings of fear and hostility toward women that are the central emotion in so many American films. Gable's vision is of the coming together in joy of a man and woman, a dream which suited the Depression because it entailed no restrictions of any kind, not even the presence of civilization. As in the fantasies of the twenties, there are no screaming babies or dreary suburbs. And as in those of the thirties, there are no breadlines or foreclosed mortgages.

Colbert is so aroused by this scenario that she can barely speak. Suddenly she appears on Gable's side of the Walls of Jericho with the simple, straightforward request, "Take me with you." Because the real man is honorable and knows that lasting joy will not be his should he violate law, decorum, and sexual convention, Gable must first return her to her father and receive his blessing before he can properly possess her.

Capra did not entirely ignore the fact that most of his audience was in severe economic straits. His hero is no Robert Montgomery aristocrat but an ordinary man suffering from unemployment. It is only such a man, says *It Happened One Night*, who can offer a woman an exciting, real, vital relationship. His rival, whom Colbert is scheduled to marry, is an effete, money-hungry playboy without a muscle, or, it seems, an ounce of blood in his veins.

Appealing to audience hostility toward the rich, Capra has Gable scorn the wealthy, arguing that the poor are really happier. The rich are boring, upright, sexually repressed, and incapable of enjoying life despite their money. "You're all a lot of hooey to me," says Gable to Colbert in the colloquial talk that bespeaks the virile man in the thirties film. A real man has better things to recommend him than money or position. Gable would convince us that the poor have more fun. The rich may dine off silver trays, but the bus passengers, all down and out, Gable foremost among them, can make life worth living by as simple an act as joining together in choruses of "The Daring Young Man on the Flying Trapeze." Ordinary people live best even in hard times. "Never knew a rich man yet who could piggyback," says Gable. Among historical figures, only men like Abraham Lincoln were "born piggybackers." How appropriate it was to the needs of the Depression that Capra should insist that manliness resides more in character than in social advantage! The poor are blessed, says Capra, and he even has Gable give his last ten dollars to a starving boy and his mother, with the lie that he's "got millions." And indeed he has, in personality, energy, wit, and joy.

At the end Gable marries the rich heiress. He achieves great wealth by rejecting it. For Colbert's father, a self-made man—offering one more testimonial to the American system—admires a man who won't take a reward. Gable wants only his lost shirts and socks replaced.

That Colbert's father and her husband-to-be seem so close in temperament despite their economic disparity suggests that all men can rise to riches as her father did if only they have that grit, determination, and will to work. Daddy also finds Gable a perfect husband for his daughter because he appreciates Gable's manly dominance: "She needs a guy who would take a sock at her once a day." Of course he is a good father, not because he is rich, but because he would move heaven and earth to get his daughter the man she loves, even as Gable would move heaven and earth to get a story but chooses to sacrifice the story to bring Colbert home.

All the good things of life are finally to be had through persistence and individual effort. They include economic security and personal happiness. That all is resolved in the metaphor of the fall of the Walls of Jericho and a sexual consummation at last between Gable and Colbert is immensely appealing because Capra has so cleverly associated sexual potency with the male's initiative and aggressiveness in the outside world. No other male image in American films of the thirties would be as influential as that projected by Gable here and in *Gone with the Wind*.

III

In the major films of Frank Capra, the male upholds the values of Americanism and illustrates how occasional corruption, seen as the ultimate cause of the Depression, can be routed. He is neither domineering nor overbearing. An authoritarian male proves to be less effective than a more homely, down-to-earth one. In *Mr. Deeds Goes to Town, Mr. Smith Goes to Washington* (1939), and *Meet John Doe,* the ideal male turns out to be a gentle and entirely unthreatening human being.

Neither Deeds, Smith, nor Doe begins as the invincible all-knowing loud-mouth Gable so flamboyantly plays in *It Happened One Night.* Corruption haunts the metropolis, but these heroes are completely naïve not only about its causes but about its very existence. Each will be initiated into adult manhood once he becomes aware of the social issues of his day. And how each man faces this corruption defines his masculinity. All share a puritanical, antiseptic attitude toward sex and an innocence about the body. But by the end they have conquered evil and discovered women, the two concomitants of Capra manhood. Joseph von Sternberg was wrong when he cautioned Capra that his Deeds would not make an appropriate screen hero because "heroes must be noble, not imbecilic." What Capra intended by casting Gary Cooper as that seeming boob Mr. Deeds was the projection of a highly traditional view of masculinity: "Cast in the frontier mold of Daniel Boone, Sam Houston, Kit Carson, this silent Montana cowpuncher embodied the true-blue virtues that won the West: durability, honesty, and native intelligence." The same qualities that won the West would now be enlisted by Capra to beat the Depression. That Deeds appears to be a rural hayseed at the beginning of *Mr. Deeds Goes to Town* links him to the Western by the same style of innocent manliness concealing overwhelming strength that Cooper had brought to *The Virginian.* Once the layers of screwball eccentricity characterizing Deeds are peeled away, what emerges is a typical male of the Western tradition with the qualities of personal courage, initiative, and determination that have always been synonymous with maleness in American culture.

Cooper as tuba-playing Longfellow Deeds of Mandrake Falls becomes heir to twenty million dollars, an escapist fantasy that could not help but appeal to audiences during any year of the thirties, when the economic system was behaving like a chronic invalid. Just as the ordinary man of *It Happened One Night* proved to be the most manly, in *Deeds* the small-town rural man exudes a wholesome virility that is sharply contrasted with the ineffectuality of the cigar-smoking shysters and sharpies of the city who would prey upon him and steal his money.

In his silence and internal composure, Deeds is the real man. Just as Gable didn't care about Colbert's wealth in *It Happened One Night,* and just as impoverished audience males were being taught that money isn't everything, so Deeds doesn't give a fig for his inheritance. His reaction to the news that he is suddenly rich is—to play his tuba. The lack of interest in material things remains an indispensable aspect of male virility. "I wonder why he left me all that money," Deeds muses. "I don't need it."

Never having been out of Mandrake Falls, Deeds doesn't even own a suitcase for his trip to town to accept the money. Once in town he refuses to succumb to the ministrations of a valet as befits his new class. A real man always attends to his own needs. Seemingly passive, Deeds is actually both morally and physically quite aggressive, as he reveals when he expels a phony lawyer from his hotel. Like Gable's Peter Warne, he relies on "common sense," an attribute accessible to every man, to instruct him in his actions.

The innocence of Deeds only conceals the strong fiber of the man, which will emerge in the last third of the film. Before he is confronted with the moral challenge at the heart of *Mr. Deeds Goes to Town*, he can be childlike, sliding down banisters, tickling the foot of a marble statue, and even temporarily abandoning slick city reporter Jean Arthur to jump on a fire engine and follow the action. His attitude toward women derives from the Western and is both ridiculed and approved by Capra. Deeds's chivalry is anachronistic but charming. His mother once told him that he remains a bachelor because he's always been in search of a "lady in distress," as if nothing would suit him but an enactment of the romantic film myth cultivated by Fairbanks in the twenties. In Depression America Deeds can still realize that myth, if in a very different manner. He writes Jean Arthur, who is exploiting him to get her story, a poem saying "Be mine." He is pained when he discovers that it was she who wrote the humiliating newspaper accounts calling him a "Cinderella Man." But his chivalry remains unshakable.

The climax of *Mr. Deeds Goes to Town* involves, not Deeds winning his woman, but an action much more appropriate to a male confronting the Depression-ridden thirties. Confronted by a begging down-and-outer who denounces him ("you never gave a thought to all those people starving in the breadlines"), Deeds is horrified. The man weeps: it kills him to take a handout. Thereupon Deeds decides to distribute his inheritance to ease the suffering of the poor. Charity is proposed as an answer to the traumas of the Depression, and Capra's Deeds gains his manhood in the process of alleviating mass suffering by paternal benevolence. The money is to be used for a farm project, and the unemployed appear at Deeds's door to sign up. Reform will spring from within the existing social order if only men with good hearts are willing to minister to the needs of the have-nots. A real man is one who cannot eat while others go hungry. In Deeds, Capra equates manliness with a social conscience.

Capra was too sophisticated not to admit that thirties America was not the "Old West," although he insisted upon the simplistic view that if there had not been selfish men in power, the Depression could not have happened. Unlike a cowboy, who could act freely, Deeds is charged with insanity, for who but a madman would give away all his money in the midst of the Depression? But at Deeds's trial the "little people" turn out in great numbers. They are there to pose the implied threat of revolutionary upheaval to those in power who would resist a Deeds-style solution —which, of course, is an analogue for Roosevelt's New Deal. Charity from the central government is necessary, Capra informs all those Roosevelt-haters who called the president a "socialist," if only because the oppressed might turn against the social order itself if their justifiable pleas are not heeded. Those who would condemn Deeds insist that he is provoking "social unrest," but Capra insists that the contrary is the case: Deeds is doing exactly what must be done to prevent people from taking to the streets in anger and frustration. The foolish court rules that Deeds be committed as certifiably insane; the crowd joins crusader Jean Arthur in so angry a protest that the decision is reversed.

Through Deeds, Capra elevates the individual and his capacity to shape his world. It is important that he manages to grant Deeds the power to help the Depression poor without so much as disturbing the status quo. The prosecutor, like the opponents of Roosevelt, mistakenly believes that Deeds is hurting the "governmental system" by his welfare plan. Actually, Deeds's action is entirely safe because it proposes no structural changes in that "governmental system" whatsoever.

"The people" carry Deeds away in triumph. And at the end Deeds similarly lifts up Jean Arthur. Of sexuality there is only the smallest of smiles, a hug, and some short, fleeting kisses. Manhood has been achieved through Deeds's actions on behalf of the poor. A real man puts his energy in neither words nor passionate embraces. From his beginnings as a seemingly passive, nonaggressive male, Deeds winds up as the strong, silent, all-knowing, self-confident Cooper hero.

James Stewart's Senator Smith is even more asexual than Deeds; there is nary a love scene between him and smart, fast-talking Washington secretary Jean Arthur in *Mr. Smith Goes to Washington.* At the end, she must write him a note declaring her love. In grateful assent, he smiles coyly up at her from the Senate floor. The theme is again manliness realized by thwarting the official corruption of a few—the sole source of all our troubles in the thirties and hence an evil which can be overcome through individual effort. The collapse of the economy is disguised as a fairy tale in which the wicked witch is thwarted by a knight in armor.

Stalwart and honest, Jefferson Smith devotes all his energy to waging war against congressional corruption. His masculinity is linked to his boyishness and forthright sincerity. As naïve as Deeds, he begins his fluke term as senator unaware of how hard it will be to function as an honest man within a corrupt system. No invulnerable male, he is attractive because of his capacity to feel deeply. His eyes fill with tears when "Auld Lang Syne" is played as he leaves for Capitol Hill. Shy and tongue-tied with women, he brings his pigeons to Washington, just as Deeds brought his tuba to town. Both men are great patriots, always important for the male hero in American films but essential during the thirties. Deeds had waxed poetic over Grant's tomb. Smith marvels at the monuments of Washington. "Gee whiz," they conclude in awe, just plain folks, if with the vocabularies of preschoolers.

Smith's virility derives from the determination, will, and energy he displays in proceeding to fight a crooked political machine that would pour money into a graft-ridden dam project. The basis, however, of his quarrel with these bad and venal politicians is that Smith would prefer the funds to go to a camp for boys. The frivolity of his challenge to the status quo corresponds to its evident amenability to change which the film is anxious to propose. For if the politicians fight dirty, it is about little more than a single example of graft, not an entire economic order.

A lock of hair falls forward into Stewart's eyes. He smokes his pipe. His dark eyes sparkle. But Smith's manliness is exhibited through action and not in relation to the opposite sex. Neither Deeds, Smith, nor John Doe has "a girl." The Capra men wait for women to come to them. If they lack female companionship, it neither disturbs them nor is it something it would occur to them to notice. However sensitive they appear, they know that manliness must be displayed first in effective action.

Smith decides to filibuster for his boys' camp. When he first speaks in the Senate, his voice trembles and his hands flutter and shake. He is everyman standing up for what he believes with such determination that nothing can keep him from doing battle with the political machine. But, just as Deeds couldn't do it absolutely alone, Smith too must be aided by "the people," that contrivance of so many populist morality tales of the thirties. They print the news of his effort on makeshift mimeograph machines when the official press is proven to be in the control of the corrupt politicians. Yet however often "the people" are invoked, the thirties film never substitutes them for a strong individual leader behind whom they rally and without whom they are directionless. The populace is shown here, not as a conscious agent, but as people to be told what to do. The specter of disaffection, never openly admitted to by the film, is exorcised by the equating of popular protest with "follow the leader." The myth of individual solutions is preserved as well, for the mass is shown to be only a body that would be lifeless without its head. "I'm not licked," says Smith. "I'm going to stay and fight. Somebody will listen to me." Man and nation conjoin. Smith may not be a romantic lover, but he is something better: the supermale who through will alone can pull America out of the Depression. He isn't named "Jefferson" for nothing.

Hence revolution is proven unnecessary. The masses need not unite to destroy the corrupt political order because the eloquence of our leader Mr. Smith has convinced the evil Senator Payne to capitulate, as if the removal of one official could alter a social structure: "Every word that boy says is true ... I'm not fit for office." Corruption, and by extension the Depression itself, were the result of only a few wicked individuals. With determined leaders like Smith (or Roosevelt) the economic system can be reformed from within. Smith wins because even the most venal government officials are not so irredeemable that they will not listen to reason. Thus the story that seems to be about revolt in fact invokes it in order to discover the willingness of the ruling few to respond. A real man in the thirties remains the figure who, in the midst of official corruption, poverty, and bewilderment, struggles often against those whose interests he would finally preserve in spite of themselves. His real mission is to keep order.

Meet John Doe completes this trilogy. Reporter Barbara Stanwyck has written a "news" story creating an imaginary "John Doe," unemployed and so despairing of the "slimy" politics ruling America that he is about to leap off a roof. "Doe" suggests that the wrong people are doing the jumping, seemingly an outrageous and highly revolutionary notion. The articles appeal so powerfully to a suffering populace that Stanwyck is instructed to manufacture a real John Doe. To play this role, she locates a failed bush-league baseball player (Gary Cooper), a man so apathetic about the state of the nation that he can think only about baseball. The thesis advanced is that the exceptional individual, if only he were awakened, could reform a temporarily diseased body politic. It will be Cooper's task to restore faith in America on the part of all the John Does at large.

Acknowledging at last at the turn of the decade the existence of the Depression, the hero is presented as an unattractive male, passive, unshaven, clothed in a torn workingman's jacket, and so hungry that he faints only to be revived with six hamburgers. The male as victim must even be deloused. Doe appeals to the viewer barely past the Depression through his utter indifference to money; as his buddy, the "Colonel," points out: "When you become a guy with a bank account, they've got you." *Meet John Doe* makes a direct appeal to the suffering poor, but it does so for the purpose of showing both the dangers of revolt and the need for an honest leader. It presents a mass movement as itself the source of a danger greater even than the Depression. The rebellious popular groups are shown to be the basis for an American fascism, thus totally inverting the real causes of fascism. For, historically, fascism has been the response of a threatened social order *to* popular revolt, seeking scapegoats against whom to deflect mass anger. The fascist movements in Europe, which are clearly in Capra's mind here, were orchestrated from above by those in power. But *Meet John Doe* shows that the John Doe clubs which spring up as the result of Cooper-Doe's public appearances are the *cause* of a fascist threat, with Stanwyck's newspaper-tycoon boss, D. B. Norton, the potential fascist dictator who would use the multiplying John Doe clubs of the poor to further his political ambitions.

For a long time Doe himself acts as Norton's dupe, reading in public speeches written for him without first perusing them, since he spends all his spare time practicing his pitching. We are well into half the film virtually without Doe's having spoken a word of his own. Yet it is up to "Coop," our individualistic hero, to see through Norton; the masses, "the people," need his help because they are so easily deceived and so fickle. Again only the strong leader, Hollywood's constant invocation of Roosevelt, can save America from evils far worse than the Depression. The fate of the nation depends on whether the pliant Cooper can pull himself together in time. "Gee whiz, I'm all mixed up," he murmurs.

Capra seeks to relate the male image on screen to the living experience of his audience, to depart from fantasy depictions of the glamorous rich. In so doing he shows us that the strong, determined male is made, not born. And the fascist threat as seen by Capra in *Meet John Doe* differs but slightly from the conventional Western in which a lone figure realizes that a corrupt land baron is scheming with the sheriff's connivance against honest farmers. In response to this scheme against the innocent, Cooper as John Doe becomes a real man. When he finally realizes that the American people are about to be oppressed by an "iron hand," he draws on his rigid self-control to unmask the traitor, Norton.

Seduced and deceived, like the duped townspeople of many a Western, the John Does among "the people" pelt him with tomatoes until, in despair, Cooper decides to jump off the Empire State Building on Christmas Eve to demonstrate his sincerity and thus win the people from the fascist deceiver. More sober representatives of the people stop him, and Stanwyck speaks cryptically of beginning the John Doe movement again because "it's still alive." On this inconclusive note, the fifth alternative ending conceived by Capra, the film ends.

Instead of dying a martyr's death, Coop will provide the people with an unselfish, disinterested, but strong leader, one they are shown to need. He lifts in his arms the ailing Stanwyck, who has emerged from a sickbed to find him. "They are the people, try and lick that," are the words on which the film closes. But without Cooper they would have been lost sheep. Having fulfilled his function as the strong leader, Cooper can now win the woman he had previously been too shy to approach. Only a male leader is sufficiently virile to master the woman of his choice.

At first the Capra male seems weak and beset by the overwhelming forces against him. He displays an abundance of "feminine" traits, which allow us to doubt his manliness. But in his pilgrim's progress to dominance such weakness is cast off and the male hero comes into his own as a leader. His vulnerability turns out to have been only temporary, concealing that nascent indomitable will and sense of honor buried within every man who would be male. In each Capra film the individualistic male is successful because he overcomes adverse circumstances through freely chosen action. His personal determination ensures success and permits his alliance with "the people" who so desperately need him. Honor is more important to this hero than sensuality. Capra's male spends neither energy nor time in developing a relationship with a woman, far less than did Fairbanks, Mix—or even Hart. His thirties films are testimonials to male individualism and male initiative, the salvation of the person as they are of society. What seemed soft turns out to be harder than steel, impermeable to deflection, and fiercely self-contained. Capra's view of manliness was wholly unrealistic in its expectations, though grand in the degree to which it supposed men capable of overcoming the overwhelmingly hostile forces which beset them.

IV

Side by side with the idealized images of male prowess in the early decades of the American film were the great comic figures: Charlie Chaplin, Buster Keaton, Harry Langdon, Harold Lloyd, Laurel and Hardy, the Marx Brothers. The clown, object of slapstick comedy, early secured an important place and a faithful audience that preferred his antics to movies about stoical, humorless giants of male prowess. The hero of comedy was more like the audience male himself, a social failure, a little man beset by circumstances; he appealed to an audience composed not of the elite but of ordinary people, for whom life was also a struggle. The clowns restored their followers to equilibrium by being even more hapless than they. From Chaplin to Laurel and Hardy, these were not men endlessly pursued by exotic, beautiful women. Overwhelmingly, from Keaton, Chaplin, Langdon, and Stan Laurel to the Marx Brothers they were physically small, and in their films—unlike the gangsters—they never found a way of making up for a paltry physical demeanor in violence. They lacked sexual prowess, and success eluded them.

So beset by hostile forces and callous social institutions are the comic heroes that they frequently assume grotesque qualities which only add to their troubles and ensure that they will remain outsiders. Harpo cannot speak. Keaton cannot alter the expression on his face. Harry Langdon is an adult man who looks like a baby and remains childlike, the opposite of the invulnerable male who flaunts his superiority to women and children. Langdon even wore baby clothes in his films, predictably buttoned in the wrong buttonhole. He was the comic figure who never succeeds on the basis of his own efforts but always by virtue of a momentarily benevolent providence, as when he wins the money to save his father's factory in *Tramp, Tramp, Tramp* (1926).

Always the comic hero must confront his powerlessness. In the Harold Lloyd films the bespectacled hero faces the countless obstacles of everyday life, exaggerated in his "ledge-hangers" when he dangles from skyscrapers, not as a result of his own initiative, but because he has agreed to help someone else. Laurel and Hardy were lovable losers, men with hearts of gold. They were, Hardy's size notwithstanding, small people put upon and defeated by circumstances, facing daily humiliation. Often they were misused by powerful men who took advantage of them. Down and out, Laurel and Hardy forever seek work. When they manage to find employment, they make hopeless mistakes, from serving tough lion's steak which they steal from a zoo to becoming housemovers for the rich and then breaking all the furniture. One thing they cannot do is reverse roles and become the kind of men who succeed by initiating aggression against others.

In the sound film W. C. Fields and the Marx Brothers added the clown's scorn of social pretension. Fields and Groucho played the little man who could and did get nasty as a means of warding off defeat. Fields made mincemeat of myths about the sanctity and protection offered by the nuclear family and the supposed devotion between parents and children. Nor did he find solace from a hostile environment in either purity or innocence. Groucho talked ceaselessly and his gags were themselves a means of survival. To stop talking was to face something no less than the world of the Depression—which Groucho could not admit into his consciousness. Instead, he occupied himself with such absurdities as filling a ship's stateroom with people until they lined the tiny cabin from floor to ceiling.

Nothing was sacred to the Marx Brothers, and their targets included nationalism and war, love of country, and personal heroism, all lambasted in *Duck Soup* (1933), their best film. All the more when he was in power could Groucho delight in wreaking havoc, as prime minister of Fredonia in *Duck Soup*, or on a university, as in *Horse Feathers* (1932). Decorum was forever being violated. Yet all their craziness led the brothers, finally, nowhere. The mad destructiveness in the Marx Brothers' films, reducing the world to chaos, was the bitter clowns' answer to the frustrations of the Depression. Harpo with his scissors, Groucho with his sharp tongue, could retain their manhood only by thumbing their noses at the world in riotous, perpetual defiance. But in such outlandish fantasies wise-guy Groucho could always outsmart the rich—and reduce everyone else to objects susceptible to his zany pranks.

Only into the thirties do we find this alternate mode of masculinity, the vulnerable comic male, existing side by side with the Mix-like hero. After he disappears from the screen, he is never replaced, and it is almost a travesty to see a crude figure like Jerry Lewis, forever the mindless adolescent attempting to approximate the greatness of the antisocial clowns. Especially in the twenties, when the choreographed athletics of the lithe comic hero so well suited the silent film, people turned with relief to the clowns, men at war even with the machine. Against the automobile they were rarely the victors, unlike those later heroes whose willed mastery of the car, from Steve McQueen's psychotic performance behind the wheel in *Bullitt* (1968) to Gene Hackman's imitative exploits with the automobile as surrogate sexual organ in *The French Connection* (1971), symbolizes the deterioration of the image of maleness. For the humanized male hero of comedy, the automobile was his enemy, a negative force beyond his control, as were machines in general.

Charlie Chaplin exists entirely outside of the tradition of the hero who would become the protector of us all. For in his view of the world, director Chaplin subscribed to no such philosophy glorifying an authoritarian leader who would always know what is best, whether he is the hero of a Western film or a political personality; Chaplin made his satire of Hitler and Mussolini, *The Great Dictator* (1940), precisely in protest against the destructive absurdity of such an idea. Charlie the screen character demanded that we choose between being good and being successful. He did it with laughter, but it was a dangerous idea nonetheless, and Chaplin's conflicts with Hollywood were no accident. Sheer brilliance and his working in what was considered the harmless genre of comedy account in part for the acceptance of so subversive a view of maleness as Chaplin offered on screen in both his silent and his sound films.

For the world refuses to bend to Charlie's will as Chaplin forces us to identify with values that are the antithesis of physical prowess, success, and social recognition. Charlie remains permanently on the brink of disaster—the audience male as he truly is, barely extricating himself from the scrapes of daily life and with no sense of permanence accompanying even his successes. From *The Immigrant* (1917) to *City Lights* (1931), from *The Adventurer* (1916) to *The Pilgrim* (1923), Charlie is accepted by no social group; but his being an outsider is not romantic but dangerous, the opposite of the mythology of the Western. So prevalent is defeat in his life that he sometimes is reduced to pretending that things are not as dangerous as they seem. In *The Adventurer* he covers the warden's shoe with sand as if this would make him disappear, a brilliant variation on the ostrich motif.

Even objects cannot be tamed by Charlie. They are not his allies, as they are for the Westerner, but additional adversaries, from the bowl of beans in which his elbow lands in *The Immigrant* to the shoe he eats in *The Gold Rush* (1924). The theme of the treadmill runs through the Chaplin films, influencing their structure as the bad things keep happening, as the loneliness of the open road remains Charlie's fate. Not even Charlie's identity remains his own, as in *The Circus* (1928) when he must become the troupe clown. Anything can happen to Charlie, while in the "serious" American film maleness has always been dependent upon a man's knowing who and what he is, and remaining so.

Charlie Chaplin in *The Gold Rush:* Charlie remains permanently on the brink
of disaster—the audience male as he truly is.

Had his genius not been such that it defied imitation, had this image
managed to influence the American film even in an altered form, different
values might have defined the ideal male in our movies. As it is, only a
Charlie, never a John Wayne or a Clint Eastwood, would find participating in authority an untenable alternative. This was a result of the radical

sensibility of *auteur* Chaplin himself, a reflection of the progressiveness of his own point of view.

By nature, as an ordinary man whose survival is never guaranteed, and as the creation of a Chaplin forever at war with injustice and in sympathy with the defenseless little man, Charlie is constantly intimidated by the powers that be, which are his ubiquitous enemy. He is the hero who is great because he defies a cruel world in which the poor are excluded from physical comfort. He is a man who values tenderness and love while knowing that the price for such purity is remaining an outsider forever. Like a child with his nose pressed up against the glass of a bakery-shop window, Charlie is often forced to be only a voyeur of human happiness, an image that appears in *Twenty Minutes of Love* (1914) with Charlie watching two lovers kiss on a park bench and then embracing a tree trunk. Forever besieged, even when he takes to the open road, as in *Police* (1916), there is a cop behind him.

Above all, Charlie consistently defines love as selfless self-sacrifice. A man who is a valuable human being in these films is compassionate and kind, even if there is nothing in it for himself, and in several of the Chaplin films Charlie, despite his goodness, does not win the heroine. Even in *City Lights* it remains unclear whether the blind girl whose sight he has had restored will love Charlie for himself. As she sees him for the first time the film ends, leaving this point ambiguous, for Chaplin was too honest to suggest that virtue is rewarded in this world. Right up to *Limelight* (1952) Chaplin persisted in defining love as asking nothing for oneself.

The Chaplin hero faced an eternal Depression; in *Monsieur Verdoux* (1947), having lost his job as a result of the actual Depression, he takes to marrying and then murdering rich women in order to support his family. Yet through his resilience as Charlie the tramp, he could always bounce back. Through a body language that defied gender, Charlie triumphed against the dehumanization of the social order in which he found himself. He was loved by audiences because he personified the soul of all who felt helpless, as he defied Hollywood's absurd glorification of aggressive masculinity and insistence upon the presumed superiority of being male. The violent and domineering characters in the Chaplin films are treated as mere brutes, pathological figures with whom it is hopeless to reason, whose very power renders them repugnant and antihuman. It is the strong, supposedly superior male who seems most sexually repellent in the Chaplin films. The weak and helpless Charlie manages to retain his virility through the sympathy he shows the weak, living proof that masculinity has nothing to do with dominating others.

In 1936 Chaplin made one of his greatest classics, *Modern Times*, a view of the powerless male overwhelmed by industrialized and Depression America. It was a film as exceptional for the decade as the persona of Charlie himself was for American film. What is rare for a thirties film (or any other) is the sight of a man actually working on an assembly line.

Rarer still is the image of a man so dehumanized by the drudgery and monotony of factory life that he goes to pieces, becoming himself a machine out of kilter in a mechanized ballet that distinguishes Charlie in degree, if not in kind, from the technology to which he has been a slave. The locations of *Modern Times,* also unusual for the cinema if not for life in the thirties, are the assembly line, the hospital to which Charlie is taken after his "breakdown," and the prison where he winds up as a radical. There one of the grisly inmates actually does needlepoint.

Modern Times concludes with a hilarious sequence in which Charlie, now a singing waiter all set to perform, must improvise in nonsense language when his cuffs, on which the words of his song have been written, fly off with his first grandiloquent gesture. It is Chaplin thumbing his nose both at what he felt was the facile arrogance of the sound film and at those expectations of the triumph which was to end the hero's travail. Charlie and his girl, the Gamin (Paulette Goddard), take to the open road, this time to be the last for the tramp. A human being forever resilient, he has survived with the person he loves. But the tramp, in taking to the open highway, has been pushed ever more to the periphery of a society which doesn't care whether he lives or dies and against which he has no power to struggle. His indomitable spirit allows him to go on, but not much more.

That the figure of Charlie has been so important in the history of Hollywood has by itself humanized the American film, offering one consistent characterization of a truly humanized male. If one would never hope to *be* Charlie, he helped audiences, men and women, to accept themselves and to recognize that aggressive means invariably bring about a shallow and dehumanized end. The Chaplin films alone teach that the price of success is the loss of the most noble part of ourselves without which "masculinity" dissolves. Charlie the tramp reminds us how sick and unworthy of approval has been the male image of the last four decades, since Hollywood decreed that life in America is too traumatic for us to let our defenses down by portraying the male hero as a sweet and vulnerable human being.

V

Despite Chaplin and the other great screen clowns, male strength, Hollywood's response to the Depression, would influence later decades of filmmakers. And in offering an omnipotent male image which young men were urged to imitate and women to adore, the thirties belonged to Gable. He epitomized the desirable male, appealing to women precisely because he was so unattainable. Despite the *pro forma* endings of many of his films in which he "reforms" to settle down, Gable's demeanor conveyed an impatient restlessness, a disdain for emotional commitment which suggested that at any moment he might skip out on the heroine and domesticity. Like the actor himself with his many marriages and love affairs, excluding his alliance with Carole Lombard, he seemed too eager for the fullness of experience ever really to settle down. The distortion of the women in so many films flows precisely from this insistence that the elusive, self-centered, and utterly self-sufficient male is the one most worth having.

Gable is never so attractive as he is as Rhett Butler at the moment when he informs Scarlett O'Hara that he doesn't "give a damn" whether she needs him or not. Gable epitomizes that restless male for whom a woman, any woman, is never finally enough, an image that has become the norm in American films. The challenge of taming such a man is substituted in these films for the joys of mutual involvement. Thus, even when Gable and his woman seem to be in the throes of a relationship, what comes across is the discrete personality of each, isolated in its separateness. The woman is defined by her success in catching and holding a partner, the man by his resistance to "settling down." Gable becomes the male ideal by never being "there" for a woman; the sadistic quality of this male approach to women is matched by female masochism expressed in women wanting only men who so comport themselves.

In *No Man of Her Own* (1932), an early but typical Gable film, our hero, tough cardsharp and con man that he is, reforms for love. At the beginning we see him as the footloose male: "What gets me," he declares, "is why women can't laugh when it's over." Small-town girl Carole Lombard, finding Gable's cool uncaring façade irresistible, manages to corral this wild spirit by playing hard to get. But what really is most in her favor is that, in the rural backwater where he temporarily eludes the police, she is the only woman around.

Yet there remains a positive aspect to this male image of the thirties epitomized by Gable which would be absent in later, more sexually threatened heroes of the fifties, sixties, and seventies. The woman who can win him is a live wire, not the pliant, passive toy who relies on looks and forever submits to how *he* sees things. In reaction to the economic violence of the Depression years a screen male emerged whom nothing could threaten, not even a high-spirited woman. Gable perfectly epitomized the self-confident male at once unrealistic and insisted upon in these hard times, responding to a historical moment when bravado was demanded and needed by official America. Lombard can always respond to Gable with witty repartee, and he welcomes and enjoys this aspect of their relationship. Far from feeling threatened, he finds it intriguing and a source of allure. But because Gable's manhood is never in question and is so overwhelming a feature of his personality, he immediately relegates to second place even the seemingly independent, spirited Lombard. Despite herself, Lombard must function in terms of *his* dominance, perceiv-

Clark Gable and Myrna Loy in *Too Hot to Handle:* The woman who can
win him is a live wire, not the pliant, passive toy who relies on looks and
forever submits to how *he* sees things.

ing that "the girl who lands him will have to say 'no,' but isn't it tough
when all you can think of is 'yes'?"

At the end of *No Man of Her Own* Gable gives up his con game. As
a real man, he had always hated the stultifying life of office routine. Yet
he is willing to succumb to a nine-to-five existence for the sake of love,
confirming that women restrict and emasculate with their domestic demands and need for security. The ending contradicts the emotional tenor
of everything that has gone before. Gable had been desirable precisely
because he couldn't be "managed." Now he serves a jail term for his
bad-boy ways and declares that it was worth it because it will win him
the woman he loves.

We are luckily spared the sight of their life with Gable as a white-collar
worker, doing business on Wall Street in 1932 as if the Depression had
never occurred. What had been exciting about him was his refusal to
assume the unmanly role of a nine-to-five drudge. "C'mere, you!" he
summons Lombard upon their final reunion. It is best that the film end
here.

Indispensable to the male mystique cultivated by Gable was the omnipresence of physical danger, nowhere better glorified than in Victor Fleming's *Test Pilot* (1938). From the beginning of the decade, aviation had proven an ideal arena for the masculine male. But as in *No Man of Her Own*, by the end of *Test Pilot* Gable has given up his dangerous occupation for the woman he loves (Myrna Loy). Yet what had made him a "real man" were precisely those constant confrontations with death in which he embodied the Hemingway mystique.

The woman who would attract and hold such a man must, like Loy, have spunk and wit and understand instantly what Gable demands when he calls her "sister" and "pal." To her, this daring male is the prince she has been waiting for all her life, the man who corresponds to her dreams. Gable's charm resides in his cool. During a baseball game he stolidly chews his peanuts while Loy, emotional and girlish, cheers madly for her team. Half proletarian and half Valentino, Gable flaunts tough-guy grammar: "Wait till you smell them honeysuckles," he tells his buddy and flying partner Spencer Tracy. Baby-faced yet brusque, rugged yet sophisticated, Gable comes across as equally unencumbered by intellect or fear of risk. Security doesn't interest him. Virility and a pseudo-working-class bravado are conjoined to *savoir-faire*. Because he shows no weakness and is resigned to its presence in women, Gable becomes the formula "macho" male of the thirties. He enjoys a camaraderie with his buddy Spencer Tracy without tainting his heterosexual façade because their interaction is generally light-hearted and relaxed. If Gable disdains women, he is nonetheless oriented toward them, and Gable and Tracy manage to be involved without suggesting that their interest in women is incidental. Lest we think otherwise, Tracy is made silently to long for Loy, who has eyes only for Gable.

But Tracy clearly loves Gable, as he shows by sticking his chewing gum for luck under the wing of each plane taken up by Gable for a test flight. The men choose women first, but the buddy relationship serves as a preparation, both an initiation and a catalyst drawing the man and woman closer together. Yet male priority endures. Gable and Tracy crash, Tracy dies in Gable's arms, revealing the inevitable meaning of his continuous presence. Tracy's last words are explicit: "Don't take anyone in my place," words which presage Gable's retirement from flying.

Whether Gable can retain his masculinity as a flying instructor and a middle-class husband and father remains to be seen—but not by us. The film, by ending here, evades the implications of the heterosexual relation for its own masculine ideal. Gable feels like a man only when facing danger and believes, interestingly, that he couldn't love a woman fully were he to retire from flying. "He's awful good up there," Tracy had said of him. At the end of the film all of the qualities which define him as the dominant man are in jeopardy, though the problem is met in part by the implication that Gable was born with a masculine core which he can never lose despite changes in his circumstances. This is the price of associating maleness with activities which exclude women and at the same time underlining women's presumed inferiority. Women are necessary at least as decorative embellishments in order to prove that the male is heterosexual despite his moving in a world of men, yet when a man abandons that world for any permanent relation with a woman, he is in danger of losing the tough qualities that were the touchstone of his maleness. *Test Pilot* ends before it can expose the paradox of the masculine male who prefers the world of men yet commits himself to a woman on the basis of a masculinity now deprived of its arena of expression.

Gable at his quintessential best would appear the following year in *Gone with the Wind,* again under the direction of his friend Victor Fleming. As Rhett Butler in Margaret Mitchell's saga, he is the exciting man with a mysterious past, a man who had been expelled from West Point over a love affair in which he failed to marry the woman. Rhett is the supermale surrounded by cigar smoke, a mannerism later adopted by Clint Eastwood. He smiles condescendingly as lesser men exude confidence over their ability to lick the Yankees without a single cotton factory in the entire South. Rhett Butler alone is scornful of those who have only "cotton, slaves—and arrogance" to recommend them.

Rhett is more intelligent than all the other men in the film, although, of course, he is neither an intellectual nor an effeminate dreamer like Ashley Wilkes (Leslie Howard). His good sense is especially apparent when it is contrasted with the faulty judgments of Scarlett O'Hara (Vivien Leigh), who prefers the pale Ashley, a man who lacks the resilience to survive after the South's defeat.

Rhett begins as the supreme individualist, the rugged fortune-seeker who makes his way in spite of social disaster. At first he refuses to identify in the slightest with his region's crisis: "I believe in Rhett Butler," he says, "he's the only cause I know." It is this very selfish unconcern which enables Rhett Butler to emerge as the sanest and most competent man in the film. He becomes the best of the South's fighting men because he goes to war out of the demands of an unruly nature, not in the name of abstract ideals, which American films have always characterized as debilitating. The foolishness of Scarlett in failing to recognize the value of such a man until it is too late corresponds to the blindness of the South in pursuing *its* lost cause.

There is another important side to Margaret Mitchell's Rhett Butler, a contribution to the male image in film which perhaps only a woman author would provide. Rhett Butler, despite his being an adventurer, is supremely paternal, not as a stern patriarch, but in a tenderly solicitous manner that in no way damages the sense of his maleness. Toward Scarlett he is protective, telling her to "blow her nose like a good girl" when the Yankees come. When they marry and have a little girl, he is tender

Clark Gable as Rhett Butler in *Gone with the Wind:* He becomes the best
of the South's fighting men because he goes to war out of the demands of
an unruly nature, not in the name of abstract ideals.

and indulgent toward his daughter. He takes delight in the raising of the child, in no way indicating regret that she was not a boy: "What good are boys? Look at me!"

An eager father, he spends much time with this "first person who's ever completely belonged to me." Wheeling the baby carriage, he cultivates silly old ladies in order to win status for his daughter and makes contributions to their charities, behavior we would expect from a mother, not a father. When the role of husband is denied to him by Scarlett, who is still lovesick over Ashley, he devotes his emotional energy to the child, refusing to insist upon a sexual relationship with his wife: "If I wanted to come in, no lock could keep me out." The scenes of Rhett as family man are the most charming of the film, transcending the conventional model of manliness.

Rhett is constant despite Scarlett's indifference; when she falls down the stairs and has a miscarriage, he becomes the worried husband, staying up all night. Real tears stream down his cheeks, a display against which actor Gable had vigorously protested, considering it damaging to his male image. He had threatened to walk off the set rather than dissolve in tears. Male-oriented though he had always been, director Fleming recognized the merit of the scene and coaxed Gable to comply, arguing that the tears would increase audience sympathy for Rhett Butler. The actor schooled in Hollywood's definition of masculinity yielded to a woman's conception of what it means to be a man and thus added a nuance to his screen persona which had hitherto been beyond him.

Throughout, Gable had to accommodate his masculine screen image to the ideal of manhood of the woman writer, Margaret Mitchell. He was given, it is true, a "rape" scene in which he carries Scarlett up to her boudoir, providing so satisfying a sexual experience that she finally falls in love with him. But he was also supplied with a share of tender qualities foreign to the brash, wisecracking persona cultivated by Gable in his other screen roles.

In the novel, with the prideful, bragging Southern slaveowners marching out on behalf of the Confederacy, Rhett Butler alone is man enough to admit that "he was always frightened when in danger, as frightened as were the brave boys at the front." He wins over the irascible Mammy by his joy that his child is a girl, and here he distinguishes himself from all other men in the book:

> "But, Lawd, Miss Melly, you know whut he say? He say, 'Hesh you' mouf, Mammy! Who want a boy? Boys ain' no fun. Dey's jes' a' passel of trouble. Gals is whut is fun. Ah wouldn' swap disyere gal fer a baker's dozen of boys. . . . He grin an' shake his haid an' say, 'Mammy, you is a fool. Boys ain no use ter nobody. Ain' ah a proof of dat?' "

And Mammy, the implicit heroine of the novel after Scarlett, admits, "Maybe Ah done been a mite wrong 'bout Mis' Rhett." Nor, in the novel, does Rhett overlook his neglected little stepson Wade Hampton, who does not appear in the film. Jealous at the birth of his sister, the boy asks Rhett whether people like girls better than boys:

"No, I can't say they do," he answered seriously as though giving the matter due thought. "It's just that girls are more trouble than boys. . . ."

And he accepts the stepchild who asks whether he'd rather have had a boy than a girl: "Now, why should I want a boy when I've already got one?"

Nor was Margaret Mitchell beyond having her male hero cry when circumstances demanded it. In the novel, Rhett's concern over Scarlett during the miscarriage is extremely effusive and tender. Melanie is shocked to see the dauntless Rhett Butler, once "so suave, so mocking, so eternally sure of himself," crying profusely:

It frightened her, the desperate choking sound he made. . . . She had never seen a man cry but she had comforted the tears of many children. When she put a soft hand on his shoulder, his arms went suddenly around her skirts. Before she knew how it happened she was sitting on the bed and he was on the floor, his head in her lap and his arms and hands clutching her in a frantic clasp that hurt her. . . .

The Rhett of the novel suffers no loss of masculinity by opening his heart to a woman:

At her words, his grip tightened and he began speaking rapidly, hoarsely, babbling as though to a grave which would never give up its secrets, babbling the truth for the first time in his life, baring himself mercilessly to Melanie. . . .

A man so closely in touch with his feelings is the projection of a woman writer for whom the deeply sensitive male is infinitely more desirable than the implacable stoic, and far less psychologically damaged.

In the film, Scarlett calls Rhett a murderer when their little girl is accidentally killed in a horseback-riding accident; at this Rhett is returned to that fantasy male persona for whom weakness or distress is unthinkable: "You think saying I'm sorry can erase everything," he tells Scarlett. He demands something "of charm and grace" in his life; if Scarlett believes she loves him now, that is her "misfortune." When she asks what she shall do without him, he replies, "Frankly, I don't give a damn," this first screen "profanity" expressive of the heightened manliness of a character who refuses to compromise or accept less than his rich nature deserves. Tomorrow may be "another day," as Scarlett muses, but it is difficult to believe such a man will reverse himself.

The plot of *Gone with the Wind* is sheer cliché and Scarlett's devotion to the weakling Ashley merely exasperating. What remains is the image of male perfection offered by Clark Gable as Rhett Butler. In his every gesture, his ease with his sexuality, his fierceness, and his physical competence as a soldier of fortune, he becomes a male model. To this image, depth is added by his gentleness with his child and his willingness to devote himself to her nurture. There is no competing male buddy to divert Rhett or cloud his sexuality, and finally no compromise with his standards for himself. The setting in times past lends romance to this male image and a credibility it could never have in a contemporary milieu.

VI

Companion to Gable and equal in grace was Errol Flynn in settings even more flamboyant. In *Captain Blood* (1935), in *The Adventures of Robin Hood* (1938), and as the savior of *Dodge City* (1939), Flynn is clearly a descendant of Fairbanks Senior, even incorporating his hand-on-the-hips stance and athletic bravado. Lacking the depth of Gable characterizations like that of Rhett Butler, Flynn's heroes represent Depression-era escapism at its most obvious. If the Capra films acknowledged that total escape from the experience of the decade was not always possible, and Hollywood had occasionally to address itself to the actual experience of people, Flynn's films represented the explicit attempt to use cinema as an entertainment—an open flight from the woes of the present. Neither as original nor as influential as Fairbanks had been in the twenties, Flynn expressed the charm of the man of honor. If in the twenties this sentiment could flourish only in settings where ethical questions were unambiguous and a man's choice of right over wrong indubitable, how much more true was this in the thirties! Depression escapist films allowed men to help others and survive so radical a response, as Flynn's Doctor Peter Blood attends a sick man regardless of whether the victim is a rebel against James II or a loyal subject. His "sacred duty" to his profession is a clear ideal, and who would argue with a doctor's insistence upon treating a sick person regardless of his politics? Safe in the Europe of the seventeenth century, Peter Blood can even be man enough to criticize a king: "What a creature must sit on the throne that lets a man like you deal out his justice," Blood scornfully tells his accuser. He feels no self-consciousness in using the word "justice." It rises to his lips naturally with neither pretension nor melodrama, and he takes it for granted that he would die for this ideal. Such sentiments were obviously inappropriate in the setting of the thirties; the need to express them at whatever risk was sanctified by their romantic transference to a pirate past.

Far more than in the Gable films, manliness is associated with physical danger and the risk of one's life, an element which defined the virility of the Flynn male in film after film. At the end of *Dodge City*, having cleaned up the town, he would move on to Virginia City, there to risk his life doing the same. As Robin Hood, Flynn would give all for Richard the Lion-Hearted. For the audience it was a comforting game since the reward for risk was a guaranteed happy ending.

Nowhere is Flynn more himself than as the dashing Captain Blood, once a doctor, sold into slavery in the Americas but remaining proud, untamable, and defiant. As a slave he refuses privileges; a real man bows to no one, even when he is in chains and his life is at stake, a philosophy light-years away from life as it was in the thirties, yet curiously speaking to what people yearned for in a world of depression and impending war. The early slavery of Dr. Blood provides Flynn with the chance to prove himself through individual rebellion, truly acceptable only in times past. Others may accept their serfdom passively, but no real man would, and through individual initiative, Blood wins all. He even becomes the governor of the very island where he was once enslaved. Audiences were not, of course, meant to apply such rebellious sentiments to life in their own time, the very point of exorcising such desires in the swashbuckling setting of distant climes.

Blood, seizing a Spanish galleon and sailing the high seas, as romantic as Fairbanks portraying "the black pirate," is so clearly not one of us that the transference of his bold rebelliousness to our own times by ordinary men is at once implied to be impossible. As Captain Blood, Flynn stood for a spirit of adventure irresistible because it was so irretrievably lost. "The sails," says Captain Blood, "will fill with the wind that's carrying us all to freedom." Swordplay with the infamous Basil Rathbone completes the adventure as white blouses blow in the wind. The sword is a scarcely disguised surrogate penis as the two men relish their struggle while the passive object over which they fight, Olivia de Havilland, anxiously awaits the outcome. The ending of *Captain Blood*, like that of *Test Pilot*, fails because the male hero was portrayed as fully masculine only in the struggle itself. Peacetime presages dullness. Marriage to de Havilland is in store, but the pursuit was clearly more erotic than the attainment could ever be.

Even more arousing as a sex object was Flynn in the role of Robin Hood. In one of the outstanding color films of the thirties, Flynn is electrifying in green doublet and tights, with flaming red hair and beard. His dimples were never more pronounced, his irony never more tinged with disdain for his wily antagonist, again Basil Rathbone. Flynn's *Robin Hood* was choreographed in the best Fairbanks tradition, a musical without music clearly foreshadowing such later Gene Kelly films as *The Pirate* (1948). The entire spectacle was constructed upon the cult glorification of Flynn's maleness. At a time when many men were jobless, their male pride severely undermined, Flynn flaunted a masculinity so unflinching that all obstacles disintegrated before it in short order.

Fearless, if not as agile as the graceful Fairbanks Senior, Flynn's Robin also climbs castle walls and swings from ropes. There is even less pretense of credibility in these feats than there was in the twenties when Fairbanks and Mix took pride in wounds suffered during the performance of their own stunts. By the late thirties the staged unreality of such scenes was taken for granted. Robin is provided with an inexhaustible supply of arrows. The spectacle of manly grace is not an embodiment of realism here, but its substitute.

Flynn's image was finally derived as much from early gangster films as from Fairbanks swashbucklers. Although transported back into romantic times, Flynn, like Little Caesar, faces a recalcitrant social order that denies its benefits to the many. He too goes beyond the law, but, as befits the far more escapist character of his films, he steals not for himself but for weaker men. Just as during the Depression the prevailing myth was that a few corrupt bankers and speculators had caused the economic upheaval, so in the Flynn films there are a few evil tyrants who must be deposed before order can be restored.

All the while, Flynn in his person stood for success made possible through the exercise of his manly attributes. His personal values, like those of the characters he played, carried no remote promise of rebellion against the existing order, despite his unrelenting persona. Indeed, his very defiance was invoked in order to enlist it for the status quo and to channel insurrection into the vanished past. Thirty years later, describing Flynn as "the most beautiful man in the world," his most frequent costar, Olivia de Havilland, recalled that when asked what he wanted most in life, Flynn had replied, " 'Success,' by which he meant fame and money." The same values are evident in his screen characters who so charm us by their brashness. "I love a man that can best me," is a line that could be spoken with absolute credibility only by Errol Flynn. His self-confidence was taken for granted, as was his capacity to lead. Nor was anyone to doubt the ability of Flynn's Robin Hood to "protect all women," as promised.

But the thirties films could not approach those of the seventies in the psychopathic impassivity demanded of the masculine male; hence there was also a softness about the Flynn image. When Robin takes Maid Marian to view the cottages of the poor who have been tortured by the evil Prince John, he is overcome with sorrow for "beaten, helpless people." Compassion is a necessary component of his eroticism, a far cry from the sadism of Dirty Harry Callahan, who wages a vicious war on the poor for striking out helplessly against the privileged world from which they have been excluded.

So sweet is Flynn that *Robin Hood* has a lyricism that transcends the

Errol Flynn as Captain Blood: For Olivia de Havilland, "the most beautiful man in the world."

swashbuckling melodrama. In the archery sequence he moves forward to compete with the grace of a dancer. The courtship of Maid Marian is conducted with joyous abandon, in the very manner of Romeo and Juliet so scorned by Gary Cooper in *The Virginian*. Robin climbs up a castle wall at night to Marian's room—solely to make her admit that she cares. Sexuality is linked not to physical violence but to mutual responsiveness, as Flynn and de Havilland embrace in the moonlight. He can offer her no material advantages, indeed can do nothing more than invite her to Sherwood Forest as a fellow outlaw, for in the thirties romance the motif of justice—that England belongs to all the people—joins man and woman together. How remote are such scenes from a seventies quest-for-justice film like *Serpico* (1973), where the hero must struggle alone, with women playing a barely tolerated and exclusively sexual role in his life! Unlike Serpico, Flynn's Robin respects his woman as he does his king; if he goes down on his knees before the returned Lion-Heart, he performs the same gesture for Marian.

The endings of the Flynn films pose the same problem as those starring Gable. Robin and Marian depart to marry, with Flynn flashing a big toothy smile of delight. Now that justice and King Richard reign, will their lives be dull? Will Robin's maleness be stunted when deprived of its performing arena? Even more than in the Gable films, we are led to believe that the man himself will remain intact no matter the circumstances of his life. Unlike Sean Connery's 1976 Robin Hood, Flynn could never be bored or be other than an exciting male. He presents an ideal in which ennui and self-destructiveness have no part. Besides, as the ending of *Dodge City* makes plain, there are always new frontiers, other areas where a man who fights for justice is needed. Commitment to a worthwhile struggle and to a woman formed Flynn's chief concerns, the pattern that made him one of the most appealing screen males of the decade. His roles proposed the ideal of an integrated life with room for neither internal doubt nor hesitation because whatever he chose to do was so obviously valuable.

VII

The gangster movie was replaced in the second half of the thirties by the G-man or police film, which perfectly expressed the official view of the Depression. The law itself occupies the center of these films. As the struggle is waged to preserve the social order against the unruly, we are expected to identify with authority, represented by the federal agent as hero. Because the concept of law and order is more important than any man, Edward G. Robinson has less personality in a film like *Bullets or Ballots* (1936) than he did in *Little Caesar*, where he was a man with egotistic moments, vanities, and fears. Such weaknesses humanized Rico. The G-man instead is a stock character, the indefatigable hero fearlessly entering dens of iniquity to break up the power of the syndicate. Those who boss the rackets turn out, appropriately enough, to be bankers in elegant attire, one of whom is a former government official. They, the "Wall Street speculators" who caused the Depression in the first place, are defeated by the determined efforts of Robinson, a servant of the public weal who refuses to coddle criminals. A forerunner of Dirty Harry, who, like Harry, is not above using brute force to smash crime, Robinson finally acts with the sanction of all. Harry in the seventies, however, considers state power insufficiently brutal and fails to convince his superiors that his strong-arm methods are necessary. In the difference lies the distance between the basic self-confidence of the New Deal and the openly fascist demands of the law-and-order films of the seventies. Having used physical force against the hoodlums before the film opens, Robinson has been forced into retirement from the police force, like Dirty Harry having gone too far in his vigilante fervor. The thirties film also meets that of the seventies in its utter intolerance of radicalism of any kind in response to economic deprivation. Strong males, say these films, correctly place law-and order before civil liberties; a man defines himself by the effectiveness with which he employs violence in the service of the law, for the identity of the villains is clear and distinct.

Robinson uses the very methods of archcriminal Humphrey Bogart, who also shoots first and asks questions afterward. Search warrants are never required or produced, for the enemy must be crushed without hesitation. If there is a woman (Joan Blondell) in strong-man Robinson's life, he makes absolutely no emotional commitment to her. "If women and home life had been in my line," he tells her, "I'd have gone for you a long time ago." But "it isn't in the cards." Robinson may be chivalrous to women, but the imperatives of his manhood, which involve pitting nerves of steel against sophisticated enemies, would be undermined by feelings of personal obligation. He will not allow himself to be tied down, refusing when he is in need to accept a handout from Blondell—even, perhaps, as the poor were enjoined to shift for themselves.

The racketeers attempt to enlist him, but Robinson becomes instead an undercover agent. His destitute condition is assumed by him to be both temporary and amenable to his personal efforts—a moral intended for the American public at large, even as Robinson's role as a government agent argues that morality requires not just refraining from attack upon the established order but actually joining it.

Thus the true male always retains the means of transcending hard times; male energy and pride come to the rescue. Undaunted, Robinson descends into the sleazy haunts of the racketeers, facing down men a head taller. Low-angle shots that look up at him stress his manliness and power, which are not undermined by his lack of height. A man of total courage, ever ready, despite his size, to use his fists, Robinson is willing to jeopardize his very life. He overcomes both hard times and a physical disadvantage. It is the other side of the coin of Robinson's portrayal of Little Caesar at the turn of the decade, which also taught the little man in the audience not to be concerned with his physical—or economic—smallness.

Before he can deliver the incriminating evidence, Robinson is shot by Bogart, whom he then kills. Robinson goes on to fulfill his mission. His shadow looms up on the wall larger than life as he enters the meeting place of bankers and executives with the marked money that will break up their racket. After calmly bidding goodnight to the men whom he has singlehandedly called to account for their crimes, he collapses on the bank floor, drags himself to the door, and finally expires. He has led a life worthy of a man. Society, we are instructed, awaits the aid of such a male, as the film ignores the fact that police departments were very often under the sway of such racketeers and hence hardly this diligent in their pursuit. A small man has won out, even as the audience male is ordered to take himself in hand.

A comic version of this call to male power and will appeared in the mid-thirties with *Ruggles of Red Gap* (1935). Charles Laughton plays an English butler "won" in a card game by an American. Through personal drive and initiative, possible only in America, Ruggles becomes a free and independent man, owner of a restaurant over which he presides at the end with competence and humility. The system of "free enterprise" in which every man can open a small business and make his way is presented as the only real vehicle for the masculine man. Economic opportunity is really for the taking, as if the Depression had never occurred. To make this myth more credible and to sustain the notion that small enterprise remains the route to fortune in America, the film is conveniently set somewhat earlier.

At the end of *Ruggles of Red Gap* the upper crust of the town dines democratically at Ruggles's new restaurant, serenading him with a rousing "For He's a Jolly Good Fellow." The effect is cathartic; the Ruggles who had been so humiliated and lonely has at last found his place. He is still a man of the working class, and the film does not propose classlessness. But Ruggles demonstrates the opportunity for every American to achieve economic independence if he has the grit to compete and succeed. A real man does not remain a butler, and America is the land of opportunity where overwhelming class distinctions do not exist. This morality tale appealed to fantasies of unexpected wealth in a society where social mobility was in startling decline. Yet the very Ruggles who had worried about "M'Lord's" capacity to undress himself succeeds by becoming a property owner. At the same time he is valued as a person, and with this comes in turn renewed sexuality, although Ruggles's choice of a woman is from his own class: a servant named Prunella (Zasu Pitts). Hollywood was not about to depict a complete overturning of class distinctions. Ruggles joins his betters, but he is at least a generation away from concealing his origins.

Ruggles, of course, is always inspired by extreme patriotism, a continuing concomitant of masculinity in the American film. In a classic scene he alone, a foreigner, is able to recite the Gettysburg Address by heart. The same values that inspired Abraham Lincoln have led Ruggles to the decision to take the risk, stand on his own two feet, and make something of himself. Lincoln, manhood, and the work ethic coalesce to form the highest good. For a moment Ruggles hesitates, disturbed to be "the first member of my family ever to let a member of his family down," for the earl would take him back to England to become a butler once more. But in America each man may be reborn, unburdened by the failures of his fathers. Zasu Pitts is there to disabuse Ruggles of his false notion of duty. If he returns to the earl, he would show thereby that he was "not a man."

We leave Ruggles presiding over the "Anglo-American Grill." There he commands his staff with new-found powers accessible to all men if they are but willing to take the risk and attempt businesses of their own. He uses force to eject an unpleasant, harassing customer, brute physical power the touchstone in the American film for a male who would at last attain his manhood. The sentimentality of the ending is overwhelming; we dissolve in tears when Ruggles replies to "For He's a Jolly Good Fellow" with "My friends, God bless you all."

Ruggles has finally found his way to acceptance, becoming an approved member of society. He has done it by conforming to a set of values we would all do well to uphold, for they chart the path to manhood, dignity, and respect. The figure of Abraham Lincoln moves through these films of manly self-help throughout the thirties, culminating in 1939 in John Ford's *Young Mr. Lincoln.* Because the possibility of success was tenuous in thirties America, the myth of a man making his own way, educating himself to the presidency, served perfectly for a Hollywood seeking to rationalize the chaos of hard times throughout the decade.

VIII

By the end of the thirties, so many films had been made which refurbished the image of the stoical, indefatigable male as America's response to the Depression that ground was laid to revive the Western as a serious film form. Having appeared to weather the "temporary" crisis, which lasted until rearmament and a world war "solved" unemployment, America could again be portrayed credibly as a frontier of opportunity. The tough male on film returned to the more comfortable setting of the Old West, and the audience could sigh with relief.

Cecil B. De Mille's *The Plainsman* (1937), however, with Gary Cooper as Wild Bill Hickok, was made in response to the uncertainty and apprehension still abroad in the public about Depression America. Unlike the heroes of Westerns to come, Coop is shot dead at the end by a lowlife just as he is about to deliver the film's scoundrels into the hands of the United States Cavalry—coming to the rescue this time too late. Hickok and his buddy, Buffalo Bill Cody, are portrayed as "men who thrust forward America's frontier." The film is set during the years following the Civil War, when veterans were encouraged to go West and seek economic opportunity unavailable elsewhere. The frontier had first to be made safe for settlers by conquering the "savage" Indians who still held sway. Hickok's role is to impose "law and order." We are returned to an epoch when a man could solve problems through physical force alone, in which the victim Indian was the villain deemed savage for resisting annihilation. The need to disguise the character of the violence of "taming the frontier" became in no small measure a cause of the brutalization of men on screen.

The Westerns of the late thirties re-create the values of early Westerns like *The Virginian*. The Westerner's manhood is again defined by his scornful refusal to reveal his feelings to a woman. Tomboy Calamity Jane (Jean Arthur) is forever telling Wild Bill that she loves him. Her heart is on her sleeve; he remains aloof. The woman Hickok does find attractive, although he would never settle down even with her, is not "masculine" Jane with her Union hat, pants, and job as a stagecoach driver. Hickok prefers Mrs. Bill Cody, the symbol of passive domesticity. Jane, who emulates him and his rough way of life, isn't "woman enough," as if womanliness resided in corsets and plumed hats. That he is unable to reconcile this contradiction without exploring his hero in some psychological depth (which no Western of this era was willing to risk) is another reason why De Mille must kill off Hickok by the end of the film. Hickok has called Cody "Bodkin Bill," strengthening the code of the masculine male which is part of both the gangster and the Western genres. Domesticity equals emasculation; the real man is one who ruthlessly roots out of his life all activity appropriate to women or carrying the taint of their weakness.

Incorporating many of the motifs which had been so successful in *The Virginian*, the Western by 1937 had become the most strident and explicit genre of the American film in its advocacy of the proper male role. A man does only those harsh "things that have to be done." When Hickok leaves on a scouting mission, Calamity Jane impulsively grabs and kisses him. So far from returning her affection, Hickok wipes his mouth of this sullying display and stalks off. The masochism and self-degradation urged on women in such films flows from the insistence, like that in many Gable films, that the uncaring, hostile, and sexually repressed male who cannot reach out and would never show his feelings is the only man worth having. We later learn that Hickok in his way does care for Jane, because he carries her picture in his watchcase. But when she discovers this little secret, he aggressively tells her that he couldn't remove the picture without scratching the case. He, the stern, noble male, would rather die than jeopardize the lives of others—or avow his own feelings. Jane, a female and a member of a weaker species, betrays the lives of others to save Bill from being tortured to death by the Indians.

And he scorns her for it: "I hope I'll never have to look at you again," says Hickok to the woman who has saved his life. He, the better person, never loses his cool throughout the long Indian siege. No woman can successfully emulate the competent male, and Jane would have done better not to try. Hickok must die because the world affords him no place. The frontier is closing, thanks to his efforts. "What room is there in the West for a two-gun plainsman?" he muses. A cowardly weasel finally shoots Hickok in the back.

At this Calamity wraps her arms around her dead beloved. She kisses him, pathetically remarking that for once he won't wipe off her kiss. A last superimposition shows Bill alive once more, riding with the cavalry. Only here, among other men, is he the man De Mille would have us remember. The woman is nowhere in sight, having been eclipsed by the purposeful life Bill led as a plainsman.

Only at the very end of the decade does film begin to assail injustice as something structural. *Jesse James* (1939), another important Western of the late thirties, attacks the railroad monopoly itself, not a few individuals, for its savage disregard of human life. Jesse (Tyrone Power) and Frank James (Henry Fonda) become outlaws because unscrupulous railroad men are grabbing up the land of poor farmers for a pittance. Those who protest are murdered. Jesse and Frank differ from their neighbors because, again as "real men," they are willing to fight. Evil speculators, the carpetbaggers of the Depression Western, make outlaws of good men who resist heroically with fists and guns, unaided by the police, who have been bought off by the railroad. The railroad has also purchased the judges who are in its employ and who condemn to death dissidents like Jesse James. Lest the film appear too uncompromising in its depiction of how the system operates, there is also the obligatory good marshal (Randolph Scott), who pleads with Jesse to surrender and receive a light sentence. Scott argues that by going straight Jesse could better expose corruption. But Scott too is betrayed by the voracious forces of the railroad. The film throughout its first half thus has a radical component, perhaps because the Depression, and with it the danger of rebellion, was presumed to be past. When the government *refuses* to reform, individuals *must* take the law into their own hands. It is in this context that Jesse becomes a hero. "When I hate," he says, "I've got to do something about it."

The second half of *Jesse James* flags, with Power as a Flynn-like swashbuckler suddenly, inexplicably, turning into an "animal, like a wolf." The reason, we are told, is that shooting and robbing have gotten into his blood. Thus to struggle against injustice outside the system, however understandable, is finally misguided if only because it will cause a man to degenerate. Lost is the issue of how to stop the powerful railroad tycoons; equally absent is any exploration of how total their control of the country has become. And gone is even the semblance of substance.

It was not until the last years of the thirties that Westerns would appear that approached the vitality of *Cimarron* (1931) with its boundlessly energetic, freewheeling lawyer-newspaperman hero, Yancey Cravat. *Destry Rides Again* (1939) is concerned with the distinction between being a real man as opposed to appearing as one. In the spirit of the turn of the decade, when the social order was regaining confidence in its basic stability, movies turned away from the present back to the Old West. In *Destry* ultimate coolness is possessed by the male who is so internally self-composed that he has no need to flaunt a flagrantly masculine exterior.

The setting is the corrupt town of Bottleneck; the hero, Destry (James Stewart), the son of a famous sheriff, is now himself called in to preserve law and order. But Destry doesn't seem man enough for the job. He is not tough. He carves wooden napkin rings. He stands around holding a lady's parasol, while all the real men laugh at him and offer him tea. A real man would order liquor, but Destry chooses milk. Someone hands him a mop—the only way it seems that he will be able to clean up Tombstone.

Destry is unperturbed. He labels first impressions "darn fool things," confident in the inner knowledge that he will be man enough when he must. His style, always the truly masculine approach to experience in the American film, is that of hard common sense. He has surrendered his gun because "one of us might have gotten hurt and it might have been me." Paradoxically, in seeming to overturn the stereotype, the film actually proposes a harsher view of masculinity, so steely that it must be concealed by seeming cowardice, expressed by Destry's pretended concern for his personal safety. The world is now treacherous, and cunning must replace brash display. Nonetheless, *Destry Rides Again* is refreshing in its insistence that real men should be judged finally by what they are and not by how they look. Appearances only decorate, and no one with any sense would confuse them with the inner reality which truly matters. Marlene Dietrich as a saloon floozy recognizes this at once.

The year of the film is 1939, when the issues of neutrality versus involvement in a European war were being debated. Destry, like Roosevelt, stands for involvement, and he disarms the local bully with the superb skill he had concealed all along. He is supremely capable of the grace under pressure that shuns bravado. Applying his standards for himself to Dietrich, he asks her to remove her make-up because she would look prettier without it.

Finally, the fearless Destry, guns strapped on, must be saved by Dietrich, who protects him by stepping in front of a bullet meant for him. She has rescued him because he recognized her value beneath the façade. She must also die, because Destry, the idol of nine-year-old boys, is at heart a loner. His inner purity and effectiveness depend upon the absence of entangling alliances, such as he assumed when he agreed to save Tombstone in the first place.

The most influential Western of the thirties was John Ford's *Stagecoach* (1939), not because of its subtlety of either filmmaking style or point of view, but because it raised John Wayne to prominence and made his the dominant male image in American films for years to come. Gangling and gawky—although he was already in his thirties—Wayne plays "the Ringo Kid," who has just escaped from a penitentiary where he has been incarcerated since he was seventeen years old. His purpose, of course, is to kill those who framed him. Then, an honorable man, he will return to prison to complete his sentence. What already counts for the Wayne character is principle, never personal comfort.

On the stagecoach that he boards, Wayne meets Dallas (Claire Trevor), a loose woman with a heart of gold whom the good ladies of the community where she lived have driven out of town. Wayne alone sees her value as a human being, proof that he is a good man. His face is sweet and open. Arrested almost immediately by a marshal who is also traveling on this stagecoach, he is still called a "fine boy" by all. Everyone likes him.

But the softness notwithstanding, *Stagecoach* contains many hints of the later Wayne too. He stares straight ahead when speaking of his murdered brother, fierce and unrelenting in his cause. He intervenes in a fight between a gambler and a drunk doctor because "doc don't mean no harm." Young as he is, he is already a leader among weaker men. Assertiveness comes naturally to him, as does chivalry. He demands courtesy for Trevor and refuses to permit the others to condescend toward her.

From *Stagecoach* on, the male played by John Wayne is above pettiness and is never diverted by triviality. It is not only that he is the superhuman male at battle (he defends the stagecoach against marauding Apaches, at one point knocking five off their horses with a single bullet). Wayne stands for a man for whom the world is large and full of possibilities, even when he plays an escaped prisoner. Always he rejects superficiality (the theme also of *Destry Rides Again*) in favor of the finer, simpler pleasures of life. He has a ranch that he loves. "A man can live there," he says simply to Trevor, "and a woman. Will you go?" The barest number of words suffices. This woman who has met him so recently immediately recognizes his merit. If she hesitates, it is not for lack of desire to accept his offer, but because she considers herself unworthy of him, particularly as he doesn't know about her past.

But such externals never distract a man of moral and physical fiber. "I know all I need to know," says the Ringo Kid. Nor will he take the woman's advice to escape, counsel that could come only from a weaker sex. "There are some things a man can't run away from," says the Ringo Kid. We have here the credo of the later Wayne character, a man fully in tune with the imperatives of his own nature, supremely confident of his purpose.

It is to this that our interest is directed, not to the creaky plot, which has Wayne suddenly shoot down the three bullies who had framed him in an anticlimactic offstage scene. Out of the fog one man emerges from this duel, into which Wayne went against three brutal men. The camera dollies in to Trevor waiting in fear. Wayne, of course, has survived to keep his word: "I asked you to marry me, didn't I?" She must wait out the one year he has yet to serve in prison, and then they will be together. An idol had been forged who encompassed the mythic values on the romantic basis of which the American continent was supposedly settled. The marshal then allows Wayne his freedom and the two ride off. "Well, they're safe from the blessings of civilization," exults Doc (Thomas Mitchell).

IX

One after another the films made at the conclusion of the decade reasserted an image of the confident, nonintellectual male. In 1939, William Wellman remade *Beau Geste* with Gary Cooper, Ray Milland, and Robert Preston as the three devoted brothers, even as in 1938 Edmund Goulding had made a version of *Dawn Patrol* with Errol Flynn and David Niven assuming the Barthelmess–Fairbanks Junior relationship. The world of men completely apart from women was again offered as a sanctuary, a harmonious redoubt where the hostility between the sexes and the enervating battle against compromising women might be evaded.

Wellman's Geste brothers love each other more than any man could love a woman. A title links this motif shared by the remake with the original. Strains of the male love affair of Wellman's *Wings* surface as well in his *Beau Geste*. Gary Cooper as Beau is totally without heterosexual interests, unlike Michael York in the spoof *The Last Remake of Beau Geste*

(1977), which deserved to be made if only to deflate the high seriousness of its predecessors. Cooper's Beau remains into his manhood a boy chasing a mouse with gargantuan weapons from the King Arthur armory of his aunt's antique collection. Only John, the youngest and weakest of the Geste brothers, can, as a consequence, care for a woman. The three Geste brothers experience no sexual deprivation nor do they hesitate at the prospect of five years in the Foreign Legion, a world populated solely by men.

The most significant alteration in the 1939 remake lies in its equation of patriotism with the love between men. Beau refuses to join the mutiny against the cruel officer, Markov, because he will not be a traitor to the French flag, for which he has fought so single-mindedly. He aids in the disarming of those justifiably appalled by the Draconian treatment to which the legion has subjected them. When he dies, Beau's face is covered with the flag at the "Viking's funeral," a further elaboration of the patriotic motif. The mood of revulsion against the mindless slaughter of World War I which continued into the thirties is ruptured at the decade's end by insistent calls anew for military heroics from the masculine male, the patriotic summons presaging American involvement in an impending second world war.

John Ford made two films in 1939 which close out the decade, *Young Mr. Lincoln* and *The Grapes of Wrath*. Here again the association between manhood and patriotism is pointedly explored. Lincoln, held up as the ideal American, is very deliberately presented as a nonintellectual. Learning derived from books is shown to be spurious, studiousness so severe a handicap that it emerges as virtually un-American. Lincoln, on the contrary, is the salt of the earth, full of country wisdom. He bites coins to check their authenticity and does all the earthy and down-home "American" things: winning rail-splitting contests, tasting countless pies, and winning tugs of war, if with a little sly cheating—the male who is a Sunday school paragon of virtue cannot be a real man.

Lincoln (Henry Fonda) establishes his Americanism by involvement in the defense of the two Clay brothers, falsely accused of murder. The moment of his decision is dramatic. Lincoln grabs the hand of the mother of the two hapless boys. "Who are you?" she demands. "I'm your lawyer, ma'am," says Lincoln and proceeds at once to stand off an angry lynch mob clamoring for instant justice. "I can lick any man here hands down," declares Lincoln. Physical strength, manhood, and Americanism are rendered synonymous. A man is soft only toward women, particularly his mother. Lincoln tells Mrs. Clay that she so appeals to him because his own mother, Nancy Hanks, "would have been a lot like you."

Ford's Tom Joad (played by Henry Fonda) in *The Grapes of Wrath* suffers a diminution of his personality because the film's primary purpose is to present Roosevelt's New Deal as the sole means by which dust-bowl refugees can be reintegrated into America, the last chance to prevent something far worse than reform, namely, open revolt. Reversing the order of John Steinbeck's chapters, Ford has the family, after all their suffering, end up in a clean government camp, thus arguing that the state is now devoted to reform and the improvement of intolerable conditions. Hence the people need not organize against injustice. As a result, Tom Joad, who had chosen to lead people to join together and to struggle against their fate, is reduced to being an isolated, foredoomed fugitive rather than an effective rebel. In the novel the government-camp episode occurs midstream and is a temporary, clearly inadequate respite from starvation. In it, the Joads learn that you "can't eat toilets" and move on to greater degradation. Paltry, token reforms were a cruel deception, and Tom knew he had to set forth to unite the oppressed in a struggle for their rights.

But Ford was never one to associate masculinity with political and social rebellion against the established order. He emasculates his hero, giving central place to the benevolent official who heads the government camp and who bears a pointed, if embarrassingly obvious, physical resemblance to Franklin Roosevelt. It is left to Ma Joad (Jane Darwell), a beaming earth mother, to assert the film's message about the capacity of people to endure. Tom is among the lost, a fugitive after killing a man in Preacher Casey's defense. He goes off to an uncertain fate before the final scene, cut off from his people and on the run.

Ford has so altered the novel's Tom Joad that he becomes more a victim than a rebel. Tom's fury may be articulated in the film ("there comes a time when a man gets mad"), but he goes off, not to fight, but to "find out" why there aren't more good government camps. In his peroration Tom asserts that he'll be "everywhere wherever there's a fight so hungry people can eat," but the film insists that the system itself will reform in response to suffering if people but make their wish for reforms such as government camps fully known. Ma's "we're the people" speech, which ends the film, implies that individual rebels do more harm than good, for the mere existence of the people who "keep a' coming" will bring the government around. Her solid faith drives Tom off stage and into obscurity, the price director Ford exacts in his refusal to allow real masculinity its component of outspoken dissidence.

Like most of his fellow directors, Ford insisted upon placing masculinity in the service of the status quo. Patriotism symbolized by the United States Cavalry was a banner which would suit Ford far better, one he could fly on the frontier or in the present. The coming years of World War II would allow the film industry to measure the male in terms of valorous, unquestioning service to his country. Only in the late forties and the fifties would Hollywood timorously begin to explore the disenchantment and alienation of the American male from the dominant values of his culture.

The Forties

If in the 1930s the "real man" engaged in little soul-searching about the causes of the Depression and the nature of the society that produced it, in the early 1940s the hero subordinated everything to winning the war. Only the man who fought fervently for his country was worthy of the name. The forties war hero is enthusiastic, full of optimism, and certain of his identity. True maleness in the American film now meant that a man, however solitary his personal impulses, would prefer commitment to battle as the only course worthy of manhood.

The end of the war, however, was to lead to an abrupt end to the brash optimism and confidence of the wartime star. The personality of the hero lost its wartime buoyancy, and in the most important manifestation of this tendency, the *film noir*, or "dark film," masculine behavior came to be characterized by its lack of self-confidence. Despite the militarization of America's role in the post-1945 period, the male hero no longer associated his masculinity with wartime patriotism. Now the society in which he had to make his way was perceived as shabby and decadent. America's importance as a world power did not lead to a corresponding sense of the screen hero's own power, but more nearly to its opposite.

While the war was in many ways an escape from the America of the present, both in life and on film, it was a harrowing one. Few returned from the war with a light heart. The combined experience of the Depression and coming home from the war to face the uncertainties of beginning life anew lent to the *film noir* a sense of finiteness, a feeling that we have a very limited time in which to create a decent life. The romances of the twenties suggest the opposite: endless time, as if we could indulge in screen daydreams and still have energy left to shape our destinies to our satisfaction. The options in the *film noir* are few and bleak as the screen hero finally faces social institutions against which the individual barely stands a chance.

The optimism and innocence of prewar years, when it was assumed that sooner or later justice would triumph, were thus replaced by a despair which flowed from the realization that the defeat of fascism did not, as promised, usher in peace, hope, or harmony. On the contrary, menace and perfidy had become the rule in the relations between the individual and his society; the dangers of nuclear incineration and economic depression lurked behind the scene. So drastically had the expectations about the quality of life altered in the initial years after the war, so shocking was the discovery that naïve hopes of an end to evil and strife were not just excessive but had been replaced by the darkest pessimism about human decency, that all aspiration seemed embarrassingly pollyanna. Thus the hero of the postwar *film noir* seems forced to confront social problems that had been too long ignored or wished away in easy invocations of reformism, as in the Capra films. He is unprepared for what he finds in America: corruption, graft, inequality, huge bureaucratic forces lined up against the individual. Hence, it is no wonder that the tone of the American film should have changed drastically to one of defensiveness and menace. Justice was inaccessible to the ordinary man; raw power had become the only reality. Dreams of a moral society dissolved. Honesty was rare; concern for another human being vanishingly infrequent. Paranoia characterized both the hero and his world as the cinematographers, borrowing from the expressionist tradition in film, became fond of the imagery of shadows looming on crumbling walls, larger than life, overwhelming the hero. Even the Westerns of the late 1940s were to be deeply influenced by such attitudes.

The most important male screen personality during these years was Humphrey Bogart, whose major films span the decade. A chain-smoker with cynicism etched onto his homely face, his hands virtually shaking, his head balding, his eyes knowing and sad, Bogart was a perfect embodiment of the postwar mood. As early as such wartime films as *Casablanca* and *To Have and Have Not*, the mood of the *film noir* was already foreshadowed in Bogart's image.

In retrospect, given the dark state of mind of so many male heroes of the late 1940s, it seems as if the problems which had so plagued Charlie Chaplin right up to *Modern Times*, but which had often been ignored in the "serious" film, now resurfaced. Having assumed in such films as *Mr. Smith Goes to Washington* and *Mr. Deeds Goes to Town* that the New Deal had solved the problems of the Depression, the hero seems to have gone to war content to let the matter slide. On screen he fought bravely, content with patriotic mythology about America's democratic institutions and concern for "the people." Chaplin had already demonstrated other truths about our social institutions, but his views remained outside the mainstream of the Hollywood film until, in a different form, they reappeared after the war.

I

The hero who discovered his masculinity in the commitment to defeat fascism was most brilliantly and consistently played by Humphrey Bogart. And in no Bogart character are manliness and political commitment conjoined with more verve and flair than in his Rick of *Casablanca* (1942). Casablanca, the city, is dubbed gateway to the "New World," the land of freedom and opportunity in danger of being undermined by a ruthlessly ambitious fascism. There, in what actually was a North African colony of France policed by the Foreign Legion, Bogart presides over "Rick's Café Américain." An expatriate, Rick believes he can retain his autonomy only by refusing to become enmeshed in other people's squabbles, particularly in European politics, the machinations of which are forever taking place under his nose. Rick's detached demeanor is pointedly parallel to America's isolationism in the twenties and thirties, now shown to be venal and sleazy. It is the profiteering Sidney Greenstreet who uses the term "isolationism"; Bogart will be the ideal tough male through whose behavior the choice of involvement becomes an imperative by the end of the film. Indeed, Bogart is converted from his cynical neutrality, his refusal to take sides. His masculinity is finally tied to the moral choice of dedicating himself to the fight of all right-minded people.

What grants this crude exercise in political propaganda its appeal is its association with Bogart's supreme style, *savoir-faire*, and romantic sophistication. His every gesture is cool and knowing, bespeaking an immense knowledge of the ways of the world. If Gable exuded a sense of unquenchable energy, Bogart expects the worst at any instant and lives for the moment. He is beyond being shocked: "I don't mind a parasite," he says in *Casablanca*; "I object to a cut-rate one." He is, paradoxically, a more powerful male than any of his predecessors because he is so cynical about his own or anybody else's capacity to create a world free of corruption and evil-doing. Tough and shrewd, he knows that life at any moment may trap him; if, despite this, we feel safe with him, it is because no event, however outrageous, seems to come as a surprise. He is far less physically beautiful than any major male star before him, whether Fairbanks, Barrymore, Valentino, Cooper, Gable, or Flynn. But his nondescript appearance only increases our admiration.

Bogart also appeals because he has little patience with phonies, valuing only authenticity and no-nonsense straightforwardness. He scorns surface advantages like inherited wealth, status, or easy good looks. Mary Astor reveals in her memoir, *A Life on Film,* that Bogart the man associated phoniness with effeminacy and being unmanly: "To him 'artist' meant someone unpredictable and fancy pants. He would have made a wisecrack if anybody had called him 'Humphrey'—or even 'Mr. Bogart.' "

As Rick, Bogart withholds his approval from anyone who enters his milieu until that person establishes his hard-boiled common sense. Ineptness and stupidity also enraged Bogart the man. Nathaniel Benchley in his biography refers to Bogart's personal "combativeness ... whether toward a man pretending to be a Marine or with a friend on whether there is an umlaut on the word 'fünf.' " His wartime screenplays have him capable of involvement, but always on his own terms. Rick's value as a man is enhanced when we learn that before his skeptical phase in Casablanca he had fought on the Loyalist side in Spain and had been a gunrunner against Mussolini in Ethiopia. His persona itself, his tough yet gentle competence, legitimizes these struggles. Disillusioned by the world's indifference to Spain and Ethiopia, he is too jaded to return to the struggle. He now devotes himself to chess, although a ray of hope may be found in his continuing contempt for the Germans. By the end of *Casablanca* he finds that he can retain his manhood only by renouncing the woman he loves. Personal happiness has become impossible so long as sadism and cruelty reign.

This new variation of the male image in the wartime forties was politically inspired. Its first law was that at moments of historical crisis a real man cannot withhold himself from involvement. If the masculine image remained tough and brutal, the ends for which men worked had altered.

Many of the male images of the late 1930s and early 1940s were shaped by Communist screenwriters and sympathizers of the party. The Hollywood Ten alone were responsible for 159 films from 1935 to 1949, while others associated with them were almost as prolific or influential.* Among their films we find *North Star, Action in the North Atlantic, Thirty Seconds over Tokyo, Mission to Moscow, Sahara, A Guy Named Joe,* and many more. Their influence, however, was not confined to the volume of their output. As John Cogley points out in his *Report on Blacklisting: Part One, the Movies,* the Communists held a "virtual monopoly on activist organization" in Hollywood. The Hollywood Writers Mobilization, a clearing house for scripts in which nearly every radio and screen writer held

---

*The Hollywood Ten were Alvah Bessie, Herbert J. Biberman, Lester Cole, Edward Dmytryk, Ring Lardner, Jr., John Howard Lawson, Albert Maltz, Samuel Ornitz, Adrian Scott, and Dalton Trumbo. Others associated with them include Lillian Hellman, Paul Jerrico, Clifford Odets, and Donald Ogden Stewart.

at least nominal membership, was Communist-dominated. John Howard Lawson, later one of the Hollywood Ten, was its first president.

No articulate or effective liberal or left-wing opposition to the prevailing orthodoxy found its way onto the Hollywood screen during these years. And because the Communists were ardent supporters of the New Deal, they could successfully compete with the right as well. Thus, as Cogley indicates, Donald Stewart, Hy Kraft, Richard Collins, Jules Dassin, and Ring Lardner, Jr., circulated a petition at Metro-Goldwyn-Mayer to halt production on a film with whose political content they disagreed, and few thought much about it. Such outrages as the evacuation of Japanese Americans from the West Coast were greeted with silence by the Communist screenwriters and directors.

Irving Howe has recently remarked on how the Communist Party during these years could be counted upon to oppose strikes and to support speed-ups on the assembly line in factories while helping to bring totalitarian methods into the trade unions. Such policies were reflected in films as well. For despite their association with the Communist Party, we do not find images of working men in the films of the Communist intellectuals, nor do we find depictions of what it was like to work in a factory. The *Daily Worker* may have bemoaned that "the redman has not yet gotten the chance to tell his side of the story" in the American film, but the screen male in the hands of this group remained white, Anglo-Saxon, and dominating. In 1938, the party convention polled its delegates as to their favorite movie stars, and among men Gary Cooper was the victor. From the mid-1930s on, the Communist-affiliated left in Hollywood played its part in shaping the image of the male, creating some of the worst stereotyping of men in the history of American cinema. Had these people honestly believed in socialism, an entirely new view of the male would have been advocated for the American film—and, ironically, the Communist screenwriters would have been "guilty" of the progressive ideas of which the McCarthy committees later accused them. Instead, the focus after Hitler invaded the Soviet Union was always on the war effort.

These screenwriters supported the war with a patriotism unmatched by their less progressive counterparts, and always in their films we find the male hero as the ultimate patriot. Other film people, such as Frank Capra and John Ford, had close relationships with the military and the government, and they too made wartime propaganda films. But they differed from the Communist screenwriters in that their views were out in the open; they did not create patriotic war heroes, staunch defenders of democracy on the front, as a means of supporting Stalin's policy of socialism in one country. For the Communists the interests of the Soviet Union took priority in their films over the needs of the working class at home. That the Bolshevik Revolution was now characterized by purge trials and concentration camps in which millions perished was denied and brushed aside by many of these people. The male heroes in their films were drawn on behalf of such unavowed politics, just as their Communist Party memberships were kept silent. Male characters were now defined by their capacity to respond to the threat of Nazi spy rings backed by some sinister, if isolated, industrialist and to the menace to "progressive" goals and the "little people" everywhere. Masculinity now required coming to the aid of the "democracies" of Europe. The general rule was not to portray the Soviet Union negatively if not to rock the boat by any open praise.

An example of the mentality which produced so many male images of the early forties was Dalton Trumbo's attitude toward his pacifist novel, *Johnny Got His Gun,* after the signing of the Nazi-Soviet pact. Trumbo found himself in a most uncomfortable position, having based his novel on the premise of American noninvolvement only to have Hitler break his promise not to harm the first "workers' state." The heroic male in Trumbo's novel was he who was sensitive enough to oppose the senseless barbarism of war. Once Hitler invaded the Soviet Union, however, real men suddenly were defined by Trumbo as those who put aside their personal inclinations and enthusiastically sought to enter the fray. In the 1959 edition of *Johnny Got His Gun* Trumbo tells us that had his book been *banned* at the time of the invasion, as was urged by those who perhaps forgot that although it was published later, it was written *before* Hitler's invasion of the Soviet Union, "I doubt that I should have protested very loudly. There are times when it may be needful for certain private rights to give way to the requirements of a larger public good." In short, after Hitler's invasion, Trumbo would not have minded the banning of his own pacifist novel, a passionate invocation of the horror of war.

Hitler, of course, had been no less menacing in 1938, and Trumbo's sudden antifascism must be seen in the light of his particular concern over the plight of the Soviet Union. One more example: in 1938 director Herbert Biberman drew up a declaration urging the immediate breach of all economic relations with Germany, an unexceptionable idea. Innocently believing in the sincerity of the project, a multitude of Hollywood artists who genuinely believed in the danger of fascism signed the declaration with no ulterior motives or loyalties; these included John Ford, Henry Fonda, Jack Warner, Bette Davis, Ben Hecht, and Groucho Marx. The gathering of signatures was still proceeding when Stalin signed his pact with Hitler. Immediately Biberman dropped the project and in the process accused himself of having mistakenly been, temporarily, a "warmonger."

Equally spurious was the fact that in the screenplays written by these "progressives," the evil was framed as national and racial. The German people were cruel, spitting out harshly accented commands. They wore monocles and were scarcely human. The Japanese were sinister and deceitful. Racism and national chauvinism against these two peoples became the terms of support for the "progressive" cause. Furthermore, when the strong male elected to fight on behalf of democracy, it was usually in European and not Asian settings. Such anti-Japanese war films as *Destination Tokyo* (1943), in contrast to those set in France and other parts of Europe, never overtly dramatized a conflict in which a reluctant hero is convinced to fight for the sake of democracy and, once again, for "the people" in the Pacific theater. Toward Europe, an analogue for the Soviet Union for these writers, the issue of involvement was repeatedly raised and placed at the center of numerous films.

The necessity for commitment on the part of virile men to the right cause was also the theme of John Huston's *Across the Pacific.* Its focus was intended to be the protection by Bogart of Pearl Harbor. When the film was made in March 1942, the fictitious target had become a reality, and Bogart's energies were transferred to the vulnerable Panama Canal. The formula remained the same as it would be in Bogart's next film, *Casablanca. Across the Pacific* differs only in that Bogart merely pretends to be an uninvolved loner, whereas in *Casablanca* he has truly become that individualistic, isolated man which he remains until the war leads him to a carefully defined involvement in the fate of humanity.

In *Across the Pacific* Bogart is a member of army intelligence in search of pro-Japanese traitors. When, in reference to the Japanese, he says he "never thought much about 'em," we are meant to disapprove thoroughly of such selfish and unpatriotic noninvolvement. But the more he pretends to be a man who will hire out to anyone who will pay for his services, "Chiang Kai-shek, Hirohito, anyone," the more discredited become all choices but that of risking self for flag and country.

Bogart's disguise as an uncommitted male allows him to pursue a romance with Mary Astor. Sexual excitement crackles between them. In the Bogart films the male's devotion to causes larger than himself is accompanied by his involvement with passionate, beautiful women, indirectly corroborating the view in these films that the politically active man is the most manly. "Women are more elemental than men," says Astor. "I hope so, honey," is Bogart's reply. Bogart is an affectionate lover, not above comforting Astor when she is seasick or sunburned. Their relationship proceeds without ambivalence or hesitation. And when Astor proves not to be a conspirator in the fascist plot, but an innocent bystander, she is awarded Bogart's tribute to all women he has deemed worthy of his love: "You're good, angel, you're very, very good." It is a line he would use as frequently as Mae West would beckon, "Come up and see me some time."

As *Across the Pacific* draws to its close at a sinister South American plantation, Bogart, wielding a machine gun, manages to blow up the plane about to leave on its mission to bomb the Panama Canal. He is the patriotic American warning his enemies cowboy-style in the manner of the Old West. "You guys have been looking for a war, haven't you?" he snarls. "You started it, but we're going to finish it!" A Nisei (first-generation Japanese American) turns out to be a Japanese spy, an apparent attempt to justify the cruel round-up in American internment camps of hundreds of thousands of American citizens of Japanese descent. Bogart exits with patriotic zeal, as he warns Sidney Greenstreet and other "spies": "If any of your friends in Tokyo have trouble committing *bara kiri,* these boys will be glad to help them out."

Casablanca makes a more compelling case for male commitment to the war because Bogart begins, not as an intelligence officer, but as a man who lives only for himself: "I stick my neck out for nobody." So much more dramatic, then, will be his about-face. The tough man comes to equate real courage with self-effacement and a soft heart, sacrificing both the woman he loves and a peaceful life to help his lover Ingrid Bergman's husband, Victor Lazlo, the noble concentration camp escapee and antifascist leader.

A masculine man has become one susceptible not only to aiding his country but to deep feeling of all varieties. Bogart's heart can break over a sentimental song ("As Time Goes By"), the tune which he and Bergman had always played. He remembers the blue dress Bergman wore the day the Germans marched into Paris, when she disappeared. Loyalty to what he loves defines his nature and makes him the kind of man worth having. His soured bravado—"I'm the only cause I'm interested in"—turns out to be only the posture of a man too hurt to risk commitment again, even though he suffers for the inability to believe in anything.

Such a man can inspire the total love of a woman. Bergman is prepared to sacrifice Lazlo and undercut his antifascist cause to remain with Bogart. "I'll never have the strength to leave you now," she tells Rick. Women are selfish, men alone capable of a larger vision. Bergman, unable to sustain her loyalty to her husband and his cause, acknowledges that Rick "must think for all three of them," such is his strength. He decides they should have one night together to revive those lost moments of their love affair in Paris. And in their parting scene he sums it up: "What I've got to do, you can't be part of . . . the problems of three people don't amount to a hill of beans in this crazy world."

Lazlo himself, survivor of the camps though he may be, is far less masculine than Rick. Basically an intellectual, and hence by the standards of American cinema effete and ineffectual despite his noble demeanor, he knows that the antifascist resistance doesn't stand a chance unless men like Bogart can be enlisted in the struggle. "Welcome back to the fight," says Lazlo to Rick. "This time I know our side will win."

As Lazlo and Ilsa (Bergman) board their plane for take-off, Bogart is left behind with the prefect of police. With no small measure of praise, the prefect, Louis, calls Bogart a "sentimentalist," his cynical term for a man of feeling and conviction. Rick's loss of Ilsa is all the more poignant because we know how he longs for her, how he would savor each moment, capable as he is of living life to the full. Rick and the prefect now commence their journey to Brazzaville to fulfill the imperatives of Bogart's new commitment. "Louie," he says, "this is the beginning of a beautiful friendship." In 1943 the war, with its camaraderie of men in combat, temporarily replaced the relationships men share with women. This particular friendship, however, cannot be said to be even latently homosexual, especially when it is compared with the subterranean erotic sensibility of the buddy films of the 1970s. Bogart is male enough to befriend man or woman; his alliance with a man never carries the suggestion of a permanent choice.

Howard Hawks's *To Have and Have Not* (1944) also partakes of the prevailing pattern of associating maleness with political commitment. Bogart plays a free-and-easy adventurer who leases out his boat to tourists. Volatile and uncompromising, he fears no one, least of all the police. Politics bores him as he moves through the waters of Martinique, guided solely by his own desires. Bogart is thoroughly heterosexual, if also profoundly superior to the women in his life. He welcomes Lauren Bacall because he can shape her into the kind of woman he prefers. "Quit the baby talk!" he demands.

Alone and penniless, Bacall remains a woman who can take care of herself, although her tough manner, imitative of a male style, remains a siren call for protection from a man tough enough to meet her requirements. The paradox of this and other male-oriented Hawks films is that the hero seems to prefer an independent woman. But if her spunkiness is attractive, it is also indicative that she has assimilated male scorn for feminine passivity and weakness. Yet she finds that infinitely more desirable than her freedom is the presence of a strong male who will take charge of her life. The independent pose is finally a ploy to win such a man by emulating his values. Equal in brashness to Bogart, Bacall earns the standard Bogart tribute to the tomboyish yet slinky woman: "You're good. You're awful good." Throughout she imitates not only his gestures but his style. "Kissing is even better when you help" is one of her typical lines.

Precisely because she seems to be a woman who doesn't need a man, her capitulation is all the more erotic. Thus, in her now classic approach, Bacall signals how her pose has been an invitation to mastery: "You don't have to say anything. You don't have to do anything. Just whistle. You know how to whistle, don't you? You put your lips together and blow." Compared with someone like Mae West, who did her own whistling, this independent woman is hardly convincing. Yet she is uninhibited enough to admit what she feels and tenacious enough to go after it. Bacall becomes thereby the ideal female counterpart to Bogart's confident male. As rootless and unencumbered as he, she becomes a female impersonator of his male style, if as pliant as Jean Arthur was in Hawks's *Only Angels Have Wings*. The male remains the person who is most self-sufficient—and most desirable.

The cause which again lifts Bogart out of himself and validates him as a real man is that of "Free France." Again maleness is conjoined to the political formulas of the Popular Front, which backed the status quo in the West. The enemy is the Gestapo, sufficient cause to wean Bogart away from his typical stance of "minding my own business." When he does help the antifascist Frenchman, Paul, it is with some degree of contempt, since Paul has, incomprehensibly to Bogart, brought his wife along on the mission: "I don't understand the kind of war you're fighting, lugging your wife [with you]." Whatever the new political needs of the moment, Bogart remains clear enough about the fact that real men do their fighting without women and children (the two are interchangeable) hanging around. It is Bogart who removes the bullet lodged in the Frenchman; the resourceful, practical, ever competent male on the American screen can do anything, including surgery. Bacall acts as nurse. Tough American neutralism, when enlisted, provides the very ingredient Europe needs to see it through its crisis. Bogart is also attracted to Paul's demure wife, who is properly deferential in manner as well as feelings, but ultimately he chooses the tough woman, Bacall. In wartime a man needs a pal, in part an explanation for these positive changes in the sort of woman a real man can now accept.

Like Victor Lazlo, Paul wishes he were as masculine as Bogart, a man for whom the word "failure" does not exist. If World War II is not yet Bogart's fight, it will be by the end of the film. The Frenchman's joy at this prospect is linked to Bacall's pleasure in being lucky enough to share life with such a man. The Bogart who described himself as a man with "no strings" winds up with both political and sexual involvements. It is both a victory for humanity and an erotic triumph as reluctant masculinity, won over, proves to be infinitely more desirable than an eager male presence that could be had without a struggle.

The war films of the forties which take place in theaters of combat are far cruder in their treatment of maleness. In *Back to Bataan* (1945), directed by Edward Dmytryk, a typical example, John Wayne plays a single-minded military leader bent on winning the war. As in the scriptwriting of all the Communist intellectuals, there is no criticism of America's colonial role in Asia. The war effort remains unqualifiedly supported. Anthony Quinn, Wayne's protégé, is a Filipino guerrilla leader whom he initiates into manhood. When Quinn is distressed to discover that his woman has become a local "Tokyo Rose," broadcasting propaganda for the Japanese, Wayne offers Quinn solace. Such a thing is tough indeed, but a real man will always "act like a soldier," not permitting personal feelings to interfere with duty.

Wayne alone is the masculine male, condescending and paternal toward the Filipinos whom he has known "since they were kids." His manner is patronizing, for they are more than ever in need of his extraordinary leadership. Always relaxed, calm, and honest, he never lies about the possibility of success. Nor does he seek personal power. Utterly altruistic, Wayne risks his life solely to help others. He addresses a child as he would a crowd: "You're the guy we're fighting this war for." At the end, symbolic of his idealism, he hands this child his colonel's insignia. The high military status which his superior abilities have achieved for him does not make him a snob. Meant to stand for the typical American, he is generous and direct. Still "plain folks," he is an ordinary American who has risen to the top and hence is an emblem of democracy. Handing a man a grenade, he even converts the war into sport, a baseball game with patriotic stakes: "How's your pitchin' arm?" he asks. As more Americans land, he is all bluff and bravado, shouting, "You're three minutes late!"

Anything is possible and victory is a foregone conclusion because Wayne is the male who acts effortlessly, with neither self-doubt nor a day of anxiety. Because his very reflexes guide him in how to be a man, he requires neither intellect nor the brutalization of women to prove himself. This is in marked contrast to paltry Wayne imitators like Burt Reynolds who, brutalizing a woman in the opening scene of *The Longest Yard*, resembles no one more than an arrested adolescent running the gamut of male emotion from A to B. Wayne, Hollywood's version of the natural man, in films from *Back to Bataan* to postwar afterthoughts like *The Flying Leathernecks* (1951) and *The Sands of Iwo Jima* (1949), seemed as if he could win the war singlehanded and without unnecessary brutality, always in the proper style.

A more fully developed glimpse of what was expected of the masculine male in wartime appears in Delmer Daves's *Destination Tokyo* (1944), written by Albert Maltz, one of the Hollywood Ten, and reflecting his sensibility as *auteur* much more than that of director Daves. The submarine presided over by naval commander Cary Grant is a microcosm of America filled with a variety of male stereotypes. There is a hot-tempered Greek (Dane Clark) and a would-be Don Juan (John Garfield), rivals in their claims to be "real men." There is also an uninitiated adolescent still tied to mama's apron strings, and hence weak and unmanly. The model for all to emulate will be the suave Grant himself, who, during this great mission—a reconnaissance into Tokyo Bay—will periodically offer lessons in manliness. Only a male as idealized as Hitler's own Aryan soldier, here a cross between Superman and Jack Armstrong, could carry off so daring and outrageous a maneuver—and all this portrayed by an English-man!

Benevolent paternalism, as with John Wayne, is the demeanor appropriate to Grant as America's skipper. He is a father figure to all, deeply concerned for the welfare of each of his men. The buddy syndrome with its palpitating if latent homosexual feeling is disavowed here as Grant is shown trying desperately to call his wife on Christmas Eve just prior to the submarine's departure. As our commander, he is also a regular guy, standing as did all the screen's warrior skippers for democracy and class-lessness. Rejecting the prerogatives of his rank, he calls each man by his first name. Grant's own status, symbolized by the "scrambled eggs" on his cap, means nothing to him at all.

The wartime film idealized the officer class, as it worshipped the military itself, so necessary for the protection of us all and so devoted and

Cary Grant in *Destination Tokyo:* Only a male as idealized as Hitler's own Aryan soldier, here a cross between Superman and Jack Armstrong, could carry off so daring and outrageous a maneuver.

altruistic in its motives. Commander Grant even hopes that he will not be promoted after this mission since advancement would mean his never going to sea again as one of the boys. So close is Grant to his men that he forgoes the customary speech to the ranks before they set sail. All is understood. Such officers, of course, are rewarded with absolute fidelity. His men, as one puts it, would follow him "to the Mikado's bathtub." Whenever a volunteer is needed, a host of men willingly offer themselves. The manliness of the leader inspires a comparable response from his men. In contrast we have the cunning, perfidious Japanese. The enemy flier who is shot down and rescued with kind treatment treacherously murders the amiable "Mike," among the best of the men.

The manliness of the Americans is contrasted with the ruthlessness of the Japanese in their attitudes toward women. *Destination Tokyo* idealizes the American male while invoking racist stereotypes. Grant is a man who chose his wife on the basis of her character. "I found you didn't need to know what a girl looks like to like her," he says of their first meeting on a blind date. The romanticism of the Americans is compared with the cold, unfeeling attitude of Japanese men toward their women: "They don't understand the love we have for our women ... they sell theirs." The film ends with Grant nearly succumbing to tears as he sees, awaiting him on the dock as the ship returns, the wife and kids he had left behind: "I couldn't be that lucky," he says, "but I am."

The American male in *Destination Tokyo* expresses feelings far more openly than in other films because he is being compared with the inhuman, cold-blooded Japanese. But Grant still retains much of the stoicism demanded of the screen hero. Even when the submarine is slipping under the nets and entering Tokyo Bay, he remains unmoved and does not lose his cool. What sustains him is the soft memory of his son getting his first haircut, resting his head on Grant's shoulder and proudly announcing to the assembled patrons of the barber shop, "This is my daddy!" Grant is also characterized as an ordinary man, one who can be as afraid as anyone. He is asked about this and at once replies, "I'll say I am, so is everyone else." The anxious sailor who had been ashamed of the fear which he thought unmanly is at once relieved. The male hero of the war film had to descend from the realm of fantasy (the Western, the swashbuckler) to the world in which American men actually had to perform their heroics instead of dreaming about them. Hence Grant must be both a man who admits to fear and a forceful leader.

But the forcefulness wins out. When the submarine is battered by a Japanese destroyer, Grant takes the offensive required to save his men without hesitation and with a sharp assertion: "I think we're tired of getting pushed around!" He manages to blow up the Japanese ship because a real man does not hesitate, however difficult the task, nor does he submit passively to defeat, whatever the odds against him. When the battle is won, he leads his men jubilantly back to a world of familiar values: "Let's get out of here!" yells Grant after accomplishing his mission. Grant and America triumph through tenacity and a desire to preserve those values distinctly American, epitomized both by his family and the familiar symbol of the Golden Gate bridge.

Such wartime propaganda drew upon the usual demand made of the male star that he achieve success and evoke manly fortitude. The war films of the forties had been prepared for by a glorification of maleness and a belief in the ability of men to master their environment, already standard procedure for the depiction of maleness in film. The war films made absolute the supremacy of men in American movies to come. Despite those forties exceptions during the war which—with various reservations—acknowledged the career woman, the superiority of the male figure became the central if unstated premise of American cinema in general. By the seventies a script such as Eleanor Perry's *Memoirs of an Ex-Prom Queen* could be rejected by the studios on the sole ground that it did not contain a single strong male figure. Hollywood allowed the representation of Mildred Pierce, the female entrepreneur, in 1945 because the wartime need of millions of women on the job made it difficult to ignore the reality of the working woman in American life. But even such token representations were allowable because so many war films had securely drummed into consciousness the superiority of the male member of the species.

II

Before 1945 a certain innocence and naïveté prevailed in the male image, against which tough guys like Bogart were set off. After the war, survival for the male hero became much more tenuous, if only as a reflection of the nuclear age. The *film noir* then came into its own, with deep, dark shadows marking its style as it bares unrelentingly the murky underside of life, replete with sinister, subterranean emotions against which a man must ever maintain his defenses. Traditionally stable relationships began mysteriously to dissolve before the corruption of the very universe. *Mildred Pierce,* (1945), *The Big Sleep* (1946), *Dark Passage* (1947), *Key Largo* (1948), *Force Of Evil* (1948), and *The Treasure of the Sierra Madre* (1948) offer but a small sampling of this genre. All reflect the same essential qualities of hopelessness and despair. Personal motives, like human nature itself, appear menacing, vicious, and in need of control. Sadism is not infrequent; men become victims of uncontrollable, destructive behavior as the universe appears not only immune to men's influence but beyond their powers of comprehension. A cynical pall descended on the screen as it did upon American life; the fantasy exploits of screen males of earlier decades were gone, having vanished with the belief that evil was always amenable to human control if only men would measure up.

Bogart was the typical hero of the *film noir*, both in its early phase during the war and in its maturity during the war's chaotic aftermath. Yet as Sam Spade in *The Maltese Falcon* (1941), Bogart not only calls the shots but he exhibits a vulnerability markedly absent from a darker post-war *film noir* like *The Big Sleep*. The more under a man's possible control the world seems, the more space exists for him to manifest a relaxed self-confidence. In *The Maltese Falcon* Bogart wins out easily over the collection of amusing eccentrics whose bumbling evil-doing is not without a certain charm as they greedily pursue the black bird of the film's title. Drugged by his enemies and as uncertain of the whereabouts of the black bird as anyone, Bogart remains at the film's conclusion in full command of his life, retaining the power to make his own choices. His confidence matches his panache to the extent that director John Huston can include a scene in which Bogart emerges from his first meeting with Sidney Greenstreet with his hands trembling. When our hero looks at this betraying hand with a will of its own, he laughs—at human frailty and at himself. *The Maltese Falcon* established the no-nonsense, supremely rational man. Free of debilitating illusions—or dreams—he is more clear-sighted than his antagonists. Mary Astor, Greenstreet, and Peter Lorre are all mesmerized by elusive wealth and power, "such stuff as dreams are made on." Bogart lives by his wits and a few basic principles, which include loyalty to his dead partner, Miles Archer. That he never liked Archer, and even had an affair with his whining, obnoxious wife, in no way jeopardizes the staunch loyalty he owes a man who worked with him.

In his appearance Bogart lies somewhere between the cop and the hoodlum of the thirties gangster film. His hair is slicked back; the cigarette dangling from his lips remains in place even while he unloads a punch on Lorre's jaw. Bogart shares in the moral legitimacy of the police because, while remaining the tough individualist, he approximates their power; he carries as well the forbidden attraction of the gangster because he too is an unbridled rebel who risks all on a chance, always demanding the freedom to act according to the imperatives of his own personality. His manliness is so manifest that he doesn't even carry a gun, always able as he is to demonstrate his power with his fists. Bogart's Sam Spade is supremely masculine because he is his own man, a quality biographer Benchley attributes to the actor as well: "The one rule he clung to above all others was that he lived his life as he wanted, with nobody to tell him what to do."

Sam Spade, of course, remains faithful to the male code. He sees women as undermining the purpose, resolution, and integrity of a man, for under the surface they are irredeemably selfish, impulsive, emotional, and unprincipled beings who, no matter how you slice it, mean trouble. The woman Bogart likes best in *The Maltese Falcon* is one with whom he has no sexual relationship: his secretary, Effie, whom he bullies and belittles good-naturedly, to her delight. Bogart admires Effie because she thinks "like a man." He pays her his highest tribute in calling her "a good man." Of course, like that of all women, her judgment is faulty, and she is easily taken in, as she shows in bestowing her blessing on the wily Bridget O'Shaughnessy (Mary Astor): "She's OK." The wife of Bogart's dead partner, Archer, is a hypocritical predator.

The worst of them all, however, is Astor herself, especially dangerous because she knows how to attract a man. She proceeds from lie to lie about the black bird, each succeeding lie conceding its predecessor in aid of the latest deception. Bogart admires her audacity: "You're good, you're very good," he purrs, even as he sees through her and tells her half-admiringly what she is: "You *are* a liar." Astor tries to disarm him with a confession: "I am. I've always been a liar." Her consistent pose is that of a helpless woman on the verge of going to pieces in the absence of a male protector. Indeed, it is the suggestion that, deceit aside, she acts as she does because her need is so great that attracts Bogart, although he pretends to be unaffected by her wiles and constantly deflates her: "Don't brag about it."

The contrived melodrama which evolves around the pursuit of the falcon is utterly incidental. *The Maltese Falcon* is no more or less than the portrait of a man of style. Bogart's image—the way he moves, the lightning-swift thought processes he exhibits—are far more precious to the director and to the film than any jewel-encrusted curio. We have before us a man self-employed and answerable only to himself, taking no orders and beholden to no one. He is the solitary male, alone but supremely self-assured. If he is capable of loving a woman, he is equally able to renounce that love when he is used or betrayed. Both Bogart's freedom and his endless adventures are inaccessible to ordinary mortals. He remains what all men would be had they the guts to take the risks or the willingness to sacrifice whatever jeopardizes their autonomy and self-sufficiency.

Fast cuts by Huston, often bisecting a scene by means of a dissolve, match the hero's capacity to make split-second decisions. The visual style of *The Maltese Falcon* is itself an emblem of Bogart's self-confidence and manliness. In a bizarre arena of eccentrics, which he calls the "wild, wild West," Bogart, free of the obsession with the ridiculous black bird, remains the only man, and hence the only human being, in the film.

Spade emerges as morally intact. Bridget O'Shaughnessy had set up his partner, Miles Archer, and for this she must "take the fall." No amount of pleading will change his mind as he turns her over to the police: "This isn't the time for that schoolgirl act." The politics of male-female relations as Hollywood saw them in the early forties becomes unabashedly explicit. For were Spade to fail to put her behind bars, she would have power over him. Spade—as would Bogart himself—will sacrifice anything to ensure that this never happens:

> I won't play the sap for you ... I don't care who loves who, I won't play the sap for you. You killed Miles and you're going over for it.

No amount of sympathy, love, or admiration for her toughness can alter the fact that letting her go would threaten his own autonomy and freedom of action. It would give her something to hold over him for purposes of future blackmail, or worse. As with her fickle breed in general, that she loves him now can never guarantee that she may not betray him later. He will remind himself of this during the "rotten nights" he is certain to suffer, even as he knows that sooner or later he'll get over her.

Elevator bars move across Astor's face in a pan as she is carried down to the jail that in a sense she already inhabits—the prison of her greedy, deceitful, feline character. Distinctly apart, Bogart takes the stairs, walking out of the last frame as he has exited from Astor's life. Sam Spade will survive alone. His principles are his own, even if it remains odd to the casual observer that he should surrender the woman he loves out of loyalty toward a nondescript dead partner for whom he never cared. Bogart remains quintessentially inviolate in this paean to masculine self-sufficiency, a level of spiritual excellence reserved exclusively to men in the American film.

After the war, the world in which Bogart attempts to survive becomes far more treacherous. The mood is analogous to that of the returned veteran who finds his society utterly unrecognizable. As Philip Marlowe in Hawks's *The Big Sleep*, Bogart is led down such chaotic byways that the film's plot becomes too tangled to unravel, even by the close of the film. A General Sternwood is being blackmailed, but how and why remains unclear throughout. Marlowe blunders through a case he doesn't understand, trading wisecracks with the general's daughters. The younger of the two immediately accosts him: "You're not very tall, are you?" "I try to be," he replies, moving on to her older sister (Lauren Bacall). The two slowly kindle a relationship which will provide a moment of illumination in an otherwise dark and confusing world. Bacall calls the sloppy Marlowe a "mess." "I'm not very tall either," he answers. What counts, we are meant to see, is the fiber of the man within. Once an aide to the district attorney, until he was fired for insubordination, and before that a gun-runner, Marlowe, like Sam Spade, is a man unafraid of danger and always himself.

Following the sexual pattern of most male stars, like Clark Gable who always first insults the woman he already knows will soon be his, Bogart plays hard to get. He is always ready to walk out of a relationship or to avoid involvement with a woman. His cynical wariness and inaccessibility are of course assumed to make him all the more appealing. Bacall compares him to a temperamental racehorse, finely bred and full of vitality, by way of accepting his casualness, and all the while craving some indication of his feelings.

Unlike Gary Cooper or Clint Eastwood, however, Bogart is willing to concede; once a woman has shown herself tough enough in emulation of the approved male manner, yet subservient to her man, Bogart will offer some display of interest. To this Bacall eagerly responds: "I like that. I'd like more . . . that's even better." What is distinctive about *The Big Sleep* is the exciting relationship it charts between a man and a woman. Through Bacall's response to him as a beautiful and intellectually independent woman, Bogart is validated as a man. Bacall's image is a confident, audacious one and these qualities make her attractive to a man like Bogart, as Bogart's own brashness conquers her. The traditional Bogart remark, "You look good, awful good. I didn't know they made them that way any more," could have been uttered in this film by either of them.

At the end Bogart asks Bacall, "What's wrong with you?" "Nothing you can't fix," she replies. What is striking here is that this is true in every sense. It flows from their mutual regard. They face each other with no need for the obligatory kiss, and the film is over. Bogart and Bacall carry off what Marlon Brando and his postadolescent Lolita, Maria Schneider, fail to achieve in *Last Tango in Paris* (1973): an experience in the present, free both of the legacy of personal repression and of the varieties of social oppression that distort people and make their interaction so painful. Bogart and Bacall do indeed "come without touching," as Brando and Schneider had put it. They are heroic enough to have achieved such a communion apart from and despite the chaos of a destructive postwar world.

In the Bogart films the male becomes heroic in managing to discover romance in spite of society's corruption. Two people could still find each other and with their intense love fortify themselves, even if they had to do so in a moral wasteland where they must forever endure the menace of irredeemable evil both individual and social. The hero of *Dark Passage*, an escaped convict framed for the murder of his wife, undergoes plastic surgery to convert him into the Bogart we know. Bacall becomes interested during his trial because his cause so closely resembles that of her father, who had also been falsely accused—of killing her stepmother. In the *film noir* as it came to fruition after the war the abuses of the world are in the grain of the wood, an emblem of the recalcitrance of social evil.

Rare moments of light break the darkness; a cab driver, himself ensnared in the dreary, dark, menacing streets, sympathizes with Bogart.

Humphrey Bogart on the set of *The Big Sleep:* The male becomes heroic in managing to discover romance in spite of society's corruption.

Only in such random encounters do people find help from others; in the world of the *film noir* you can rarely trust those you know. Evil people like Madge (Agnes Moorehead), the woman who framed Bogart, appear to have been born that way. The good, like Bacall, the cabby, and the doctor who performs Bogart's plastic surgery, lack plausible "motive," as if a conscious commitment to justice or kindness would render both unlikely.

The surgeon proposes to make Bogart "look older, but good—as if he's lived," a rather apt description of Bogart as we know him. "I hope I'm not a coward," Bogart offers, enough in touch with himself to admit to fear. "We're all cowards," replies the doctor. In the *film noir*, myths of male invulnerability are surrendered because they presuppose the accessibility of things to change. Thus in these films the male image can transcend the facile assertion of male infallibility normally invoked by Hollywood.

When his best friend, George, is murdered, Bacall becomes for Bogart "someone to watch over me." "Their song" is played on a record the reverse side of which is "You're Just Too Marvelous, Too Marvelous for Words." The music is poignant for them both, as in *Casablanca* Bogart and Bergman shared the resonance of "As Time Goes By." Both songs express the lovers' sense of the uniqueness of their relationship in a menacing world.

At times Bogart does participate in the typical responses of the screen male. In *Dark Passage* he moves through disquieting events without betraying emotion. But the formula is altered here because his power is limited. His shadow stealthily trails behind him, an oft-repeated symbol in the *film noir* universe. Malicious people dog his steps like furies. And he would certainly have suffered capture and incarceration once more had he not been saved by an entirely fortuitous happening. In a bus station he overhears a forlorn man making friends with a lonely woman: "We have something in common—being alone." The words vividly remind him of how precious his relationship with Bacall has become. He had been planning to flee without her. Now he steps into a phone booth to call. Had he not ducked into the booth at that precise moment, the policeman on the scene who was looking for him would have ended their chance for happiness forever, so tenuous is our control over even the most personal aspects of our destiny. The smallest chance happening can either ruin everything or sustain us forever. "If God's good to me," Bogart tells Bacall, "I'll be waiting for you."

The closing scene takes place in a bar over strains of "You're Just Too Marvelous." Bacall has arrived in Peru. That the law and the state still believe that Bogart is guilty is something they will have to live with. As at the end of many of the Gable films, we have no doubt that their relationship will be sustained: it is all they have. The confidence in their love shared by Bogart and Bacall as mature adults appears in retrospect touchingly rare for the American film, even if, in part, it remains a measure of the insecurity and sense of inadequacy people felt in the culture of the time.

Key Largo bridges the theme of *Casablanca* with the mood of the *film noir*, acknowledging the decline of hope but demanding one more round on behalf of the world of order. The strong man is asked to transfer his commitment from fighting the war to ridding the postwar world of the lawless. If the prewar gangster like Little Caesar was a rebel *manqué*, a self-made man gone astray because times were awry and social opportunity absent, the old themes are renewed here with a twist. The gangster-rebel is now wholly despicable, an unadulterated menace to a world he has considerably corrupted. Bogart renews the note of *Casablanca* prior to his return to the fold of the committed: "I fight nobody's battles but my own," he says. "Me, die to rid the world of a Johnny Rocco?" For this cynicism he earns Bacall's contempt: "If I thought your way, I'd rather be dead."

But the issue which she considers gives purpose to life is no longer, as in *Casablanca*, an international fight for justice and human progress. The cause invoked in the postwar American film is that of combatting ubiquitous malevolence, which will always be with us. And that combat is waged in the name of the status quo. It is a very different commitment which now calls for struggle no matter the odds. Bogart grants that his head says one thing and his whole life another, but he fails to articulate why he has abandoned a committed life in keeping with his reasoned sense of the way things are. He acts almost out of old habit, telling us that with such ambivalence the head always loses. Wounded himself, he manages to thwart the evil Rocco, whose delight in humiliating his pathetic alcoholic mistress (Claire Trevor) is matched only by his unrelieved cruelty in the other aspects of his life. He is a crude stereotype, a slight reconstruction of the German or Japanese villains of World War II films.

Bogart's reward is again that sense of peace which comes only to those large enough in moral stature to abandon defining the world solely in terms of their own ego. Out of the fog engulfing the characters throughout the film, Bogart, half-smiling, sails into Key Largo at the end, the job done. But it is a willed conversion without much conviction. War turns out to be a permanent condition, its theater of combat simply brought home. Despite victory, a man must still be ever ready to risk himself, however futile he now knows the effort may prove in the long run.

In only one Bogart film of the forties does any direct criticism occur of the ossified shell of masculinity in which he so often encases himself and which he retains despite his many moments of vulnerability and honesty. John Huston's *The Treasure of the Sierra Madre*, made shortly before *Key Largo*, features Dobbs, the Bogart character whose "masculinity" is conjoined to selfishness, greed, and inhumanity. Masculinity is in fact perceived by Huston as a function of economic well-being. The down-and-out Dobbs, who carries all his possessions wrapped up in newspapers and whose clothes are filthy, is presented by the camera as a lesser man than the more solvent Sam Spade of *The Maltese Falcon*. B. Traven, author of the original novel, was concerned with how greed and the lust for possessions reduce and destroy men. And he held a specific social order to account both for pauperizing men and for conditioning them to want the things taken by their oppressors. Huston is more ambiguous, suggesting that venality is latent in human nature, and that ultimately the difference between the behavior of the possessors and the dispossessed is that the latter want what the former have.

In the film Huston reveals that to be a man requires means. At the beginning Dobbs and his buddy, Tim Holt, are cheated of their pay by a wily foreman. They beat him up only to take what is coming to them, leaving the remainder of his money with him. The greed of Dobbs has not yet surfaced. But prospecting for gold with a gambler's compulsion to hit it big unleashes the worst aspects of male selfishness. Dobbs begins to distrust even his closest buddies, whereas earlier he had clasped in friendship the hands of his partners, Holt and Walter Huston, as they began their mutual project. Egotism is presented here as an emblem of depravity. Dobbs furtively hides his share of the wealth each night.

Such a man has the most predictable of male fantasies: a turkish bath, new duds, food in a "swell café," and, of course, a woman. Heterosexuality is seen as an obligation to which every man must give obeisance, even if he doesn't feel it. Huston calls the mountain where they are prospecting a woman, to whom he speaks as to a reluctant mistress. For Dobbs, "She's a lot better ... than any woman *I've* ever known." In this honest portrayal, the more crudely male a character appears, the more hostility and distrust he feels toward the opposite sex.

But unlike Mike Nichols, who delights in the arrogant males of *Carnal Knowledge* while ostensibly criticizing them, director Huston distances himself sharply from the Bogart character. Extreme male dominance is seen by Huston as a form of insanity. Dobbs loses control, dementedly muttering to himself, "You won't catch *me* sleeping ... the day you try to put something over on me ... a little more lip and I'll let you have it." The extreme male personality, unsoftened by concern for others, disintegrates. Dobbs begins to speak of himself in the third person. Alienated from others, he is dissociated from himself. When he finally pulls his gun on Holt, his mad laugh resounds into the night.

The Treasure of the Sierra Madre is unique in its uncompromising hostility toward the competitive, overbearing, self-centered male and the capitalist romance of his drive for gain. Dobbs here is compared to the desert lizard, something less than a human being. Having shot Holt,

Dobbs, mistakenly believing him to be dead, decides not to bury the body: "In a week the buzzards and ants will get him." He changes his mind only out of fear that the buzzards will give *him* away. Paranoia stalks the man who lives only for himself.

Such a man cannot survive alone. Dobbs is murdered by bandits, who steal his burros and throw away the gold dust, failing to recognize it, as if it had no value at all. The male persona Dobbs represents has been utterly demolished. Holt survives to visit the widow of a man who died fighting with them. Huston in his old age has learned from a life of questing for gold; he chooses to live among the Indians as a medicine man, repudiating the false values which turned Dobbs into a predator. These two gentler male alternatives endure in an ending full of poetic justice. They are able to laugh in cathartic release at the irony of having the bandits mistake the gold for sand used to make the burros weigh more and scatter it to the winds. Maleness, director Huston shows us in this film, as in *The African Queen* (1951), has nothing to do with a tough, silent, unfeeling approach to life. *The Treasure of the Sierra Madre* anticipates the fifties, when the male hero will once again examine his personality, openly exploring the self in all its anguish and neurosis.

III

The innocence of the first half of the forties was well reflected in Tyrone Power swashbucklers like *The Mark of Zorro* (1940) and *Blood and Sand* (1941), and in films like *Knute Rockne—All American* (1940) and *Gentleman Jim* (1942) where sports enable a male to rise à la Horatio Alger from obscurity to fame. These were Hollywood's typical products, against which the stylistic, if not the thematic, achievements of Orson Welles's *Citizen Kane* (1941) might be measured. Yet despite its overwhelming superiority as a motion picture, *Kane* never distances itself from Hearst's style of masculinity, however much it challenges and condemns Hearst as a political figure and as a human being. It is not Kane's exploitative attitude toward women that interests Welles but his cancerous infatuation with power, and one feels that had Kane been truly concerned with bringing the news to the people, had he not been a hypocrite, his coveting beautiful, dumb singers or decorative nieces of presidents would not have bothered the director. *Citizen Kane* sees itself as concerned with far larger issues, though in reality Kane's maleness is interwoven with his preoccupation with power.

The two Tyrone Power films, remakes of Fairbanks and Valentino originals, sought to resurrect a hero for whom the choices and moral issues were clear, simple, and unambiguous, exactly the opposite of what happens in *Citizen Kane*. As Zorro with his pencil-thin moustache, Power is violently virile or predictably effeminate as the plot requires. The humor of his effete Don Diego consists in the performance of one of the rare film sneezes permitted a male star. The ending is conventionally absurd as well. The gallant, swashbuckling Zorro, who has been disguised as Don Diego all along, decides to settle down with Linda Darnell, "marry, raise fat children, and watch our vineyards grow."

As Juan Gallardo in *Blood and Sand*, Power imitates Valentino entertainingly. He is dark and slim as he glowers from under thick, dark brows. As in so many American films in which the implicit sex object is the man, Power has two women after him, the good and truehearted Carmen, his wife (Linda Darnell), and the evil and hence more desirable Doña Sol. Reversing traditional symbolism, the dark woman is here the faithful wife and the light—Rita Hayworth, a glorious redhead—the seducer. For her, fame and success provide the strongest aphrodisiac, as she pursues Power with brilliant blood-red fingernails and lips. She serenades Power with her guitar. Like one of the bulls he fights, he is corralled by Hayworth, as will be Anthony Quinn, his successor as number one bullfighter.

The social dimension of the Valentino original has vanished. Missing as well is the unpredictable quality of Valentino's passion. Power's sexuality appears totally on the surface: hard, shell-like, and lacking all spontaneity. At times he seems but one more prop in this technicolor spectacle and extravaganza. All is a tediously foregone conclusion, since according to the film's premises no real man could withstand the advances of so alluring a woman as Doña Sol.

Nonetheless, although his masculinity demands Power's sexual capitulation, the film must punish and kill him for his breach of the canons of marital fidelity. Like *Little Caesar*, *Blood and Sand* returns at its conclusion to a morality to which it earlier has shown no virile man could submit and still consider himself masculine. Having set us up, the film coyly takes back its arousing proposition. We are told that a bad woman has, by tempting him, robbed our hero of his manhood, forcing him to use up the juices he badly needs to face and destroy the bulls in the arena. Fear now stalks him.

The "good" woman has waited patiently "for the sickness to pass," but must lose him because he is, finally, most intensely himself in his passion for Doña Sol. This obsession ended, little would remain of Juan Gallardo's vitality. *Blood and Sand* spares us the sight of an unmanned if faithful Gallardo returning with his ever-loyal wife to the provinces to raise bulls for other real men to fight. Had he survived, this was his plan.

Sports films of the early forties were even more naïve in glorifying the "masculine," sportsmanlike male. Male prowess is their central theme. *Knute Rockne—All American* even displays an opening message declaring

—in case we sleep through the next ninety minutes—that it is dedicated to "ideals of courage, character, and sportsmanship." In these sports sagas athletic ability is linked to patriotism and to psychological normality, promulgating the insidious command enforced in every public high school that the best Americans and the most manly men are those good at sports. "America the Beautiful" drones through the soundtrack. As a small boy Knute gets his nose bashed in playing football. But he is not too incapacitated to instruct his immigrant father not to talk Norwegian: "We're Americans now!"

An ideal man, says this simple exercise in propaganda, would be both an honor student *and* captain of the football team. But it is the latter that counts. Chemistry could never capture the heart of a Knute Rockne; he devotes his life to coaching football, and before this high-minded purpose his wife will take second place. Knute will live to give "the boys" on his team a model for "a right way of living." Intellectual pursuits, the moral issues of daily life, love—all are virtually nonexistent in the lives of the men trained by Rockne (Pat O'Brien) and led by his disciple Gipp (Ronald Reagan).

Particularly in the sports film is the ability to withstand pain without flinching granted virtually a religious sanction. When one of the players dear to him dies, Rockne neither cries, breaks down, nor displays open emotion because, as we have been shown endlessly by Hollywood, a real man does not express his feelings.

Rockne represents a true dehumanization of the male personality. He insists that sports provide the most desirable vehicle for that goal of goals, "the spirit of combat," an essential component of every "red-blooded young man." A man who is not a fighter and an aggressive competitor —who is not sufficiently male—becomes repellent. For Rockne, hardness is synonymous with "purity," and sports the sole means for a man to avoid "getting soft." And, unawares, the film reveals that while callousness and unyielding determination to dominate and defeat others may win football games, such qualities forge as well intolerant, brutal, and finally pathological people.

Gentleman Jim (1942), with Errol Flynn as boxer James J. Corbett, is also about what it means to be a man. The pseudo-democratic mystique with which it launches Flynn's masculinity is that the working-class male is far more virile than his effete, wealthier counterparts. The rich athletic-club members who are his antagonists are stuffy and arrogant. Flynn, brash and self-confident, is much more the man. The physically potent male, because of his agility and superior strength (and hence personality), never abandons belief in himself. In one of his fights, in which Corbett "dances" in the manner of Muhammad Ali, he is called "a Greek god if not an old woman's mirage." Success is all. Once Corbett defeats John L. Sullivan to become champion of the world, Alexis Smith, the rich woman he craves, confesses that she was wrong about him. The man of assured physique who knows, consequently, his own worth, will go far. As Flynn puts it, "A swelled head is a guy who thinks he's good, but isn't." Gentleman Jim's head may be empty, but the swell of his biceps permits him to swagger to the top.

IV

Some of the most striking postwar sports films partake of little of this sunny optimism. The athlete and his environment are at odds; the man who would use his physical abilities to rise to the top must do so in an arena infested by sharklike gangsters. Fixed prizefights are the norm; corruption has suddenly invaded all social institutions, including sports, and no sport more thoroughly than boxing. Sports films made in the era of the *film noir* reveal that far from granting him success and fame, the athlete's physical ability only renders him vulnerable to malevolent predators who would abuse his purity and talent.

Body and Soul (1947) and *The Set-up* (1949) both demonstrate that strength and self-confidence are insufficient to sustain manliness or guarantee survival. Both films are grounded in a postwar America far closer in spirit to the world of King Vidor's *The Crowd* than to that of Fairbanks Senior's romantic escapism.

It is with bitter irony that John Garfield is called "the champ" in *Body and Soul*. The film opens with a hero already gone to seed, laden with "whiskey fat, thirty-five-year-old fat." Something has gone awry with the cult of maleness glorified in *Knute Rockne* and *Gentleman Jim*, films which never hinted at, much less confronted, the moment when an athlete who had defined his manhood by the ripple of his muscles must face the erosion of the years.

A Garfield over the hill is forced to bet his entire purse against himself, as the body is enlisted in the utter degradation of the soul. The male obsessed by success turns out to be at war with himself; the ethic of "every man for himself" has come full circle. Those who are really out for themselves have destroyed all others in their path, strong and weak alike. The world which preaches that success will bring happiness turns out to be barren, and the American boy who grows up in circumstances not very different from those faced by Knute Rockne, believing that "it's better to win than to lose," is in for a rude awakening.

Charley (Garfield), refusing to accept "handouts," acts at times as if he were in 1933 rather than 1949. What the two periods have in common is despair, but in films set in the latter period all hope has been abandoned.

John Garfield in *Body and Soul:* He has regained his manhood not so much by returning to an honest course as through the prowess of his body—what the male in American films has always relied upon.

Struggling desperately to survive, Charley permits anyone to own a piece of him as he claws his way to the top. The ending is disappointing. Screenwriter Abraham Polonsky loses his focus and resorts to blaming his main character for lacking enough soul to combat the corrupt world in which he moves. Charley has accepted the society's view that money is everything and will make him a man, a feared and dominant figure. He has done what is necessary to succeed in his society, and yet it is he who is treated as a fall guy, accused by the film of personal corruption.

Polonsky's ending only confuses the issue. Charley is double-crossed. He agrees to throw a fight if it will be a fifteen-round decision, only to discover that his opponent has every intention of knocking him out. The moral issue is now easy, if a little odd. For, his pride aside, his willingness to throw a fight in fifteen rounds is hardly less dishonest than allowing himself to be knocked out. What emerges is that his male pride would be violated beyond repair if he were knocked out. To become a real man Garfield must finally do exactly what Knute Rockne and Gentleman Jim did before him: he must fight to win. And he does so, ferociously; someone even compares him to Blake's "Tyger." Charley wins and retires, invoking that male behavior as traditional to the culture as the obsession with money and success which the film nominally opposes. And Charley is transformed into the supercourageous male as he confronts the evil promoter: "What can you do? Kill me? Everybody dies."

Full of soul and self-assertion, he proudly announces, "I never felt better in my life." He has regained his manhood not so much by returning to an honest course as through the prowess of his body—what the male in American films has always relied upon. A worn-out fighter, out of training and out of shape, nonetheless carries off a physical tour de force. Maleness still requires pitting one's physical power against evil—and winning. Despite the aura of grim realism, the film in its ending perpetuates a myth as fantastic as the exploits of Fairbanks Senior sailing through the air on his magic carpet at the close of *The Thief of Bagdad*.

The Set-up is more honest in refusing to permit aging, second-rate boxer Robert Ryan to win out over the mobsters who control the world of boxing. All he can do is hang on a little longer, not in the cause of his male identity, but because he is trapped in the only way of life he has ever known: "If you're a fighter, you've got to fight." Ryan offers a unique image of the prizefighter—or the screen male. He is gentle and soft-spoken. If he is a boxer, out of the ring he is complex and often emotionally insecure, and he shuns aggression as the norm of male behavior. He is quietly devoted to his wife (Audrey Totter), and it matters a great deal to him that she attend his fights.

The Set-up bears the same relation to fight films as does its main character to the typical screen male. Ryan is not even a main-eventer. He is the average boxer fighting for peanuts under appalling conditions and suffering entirely unromantic damage in each encounter. The film shows how ninety-nine percent of fighters really live, debunking the myth of glamour, fortune, and fame that attaches to the very few. The character portrayed by Ryan is a very ordinary, if decent, fellow. He is neither heroic nor vicious. His physical attributes are unexceptional and workmanlike. He is, in short, a real person. It is interesting that by showing the boxer as he usually is, the film, despite the subject of prizefighting, humanizes the male image itself. Its hero is a male freed of the burden of being number one. If he is like most fighters in reality, he is also like most men. The result is a person who neither strikes absurd pathological poses of supremacy nor is anything but natural to those he knows.

Everyone but Ryan is aware that the event around which the film is centered has been fixed—a situation that enhances his powerlessness and victimization. A flabby, over-the-hill Ryan, his timing long gone, is matched with a younger, stronger if ungifted man, and he takes a terrible beating. Near the end of the fight, discovering that it has been fixed, he fights so hard that despite the pummeling he endures, he knocks out his opponent.

But in the *film noir* neither principle nor physical prowess ensures success. By winning, Ryan has double-crossed the mob. His manager and trainer, now in jeopardy, disappear and Ryan's moment of male pride rapidly turns sour. No sooner does he stagger to his dressing room than the mob's hoods begin to stalk him to exact their revenge. Unlike other films about the phoenix-like rise of a defeated man through a heroic gesture, *The Set-up* does not, indeed cannot, close on a note of triumph, for Ryan's "victory" can lead nowhere. Not even a decision to retire with dignity would serve, although such an ending would have allowed the director an upbeat finish in keeping with most such films. But *The Set-up*, infinitely superior as a work of art to a watered-down descendant like *Rocky*, has already raised too many issues. The boxing profession, and the larger society which requires it, have been exposed to us, and it is too late to conceal their workings.

In the dark postwar world the forces trampling down the isolated individual are overwhelming. In a grimy alley behind the dressing room, gangsters work Ryan over. The beating they administer to him outside the ring reveals that the boxing arena is but an emblem of the entire society. Since he has briefly, quixotically, defied them with the tools of his trade, these are taken from him. Stomping on his right hand, the head thug informs the audience, "He'll never hit anyone with that hand again." If Ryan has risen to a defense of his integrity and manhood, it is out of a sense that he no longer cares what happens to him, that because all is so hopeless there is really nothing to lose. His "victory" in the ring was a gesture enacted at the price of survival. And death itself awaits the man who stubbornly resists or who attempts to approach life on his own terms.

Robert Ryan in *The Set-up:* Ryan offers a unique image of the prizefighter —or of the screen male. He is gentle and soft-spoken. If he is a boxer, out of the ring he is complex and often emotionally insecure, and shuns aggression as the norm of male behavior.

This despairing sense of a man's ultimate limitations pervades one of the best and most typical examples of the *film noir*, Abraham Polonsky's *Force of Evil*, which he directed as well as wrote. The hero is no athlete but lawyer John Garfield, a man who recognizes that wealth and success are attainable only via that nether world just beyond the law. His task is to make the numbers racket legal and profitable. Young, vital, and energetic, Garfield is prepared to do whatever is necessary to succeed, including the coaxing of his elder brother, Leo, to join the racketeer's combine. Brash, cool, and sure of himself, Garfield places his masculine energy in servitude to expediency. His dark shadow, a sinister alter ego, pursues him in silhouette, that emblem of the *film noir*. With the murder of his brother by the mob, Garfield renounces his corrupt way of life only to be left at the end penniless and without prospects. Success and corruption have proven to be inextricable, the efficacy of individual rebellion but chimerical. Garfield must survive with a diminished sense of a man's possibilities. Stripped of his confidence, he becomes hesitant and plaintive: "Is that what life is?"

In so mordant a world, new criteria for manliness are necessary. Garfield discovers his "soul," the love for his dead brother, which grants him the courage to stand up to his betrayers by testifying against them. In a long shot under the bridge where he searches for Leo's body, Garfield appears small and vulnerable. Leo's body is called "an old dirty rag nobody wants" and a piece of rubbish, images which apply to Ryan in *The Set-up* as they do to Garfield himself both here and in *Body and Soul*. Garfield and his girlfriend, Doris, clamber up from the rocky riverbed. Success has neither been regained nor promised, despite this climb upward. They are alive and have made their own choices, but survival as a consequence may be even more tenuous.

In the light of a postwar society in which orthodoxy is enshrined, expectations of maleness are narrowed. *Force of Evil* does not propose an alternative definition of masculinity and is far from suggesting that men and women should be viewed as having equal capacities. But it does perceive men as more limited, vulnerable, and powerless before authority than they had hitherto been presented in the American film. The *film noir* insists that they are no less male despite their being powerless, and in this insight born of the need to reconcile male prowess with the notion of the futility of change lies the positive contribution of this genre to the male image on screen.

The *film noir* of the late forties continued to reinforce the culture's notion that only men are to be truly valued. In *film noir*, as in preceding genres, male capacities remain superior. Even when the men suffer or are reduced in status and dignity, they remain capable of gratuitous moral gestures that earn them our respect, as does Robert Ryan's in *The Set-up*. It is always a male who finds his precarious way out of the darkness of the *film noir*.

Although *film noir* challenges the viability of such traditional masculine qualities as competitiveness, it nonetheless replaces them with traits considered accessible only to a male hero: uprightness, moral courage, and, as in *Body and Soul* and *The Set-up*, the willingness and ability to endure punishment as the price of integrity. In the American film these options have belonged exclusively to men. And even in later, supposedly feminist films like *Alice Doesn't Live Here Any More* (1974), women's choices will not embrace the possibility of integrity or a moral commitment to some goal requiring self-sacrifice. Unlike the heroes of the *film noir*, Alice (Ellen Burstyn) is granted no ennobling traits of character which would make her defeat tragic, no strengths to match her weaknesses. Her conflicts reside on the sexual plane, and she is deprived of the wider arena awarded to screen males within which their defeat may result as much from the corruption of their society as from personal inadequacy. Lacking talent, Alice can be given no choices to weigh about her barely begun singing career. She must decide only whether or not to accept the protection of a new and better man (Kris Kristofferson). One asks for Alice, not the spurious achievements of a John Wayne, not a new distortion on behalf of women, but, at the minimum, a chance for the woman in film to be treated as a being worthy of the same opportunities to rise and to fall as the male hero.

This purportedly feminist film of the seventies is, however, more insistent by far on the image of woman as an essentially helpless dependent than were some films of the forties in which certain strong, independent women were allowed on screen. Although, unlike the men, they were never permitted the capacity to triumph over the pressures and obstacles of the sleazy universe in which we are all shown to be mired, some of the women of the *film noir* were strong and independent in a manner entirely lost by the seventies. But again, their strength was used against them. The condition of Joan Crawford in *Mildred Pierce*, a typical *film noir* about a dominant woman, bears certain similarities to and yet distinct differences from that of John Garfield in *Force of Evil*. Crawford also discovers that the quest for money and success exacts too great a price and does not provide happiness in a dog-eat-dog world. Garfield loses a brother. Crawford loses one child to an illness for which she is blamed and the other to the false values by which she herself has lived: competitive individualism, success at any price, and an all-consuming materialism, values all shared by Garfield. Flourishing restaurant owner though Mildred may have become, her daughter, a caricature of her own quest for wealth and status, has become a murderess. The degeneracy of Mildred's own values finds expression in her dehumanized child.

At the close of *Mildred Pierce*, Crawford, defeated, leaves the police station where this daughter, Vida (Ann Blyth), has been incarcerated. Totally alone, Mildred accepts the company of her first husband, a man both sexually and emotionally lacking. So the venture into independence and a career has proved calamitous, analogous to the indulgence of her daughter. In the end the husband and the marriage, which we are meant to realize she should never have deserted, are her only refuge, a bitter lesson learned at a terrible price. The future seems bleak and empty of promise.

Ironically, Mildred had pursued success in large measure to please her parasitic daughter. She passes now between the lowered heads of jail-house janitors on her way out. Having briefly transcended her own working-class origins, hungry to be someone besides the wife of a strug-gling salesman, she finishes no better off than these unskilled laborers bowed down by life in a jailhouse, an image that suggests the limitations imposed on us all. *Mildred Pierce* has been justly praised as one of the few films of the forties picturing a woman who achieves financial indepen-dence through her own initiative, drive, and imagination. But as these very qualities lead her to disaster, they are invoked finally in order to be discredited. Punished for her hubris in aspiring to be something she was not meant to be, Mildred has become little more than an empty shell. Even her final self-sacrificing attempt to right the wrongs she herself wrought by taking the blame for the murder her daughter has committed proves futile.

In telling contrast, Garfield emerges with real dignity at the end of *Force of Evil*. Cleverly leaving the telephone receiver off the hook after surreptitiously dialing the police, he traps the racketeers into an unwit-ting acknowledgment of their crimes. Garfield will further avenge the death of his brother by testifying courageously against the mob, a theme anticipating *On the Waterfront* with its justification of informing to con-gressional investigating committees and the police. As a result, Garfield earns the respect of a woman whom he genuinely loves. Through his decision to go straight he has matured enough to discover what really matters, a development in sharp contrast to the fate of Crawford at the conclusion of *Mildred Pierce,* who emerges a broken woman in expensive clothes.

V

The comedies of the forties glorified maleness more subtly. The best of these, *Adam's Rib* (1949), appears to depart from the pattern, giving the impression that in the struggle of men and women to create a harmonious life together, neither need be subservient to the other. Husband Adam (Spencer Tracy) seems a superbly enlightened male with that maturity and self-confidence required in a man who has chosen a woman of capacities equal if not superior to his own. Wife Amanda (Katharine Hepburn) is an attorney like himself, as successful and shrewd as he.

At first theirs seems to be a relationship of true equals. After a hard day's work they take turns giving each other a massage or they prepare supper together. Neither considers the other to have a fixed province, nor is the woman assigned to the kitchen when it comes to meals. Vulnerable despite his power as an attorney and subject to anxieties such as we all have, Adam, his masculine strength notwithstanding, makes noises in his sleep when he is troubled. Relative to the entire history of the image of men in American films, this is an emancipated portrayal indeed.

When Amanda defends Judy Holliday, a woman who has shot her unfaithful husband, Adam as assistant district attorney is assigned the role of prosecutor. The film now centers not only on whether the law is capable of treating men and women equitably but on whether Adam and Amanda are in fact equal in ability and equals in their relationship.

Hepburn succeeds in clearing her dumb-blonde client of attempted murder, but largely through resorting to histrionics, emotional appeals, and such stunts as bringing to court a female wrestler and circus performer who lifts a dismayed Tracy right off the ground in absurd, if also convincing, proof that women may be the physical equals of men. But Hepburn's victory in court is followed by a series of events that undermine the film's feminism.

Surprising Hepburn in an innocent tête-à-tête with her admiring neighbor David Wayne, Tracy, seeming to revert to macho type, pulls a gun. Feminism is revealed to be defenseless before the masculine mystique. If Holliday, Tracy declares, was justified in shooting her husband to protect home and hearth, why isn't he? Genuine terror invades Hepburn's face. "You have no right—no one has the right," she stammers. Tracy now moves in for the kill: "That's all, sister . . . no one has the right to break the law." The gun is made of licorice, but nonetheless Tracy has devastatingly established his point and won the case out of court if not in it. And in terms of the rhythm of *Adam's Rib*, he has broken through the façade of Hepburn's competence.

Logic becomes the male prerogative, as Tracy is proven entirely correct in his contention that Holliday's excuse of passion would allow us all to be murderers, a position in defense of reason which had been thwarted solely by Amanda's resort to the emotional. "You're shaking the law by its tail," Tracy had told her, unmoved when Hepburn, incapable of any other resort, had collapsed in tears. These tears lay the groundwork for Hepburn's final capitulation to Tracy's demand at the end of the film: "I'm old-fashioned. I want a wife, not a competitor." Hearing these words, Hepburn first shoves him back against the wall. But hers proves to be a brief resistance, followed by that acquiescence in the last minutes of the film when their relationship has evolved precisely to such an "old-fashioned" apportioning of power.

But first a seminal scene occurs. Their marriage seemingly in shreds, the two meet at their lawyer's office to iron out their finances. Under the stress of it all Tracy bursts into tears. At once Hepburn consoles him as he weeps and weeps. Their quarrel now forgotten, she takes him to their farm for the weekend. Have we here one of those rare expressions of male vulnerability in film? What in fact emerges is that Tracy is using a woman's typical ruse, even as Hepburn as a lawyer had deployed a defense of her client based upon emotion.

The ending finds the two in a four-poster bed, an image of the "old-fashioned" quality of their renewed relationship. Tracy announces he will run for judge on the Republican ticket. Hepburn jokingly asks if they've yet selected the opposing Democrat. "You wouldn't," says Tracy, "because I'd cry." And the tears, which we now see he has learned to turn on whenever he wants his way, begin to flow, exactly as they had in the lawyer's office. We are left in no doubt that this time she has given up competing, as any good wife should. Settling down in bed, she seems almost about to accept the profession of mother. Male dominance is, however tenuously, restored and depicted as necessary to a balanced relationship. The last line of the film even belongs to Tracy. Hepburn had continued to maintain that the fact that they both can use tears to win an argument reveals that there is "no difference between the sexes. None. Men, women. The same." But Tracy asserts, "*Vive la différence* . . . which means: Hurray for that little difference!" His triumph over the brilliant Hepburn seems slight, but it is no less present.

VI

While the Western of the forties sometimes seemed as fraught with peril as the *film noir*, its heroes were frequently able to rise above it. But at times even the Western found chinks in the armor of the supremely powerful male, and manhood itself became an explicit issue in the way it never had before. As early as 1943 *The Ox-Bow Incident* ponders directly what it means to be a man. And if it chooses rather anxiously the strident "macho" characters over gentler examples, it does so with some hesitation. Henry Fonda, the most important male in the film, is hardly a hero. But he is, despite his acquiescence in the event, appalled by the mob brutality and lynching which the film has been made to deplore. He remains "masculine" in all other respects. Tentatively acknowledging the legitimacy of alternative styles of maleness, Westerns of the forties quickly cover themselves in retreat, surrounding their characters with reassuring attributes of raw physical courage, stoicism, and skill in violence, reaffirmed as the true touchstones of masculine identity. Hence, lest we associate Henry Fonda's distaste for the lynching with softness and effeminacy, he is quickly introduced as a man who loves nothing more than a good fight; indeed, brawling for him is such a delight and natural passion that even if he has lost, he feels "fine." Having established Fonda's masculinity, director William Wellman now feels able to risk condemning the Major, leader of the lynch mob, as a pathological brute who goes beyond delight in harmless brawling and requires mindless, cruel bloodletting and force to establish his masculinity. The cruder notions of maleness are thus timidly held up to critical scrutiny.

The Major wishes to have the lynching above all to initiate his sensitive son, forcing him to join the mob because it will "make a man of you." But here the son's revulsion for weapons and physical force is perceived to some extent by the film as weak. Trying to make a nonviolent male into something he cannot be is cruel, and contriving a setting for maleness unwarranted by normal circumstance is dangerous because it is false (the men who are lynched are innocent). What is at issue, in fact, is not the cruelty of the hanging but the illegality of doing it without a trial. The film defends legal due process and suggests that the ways of the frontier, once appropriate, are no longer so—which is why *The Ox-Bow Incident* is scorned by many as an anti-Western. A new order might prevent all such lynchings by appropriating male power and institutionalizing it, thereby making its lawless demonstration unnecessary. When violence and the need to demonstrate male prowess come into conflict with the social criteria for right and wrong, such violence, however understandable, must be disciplined.

The Fonda character, although he is unable to prevent the lynching of the suspected murderer (Dana Andrews), is still a hero. His restraint proves warranted; an abiding faith in the justice and stability of American society still pervaded the American film during the war. Fonda thus has no need to become a vigilante—as Bronson will in *Death Wish* when the official order feels far more threatened.

In *The Ox-Bow Incident* poetic justice vindicates the society. The Major, who was contemptuous of one of the victims for crying ("takin' it like a woman") and who called his son a "female boy" for his reluctance to take part in the hanging, is defeated. A softer conception of manhood is finally validated. The Major shoots himself, while his son, labeling himself a "coward" for not having rebelled, calls his father an "animal." Fonda is left to read aloud a letter written by the dead Andrews. It says that law is everything people have found out about justice, the root of right and wrong. The innocent man, in a letter to his wife, articulates how adherence to the rules is equivalent to civilization, reason, and the social good. The male hero of 1943 was just such an innocent; only in the seventies would films consistently explore the divergence between law and justice. The seventies hero finds the law an impediment to the true defense of the established order, a shield behind which malefactors hide from their just punishment. Such heroes as Dirty Harry express *on behalf* of the social order the mentality of the lynch mob pilloried in *The Ox-Bow Incident,* which challenged the association of virulent and mindless violence with masculinity.

The greatest Western of the forties, Howard Hawks's *Red River* (1948), centers also on what it means to be a man. Two definitions of masculinity are advanced, with a composite portrait presented by the film as the ideal: the indestructible toughness of John Wayne merged with the sensitivity and fairness of spirit of his surrogate son, played by Montgomery Clift. The result would combine the virtues of the paternal, the youthful, and the man at the height of his powers: a gentle superman.

Wayne and Clift share an uncommon ability to lead others in the all-important task of taming the frontier. Together they accomplish the first great cattle drive, forging the Chisholm Trail. Their success depends on each of them, although Clift must complete the drive without the help of the stubborn, temporarily estranged Wayne. By carving a great ranch out of the wilderness, Wayne has accomplished the most demanding part of the undertaking. In the process, his personality has deteriorated as he became intolerant and insensitive to the weaknesses of others. Clift, as the beneficiary of Wayne's raw energy and strength, can afford to temper stern resolve with fairness and mercy.

For the first third of *Red River* the film idealizes Wayne with little reservation. Having come West with a wagon train, he swiftly declares his self-sufficiency and independence by separating from the group: "I'm startin' my own herd." A real man acts alone, responsible solely to himself. The risks are thereby his and so are the rewards. No amount of personal jeopardy can dissuade him from this course; as his buddy and sidekick Walter Brennan remarks, he's "a mighty set man when his mind's made up."

Wayne's stubbornness will emerge as at once his greatest strength and his most destructive weakness. But early in the film the man who listens only to himself and does his own thinking is far and away the most inspiring and arousingly masculine figure.

The fortuitous death of his woman early in the film leads Wayne to forgo forever a domesticity which might have removed some of his masculine aura. The woman he loved had pleaded with him to take her along when he left the wagon train, but he had refused, telling her, "It's too much for a woman." And he is a man who does not change his mind. He intended to return for her upon establishing his stake. That she is massacred by marauding Indians is treated as an inevitable consequence of the heroic, danger-ridden life all who move West have chosen. Her murder also permits Wayne legitimately to remain without a woman for the remainder of the film without having to establish again, in some gratuitous encounter, his heterosexual credentials.

The sole survivor of the massacre is the boy Matthew, who as a grown man is portrayed by Clift. Wayne adopts this lone survivor—symbolically an emblem of himself. For even as a stripling Matthew is tough. Wayne initiates him into the violence required of men, removing Matthew's gun from him as a test. Matthew is humiliated, but, respecting the ritual, agrees not to use his gun against the older man. Asserting himself, he adds, "But don't ever try to take it away from me again." "He'll do," comments Wayne approvingly to Brennan, taciturnly and in top male form paying the boy his highest compliment. Although he has just had to watch all those he loves being slaughtered by the Indians, Matthew reveals no weakness. He is already stoical and repressed, capable of the "manly" quality of scrupulously concealing his pain, the central behavioral code and moral in which Wayne would instruct all the young men and women in his audience.

For much of the film *Red River* extols Wayne's stern aggressiveness as essential for the building of his ranch. But simultaneously it begins to deplore the resulting hardening of his personality. To take the land by brute force, as Wayne does, is both heroic and corrosive. Yet Hawks, speaking now for pioneer America, rationalizes that the Mexican occupants had earlier stolen the land from the Indians, and since Wayne is only doing what others did before him, he is somehow absolved. In the West moral codes are rapidly proven irrelevant. Seven graves on Wayne's property mark failed attempts by others to do the same to him. *Red River* can never quite decide whether to condemn this callousness or applaud it as a demonstration of the hero's masculine power. It is an ambivalence which lies deep within our history: the romance of immigrants escaping unjust societies as opposed to the disgrace of conquest and genocide of indigenous people ruthlessly displaced.

A deep and loving relationship grows up between Wayne and Clift, intensified by the post–Civil War depression which draws them together out of need. The Civil War has taken all the money out of the South, a situation analogous both to the depression of the thirties and to the disorientation of the returning veteran after World War II. *Red River* proposes a model of behavior: how a man ought properly to conduct himself under such conditions.

The qualities he must enlist are daring, imagination, and invincible courage, all in the service of an essential personal initiative. Nor would anyone who calls himself a man accept a handout or charity, however dire his circumstances. A real man discovers an answer none before him considered—and acts upon it. Wayne decides to take his cattle cross-country to Missouri, becoming the first man to travel the Chisholm Trail, the event commemorated by the film.

Only the strongest of men could accomplish such feats. *Red River* supports the Wayne style as reflected in the following incident. Choosing to base right upon might, Wayne has taken to branding with his own mark any of his neighbors' cattle that stray onto his property. One of these cattlemen, accompanied by his foreman, Cherry (John Ireland), angrily accuses Wayne of theft. Yet although he is clearly in the right, the owner backs down before Wayne's bravado. Cherry at once quits this weak boss to join up with Wayne. *Red River* again displays its ambivalence: it knows Wayne is wrong, yet it cannot help but advocate his assertiveness, physical strength, and manly dominance.

It is the same rationale which underlies the Western's basic approach to the American past. It knows the land was taken by conquest from the Indians, even as the small homesteaders were displaced by mine owners, banks, and railroads. But Hollywood was in the business of ratifying American history, not indicting it. Here the male image comes together with the legacy of the country. Despite its escapist and romantic setting in the frontier past, the settling of the West poses all the problems of an unjust society in which force and profits go together.

The male persona of rough dominance cannot be separated from this past because such a male image is designed to legitimize the harshest aspects of American history and to perpetuate similar male behavior in the present and future. Stealing other people's cattle because they stray onto one's property is, finally, little different from the theft of that same land from Indians or Mexican settlers. And since the male bravado romanticized in either case is the same, it becomes difficult to call into question the callous consequences for the male individual of such behavior without indicting at the same time its social rationale and historical roots.

Red River attempts to humanize the male image by using the character of Clift as a foil. Having been victimized himself as an innocent child whose parents were cruelly killed, Clift, if tough, knows from experience the consequences of Wayne's values. In the 1940s American society was seen in such films as deserving of its citizens' approval. The Western had to project an acceptance of the present by both assailing and glorifying the past. The problem is handled by Hawks's choice of a dual male hero, two intimately connected characters who complement and accept each other, but who represent two distinct male types.

In Westerns like *Red River* men feel most at home with male buddies. Wayne has Brennan, and Clift enters into a similar relationship with Ireland, a male as rugged as he, a man who admires "a good gun, a Swiss watch, or a woman from anywhere." So close do these buddies become that they never have that physical confrontation everyone else in the film expects. They share a common definition of what it means to be a man and are set in sharp contrast to Dan, the married cowhand.

Thoroughly domesticated, Dan signed on the cattle drive in order to buy his wife a farm and a pair of red shoes. The man whose life is ruled by women and an involvement in their needs can only be a weakling. Dan stutters, an expression of his uncertain male status. When there is a stampede, as the least able to fend off the dangers facing a man he is the first killed. The American film repeatedly ridicules the man whose main emotional commitment is to a woman. Since women are weak and unworthy, men who fail to disdain their whining incapacity are presumed to partake of it.

But the violence of his way of life has taken a lasting toll on Wayne. He becomes so desperate to complete the cattle drive that he descends further into brutality. He threatens to kill those who would desert, as both Wayne and the film unconsciously acknowledge that only terror can induce in young men the more strenuous aspects of male behavior: "There'll be no quitting along the way. Not by me and not by you." Hawks sees Wayne himself as a brutalized man, yet one who, like the settlers he represents, had no choice. For had he not abandoned that wagon train and taken off on his own at the beginning of the film, he would have long since been dead.

The Wayne who would kill quitters "not good enough to finish what they start" is replaced by Clift, who represents the modified male behavior advocated for today. As the beneficiary of Wayne's fierce battle with the wilderness, he has not had to pay the psychic price for taking the land exacted from Wayne. Yet having absorbed the essence of his surrogate father's masculine credo, he is Wayne's equal as a man. He saves the deserters Wayne is about to hang only to be accused by Wayne of being "soft," unmanly.

A real man is now one strong and confident enough *not* to dominate others crudely. The success of the drive, like the triumph of the settlers, provides a retrospective justification for Wayne's harshness. But without Clift's softness it would have fallen apart somewhere along the way. The woman Clift chooses is another of Hawks's daring, loose women, a reincarnation of the male-emulating woman played by Jean Arthur in *Only Angels Have Wings*. Joanne Dru plays a saloon girl bound for Las Vegas who is ready and willing to fight off the Indians when need be. But despite this, as in nearly every American film, she is inferior to the male and hopelessly illogical. Why did she expose herself to danger and fail to duck down as Clift had instructed her? Not out of bravery or calculation, but "because I got up!"

Clift evades her, displaying that essential instinct, the Hawks code of male style: Be wary of women. As he keeps watch over the cattle in a deep fog, she seeks him out, only to discover this strong male actually trembling. Hawks can allow the male who has established his prowess to reveal such vulnerability because Clift expresses the character to transcend it. Dru wins him by articulating and accepting that his first love will always be Wayne: "You love him, don't you? He must love you. That wouldn't be hard." It is she who kisses him, the passive love object who at any moment might depart, leaving his woman behind to yearn.

The triumphant arrival of the cattle in Abilene is rhythmically matched by the final confrontation, the showdown between the estranged father and son, Wayne and Clift. "You're too much like him," Dru tells Clift, as indeed he must be if he is to be a man. Nor will Clift draw first, although Wayne taunts him, calling him "soft" and a "yellowbelly." "Won't anything make a man of you?" yells Wayne. Only when Wayne beats him with his fists does Clift fight back.

Yet the last moments of *Red River* form a paean to male love, which is why this Western is one of the most popular ever made. Hawks himself once described his *A Girl in Every Port* (1928) as "really a love story between two men," as, in fact, are so many of his films, including *Red River.* The woman functions basically as the catalyst bringing the men together: "Anyone with half a mind would know you love each other." (It would only be a Hawks woman who could speak about having half a mind!) Women are needed, however, to speak words on which a real man by the standard of the American film would choke.

"You better marry that girl, Matt," says Wayne, approving Dru's sanction of the love he shares with Clift. "When are you gonna stop telling people what to do?" replies Clift. The promise of the film is fulfilled as Wayne draws a new Red River brand in the dust, now with a large M for "Matthew" on it. It is really Clift and he who are getting married, with Dru looking on as if she were the best man! The two men smile at each other as Wayne tells Clift, "You've earned it," on which note of union the film ends.

The Western of the forties offered perhaps the most important lesson in how a man behaves, and Wayne was its main instructor. Never would he be so weak as to waste words, and he would always feel more comfortable with other men than with women, the reason perhaps for Dustin Hoffman's exasperated assertion in *Midnight Cowboy* that John Wayne was "a faggot." Although he would reluctantly have to temper it with mercy toward weaker males, his physical strength was indispensable. Even physical size could take second place before raw power, for although Wayne in *Red River* was a splendid specimen, Clift was quite small, if all the more tough. Stoicism in the face of adversity was taken for granted, and vulnerability before one's opponent was unthinkable. In the major John Ford Westerns of the forties these would be the requirements of maleness propagated in film after film.

John Wayne and Montgomery Clift in *Red River:* "Won't anything make
a man of you?" yells Wayne. Yet the last moments of *Red River* form a
paean to male love.

My Darling Clementine (1946), with Henry Fonda as "retired" marshal
Wyatt Earp, poses the wartime issue faced by Bogart in film after film:
Can a man worthy of the name evade involvement in the affairs of his
community? Earp wants only to drive his cattle undisturbed to California. But the marshal of Tombstone has not been man enough to wipe out
the marauders wreaking havoc on the town. Enter Earp, a man of few
words but supreme competence, instantly effective: a model man. When
his youngest brother, James, is killed by these thugs, Wyatt, tormented
by the boy's face pressed in the mud with the rain beating down on his
body, chooses the only manly course. A fast cut has him knocking on the
mayor's door and accepting the position of marshal of Tombstone.

Its plot random and unwieldy, *My Darling Clementine* is a film about
the male character, dotted by *tableaux vivants.* One such set piece occurs

as the surviving brothers are pictured as black shadows in the driving rain. Loyalty to one's kin inspires a male rite, as does the avenging of a wrong against one's own. Motivated by such obligations, a man dedicates himself to the quest for law and order. For with the Indians defeated and the settlers now constructing towns, the lawless quest for land, as in *Red River*, must be institutionalized. Moreover, because marauding had been both romanticized and the norm, now that those who perpetrated the violence have the fruits of their efforts to defend, peaceful development becomes necessary. This reversal is expressed, of course, in the transformation of such gunslingers as Wyatt Earp and Doc Holliday into marshals and lawmen.

Against the postwar confusion, Ford pits primitive, eternal values which always involve love of country and a fervent patriotism. At dusk Wyatt Earp visits the freshly made grave of his dead younger brother. The clouds are luminous above, like hovering presences, intimations of a God thoroughly approving of Earp's manly ways. "When we leave this country, maybe young kids like you will be able to grow up safe," Earp whispers to the silent grave. At dusk, that magical hour for director Ford, it is best that a man be alone with his feelings; it is the only time he can indulge them without appearing weak, and he is able to do so only alone in such a place.

Fort Apache (1948) studies the value of two alternative male postures. Lieutenant Colonel Thursday (Henry Fonda) and Captain Kirby York (John Wayne) offer distinct approaches to the "Indian threat" with which the United States Cavalry must deal. Dour, humorless, and sour at having been sent to a godforsaken outpost, the rank-conscious and graceless Thursday embodies all the bad traits of which the spontaneous Ford hero is usually free. A stickler for appearances, he demands that the men always wear full uniform, a type of army discipline Ford scorns, as he insists that what counts is the fibre of the man beneath. Equally unmanly is Fonda's lust for glory. His ambition leads him to underestimate the power of the Indians, a mistake unworthy of anyone who would survive in the wilderness. A better man would recognize not only the masculine warrior bravery of the Indians but, in this film at least, the objective merit of their claims. Ford is an advocate of the idea of the hero, a condition to which the noblest men may aspire. Were the Indians not viewed as equal in manliness to the Ford heroes (but not their superiors, despite the admitted justice of the Indian cause), the triumphs of the cavalry would be diminished. But the unusual admission of legitimate Indian grievances is still outweighed by the superiority of the civilization defended by the cavalry. By taking Indian claims into account, yet still siding with the settlers, Ford shrewdly anticipates those who would point to the cruel conquest of the Indians and the theft of their land.

In *Fort Apache* Fonda is present to provide an example of what a man should *not* be. A real man is free of petty ambition, motivated solely by large, patriotic goals. In this sense the deeply conservative Ford scorns empty materialism. What really counts for Ford is what you do and have done, not what other people believe you have done, the theme as well of his later film *The Man Who Shot Liberty Valance.*

Predictably, Fonda makes a mess both of his command and of his personal life. As a strict, unrelentingly class-conscious father, he forbids O'Rourke (John Agar) to court his daughter (Shirley Temple) because Agar failed first to secure Fonda's permission. He sends out too few men and too little ammunition on Indian patrols. Wayne would parlay with Indian leader Cochise; Fonda, indifferent to the actual demands of the situation, desires mainly the glory of bringing him in. It is out of respect for his enemy, and because of his own shrewd ability to understand the other side, that Wayne arranges a meeting with Cochise. Disregarding the plan and the fact that Wayne has given Cochise his word, Fonda orders out his regiment, commenting in disgust, "Your word—to a savage?" In at least this Ford cavalry Western, historical justification does not require contempt for the Indians as people. The true man views the Indians as worthy of respect, and crude racists like Fonda are in need of proving their superior worth precisely because they do not really possess any distinction as men.

In the ensuing massacre, Wayne must rescue a besieged Fonda from his own folly, and later must lie to reporters in order to imbue the army with legends that will preserve its authority and power. An oil portrait of the now-dead Fonda glorifies him, and Wayne assents to a reporter's myth-making adulation: "He must have been a great man." "No one died with more honor or courage," echoes Wayne, affirming that men like Fonda will remain alive "as long as the regiment lives." The truth about any individual is less important than the survival of what Ford believes is a noble institution. Wayne wears a scarf exactly like that of his former adversary and asserts, "Thursday made it a command to be proud of."

Men must be large enough to perceive their own smallness and to protect the great institutions through which they have gained the priceless opportunity to live and die as real men. In *Fort Apache* neither Fonda nor Wayne has a single woman in his life, though both are mature men in their prime, nor does either feel the slightest sexual deprivation, an emotion openly to enter the American film only with the introspective heroes of the fifties. Nor would Ford's assertion that army life offers a far more fulfilling alternative to the dubious pleasures of conjugal bliss be credible in the decade to come, even in a John Ford film.

In *She Wore a Yellow Ribbon* (1949) Wayne plays an aging cavalry man, the old warhorse and hero on the verge of retirement. The Indians are now a mindless enemy who must be wiped out if the West is to be opened to civilization. Grey and moustached, Wayne dreads his retirement. Approaching old age, he remains his intractable self. "Never apologize, mister, it's a sign of weakness" is his motto. At one point a lyrical full shot offers a frame filled with buffalo, like Wayne a dying breed. The mood is one of nostalgia for a male personality full of grandeur and purpose now vanishing and increasingly obsolete; it is as if the actor John Wayne were stepping aside at the close of the decade for new male personalities like Marlon Brando and James Dean. Funereal tones of "Bury Me Not on the Lone Prairie" come and go on the soundtrack. The nostalgia for a style of manhood like Wayne's is Ford's response to the world of 1949, the period of the cold war, during which Ford would consider such male qualities more necessary than ever.

Ford offers as a model for all time John Wayne, a man with the courage of his convictions and an inspiration to all. It required nine years for Wayne to agree to call the John Agar character "Flint," not that much longer than it took him to add the M for "Matthew" to the Red River brand in Hawks's film. Flint doesn't mind the long delay in securing Wayne's approval: "It was worth waiting for." As an older man in these later Ford Westerns, Wayne assumes the mantle of mentor, creating for younger men rites of passage into manhood.

The Ford Westerns consist of a series of such initiations. Masculine credentials are not bestowed at birth by mere possession of the right physical equipment; they have to be both proven and earned. An older man who has already established his own can confer male sufficiency upon a youth, his most essential and precious gift. Finally only the fullness of years, indicating that one's manliness has already been put to the sternest tests, can create such a man as Wayne.

Another such rite involves the passing from command of the old soldier. As Wayne himself puts it: "Lieutenants jump when you growl one day ... glad if a blacksmith asks you to shoe a horse the next." It is sad when great men pass from the scene, and Wayne even sniffles—without, of course, actually shedding tears—when he is presented with a silver watch. He must now use eyeglasses to read the inscription: "To Captain Brittles. From C Troop. Lest We Forget." The inscription is sparing in its emotion, consistent with the personality of its recipient, whose credo eschews all such gratuitous outbursts of feeling. Finally Wayne is made Chief of Scouts, permitting him to remain with his sole love, the army. The only "woman" on the scene is, in fact, his male buddy, played by Victor McLaglen, who greets him at the end with a feeling "Welcome home, Colonel darlin'." These two brusque Irishmen, says Ford, a dual nationalist, know how to love each other well.

In *Rio Grande* (1950), which completes the trilogy, Wayne, again as Kirby York, is father to Claude Jarman, Jr. He is a rigid, discipline-loving ramrod, a martinet, ashamed of a son who has failed at West Point only to enlist in the army the next day as an ordinary recruit. Wayne, a father who cannot forgive defeat, makes it doubly, even sadistically, hard for his son: "You've chosen my way of life. I hope you have the guts to endure it." By the end Wayne is reunited with his estranged wife (Maureen O'Hara) and endorses his son, who outdoes Wayne in toughness. "Our boy did well," he affirms, smiling proudly to himself but still not revealing to others his pleasure in his son's fortitude.

When they are present at all in the Ford Westerns starring Wayne, women function as foils for the qualities of their men. O'Hara pleads with Wayne, whom she has not seen in years, to let her buy their son out of the army. Wayne insists upon seeing their son through the necessary male rituals by which he will gain his manhood. Strong-minded though she is, O'Hara is quickly overwhelmed by Wayne's strength, manly courage, and stoicism. She works at her washboard in camp while he leads the troop to the Rio Grande against the Indians. Men and women return to their appropriate functions. O'Hara, who in buying their son out of the army would have kept him a boy, clearly manifests the danger women represent to real men, whom they would domesticate and, by implication, at once emasculate and feminize.

Meanwhile a "sense of duty," essential to manliness, can be taught only by the father. Sometimes it involves obedience to an unjust course of action, as in *Fort Apache*. The Ford Westerns are far too simplistic to explore this contradiction, which implicitly undermines the code of masculinity running through all these films. For ultimately, can we believe that a man who behaves unfairly and unjustly should be awarded his masculinity through such actions? Ford repeatedly insists that honor determines a man's worth and demands of his heroes that they accept their orders and act in the name of the flag, whether at Wounded Knee, Fort Apache, or—by implication—My Lai.

All ends well in *Rio Grande* as O'Hara is left to sputter good-naturedly, if with rueful accuracy, about her "only rival—the United States Cavalry." She is made to love her man precisely as he denigrates her judgment and is allied to something "grand" in which she, as a woman, cannot be included. The cavalry provides for John Ford a pure world, more just than that of weak civilians, where a marshal can charge a recruit with manslaughter based upon an incident involving the honor of his sister. Throughout *Rio Grande* Wayne protects this man from civilian "justice," as Ford acknowledges a discrepancy between justice and law in American society and answers it with the iron discipline of a military almost Prussian in its rigor.

The final rite of manhood is granted to Wayne's son. An Indian shoots an arrow directly into Wayne's chest, and he demands that his son pull it out. The young man does so without flinching and, having passed muster, is rewarded by a rare show of dependence by Wayne: "Son, help me to my horse." Like all men, Wayne welcomes his continuity in a son.

But he will accept him only if and when the son has become a man in the father's stern image.

The forties came to a close espousing this unrelieved and unattainable male ideal. The coming decade would offer far more nuanced and complex images of men. But the distance of Brando, Dean, and Newman from the values and style of John Wayne was perhaps not as great as people believed at the time.

The Fifties

To most observers the fifties stand for conformity, a vapid celebration of the established order, and a fearful atmosphere of repression. Loyalty oaths were prevalent, as if disaffection were potentially epidemic and constant declarations required to assure that the infection had not incubated.

But had the forties differed so fundamentally, or were the categories of conformity, determinedly pursued, merely altered in the fifties? During the war, patriotic propaganda was pervasive, particularly in movies, and not in war films alone. Because Russia and America were allied, those sympathetic to the Soviet Union were patriots, more insistent than most on total abdication of the struggle for social change within America. Indeed, the Smith Act, which made advocacy of violent overthrow of the government a crime, was directed against trade unionists and their sympathizers, who continued during the war to press for higher wages, strikes, and political action independent of the New Deal, as opposed to "no strike" pledges and faith in the government of Franklin Roosevelt.

The Communists did not defend the first Smith Act prisoners, those leaders of the Teamsters who did not subordinate social struggle to support for the Democratic Party. They also were silent in 1941 when a group of Minnesota Trotskyists were tried and convicted under the same statute. (The *Daily Worker* then wrote that the Socialist Workers Party deserved no more support than the Nazis.) Thus, ironically enough, the witch hunt actually began in the early forties with support from Communist screenwriters, who were shortly to be hoist with their own petard.

As Cogley puts it, "The 'blacklisting of anti-Communists' was highly informal. It was a question of discrimination and mild treachery"[1] which relied largely on apolitical gossip and innuendo to keep their political opponents out of the industry as much as they could. ("She's such a terrible reactionary and a troublemaker too, I don't know why you'd want to have her around.") The writers in particular exploited their close relationships with producers to discourage them from hiring anticommunists of the left and right. Such "reactionaries" as John Wayne and Gary Cooper, of course, could not be touched, although the Communists tried; the profit motive overpowered their influence in these special cases. But as Cogley meticulously chronicles, the Communists' campaigns against their opponents in Hollywood constituted a mini witch hunt.

> "Trotskyite" became a hate word, endowed with loathing and horror. Enemies of the Party could be destroyed by the label. In Hollywood, philosopher John Dewey's investigation of the Moscow trials was publicly denounced in newspapers and by Party members and sympathizers. So, too, Dewey's Cultural Freedom group, which was fighting Communist influence among liberals, was the object of a bitter hate campaign. The only opposition the Communists got in Hollywood was identified by them as being anti-labor and racist-minded.[2]

In their history of the American Communist Party, Irving Howe and Lewis Coser aptly describe what can only be termed the witch-hunting mood of the Communists of the day:

> Anyone during the war years who disagreed with the Communists from the left could expect to be called an "agent of Hitler." Frequently informing to government agencies against left-wing dissidents, the Communists contributed to the corrosion of civil liberties from which they themselves were to suffer in postwar America.[3]

When World War II ended, the United States not only was the supreme military power on the planet but also had a monopoly on the atomic bomb. President Harry Truman quickly concluded that an alliance with Stalin was unnecessary and that open hostility might weaken the Stalinist regime and "roll back" Russia's sphere of influence in Eastern Europe. Fear of Russia was carefully orchestrated, even as the fear of the anticolonial revolutions spread. As social unrest increased abroad, a major recession broke out at home in 1947 in the absence of arms production. This was the setting in which the witch hunt was launched.

The cold war with Russia became the justification for identifying any

---

[1]John Cogley, *Report on Blacklisting: Part One, the Movies* (1956; reprint ed., New York: Arno Press, 1972), p. 32.
[2]Cogley, *Blacklisting*, p. 40.
[3]Irving Howe and Lewis A. Coser, *The American Communist Party: A Critical History* (1962; reprint ed., New York: Da Capo Press, 1974), p. 418.

social challenge—to rearmament, racial discrimination, or economic de-privation—with foreign subversion. The Smith Act became the basis for the entire witch hunt. Those who in the late thirties and forties had conjoined their communism to a patriotic endorsement of the established order were now persecuted by the superpatriots of the fifties. The witch hunters knew that the Communists they persecuted had been patriotic during the forties, if only because Stalin had then sought favor with the West. But with Russia as an enemy, all social dissent could be labeled pro-Soviet subversion and foreign in origin.

As always, Hollywood conformed to the orthodoxy of the moment. Films glorifying the "red squads" of the FBI as well as those excoriating the sinister Communist menace began to be made. The Communist screenwriters, moreover, were not merely so prolific following the war. The cold war had begun almost immediately, and the demands of Ameri-can culture this time could not be made to mesh with their own point of view. Nevertheless, the presence of numerous fellow travelers or Com-munist screenwriters was used to suggest that Hollywood was a hotbed of subversives.

Thus did the congressional investigating committees, from those of McCarthy and Jenner to the House Un-American Activities Committee of J. Parnell Thomas and Richard Nixon, foster an atmosphere of terror in America. People were threatened with being blacklisted and rendered permanently unemployable or imprisoned if they did not inform on innocent acquaintances. Loyalty oaths were required for jobs, grants, and passports. The "Communist menace" was used to equate independence of thought with treason and thus to cow the entire population into unthink-ing submission. And because the targets had once defended Stalin's regime as progressive, their invocation of civil liberties and individual rights in the fifties, often as courageous as it was correct, was cynically received.

The last half of the 1940s and the first part of the 1950s were a feverish time, a period of paranoia elevated to a norm. Joseph McCarthy and Richard Nixon redefined the New Deal as a decade of treason. McCarthy invented endless lists of Communist subversives as the FBI, congressional committees, the mass media, and cottage industries of blacklisters made careers out of informing, blackmail, and terror.

Paranoia was already reflected in the aesthetic of the *film noir*, which clearly foreshadowed the mood invoked by McCarthy and his friends with its imagery of pursuit in which nameless, ubiquitous forces chase the hero down dark alleys and attack him on deserted streets where observers at their windows pull down the shades and refuse to become involved. Often the shadow of the enemy methodically makes its way up a staircase while the hero, petrified, waits above for his malevolent foes to do their worst.

Few voices were raised against the McCarthyite reign of terror during the first half of the fifties. This climate easily facilitated the decision by the Supreme Court to refuse to review the contempt convictions of the Hollywood Ten, who had invoked the First Amendment in declining to testify or name names before the House Un-American Activities Committee as "friendly" witnesses. But in this cold-war epoch of loyalty oaths and conformity to the status quo, a defense based upon the Bill of Rights and its guarantees of freedom of speech, thought, and association was labeled subversive.

The American screen, like the culture at large, devoted itself in the early 1950s to the glorification and reinforcement of individual success and crass material gain, and to the most straitlaced adherence to puritan values. Prudery toward sex and all erotic feeling fueled the demeaning of women and their distorted representation on the Hollywood screen, as the camera focused on the breasts of blondes from Marilyn Monroe to Jayne Mansfield. Anti-intellectualism became rampant, both as a defense mechanism against the investigating committees and as a means of keeping business in full charge of the state. Under the pall of such moral surrender, the decade was relieved only in its last years by renewed social protest, signaled in 1957 by the Montgomery, Alabama, bus boycott led by Martin Luther King.

In retrospect, one would think that the films of the fifties would reflect the fear in the air, glorifying John Wayne and his style of masculinity with a zeal surpassing even the cavalry Westerns of John Ford. But this did not happen. It was the retrograde image of *women* in fifties films that reflected the official mood of the day. Women were sent home from the wartime workplace where they had accumulated seniority, and were encouraged not to compete with but to serve men. To make sure that the message took hold, after 1950 women were repeatedly characterized on the screen purely as sex objects. Yet in this same decade, we find for the first time since the twenties a host of films offering a complex and nuanced examination of the male psyche. Where men were concerned, the American film turned inward.

Indeed, in a society where dissent meant the loss of one's job and suicides matched in frequency those of the Depression, there was nowhere to turn but to the individual self. Alone in the privacy of one's consciousness, individuality and integrity might still survive.

The purging of the "non-anticommunists" left Hollywood depleted of much of the talent of the forties. And those who would still work in the industry had certain guidelines to follow set down by the Motion Picture Alliance for the Preservation of American Ideals. The "text" was called a "Screen Guide for Americans"; its author was "friendly" witness and reactionary Ayn Rand. American films were not to "smear the free-enterprise system." They were neither to "deify the 'common man'" nor to "glorify the collective." Nor were they to "glorify failure" or "smear success." And, perhaps above all, they were not to "smear industrialists." In 1956 the Fund for the Republic published John Cogley's *Report on Blacklisting, I: Movies,* for which, by the 1984 logic of the fifties, Cogley himself was then blacklisted!

Social rebellion was obviously denied to the screen male, for even pseudo-rebellion in which the government ultimately reforms, such as that pictured in *Mr. Smith Goes to Washington,* could be challenged for its loyalty. It is a sad irony that those accused by the Un-American Activities Committee, from screenwriter Dalton Trumbo (as Richard Corliss points out, Hollywood's highest-paid writer at the time with the possible exception of Ben Hecht) on down, had never in their films proposed that the hero define his masculinity in rebellion against the American social order. Their films were the most gloriously patriotic, the most unquestioning in their loyalty to the American war effort. They had never asked for a male who would attack injustice at its roots, as Steinbeck does in *The Grapes of Wrath,* but for men who would speak on behalf of the established order about defending "the people"; their eyes had been focused on the needs of the Soviet Union, and they had never in their art depicted an honest struggle against those injustices haunting America. That Stalinist left which had been so influential in Hollywood until after the war never admitted what it was they *did* believe.[4]

The films of the fifties reveal the psychic price the culture paid for repression of the right to disagree with social policy. The right even to propose alterations in an inhospitable world was inaccessible. This repression led to an outpouring of frustration and rage, depression and confusion, which could not help but surface in the American film. Many of the screen males of the fifties for whom politics holds not the slightest interest nevertheless feel deeply alienated from the world, that society to which earlier heroes had no trouble adjusting.

The stress upon conformity thus only brought to light the lurking presence of the need to form individual judgments. The rebel appeared for the first time as a positive male model in the American film. Whether he was tamed or chastised by the closing scenes, his presence produced a positive result, a real deepening of the image of men in film. Men were given intellects, ideas which put them in opposition to the demands made

---

[4]Typical of their Communist Party memberships, as cited in Cogley, was Sidney Buchman's, from 1938 to 1945; Budd Schulberg was a member from 1937 through 1940; Edward Dmytryk, from 1944 to 1945. And so it went. But Dalton Trumbo depicts, in his letters published as *Additional Dialogue* (Philadelphia: M. Evans, 1970), the issue of membership with the most wit and cynicism: "I joined the Communist Party in 1944 and left it in 1948 on the ground that I should in future be far too busy to attend its meetings, which were, in any event, dull beyond description and about as revolutionary in purpose as Wednesday evening testimonial services in the Christian Science Church" (p. 459). These words, one might add, reveal Trumbo speaking in the late fifties.

upon them by others. They were humanized. In certain areas of the culture the same pattern prevailed. A new interest in psychology was nurtured by the political repressiveness of the time. Robert Lindner wrote a book called *Must You Conform?* (1956), offering a strange paradox. The very renewal of concern for the health of the inner self led inevitably to the expression, if not the successful implementation, of social rebellion. The original need for repression produced a new concern for the impera- tives of the self. And once it knew what it was, this self turned, inevitably, to experiences in the outside world in which it could be realized. Lindner argued that the fifties' demand for a "mass man," a conforming male whose life was controlled by pressure from without, led to the develop- ment of a psychopathic personality. Every human being, wrote Lindner, has an instinct for rebellion that must be given some arena for expression. Postwar American society offered it none:

> Forced from without to conform, and from within to rebel, he makes a
> compromise: he rebels within the confines of conformity, he discharges his
> protest within the limits set by the social order he has by now permitted
> to be erected around him. [p. 27]

Films of the fifties like *The Blackboard Jungle* (1955) and *Rebel Without a Cause,* based loosely upon one of Lindner's own studies by the same title, admitted the prevalence in the tame fifties of an antisocial personal- ity. A variety of films were made about rebellious youth and the turmoil within the psyches of those who had been deprived of rebellion in other than irrationally destructive forms.

Thus there appeared on the screen male personalities crackling with undirected energy, sexually alive precisely to the degree that they did not conform. Marlon Brando and James Dean seemed to be pure and total rebels in those fifties films—an impression that is less than accurate, for by the end of many of the films that offered alienated, tormented heroes, traditional values were reasserted. The hero was brought around and forced to conform, or he saw the desirability of acceptance. But these "resolutions" fooled no one, and audiences responded to Brando, Dean, and Montgomery Clift because people cherished their independence and the irrepressible energy they exuded. In the same way, we remember Katharine Hepburn in *Adam's Rib* for her self-assertion and are willing to forget the ending in which she capitulates to husband Spencer Tracy's demand that she cease competing and, by implication, become more "feminine."

Film males were being granted new and greater psychological space than screen heroes modeled on Cooper or Wayne. Anyone who protested against the fifties paranoia and its emasculation of individual expression would presumably find little fault with a Hollywood which glorified rebels. It seemed liberating that despite the limitations imposed by a repressive society, film recovered for men an individual self with a distinctive identity and a flourishing ego. Marlon Brando and James Dean, the most electrifying male stars of the fifties, offered in their personal magnetism and inward exploration Hollywood's inventive obeisance to those frightened by official political terror and the frantic orthodoxy engendered by the witch hunt. Thus did individual Americans who identified with their male stars still retain autonomous personalities with the right to imagine themselves free and self-determined. Even when these heroes are forced to adapt to convention or social pressure in *pro forma* endings, they concede with grace and self-possession. They display an assertiveness and flair, as well as sensitivity and concern, a combination of qualities that compares in its diversity to the range of attributes displayed by male stars of the twenties.

Brando, Dean, Clift, and Paul Newman played characters so intriguing that they beguiled us into forgetting the nature of the times, suggesting that the grey oppressiveness was but an external, surface condition. If a man in his own life feared that the slightest dissent might rob him of his job, on screen he could identify vicariously with proud, rebellious spirits whom no one ultimately could tame. The parallel with the thirties is striking. Screen males of the thirties, from Gable to Flynn, distracted out-of-work audiences from their troubles and that real emasculation caused by the inability to function imposed by the Depression. These male stars were the strong, untrammeled figures men might be in their dreams.

As in the thirties, fifties Hollywood compensated for the absence of indispensable components of a fulfilled life. If bread was lacking in the thirties, intellectual freedom had vanished in the fifties. Films offered images of men capable of forging exciting lives, personalities larger than life and far grander than the audience male could be. In an era of nationally orchestrated paranoia, Hollywood on screen turned with unprecedented openness and intensity to the exploration of what it means to be a man.

Agonies of self-examination pervade films of the fifties. In the knowledge that advocacy of dissent would induce a summons before an investigating committee or feed the predatory blackmail industry epitomized by *Red Channels* and *Hollywood Confidential,* Hollywood replaced social dissent with a fascinating and serious examination of *sexual* politics. The assumed definitions of the male sex role were challenged as films discovered the male capable of sensitivity and an open expression of tenderness, feelings which in the forties were ridiculed as effeminate. Out of the depths of cultural reaction, films began to recognize that men could not nor should they wish to be male in the manner of John Wayne. It was a touchstone of this era that any man might be susceptible to the charge that his ideas were unorthodox and jeopardized "national security." In so overwhelming an atmosphere, the vulnerability of the ideal screen male became the experience of all, and on the screen it was now not merely acceptable but desirable, an indispensable aspect of male sexuality.

Screen males whose private lives were explored so microscopically were given sufficient license to look inward, not just to divert from, but to compensate for what was denied the audiences in their political life in the real world. It was not merely television that threatened the film industry. Movies could not survive as a form of entertainment by internalizing in all its bleakness the mentality of the "grey flannel suit" which dominated the fifties. No one's imagination could be stirred by so boring an ideal as that of the organization man. Brando and Dean relieved us of our boredom and permitted Hollywood to regain an audience which in its demoralization had been captured by pathetic television fare consisting of pratfalls and the banalities of Milton Berle.

Besieged audiences were bolstered by Hollywood in the fifties by being shown that it was all right to be shaken, to experience a crisis of self-confidence. It was a relief to find affirmation on the screen that there were worse offenses than not living up to the image of Humphrey Bogart's Sam Spade or John Wayne's John Wayne. Hollywood in the fifties provided us with a fascinating paradox. In the world of America men could neither move nor think freely or without inhibition. On celluloid the male, driven inward, returned with a heightened consciousness. For the first time since the advent of sound, men in films were sentient, thoughtful, understanding of weakness (including their own), and quietly perceptive.

I

If anguish and tortured self-examination have always been part of the male experience, they surface at last on the American screen with Kirk Douglas as the obsessive, misguided hero of *Detective Story* (1951). In spite of its police setting, gone is the male ability to resolve problems in physical combat, whether on the sands of Iwo Jima or in battle with crime. Physical action is seen in *Detective Story* as an *evasion*, a false means for a man's realizing himself. In its denial of consciousness in favor of force, physical activity is portrayed as inauthentic and scarcely "masculine."

Douglas plays detective McCloud, an antecedent of Eastwood's Dirty Harry Callahan, who is not above using a rubber hose to extract a confession from one of the "criminals" he ensnares. But McCloud's forays into police brutality are not applauded here as they will be in *Dirty Harry*. In *Detective Story* they are facets of a psychopathic, rigid male personality whose aggression flows from unresolved childhood pain. The adult detective who abuses his power is accurately revealed as a sick person who ruins his life and those of others through his inability to free himself from the traumas of his early years. Given the frequent association of male sexuality with violence in the American film, the unequivocal exposure of McCloud's underlying motives, joined to disdain for the brutality of his police methods, represents a distinct departure.

McCloud is a manic detective who cannot stay away from the police station. Neglecting a beautiful and loving wife (Eleanor Parker), he prefers to hang around the precinct office even when he is off duty. At times he fails to go home for days. His compulsion to "clean up" the streets is seen by director William Wyler as pathological, an impulse drawn from low self-esteem and projected outward into the world.

With the ferreting out of hidden motivation so characteristic of the fifties, *Detective Story* probes McCloud's character, focusing on his consuming hatred of his father, whom he despises as an "abortionist" and for whom he was never good enough. In keeping with the new-found introspection of the hero, Freudian ideas, more or less bowdlerized, make their appearance in many fifties films, and they are handled in a far more conscious manner than they were in the twenties or thirties. But despite the easy Freudianism into which it falls, *Detective Story* consistently and intently explores the inner life of this character, offering a style of interior examination new to the American film. McCloud is neither an anti-hero nor a villain disguised as a hero soon to be unmasked. He is a man with personal strengths and devastating limitations—a recognizable human being.

A further insight of this film into the conventional male psyche is its recognition that extreme violence is usually accompanied by rigid sexual repression; dread passes as puritanism. The film centers on McCloud's discovery that his own wife once had an abortion, yielding to the knife of the same "butcher" he as a policeman has been bent upon nailing. His wife pleads for forgiveness, explaining that she dared not tell him for fear of his disgust. But McCloud responds as if she had confessed to a mutilation murder. Fifties morality, if critical of this man for his inability to forgive one lapse, still maintained that the woman was expected to be virginal and that abortion was a seamy, sordid act, unworthy of any decent person. Men still saw themselves as possessors of women and arbiters of their bodies, without much irony on the part of the director.

In his vindictiveness toward the abortionist Schneider, whom he has already been attempting to put in the electric chair and "personally to pull the switch," McCloud loses all rationality. The obsessive quest to punish Schneider dehumanizes him; he even attempts to induce a girl in critical condition to identify Schneider as her abortionist. In the paddy wagon, McCloud brutally beats the man up. In all these acts McCloud is seen as self-destructive and unjust, a man whose childhood trauma has blinded him to the realities of the present.

McCloud loses his wife, who is otherwise devoted, passive, and demure, because he cannot purge his mind of the "dirty" images she has put there through confessing to the premarital affair that led to her abortion. A full shot focuses on his clenched fist. His rage is at once frenzied and unjustifiable as he shrieks, "I'd rather go to jail for twenty years than find out my wife is a tramp." In what the film perceives as a distortion, he now sees his wife as "everything I hate." In saner moments McCloud recognizes that he needs and loves her, but so out of touch is he with what matters to him in the present that his compulsion paralyzes him and he loses all.

His conflict leads McCloud to break down, and, like many fifties heroes, he cries. "I couldn't go home if you weren't waiting for me," he tells his wife, the very next moment humiliating her viciously: "How many others were there?" In the process of humanizing the male image, fifties films, unaware of the direct relation between male rigidity and female passivity, still insisted endlessly upon the virginal purity of the woman. She must never have had a man other than her husband and certainly must never have become pregnant or allowed herself to fall into the hands of an abortionist. If men look inward, women in the fifties films continue to have *tabula rasa* minds, waiting to be imprinted with male values. McCloud is clearly condemned for intolerance. But the film endorses his disgust with the good woman who turns out not to have been "good" at all. Her crime remains that of presenting herself as a domesticated nice girl only to be revealed as a loose woman at heart.

McCloud becomes a victim both of his own irrationality and of fifties America's sexual puritanism with its insane notion that unmarried women must repress any and all sexual appetite. Under the stress of his own desperate need for control over her, parallel to his need to hold down his own self-hatred, McCloud disintegrates. "I wish," he declaims, "I could take out my brain, hold it under the faucet, and wash away the dirty picture she put there." McCloud has become, in spite of himself, everything he hated in his own father.

But part of the subtlety of *Detective Story*, and what makes its psychoanalytic treatment of the male psyche far less simplistic than other Freudian borrowings on screen, is that it recognizes that knowledge is not enough. Detective McCloud can finally do nothing to change the fact that he has built his whole life on hating his father. He may at some level become aware of this, but he is unable to achieve release because he has not been brought to re-experience the pain of the past in the present. Without some emotional confrontation with the roots of our personal behavior, just discovering intellectually what they are will not suffice. *Detective Story* raises certain issues about the psychic origins of the masculine mystique, but it does not pursue what change finally requires.

Near the end McCloud attains some sympathy for the adversary who has haunted him all his life. He calls his father a "poor devil," and admits that "maybe he couldn't help himself either." Convincingly, the moment does not lead to any easy liberation for McCloud, although it is authentic and fine, allowing an honest glimpse into the psyche of the violent male. In the end McCloud loses his life, as Wyler proves unable to resolve the psychic paralysis of his hero.

Detective Story achieved a departure for the male image on screen, taking psychic conflict as a major theme and examining how unresolved childhood trauma directs adult behavior, even to a man's ruin. It defined violence as an expression of insufficient masculine maturity, and presented maleness in terms of action derived from felt emotion instead of from the repression of all softer feelings on behalf of unremitting combat with the world. So obsessed, a strong and vibrant man like McCloud will, in his own words, "drown in his own juice," undermined in his case by his terror and hatred of his father, unavowed for so long and projected into the present. The anatomizing of McCloud's personality set the tone for a number of penetrating glimpses into the male psyche in films during the fifties.

The psychological space which opened up in this decade provided Humphrey Bogart with his most unique role, as Charlie Allnut in *The African Queen* (1951). It was his first Academy Award performance, one entirely deserved and allowing Bogart one of the few opportunities in his career to play the male as he most often is. John Huston, who had directed Bogart as the indefatigable Sam Spade in *The Maltese Falcon,* now gives us a hero who is the polar opposite of that immovable tough-guy detective. If, as a riverboating trader in East Africa, he operates in an exotic setting redolent of romance, Bogart is here both unromantic and entirely ordinary, a grubby, unshaven fifty-year-old, more the beach bum than the lifeguard. He belches, scratches, smells, and blinks with incredulity. Precisely because he is an unpretentious human being, free of the need of violence, he can rise to both heroism and tender affection without bravado or a catatonic surrender of his facial mobility. He has moments of doubt, and he experiences danger with rational fear. He is, in fact, a normal man without the need to play supermale or to regard women as either threats or objects to be subdued.

Living at the time of World War I, Charlie Allnut has nothing in particular against the Germans and doesn't even know what the war is about. Until he meets spinster missionary Rosie (Katharine Hepburn), he lives hand to mouth, answerable to no one, improvident but carefree. In a reversal as unique as it is psychologically liberating for the male image, it is only by falling in love with a strong, heroic woman, whose independence and audacity allow him to ignore her missionary, spinsterish exterior, that Allnut discovers his own male potential. Bogart, who both by

Katharine Hepburn and Humphrey Bogart in *The African Queen:* He belches, scratches, smells, and blinks with incredulity. He has moments of
doubt, and he experiences danger with rational fear. He is, in fact, a normal
man, without the need to play supermale or to regard women as either
threats or objects to be subdued.

Hollywood's sexual standards and his own had been teamed with Lauren
Bacall, a woman half his age, falls in love here with a skinny, aging
Hepburn, a woman tougher, more spirited, and far more capable of
initiative than he.

It is Hepburn whose vision embraces braving a river never explored,
rapids that will almost certainly smash their patched-up little steamer into
fragments, to sneak past armed fortifications and torpedo the German
ship *Louisa* stationed on Lake Victoria. Charlie, sensibly, considers her
rash and reckless, convinced that they'll never make it. It is she, in a
reversal of Hollywood's male and female roles, who is undaunted and
supremely confident. Charlie is a lazy little man, addicted to drinking gin
straight out of the bottle. Rosie has more of the qualities we are accus-

tomed to appreciate in men: courage, stamina, determination, the love of adventure and risk—true grit. And these seem, not the result of her upper-class origins in contrast to Charlie's proletarian background, but aspects of the personality of a woman who only happens to be of aristocratic birth. They are equals, not because she matches his male superiority with class supremacy, but because of their capacities as human beings. Yet he has the know-how with respect to the boat, its failing engine, and the perils of navigation.

Their relationship becomes one of the most equitable and mutually respecting in the history of American cinema, including those films in which Hepburn was teamed with Spencer Tracy. In the Tracy films, the man had the edge, that moment of superiority which differentiated him from the woman. Bogart as Charlie is more a man who can take the lead from a dynamic woman. His masculinity is actually stirred and developed by *her* sexual awakening, which emerges, delightfully and symbolically, with their furious descent down the rapids.

The days when she called him a "coward" for his caution and he, with equal justice, retorted by dubbing her a "crazy old maid" have passed as they draw together under the spur of her irrepressible spirit. They become intimate, true partners, the woman as physically capable as the man. He dives down to the river bottom to examine the damage to the rudder. She descends after him to help remove the shaft. Side by side they work to fashion a new propeller. The grubby, solitary Bogart, now romantically transformed, compares himself and his woman to Antony and Cleopatra on their barge. Nor is Bogart diminished as a man by his physical weakness. At one point leeches attach themselves to his back as he shudders in revulsion. He removes his shirt, exposing a scrawny body, not without some flab, hardly the physique of a Charles Bronson muscled like that of an arrested adolescent. Charlie Allnut is more a man, a person of maturity and emotional range, precisely because he has weaknesses familiar to us all. No matter that he is self-conscious about his body: "Fine specimen of a man *I* am," he regrets, shaking all the while with fever.

The sexual arousal and consummation between Hepburn and Bogart in this film is touchingly reciprocal. He puts his hand shyly on her shoulder. She covers his diffidently with hers, a gesture of discovery and trust that causes him to become newly aware of his masculinity. "Nothing a man can't do if he believes in himself," exults Charlie Allnut. Neither is coy nor tries to dominate the other. They emerge as equal in every way, so much so that each insists that the other leave the boat while the one remaining risks death in the blowing up of the *Louisa*. They resolve their genuine effort each to preserve the other by going together, he at the engine, she at the rudder. Far from feeling threatened either by Rosie's leadership or her help, Charlie needs, accepts, and welcomes both.

Captured by the Germans in a marvelous fantasy ending, they each confess to the crime of attempted sabotage. Neither would dream of outliving the other. Sentenced to death by the Germans, they ask as their last wish to be married before being executed. And in homage to this terribly moving relationship, their Nile barge the *African Queen*, as if of its own volition, responding to their natural royalty, torpedoes the *Louisa* alone as the big ship strikes the hand-fashioned missile now protruding from the *Queen's* capsized hull.

But Bogart and Hepburn are already safe in the water, married and alive. Singing in glee, they swim out of the frame. Wayne and Cooper never knew what they were missing in so studiously avoiding women equal in spirit to themselves instead of welcoming this exuberance as part of their own fulfillment. Only when we see, as in this remarkable film, how much emotional abandon is liberated by an unrepressed acceptance of the opposite sex do we register fully the distorted demeanor of the stolid and emotionally crippled male visited upon us like a contagious pathology by so many Hollywood films.

II

In terms of the male image, the fifties were illuminated most by Marlon Brando and the male personality he brought to the screen. In his roles of this period, Brando conveyed how the traditional toughness and tight-lipped invulnerability of the male hero were actually defense mechanisms as opposed to emblems of masculinity. The more unfeeling the screen male, Brando showed us, the more disturbed he was and the more to be pitied. With Brando the male ideal became a person capable of expressing feelings. Through his sensitivity Brando demonstrated that the tougher and more unyielding a male, the less in control of himself he really was.

Brando projected an enormous physical vitality. If he was sensitive, he was also strong. Sometimes the raw masculinity he brought to the screen prevented the tender aspects of his personality from surfacing, as in *A Streetcar Named Desire* (1951). Stanley Kowalski is a fifties swashbuckler one step down the social scale. In torn T-shirt, biceps bulging as he yells "Where's my woman?" he is the cave man set loose, a Lawrentian fantasy of the earthy, animal, proletarian male. He is an early "midnight cowboy," born of a homosexual imagination. But there is a difference between Brando even as Stanley Kowalski and someone like Burt Reynolds playing himself in the seventies.

The Brando performance offers an implicit rejection of Stanley Kowalski all the while that it appeals to us with its uninhibited sexuality. The association of sexuality with violence is challenged, for the Stanley who rapes his wife's sister and engineers her commitment to an insane asylum is no ideal male. There is something utterly repellent about him, even though he offers the ultimate sexual gratification to a woman, an ability testified to by his passive wife, Stella (Kim Hunter), who can "hardly stand it" when Stanley is away for a single night. The sensual male has a great deal going for him, but Brando's stunning, complex performance makes it clear that a Stanley Kowalski, with his drunken all-night poker games which degenerate into mindless brawls, is not ultimately the most desirable sexual partner. The "real man" in Stanley's world is what Blanche calls him, "an animal, subhuman, bearing raw meat home from the jungle," and in this the film endorses Blanche as much as it sides with the male.

However much the audience is to thrill to Stanley as the vital, physical male whose sexual virtuosity is never in doubt, the image is modified by the perception that Stanley is often no more than a scared little boy, an aspect of the film's psychology that fits in well with the fifties interest in exploring the hidden aspects of the male personality. When he is sober, Stanley calls for Stella as if she were his mother. Without her, he feels helpless. When his needs are not immediately gratified Stanley bursts out crying and yells like a baby. Far from the domineering cave man he seems, Stanley is revealed as the male in need. His anger at Blanche flows from his fear that his symbiotic relationship with Stella will be ended by her sister's snobbery and jealousy. Stanley's bravado is clearly a reaction to his actual powerlessness. Director Kazan takes pains to visualize the shabbiness of Stanley's world, the tiny apartment symbolizing how little, finally, he has to offer Stella. For all his loud pretense, Stanley has no real control over the circumstances of his life, and out of this actual impotence concealed by sexual prowess, Stanley invokes, absurdly, the "Napoleonic Code" which would protect his interests in "Belle Reeve," the family estate of Blanche and Stella. All Stanley really has is himself, a self confused, uncertain, threatened, and like real men everywhere, vicious when crossed, violent when abused.

It is from this fear and powerlessness that Stanley finally destroys Blanche, who has so invaded his life. If he strikes out at her sexually, it is the only device he has been taught. And in his betrayal of Blanche to the naïve Mitch, her suitor, Stanley behaves like a cornered animal safeguarding his turf against a predatory invader. Quoting Huey Long, he declaims, "Every man's a king, and I'm king here," but his need to announce it expresses nothing so much as his self-doubt. Blanche's taunt that he is a "Polack" and hence a "swine" enrages him because of that persistent feeling of inferiority which Brando the actor manages to slip past the cruel, egomaniacal antics of Stanley Kowalski.

In each of Brando's fifties roles he portrayed a male who had to become a man despite weaknesses, whether physical, economic, social, or intellec-

Marlon Brando with Vivien Leigh in *A Streetcar Named Desire:* The "real man" in Stanley's world is what Blanche calls him, "an animal, subhuman, bearing raw meat home from the jungle."

tual. In *The Men* (1951), his first film, he played a paraplegic, paralyzed from the waist down during the war and struggling to remain a man despite this handicap. The paralysis is symbolic of the general powerlessness felt during the repressive fifties with its blacklists and insistence upon conformity. More skillfully and feelingly than any actor before him on the Hollywood screen, Brando brought the mood of the ordinary man to his screen characterizations. His instant acclaim was a response to the weakness he projected as well as to the human strength he summoned to see him through adversity. His anger and passion transcended his roles, breaking through the screen as his own.

The Men is also exceptional because its protagonist is not afraid to admit to fear: "I was scared ... I couldn't feel anything from the waist down ... I was afraid I was gonna die. Now I'm afraid I'm gonna live." He remains finally a man who must spend his life in a wheelchair, a man who "cannot make a woman happy." Yet he will still marry his old girlfriend (Teresa Wright), for in facing his limitations and accepting them he can offer her much, more perhaps than if he were "whole" but unable to give of himself. It is in this emergence that he finds purpose and a reason to live, revealing how truly crippled are most men, who, lacking self-discovery, never arrive at such a point of consciousness.

What was revolutionary about Brando was his presentation, his joining an indispensable sensitivity to the characterization of a male who was as violent and "macho" as any screen hero before him. If he is a soul-searching paraplegic, Brando retains power and the force of a passionate temperament. A man of highly conventional values, he was once an athlete. The grit of the one-time athlete leads him finally to reach for the hand exerciser and begin the struggle to remake a life for himself.

But for all this, Brando remains far from completely revolutionizing the male image on film. He often reverts to the most archaic, shopworn imperatives of screen masculinity. A real man does not give up; neither does paraplegic Brando. Courage is still what counts as Brando in *The Men* harks back to and revives that rough, mythic masculinity of the man who fights on no matter the odds. Despite his paralysis he remains a physical specimen with powerful chest and biceps. The more restricted his body, the more he pursues athletics—which have, fortuitously, become irrelevant: bowling, basketball, and swimming—as if these endeavors remained essential tests of manliness. The cultural pursuits one would expect to be at least a dimension of the life of the sedentary person remain remote.

What was unique in *The Men* was the open theme of the loss of manhood, the explicit acknowledgment of the existence of sexual impotence, even if it was shielded from being shameful through attribution to physical paralysis. Brando's sensitivity is in evidence, as when he is allowed to cry, expressing openly the pain of his condition and departing from the obligatory suppression of feelings of despair in the manner of

John Wayne. The Brando male thus presents a leap into screen maturity, for he is a person who learns to accept and live with weakness—a permanent rebuke to those then and now who fawn sentimentally on the male image of "the Duke."

In a particularly painful scene, Brando insists, while getting married to Wright, upon standing up unaided without holding on. He loses his footing and slips, no facile Western hero who can overcome any obstacle. At home with his bride, he reacts to her nervousness by going into spasms. In a credible loss of nerve, he feels he can no longer live with his condition and retreats to the hospital, only to be forced to return to married life by his fellow paraplegics. The ending is no less explicit. "Do you want me to help you up the steps?" asks his wife. "Please," he must respond, for he knows he cannot make it alone. The admission of this failure, including his lack of sexual function, does not render him unmanly. In this rather small and aesthetically insignificant film, Brando participates in moments which fully transcend the traditional image of men on screen.

Viva Zapata (1952) added dimensions to the Brando screen persona missing from both *Streetcar* and *The Men*. To what had become in Brando an earthy, primitive, and spontaneously sensual image was added the quest for social justice. Even in the repressive fifties, Brando's films could associate maleness with social rebellion. His performance in *Viva Zapata* in particular rises above the film's own suggestion of an inherent corruption in revolutionary power. Elements of Kazan's own left-wing past emerge in the image of Emiliano Zapata; and Brando as Zapata, riding a white horse, a vibrant image of the male as liberator, transcends the jaded personal politics of Kazan in the fifties.

Part of the Zapata portrayal draws upon Brando's Stanley Kowalski. Zapata is fundamentally a physical man, as restless as a horse that "has got the scent of a mare." His illiteracy is intended to add to his sensuality. Simplicity allows him to be close to his real feelings. He is a man who can send a friend to Texas to look at Madero's face in order to determine whether he can be trusted. Primitive energy bubbles up in Brando's Zapata, as if from an underground stream of violence which may gush forth at any moment—a frequent characteristic of Brando on screen.

However pleased he is to be simply a husband and father, Zapata defines his manhood in terms of his inability to stand by without intervening as people are tormented. Living amidst injustice, he has no choice but to struggle, and he leads an armed band, a motif extraordinary for the fifties, and permissible in part because the setting is so exotically foreign.

Kazan immunizes his subject by suggesting that power itself corrupts, whatever the social order. Only Zapata's selfless abdication spares him from assuming the role of oppressor himself. But by returning to the countryside he leaves the field to a professional "revolutionary," who cynically re-creates the cycle of repression and exploitation in the name of the revolution. In the cold war this patent allusion to Stalinism was particularly welcome because Kazan equated all revolutionary conquest with this result. Zapata, as the conscience of his people, walks away from power and renews the struggle only to be betrayed in an ambush into which he is lured.

Hence, despite its nominally revolutionary subject and its identification of masculinity with revolt, Kazan deployed these themes for a deeply antirevolutionary conclusion, one much favored in the Hollywood of the day. He never conceived of a revolutionary struggle that had democratic results, as if, unlike his own character Zapata, whose point of view was the reverse, Kazan himself saw the people as sheep incapable of preserving popular control. Kazan separated psychological nuance in the male from a successful realization of dissident social ends.

Viva Zapata is in striking contrast to John Huston's more daring film *We Were Strangers*, made three years earlier in 1949 before the blacklisting was in full sway. John Garfield as the American in Cuba who joins the revolution may die, like Zapata, but the revolution is both triumphant and liberating. His Cuban comrades mourn him with a tribute meant to inspire Americans at large to remember their own revolutionary tradition. Garfield's performance, and Huston's film, unlike Kazan's, corresponded to the actor's defiance of the congressional committees and the witch hunt. Garfield's personal stand led to his virtual blacklisting, and it is possible that the hounding he endured led to his death from a heart attack at the age of thirty-nine in 1952, ironically the very year of Kazan's *Viva Zapata*.

It should also be noted that Kazan's conception of the revolutionary did not include any transcendence of the most macho approach to women. Rebel Brando never prefers women who are themselves rebels, and in this he is no different from Gary Cooper in *High Noon*, who prefers the passive, cloying Grace Kelly to a woman in his own style, the character played by Katy Jurado. Zapata too chooses the well-bred, repressed woman of strict morality before whom he can be dominant and superior. Like all the Brando screen marriages—with, of course, the exception of *The Men*—theirs promises strong sexual fulfillment and the prospect of procreation. Yet, unexpectedly, the nuance and sensitivity we have come to expect of Brando on the screen surface in *Viva Zapata* as well. Naked to the waist in the tradition of the Hollywood male, the illiterate Zapata sits down to his first reading lesson with a teacher—his wife.

Remarkable as well in Brando's Zapata is the refusal of the hero to assume the mantle of leadership so willingly accepted by the Wayne-style screen male. Upon winning, Zapata demands the distribution of the land to the peasants, refusing to settle for less than the revolution for which he originally fought. He wants nothing for himself and refuses to accept power without substance. He is incapable of acquiescing in corruption in order to retain that power or of equating his person, let alone dictatorial rule, with the revolution.

Nor would he preserve revolutionary power itself if so doing entails violating the original aims for which the revolution was fought. Brando's Zapata, superb as he appears, insists that men like himself are not needed, but that ordinary men must believe in their own power to shape their lives: "There are only men like yourselves," he says, "no leaders but yourselves . . . a strong people is the only lasting strength." He will stake his life and die, refusing the patriarchal role of "protector" of weaker men, women, and children. In implicit judgment upon the authoritarian, patronizing role of the male as protector and strong man—the dominant masculine image in American films—Zapata argues openly that such people and such a role insult those so "protected" and deny them the opportunity to develop their own potential as adult human beings. And, finally, Zapata's death functions as another instance of the freedom of the Brando screen male from the burden of invulnerability.

In *The Wild One* (1953) Brando brought to the screen the alienated adolescent of the fifties, Robert Lindner's rebel without a cause. Garbed in a black leather jacket, mounted on a motorcycle, and surrounded by a gang of cronies in the same style, he unfolds the confusion and lack of self-worth of gang members. Their effort is to forge a subgroup to which they can belong with a code, dress, and language rendering them both different and accepted. In their utter conformity to the norms of this surrogate family, these youngsters announce their need to win approval and affirmation, even as their posture of defiance is a complaint against a society that does not value them or see them as anything more than victims to be forced to conform.

Responding to the anguish of all those youths of the fifties, Brando presented the defiant young male, all the while revealing a pathetic emptiness and the thinness of their tough veneer. Johnny (Brando) at one point is asked, "What are you rebelling against?" He doesn't know. His credo, we learn, is a kind of petulant self-assertion: "Nobody tells me what to do."

Like the hero of *Viva Zapata*, Johnny prefers a "good" girl to whom he can condescend as opposed to a rebel like himself. His attraction to the hard-working waitress renders him deeply sympathetic, proof to us that he has a good heart, an inner core of decency for which he has no outlet. The whores with whom he has been acquainted are now unceremoniously brushed off. Brando as rebel is simultaneously appealing and innocent, and he is never the instigator of gang warfare. In *The Wild One* Brando portrays the rebel as a positive hero, his isolation from conventional norms necessary for the integrity he seeks to preserve. Beneath an outward show of strength his tenderness awaits release by the right woman. Beyond his violence lies vulnerability, a personal configura-

In *The Wild One* Brando portrays the rebel as a positive hero, his isolation from conventional norms necessary for the integrity he seeks to preserve. His tenderness awaits release by the right woman.

tion through which Brando created an entirely new sexual ideal. When he is beaten by the "good citizens" of the town, who mistake him for a marauding thug, Brando's Johnny sits down and cries, a man clearly in touch with his feelings and, as such, an appealing model.

The Wild One is too honest to provide Brando with what so many of Gable's films imposed on him. Brando's inner-directed male is not at the film's conclusion mired in domesticity of a kind which would rob him of the freedom to be autonomous (although the ending of *The Wild One* sustains the male myth that commitment to a woman deprives a man of full masculinity). But settling down would have violated the questing, restless, rebellious spirit Brando imparts in this film, and fortunately he is not made to renounce the open road for a routine life-style.

The integrity of the character requires that he retain the capacity to rebel, and to defy all conventions that would rob him of his dissidence, however undirected it may be. If the vehicle of the gang proves limiting, requiring a conformity of its own, it had first involved a repudiation of stultifying "straight" society, foreshadowing the counterculture and radicalization of the sixties, of which it was a causal antecedent. Johnny cannot become another hypocritical "good citizen," although the gang's ways have proven to be but another sham. Brando in these vibrant films of the fifties gave the screen an autonomous, quick-witted, shrewdly critical male bursting with energy and honesty, a figure whom society had denied any meaningful outlet for his unique and untamed persona.

Brando's finest characterization of the fifties would be as Terry Malloy in *On the Waterfront* (1954). Starting as a brooding, confused, and punchdrunk ex-boxer, Terry discovers how to be a man. Weak, uneducated, and used by union thugs for dirty jobs, Terry Malloy is a man always at the bidding of others. His first act in the film is to betray a friend, Joey Doyle, who as a consequence is killed for his opposition to the gangsters controlling the union. Doyle is the brother of a girl, played by Eva Marie Saint, with whom Terry will fall in love, precipitating his own rebellion against the hoods who use him.

No anti-hero, Malloy is at first virtually anti-human. Unable to speak clearly and unaware of who or what he is, Terry Malloy spies for the corrupt union oligarchy. Nor is he at this point the conscience of the film, a role occupied by the priest, played by Karl Malden, who rallies the union rank and file with such patriotic claptrap as "We in this country have a way of fighting back." Terry, like so many screen heroes before him, begins by thinking only of himself: "Me, I'm with me."

Yet Terry has many positive qualities, all at odds with the rough masculine stereotype associated with a former prizefighter. He raises pigeons to which he is devoted. He is capable of intimacy and of very sweet gestures: as he and Saint walk and talk during a bitterly cold December in New York, he puts on one of her gloves so that she is wearing one and he the other. The vulnerable aspects of his nature intermingle with those predictable on screen in the stridently masculine male. In parochial school he was always being whacked by the sisters— rather as expected, since real men are supposed to be obstreperous as boys. But Brando relates this to the girl, not as bravado, but as a way of showing his hurt, and her response to his confidence returns us to the psychological treatment of the male personality characteristic of these remarkable films of the fifties. Saint would have used "more patience and kindness" on Terry the boy. Brutally masculine male behavior does not flow from innate aggressiveness, as Lionel Tiger, an apologist for rigid and established mores, contends in *Men in Groups*. Rather, such young men are violent as a result of lacking love, of being starved of essential affection and acceptance as themselves, deprivations which result in projected rage and a morbid fear of feeling, which is then mediated by a rigid, repressed personality—the very model extolled previously on the Hollywood screen. When men are tough on the outside, it is solely because they have been conditioned to be, not because it is their inherent disposition.

Softness and vulnerability are expressed through the Brando portrayal in *On the Waterfront* as wholly desirable male characteristics. Although Terry, as a boxer, has conventional male credentials, these are not presented as grounds for pride but as an indication that his real self has been suppressed. His love for his pigeons is shown to flow from their affection for each other, which touches a deep longing in himself. The pigeons, Terry wistfully relates, "marry and stay that way until one of them dies." He would like to be loved in the same way. The masculine myth of domesticity as emasculating is swept away, revealed as detrimental to male well-being because it equates the need for love and companionship with menace to the self.

Terry must recover his soul, spiritually and in social terms, for union racketeer Johnny Friendly (Lee J. Cobb) literally owns him. When Terry was a boxer, Friendly had "bought a piece of me." Emotional deprivation, rooted in his having been raised in a children's home, accounts both for Terry's lack of economic autonomy and for his personal belligerence and his philosophy of "Do it to him before he does it to you. Down here it's every man for himself." Before the fifties such attitudes were often regarded as perfectly befitting the masculine man, although they might be temporarily suspended in favor of such commitments as World War II —or ridding a town of unpleasant desperadoes. *On the Waterfront* stands out for insisting that a man's very sense of self requires compassion and the capacity to offer love.

Conflict arises for Terry when he is served with a subpoena by the state crime commission. Saint calls him a "bum" when at first he decides not to testify. Redeemed by his feeling for her, he agrees, although he knows that he is putting his life on the line. A tortured scene follows in which a man's ambivalence about assuming difficult social obligations to struggle against injustice is shown to affect deeply his capacity to express love for a woman. In a car with his brother (Rod Steiger), a lieutenant of the mob, Terry reminds him of how he, his own brother, had made him throw the fight which would have led him to a title match because the racketeers demanded it: "I could have been a contender. I could have been somebody, instead of a bum, which is what I am," says Terry in one of the most sensitive expressions of self-awareness spoken by a male hero in the history of the American film. Most heroes strive to be "somebody," and Terry is no exception. What is unique about the characterization of Terry Malloy is that his masculinity arises from the admission of failure. His violence too, leading him to break down Saint's door to force her to admit that she loves him, flows more from feelings of inadequacy and confusion than from any acceptable male prerogative.

The spurious premise of the film is that Terry's testimony before a state crime commission will clean up a corrupt union. This glorification of informing with its easy justification of the act by rendering those on whom Terry informs so absolutely villainous must be seen in its historical context. As an informer himself, Kazan attempts to make informing the manly thing to do. It must be remembered as well that the victimized members of the Hollywood Ten insisted upon going to jail rather than discuss their political views or name others, as did Kazan, as they refused to assent to the destruction of the First Amendment. Informing, of course, has an ancient and ignominious history, as Dalton Trumbo, the best-known of the Ten, comments in one of the letters published in *Additional Dialogue:*

> In each historical crisis the informer has always sprung up as a bondservant of tyranny. Gibbon devotes pages to denunciation of "that reptilian tribe" as they corrupted Roman society and prepared the way for absolutism. The Reformation swarmed with them. Puritan New England, as it sank into despotism, gave them free rein ... the curse upon the informer which characterizes all religions and all philosophies lies at the very heart of the social compact: that without it there can be no decent relationship anywhere for anybody: that informing as a crime is worse than murder or rape, since the murderer and the rapist harm only specific victims while the informer poisons and destroys the spiritual life of whole peoples.... [5]

Despite the attractiveness of the conception of maleness offered by Brando in his sensitive performance, it is colored by our awareness that Kazan deployed him in this role at a time when the jobs of tens of thousands of people hinged on this issue. The unwholesome spectacle of the hero as informer works in utter opposition to the film's theme of heroic resistance to gangster control through terror of the livelihoods of

[5]Trumbo, *Additional Dialogue*, p. 388.

hard-pressed longshoremen. That Terry informs on "bad" people does not quite alter our knowledge that bad people inform. That Terry himself is blackballed from the union and hence from work, that his pigeons are slaughtered and he is beaten up, serve to create an atmosphere of emotional violence intended to elicit sanction for his act.

This elevation of the act of informing in turn leads Kazan to sacrifice much of the charm and nuance of his approach to maleness in the final scenes. Terry becomes "heroic" in the best macho tradition. He grabs his longshoreman's hook, John Wayne style, determined now to demand the right to work. Garbed in the cloak of justice—murdered Joey Doyle's old jacket—he goes down to the docks, unhindered by the slightest fear. Incredibly, melodramatically, as Kazan reverts to the superman male tradition, Terry gets his chance to confront the evil boss, Friendly, face to face: "I was ratting on myself all those years and I didn't know it . . . I'm glad what I done to you." Lest this seem too absurdly contrived, Terry is now beaten to a pulp by Friendly's henchmen.

But, like Lazarus rising from the grave, Terry keeps going, staggering toward the gate through which he must pass for work, the astonished men watching to see if he makes it before following. Terry assumes the role of leader in a burst of elitism which ends the film, making a mockery of the theme of *Viva Zapata*, a film that challenged the conception of the all-powerful, savior-like leader with a mass of passive followers. Terry alone rallies the longshoremen, who, inspired by his example, will now get back their union. Summoning a superhuman will, Terry rises to his feet, holding his battered chest together. The camera lens distorts the image, reflecting his shaky vision as he strains his smashed body forward to demand his day's work. John Wayne's grit was never more truly manifested. Nor does the upbeat ending quite conceal that in the midst of the fifties we have been given a film glorifying the role of the very congressional committees which attacked the slightest suggestion of intellectual and political independence. The sensitive, complex performance of Brando does not quite conceal that Kazan has cast the informer in the role of emancipator.

III

No less than Brando did James Dean, in his three-picture career, bring to the fifties screen the image of the sensitive, sentient male. In his first two films, *East of Eden* (1955) and *Rebel Without a Cause* (1955), Dean played a youth of high school age, not yet hardened by life or alienated from his feelings.

The Dean personality appealed so powerfully to the young of the fifties, who immediately transformed him into a cult figure, because he evoked their own submerged pain, the sense of being stifled and smothered by values not their own. Dean raged. He refused to conform to someone else's idea of right and wrong. He wouldn't do it. And he managed, like the most sincere and caring young men, to make his world in some measure respond to his own outcry. Dean waged war on society's amoral dictate demanding success at whatever human cost. In his films he quietly insists upon respect for the autonomous individual and wreaks havoc within the confines of the nuclear family until he gets his way. If the fifties could present the man in social revolt as the informer of *On the Waterfront*, the Dean films demarcated greater freedom for the male by restricting his struggle to the privacy of the family. It is no accident that Kazan also directed Dean in *East of Eden*.

In *East of Eden* Dean plays Cal, the "bad" twin. He aches to be loved for himself by his stern, authoritarian father. All his wildness stems from the primal trauma of rejection by the person whose approval he wants most. *East of Eden* manifests the sensitivity toward the male personality that characterized many films of this decade by exploring Cal's crisis of identity: "I gotta know who I am. I gotta know." He is the real-life male demanding confirmation of himself from his parents. He pleads both with his straitlaced father ("Talk to me!") and with his whorehouse madam mother ("Let me talk to you!"). He is the moody, unloved outcast who cannot please his parents in a culture where, traditionally, parents demand that their children conform to their own needs and commonly take minimal pains to discover and nurture the unique personalities of their sons and daughters.

In his quest for meaning out of his distress, Dean emerges as a new kind of hero. Lonely adolescent that he is, he cares both about himself and about others. He is not content to live an unthinking existence, something with which Wayne or Cooper or Eastwood have no difficulty. Like them, he is capable of initiative, and Cal ambitiously raises beans during wartime to win the approval of his father. He is versatile and open-minded enough, in this puritan community in which he was raised, to make friends with his suspicious mother. When she hesitates to lend him money for his crop, and later when she betrays a lack of interest and confidence in him, he coerces her, threatening to inform his father and brother that she's in town.

The famous Dean giggle issues forth as his mother accuses him of blackmail, the giggle he would always affect when the truth was near. His very physical being forces him to acknowledge reality. He admits that he, unlike "good" brother Aaron, is like her, independent in judgment and untamed in his sexuality. She had left his father out of a love of freedom identical to his: "No one tells me what to do." It is this credo which led countless young people in fifties America to take Dean to their hearts.

In his relationships with women, Dean borrows from Cooper. Like Brando, he remains aloof and wary, rejecting loose women who come his way. He prefers a "good" woman, his brother's girlfriend Abra (Julie Harris), wanting her as he was denied that prior possession of Aaron, the love of their father. In the love scene on the ferris wheel, Dean kisses Abra, managing, as Brando did so well, to be simultaneously tender and tough. But like Cooper and so many similar males of the frontier, Dean in *East of Eden* is more concerned with his relationship to larger issues, in particular the one with his father. A woman still takes second place. Cal's goal is to prove that *he* is the better son, which he attempts to do by giving his father the money he made on the beans, a birthday gift that would offset his father's losses in lettuce. Full of zest and boundless physical energy in the hope that he will be accepted, he jumps from the roof.

When his father coldly rejects his offering, refusing self-righteously to take a profit created by the war, Cal sobs from the depths of his being, as only a fifties male could. His devastation echoes that of so many young people who could not, no matter how frantically they strove to wrench free of their parents and authority, locate an essential, life-sustaining acknowledgment of their identity. They could find no source in the culture to ease their sense that nothing they might do would be of any use. Stunned by rejection, Cal performs such vengeful acts as introducing his puritanical, innocent twin brother Aaron to the mother of whose life-style he knows nothing. He accuses his father of having failed him utterly: "Tonight I even tried to buy your love. But now I don't want it. I don't need it any more ... I don't need any kind of love."

Here is a revolution in itself, the spectacle of the male hero speaking with such candor about his deepest and most agonized feelings. Equally unique is the extent to which the Dean character is in touch with himself, able to encounter and face such racking emotion. Dean added an enormous dimension to the screen male with his unprecedented freedom in acknowledging his hurts and disappointments so openly and without shame. His image confirmed and rendered acceptable the fact that men are as tormented by feelings of rejection and loneliness as women. A male, Dean suggested by his demeanor, was still manly even when revealing his weakness and vulnerability.

Presenting a radical reversal of sex roles in which gentler characteristics and their graceful expression, previously the exclusive domain of screen women, are claimed for men, Dean becomes tender and solicitous when his father suffers a paralyzing stroke which renders him helpless. Abra, emulating Cal's candor, tells his father that unless he gives Cal an open sign that he loves him, "he'll never be a man." Joining *Detective Story,*

East of Eden admits that what makes a man whole is approval by the first male in his life, his father. Elucidating this father-son relationship, *East of Eden* penetratingly unfolds how the enslavement of a son to an author-itarian father emasculates the young man unless infantile ties can be broken and the unresolved need confronted and relinquished. A man needs his father's help; Cal, an existential hero, is willing to ask for it, explaining, "Man has a choice and the choice is what makes him a man."

Kazan's flawed reliance on dialogue to dramatize Cal's psychic work-ing causes *East of Eden*, like his other films, to seem more like filmed theater than like cinema. *East of Eden* retains merit through the nuances of its theme. Cal rejects the male model proposed by the strong father, Adam, selfish with his praise and incapable of expressing physical affec-tion for his sons. He is the very male type exalted in films of the thirties and forties, parsimonious with his feelings and grudging in their display. Here we see him psychologically undressed as an antediluvian monster, mindlessly destructive. The best he can do at the film's close is to give enough of himself to allow his son Cal to do something for him, by asking him to hire a new nurse.

Dean, his psychic opposite, offers an infinitely more positive male image. He is able without shame to cry, show tenderness, and win a woman because he is a loving man. It is his capacity to give and to love, the very qualities traditionally allowed only to passive, dependent women, not to vital men, which makes him maturely responsible. In the last shot Cal sits down at his father's bedside, redeemed by his father's acceptance of his own need. To offer his love to his father, and then to others, is what Cal has sought all along.

Robert Lindner defined a "rebel without a cause" as "a religious dis-obeyer of prevailing codes and standards . . . an agitator without a slogan, a revolutionary without a program . . . incapable of exertions for the sake of others." Lindner's male subject, Harold, had been oppressed by a brutal, sexually threatening father. Lindner himself had believed, in keep-ing with a dominant motif of American culture and cinema, that "no great man in history ever aspired to get married." Nicholas Ray's film adaptation retains only the bare bones of Lindner's case study. His hero, Jim (James Dean), is no recalcitrant "psychopath" but a sensitive and immensely attractive teen-age boy whose *weak* father (Jim Backus) has failed to provide him with a strong masculine image. The film inverts the meaning of Lindner's insight by placing Dean in need of the very kind of dominant, assertive, self-confident father who caused the original Har-old to become psychopathic in the first place. Dean's rebellion in the film is thus thoroughly emasculated by the backsliding notion that firm au-thority offers the solution to a tormented, alienated adolescent's quest to discover how to be a man. In the film's culmination, as dishonest as that inflicted upon *On the Waterfront*, the solution to Dean's distress is presented in the most banal and mindless of fifties terms: a strong father in command would have solved everything. The henpecked nonentity Backus is shown to be the cause of the problem because he was incapable of offering his son a strong male model. Dean himself urges this perception: "If he had the guts to knock Mom cold once, maybe she'd be happy and stop picking on him. . . . I don't ever want to be like him . . . how can a guy grow up in a circus like that?" In the end, father Backus takes charge. The shrewish mother melts at once before his newly acquired authority. Now the future begins to look bright for the victimized, troubled, and betrayed adolescent at the film's center.

Authority is unabashedly sanctified in this film. The Dean giggle is accompanied by drunken incoherence in the first scene as he is hauled into a police station, alcoholism being the fifties equivalent to the "uppers" and "downers" of the sixties and seventies. Jim is set on the path to health by—appropriately enough for this film—a benevolent police officer named Ray. (When but in the fifties could a policeman be portrayed as the kindly, gentle catalyst of psychic health?) In addition to his other talents, policeman Ray is an amateur psychologist; he has Jim smash his desk with his fists to provide an outlet for the boy's rage.

What saves the film from such banalities is solely the image of Dean. He is sensitive and tender, while raging to be heard, like Cal of *East of Eden*. He bonds with a girl named Judy (Natalie Wood) and a younger boy named Plato (Sal Mineo), each of whom has also been deprived of parents who can accept them. Judy's father is so overwhelmed by his sexual attraction to her that, projecting, he calls her a "dirty tramp." Plato's mother leaves him in the care of a maid. Together the three waifs attempt to create a family, bestowing upon each other the tenderness and support denied them by the adults in their lives. Jim offers Plato his red jacket, a symbol of his love.

Like Brando in his roles, Dean was given the opportunity to play a male who could voice his innermost feelings. "You're tearing me apart," he yells at his parents. "You say one thing and he says another." He cries. He wants to "belong someplace," a traditional feeling married to a new definition. He will accept no façade or macho defense, valuing his feelings above all and attempting with resolve to cope with them: "If I had one day when I didn't feel confused, didn't have to feel ashamed of anything . . ."

Rebel Without a Cause recognizes that however sensitive a young male may be, he must confront a brutal, deforming masculine culture outside. A male must not be "chicken"; Jim becomes enraged when this term is applied to him because he feels the conflict of having to be both true to his feelings and strong. A male must be accepted by his peer group even when they are callow brutes in black leather jackets and motorcycle boots. Jim's heart isn't in it, but he knows he must play the game, even to the extent of participating in the "chicken run," in which revved-up jalopies race to the edge of a cliff and the drivers throw themselves to the ground at the last moment before the car goes over. The first to hit the dirt and so escape is labeled "chicken." His rival, Buzz, catches his leather jacket strap on the door handle, causing him to soar to his death, a probable outcome of this death-seeking "test" of masculine courage.

Having played the game and "won," Jim can now risk being himself, a sensitive, caring friend to the weaker Plato. The younger boy longs to be a prototypical masculine male and has pinned a photograph of Alan Ladd on his locker door—a short but manly man whom he can hope to emulate. Jim is tormented by more serious questions of honor and integrity. He asks his father, who is dressed in a frilly apron as he brings Jim's mother supper on a tray, what it means to be a man. His father is befuddled. Unmanned himself, he neither comprehends what his son is seeking from him nor knows what is lacking in himself. Toward Plato, Jim is gentle, kind, strong, and understanding, providing the younger boy all the things his own father has failed to give him. "He doesn't say much," says Plato of his new idol—Alan Ladd having been supplanted—"but when he does, you know he means it. He's sincere."

After the death of Buzz, Jim wants to go to the police and assume responsibility for what has happened. His father, a moral coward, urges him against this: "You can't be idealistic." "I am involved," says Dean, "we are all involved . . . just once I want to do something right," speaking lines which in the fifties go beyond their specific reference. Alternating between harshness and gentleness, Dean is irresistible. He screams for his father to "stand up for me!" He begins to choke the man who has so failed him. Yet his tenderness is always apparent. "Your lips are soft," Judy tells him, as once more in the fifties the physical distinctions between man and woman are torn away.

The climax takes place at an old haunted house where Jim and Judy can pretend they are grown up and married, having escaped the parents who do not understand them. Their aspirations are highly traditional. *Rebel Without a Cause* is simplistic in its moral that the juvenile delinquents and "bad boys" would not choose a life-style alien to that of their parents if only they were "understood." We are not yet in the counterculture sixties. All Jim and Judy want is to have children, roots, a home, and understanding They seek "love."

But Judy offers us a new definition of the ideal male as *Rebel* and so many fifties films saw him: "One who can be gentle and sweet, like you are . . . who doesn't run away . . . being Plato's friend—that's being strong." Strength is redefined as tolerance of the weaknesses of others and acceptance of one's own. Judy is first to tell Jim that she loves him, so deeply does she trust him: coyness and aloofness would be inauthentic. "I'm not going to be lonely any more," Jim says, "not me or you." A male

Sal Mineo, James Dean, and Natalie Wood in *Rebel Without a Cause:* Judy offers us a new definition of the ideal male as *Rebel* and so many fifties films saw him: "one who can be gentle and sweet, like you are . . . who doesn't run away . . . being Plato's friend—that's being strong."

admits here to need before the woman he loves. Their relationship is not undermined because they express how they really feel. All these elements redefine and redeem the male image in the Hollywood film.

The last scene finds Jim capable of traditional male behavior. He faces gunfire to save Plato from the police, shielding the boy with his jacket and in so doing exposing for the camera bulging biceps that would rival those of Stanley Kowalski. But he is not successful; Plato is killed by the police. What remains is Jim's involvement and his having retained his sensitivity. Overcoming the police is something only John Wayne could do.

But in its last moments *Rebel* reverts to the tired view that old-fashioned male authority can ease the pain of the young. In defeat Jim weeps over Plato's body, then cries on his father's shoulder, once more in a plea for help. This time, implausibly, his father rises to the occasion: "I'll try to be as strong as you want me to be." As Jim gave Plato his jacket, his father now gives Jim his. An understanding family, led by a male in command, can set things straight.

Dean and Brando frequently fulfill traditional expectations of the American male. Just as often, however, they defy them, insisting upon a more honest portrayal of the male and his feelings. If they can be "cool," they are also frequently sensitive. They emerge as their own men, living by personal values. They can cry without forfeiting the regard of their women. (Only in *Giant* does Dean fail to win the woman he desires.) Most significantly, unlike scores of leading men, they do not permit their physical beauty to prevent them from the full exploration of their identities.

IV

In contrast to the Brando and Dean films in the fifties, and yet in many ways similar to them, was *Marty* (1955), one of the only films made in America that took as its central theme and character a man who fulfills *none* of the culture's expectations for the male. Unlike Brando and Dean, Ernest Borgnine's Marty is not physically attractive. Heavyset, homely, and balding, he has as well a low-status job: he is a butcher. Unlike leading men who find independence to be theirs for the taking, Marty is tied down with a widowed mother and a sour, nagging aunt. Yet because he is so good-natured, he wouldn't dream of setting himself free if that would mean leaving his relatives to founder in neglect and poverty. Not since King Vidor's *The Crowd* had there been so sympathetic a portrayal of the average man.

As lonely as Brando and Dean, Marty has taken a refuge common to men everywhere. He spends his time with others like himself, single men who share the details of their supposed conquests when they are not escaping from reality through the recitation of baseball statistics. None is good-looking, yet they all desire women who fulfill the standards set by Hollywood, particularly in the fifties. And in keeping with the highly conventional morality of the decade, *Marty* suggests that such men could escape from their ennui and emptiness by getting married, the ideal way of life for the average male.

"What do you feel like doing tonight?" his best friend Angie asks Marty. "I don't know, Angie, what do you feel like doing?" is Marty's reply, an exchange that became part of popular jargon, so closely did it touch upon the sensibility of the decade. These were words that could never be spoken by Gable, Wayne, Bogart, or Cooper. None of *them* would be forced to spend Saturday night watching the "Hit Parade" on television because they couldn't get a girl to go out with them. No supermale would venture into the cattle-market of the Stardust Ballroom in desperate search of a pickup. Or, if driven to it, fail to find one. *Marty* brought a breath of fresh air to fifties cinema by describing men's lives as they were.

His family pressure Marty to get married, yet he is unattractive to women. Heavy-browed, potbellied, at thirty-four he feels as if he has spent every Saturday night of his life looking for a girl. The stigma in *Marty* is, with unique honesty, on the man who cannot find himself a wife, a figure as uncomfortable and unhappy as the old maid. Masculinity involves being selfish and self-centered, and consequently Marty's good heart is an undesirable commodity in American culture, hinting strongly at sexual impotence. Lacking all self-confidence, Marty doesn't begin to know how to approach a woman. In this film which at last explores the terror of the male who always has to make the first move, always submit to the possibility of rejection, he calls a girl on the phone. His voice shakes as the camera dollies in to him, only to dolly away once it is certain that he has failed again. "Whatever it is women like," says Marty, "I don't have it . . . I'm just a fat, ugly man . . . I'm ugly, I'm ugly, I'm ugly." In his mid-thirties, Marty in despair wants only to be left alone.

On this particular Saturday night at the Stardust Ballroom, Marty meets Clara (Betsy Blair), whose blind date is trying frantically to pay a lone male to take her off his hands. But this presages no fantasy romance, transcending the demands upon maleness in a culture which idealizes Wayne and Bogart. Marty actually finds a girl only to have her labeled a "dog" by his friends. She is what in the fifties was designated the "old-maid schoolteacher." Although his mother had wanted him to get married, egged on by his aunt she conspires to persuade Marty that Clara is wrong for him, and that college girls are really whores, but one step up from the streets.

Yet, as in the films of Brando and Dean, the differences between male and female are blurred, revealing that each is capable of similar sensitivity and similar fears. Clara cries. Marty admits that he also cries a lot, dubbing himself the "professor of pain." If he is not good-looking by Hollywood's standards, neither is she. "You're not such a dog as you think you are," he remarks in guileless if good-natured gaucherie, "so I'm not such a dog as I think I am," he concludes with a winning smile. Her seeming failure to conform to the social ideal gives him the strength to accept himself as he is. They laugh uninhibitedly.

Professionally as well, they have much in common as two people afraid of risks and change, afraid of being hurt. Clara fears a new job which would force her to leave the home of her parents. Marty dreads going out on his own as a butcher. "I know you're a good butcher," says Clara. How much easier it is to expose the fallacy in someone else's self-assessment! Marty encourages Clara equally. She, he observes, only pretends out of timidity and fear that her father needs her to live at home. Marty is provided with a new sense of his manhood by the release offered through this frank confession of his doubts about himself. "Anything you want to do, you'll do well," Clara tells him. The evening ends with her afraid to kiss him, a reluctance born of inexperience rather than the absence of desire. He misunderstands, assuming rejection, as always. But they have already established a rapport which allows them to overcome such mishaps, and all is made right.

In the end, despite the objections of his selfish family, ranging from male cousin to mother and aunt, and including his taunting buddies who hate to lose a member of the group at whose expense they could feel whole, Marty chooses Clara. His buddy Angie is particularly jealous of a woman who would come between them, as the film is unrelentingly honest in exposing the distorted homosexual component of male bonding. Angie actually eats out of Marty's Sunday dinner plate and challenges his friend with explicit pleadings: "Do you want to go with me or with that dog?" Marty, a man who had needed such bonding in default of an alternative, chooses heterosexuality.

Marty offers an alternative vision of masculinity. It describes the male bonding so common to our culture only to reject it as neither desirable nor adult. *Marty* departs from the pattern, later to appear in scores of seventies films, which finds the relationship between two men the safest, most comforting, and most satisfying. *Marty* recognizes the infantile quality of "buddy" relationships, nowhere more effectively than in a scene in which one of the bachelors in the group recounts a Mickey Spillane story to the others in all its gory detail. "Miserable and lonely and stupid," says Marty a little later. "What am I hanging around with you for? She's a dog and I'm a fat, ugly man. You don't like her, that's too bad." He bangs the phone-booth door closed on the hovering Angie.

The male bonding in *Marty* is treated, accurately, as a distortion of male friendship rather than as its fulfillment. Were it not perverse, screenwriter Chayevsky and director Mann suggest, it would not be dependent upon the absence in the lives of these men of permanent relationships with women. That Angie finds Clara a threat to his relationship with Marty and attacks her almost at first sight makes it clear that theirs resembles one of those friendships found among preadolescents in which boys leer and talk about girls, but prefer finally to be together. Thus it can be a triumph when Marty rejects a male friendship into which he had escaped out of fear and self-hatred.

Marty's tenderness permeates this film which so values his generosity, consideration, and fatherly impulses. He says of his cousin's baby that he's "no bigger than a leg of lamb." Marty's manhood emerges out of a determination to do something about his lack of self-esteem. Fearing sexual rejection, subject to tears and loneliness, he is nothing less than normal. When he meets a girl he likes, he is willing to "get down on his hands and knees" and beg her to marry him. The male principle is not undermined but redeemed by this characterization.

V

Many films of the fifties depicted males with psychic or social limitations about which they could do little. Far from being invulnerable, they were frequently thwarted in the effort to become their own men. They were shown as weakened by flaws of character. Compulsions held them in their grip beyond the final fade-out. The fifties male frequently failed to regain purpose or to rouse himself from the malaise of a pointless existence. The supremely capable male was gone from the center of the film.

In his last picture, *The Harder They Fall* (1956), Bogart plays Eddie, a has-been sports columnist who prostitutes himself to a corrupt fight promoter portrayed by Rod Steiger, a ubiquitous type in these fifties films. Because of the money, Eddie agrees to be a public relations man for boss Steiger, building up "powder-puff fist" and "glass jaw" Toro Marino (a real-life figure). He will lie to the man and to the world in his insistence that Marino is a serious contender. Eddie, broke, is willing to do anything for a bank account. That moral compromise accompanies the acquisition of wealth locates *The Harder They Fall* in the fifties, although it could easily have been made about the prospects of success in Depression America. "What are you trying to do, hold on to your self-respect?" leers Steiger. Tom Mix or Douglas Fairbanks would have gone their own way, toppling the tyrant as a matter of course. Bogart as a fifties hero compromises: "Money's money no matter where you get it."

The boxing scenes in *The Harder They Fall* are shot in a manner exposing the repulsive brutality of this "sport." Barbaric display in the ring proffers no attainment of masculinity; Toro can win only by destroying a fighter named Dundee who had suffered brain damage during his last appearance in the ring. The sick, staggering Dundee is banged around brutally until he drops. He is soon to die, and will remain of interest only to the two opponents who each demand "credit" for killing him. The bodies of the fighters are thick, beefy, fat, and asexual. Animal-like in their sluggish motions, they are also dull and stupid. It is to perpetuate this sordid world that Bogart has sold himself.

A humane man at heart, Bogart finally rouses himself sufficiently to refuse to cheat the bewildered fighter. "He's not a horse, he's a human being," Bogart declares. He gives Toro his own $26,000 share of the enterprise so that Toro will not have to return to South America with only the meager $49.07 which Steiger thought him worth. Bogart then reclaims his integrity by writing a series of articles exposing the corrupt promoter. Traditional male aptitudes come to his rescue. Physical courage accompanies him on his return to integrity, and he remains undaunted by Steiger's threats: "You can't scare me and you can't buy me ... I'm fighting you for Toro and myself and everyone."

He sits down at the typewriter to begin his manuscript—entitled, not surprisingly, "The Harder They Fall." It urges the outlawing of boxing. If Bogart is once again a real man, one who stands for truth, justice, and compassion, he and the American film have learned that these are not commodities that come cheap. The truth demands sacrifices, and we find Bogart writing in a shabby tenement apartment, his life made easier by none of the conveniences that money can buy. For the hero justice is no longer his for the taking. It must be fought for at great expense, the central insight of the film and one which grants it an authenticity that renders it as pertinent to the present as to the fifties.

With a similar assessment of power, *Paths of Glory* (1957) asked what it means to be a man when the decisions of one's life are all made by higher-ups. The milieu is the army, where men are grouped in accordance with a rigid hierarchy. Simply *knowing* what is true or just is not enough, as Bogart found out in *The Harder They Fall*. Colonel Dax (Kirk Douglas), our hero, knows that the mission of taking the "anthill" is suicidal and absurd. Yet as a member of an organization he is pledged to obey his superiors, even if it requires presiding over a brutal injustice. When a soldier shows fear in this world ("I'll never see my wife again!"), he is slapped by a general and transferred out. Masculinity in this context is for director Stanley Kubrick not a matter of invincibility but the recognition that all rational men are ambivalent about danger and are subject to terror. At a time when America had suffered for a decade under McCarthyite investigations and the Bill of Rights was under grave siege, small films like this and *The Harder They Fall* were beacons of courage upholding dissent and a claim for that justice denied the community.

Colonel Dax is a man of higher consciousness, if with little power to enact his principles. He quotes Samuel Johnson's telling aphorism that patriotism is "the last refuge of a scoundrel," a perception light-years away from those John Wayne gung-ho cavalry fanatics of the late forties. Dax realizes that to be a man means above all to question authority and dispute received wisdom, all the more so when human lives are being senselessly destroyed in their name. A general orders the men to fire on their own positions in order to force forward those in the trenches.

Colonel Dax, a criminal lawyer in civilian life, is called upon to defend three scapegoats court-martialed for "cowardice in the face of the enemy," a ploy designed to intimidate the others as well as conceal the general's perfidy. To restore flagging morale, three men will be sacrificed.

Dax brings to bear not only moral indignation but, in the best masculine tradition, the courage to risk his own status to denounce a preposterous trial in which the prosecution can produce no witnesses. But he loses. He goes to the length of trying in vain to reverse the decision by exposing the general for ordering the firing on his own men.

The three innocent men are executed, and Dax is reduced to uttering words of impotent rage. He calls the commanding officer "a degenerate, sadistic old man," only to be labeled in turn an "idealist" and "sentimental." Dax may "pity" the oppressor, but he has been thwarted. He is able only to offer his troops a few extra moments in a café before ordering them to the front, a paltry moment of compassion entirely inadequate as recompense for his inability to save three lives and prevent the loss of more. But defeat and failure in this more honest approach to male sufficiency do not diminish Dax, for it is his values and commitment, not success, which here define his manhood.

Another revisionist look at the male image occurred in Arthur Penn's *The Left-Handed Gun* (1958), a remake of the story of Billy the Kid. Paul Newman, substituting for the now deceased James Dean, for whom the part was intended, carries the tortured, introspective male to the West. In this version of the legend, William Bonney is a totally inarticulate man, stupidly and obsessively loyal, to the point of sadism. The characterization of Bonney as a willful juvenile delinquent *with* a cause in this instance—to avenge the murder of the rancher who had been kind to him—recalls Lindner's "psychopathic" fifties personality. Like so many screen males of the decade, Billy is a man hungry for love and acceptance, a sensitive, misunderstood youth. At any moment his eyes may fill with tears. Shy, lonely, yet in touch with his feelings, when his fatherly boss is murdered, Billy gives himself uninhibitedly to tears, rocking his head back in pain. He is here in diametric opposition to the Hollywood convention of the revenge-bound cowpoke. Instead, Billy is a feeling man whose actions flow from intense emotion.

These are emotions which last. Disconsolate about the killing of a man he has barely known, Billy devotes his entire life to avenging that death. The boss "never said more than ten words to Billy," says one of the hands. No matter. Kindness, however brief fate allows it to be, suffices for Billy to feel as if he "belonged" to the compassionate rancher, and that is enough: "I *knew* him," Billy declares. Indeed, the very brevity of his experience with this man's kindness magnifies its loss, particularly as it was cruelly taken from him.

It would be the sheerest understatement to observe that Billy defies

Robert Warshow's famous definition of the Western hero as the "last gentleman." Penn adds an important element of realism by making his Westerner truly a man without culture, as so many in the West actually were, a rootless lowlife with none of the innate dignity or self-possession we have come to associate with the Westerner. It is not simply that this Billy cannot read and write but that his responses to people are often crude and vulgar. Because he doesn't know any better, spontaneity is his only option.

Toward women he displays none of the chivalrous restraint we have come to expect of the Westerner, a pattern established by Broncho Billy Anderson and William S. Hart and continued by Tom Mix and John Wayne. In the same sense his mission differs markedly from that of the heroic Westerner. The Western insists upon justice outside the law, since the law has been corrupted by the malevolent; lawyers, sheriffs, judges, and juries who have been bribed or who themselves initiate wrongdoing are a standard feature of the Western film. The hero then violates the law, pursuing justice on behalf of the community both of the present and the future. Billy also seeks a justice denied men by a corrupt legal system, but he does so for himself personally. He is too egotistic and insular a figure to consider the fate of others; Penn's Billy the Kid might be called "smaller than life." And unlike the Westerner, who above all else is a survivor, Billy dies at the end, suffering exactly the fate he deserves.

The film rapidly deteriorates as the sensitivity of the hero is translated overly in terms of hysterical violence. A girl says of Billy, "It's the same wherever he goes—pain," as he projects upon the world what he has himself suffered. Billy's willful "I do what I want" renders him less the tormented adolescent than the psychopath whose traumatic rage is incommensurate with his injury. As in so many fifties films about the traumatized male, society is perceived as corrupt and murderous, overwhelming in its disregard for the needs of the individual. Billy, like others, seeks to live by his own values and even in failure enjoys moments of grandeur. But his defeat itself returns us to the repressive fifties.

For finally, Billy's insanity does not so much transcend the fifties' demand for conformity as it discourages rebellion by presenting it as inherently destructive. Resistance is assimilated to deviation from the norm and perceived as foredoomed to failure, even as Billy fails to find peace or companionship through his unrelenting vendetta. Within the texture of *The Left-Handed Gun* there are moments of authenticity. When Billy replies to the caution, "They'll kill you," he responds in the manner of Dean and in the mood of the troubled times, "They've *been* killin' me." But his compulsion leads to degeneration. Billy becomes self-indulgent in his purpose and demonic as it passes over the line from painful duty to pleasure. He kills even those who were following orders in the assassination of his boss with as much fury as he murders the ringleader. He disrupts the wedding of his friend Pat Garrett, and excuses himself by implying that his own feelings are all that count: "All I know is how I feel," an assertion which in its context warrants our disapproval. For if he presents a passionate male image, Billy's emotion dehumanizes and is tied to a brutality evocative of the old male avenger of the West rather than of the man of feeling with whom we began.

Penn's Billy the Kid thus loses touch with his reality; he looks "surprised" when a judge orders him to be hanged. Compulsive to the end, he faces down Pat Garrett unarmed, in effect committing suicide. In fairness to Penn, it must be said that he clearly intended to demystify the male hero, offering us an intensely feeling man with an entirely understandable share of human frailty. Cut by studio hacks without Penn's having the right to object, the final version of *The Left-Handed Gun* harks back to an earlier Hollywood version of the male ideal and thus projects an ambivalence toward the hero that is thematically confusing, an incoherence unwittingly expressive of the times. Being a feeling man, the contribution of fifties cinema, becomes tenuous in *The Left-Handed Gun*, no doubt because it passed through so many hands. The film remains interesting only at those moments when neurotic behavior appears indistinguishable from the normal.

The compulsive, scarcely invulnerable hero even appears in a John Ford film of the fifties, *The Searchers* (1956). A director whose work embodied Hollywood's sternest depiction of men, Ford was hardly known for his interest in psychology or analysis of the traditional view of masculinity. Failing to perceive *The Searchers* as an adaptation to the new approach in the fifties to the male psyche, an admirer of Ford, director Lindsay Anderson, found the Wayne character a "neurotic" and seriously underrated the film. What Anderson failed to perceive was that Ford, evidently affected by the emancipated evaluation of the male in the fifties, is uncompromising in his assault upon the very style of masculinity approved and applauded in his earlier films. Ford's Ethan Edwards in *The Searchers* is essentially irredeemable. He comes to us a hero with a complex and fully formed psychology, and if he bends near the end of the film, he does not change.

Wayne, as lonely Uncle Ethan, is a man who devotes a good portion of his life to an obsessive search for his niece Debbie, kidnapped as a child by Indians. Ford here is ironic toward this romanticism in Ethan Edwards, seeing his sober high purpose as anachronistic as the cape and saber he has brought back from the Civil War. The war has ended three years earlier, but Ethan has only just come home. He is a man who refuses to allow unpalatable realities to temper his spirit. Unbending in the face of the inevitable, he has refused to be present at the capitulation of the South, asserting, "I don't believe in surrenders." Nor would he turn in his saber or join the Texas Rangers, the better to continue a life given to certain values: "A man is good for only one oath," says Ethan, his to "the Confederate States of America." He is rigid and severe, as Ford utterly refuses to applaud him for a posture which has enclosed him in a narrow confine, preventing him from being at ease anywhere on earth. Parallel to his devotion to the South is his unspoken love for his brother's wife, Martha, little Debbie's mother. Despite the hopelessness of this passion and her death at the beginning of the film, his is a commitment for life.

For twenty years Ethan hunts for Debbie, a search tinged with irony as Ford alters the typical Wayne rejoinders so that they sound almost psychopathic. "You wanna quit, Ethan?" he is asked. "That'll be the day!" is his reply, repeated time after time. He would even shoot at Indians while they are helpless, carrying their dead and wounded off a field of battle. "Maybe the land needs our bones in it before it can be civilized," someone says, a despairing comment which applies equally to the behavior of Wayne and his Indian adversaries, locked in senseless combat. Sadistically, Wayne shoots at a herd of buffalo so that they won't feed Comanches during the long hard winter.

Wayne's Ethan Edwards is the male hero possessed, lonely and miserable, hanging on to an existence through an obsession long since departed from the rational—in this case, the quest for the missing Debbie. It is a telling commentary on the earlier conventions of male prowess.

But Ford's harshest criticism of his "hero" comes in the open exposure of Ethan Edwards's racism, which leads to cruelty. When he does find Debbie, she has been happily integrated into Indian life; it is the only way of life she remembers. Debbie wishes to remain, and when she tells him simply but firmly, "These are my people," Ethan takes out his gun. He would shoot her for this choice precisely because he has come this far on behalf of an obsession, that chimera now seen as the male quest itself. For "living with a buck" Ethan renounces Debbie as his blood kin. Appalled, Martin, Ethan's young companion and Debbie's cousin, passes judgment on Ethan Edwards and his ethos: "I hope you die!" "That'll be the day!" says Ethan. He lives now solely to punish Debbie for her loyalty to those who have raised and shaped her, her life reduced by Edwards to the terrible sin of miscegenation, tainting the blood for which he had fought in the Civil War.

We see that Ethan Edwards had searched for Debbie so relentlessly, not because he valued the girl, but because she represented a racial purity, a white supremacy he had unsuccessfully defended in the Civil War and which was best embodied for him in Debbie's mother, murdered in an Indian raid and the only woman he ever loved. He has become a "searcher" out of a misguided love for the distorted ideal of the purity of such a woman, as of her race. His psychopathy becomes obvious as we realize that the person Debbie, the real woman, scarcely interests him at all. She is incidental to this real search, which concerns his inadequate sense of who he is—the essence of the masculine ideal of a tough, stern man of action celebrated by Ford in other films.

By showing Edwards to be a racist, Ford is more searing in his condemnation of the values on behalf of which America was settled than he was or would be in any other work. The "good" women of the town don't want the sullied Debbie back either; they no less than her Uncle Ethan designate her "the leavings of Comanche bucks." Only Martin, part Indian himself, declares that she will be abandoned "over my dead body," after Ethan himself wishes her dead because "living with Comanches is not being alive." The legendary toughness of the masculine Wayne hero is fully exposed as maniacal, replete with the rot of racial hatred. As we perceive that Wayne is propelled by feelings opposite to his professed motive in searching for Debbie at all cost, the nature of frontier "masculinity," repressed, celibate, and brutalized, is revealed.

Only when he is in touch with contrary values do we by contrast observe the damage wrought by Ethan's earlier male demeanor. Inspired by the real love he felt for her mother, Ethan surmounts his racism; in a redeeming, tender moment, rendered beautiful because Ethan has had to rise above himself to be capable of it, he lifts Debbie tenderly in his arms. Martin rushes over in fear that Ethan may still kill her. But Ethan, released from his obsession, says quietly, "Let's go home, Debbie." If he has been a cruel fanatic, he is now human, the contrasting modes of male behavior providing their own commentary. It is instructive, however, that his humanity does not rise to leaving Debbie with her Comanche people nor in allowing her the will to make her earlier declaration stick.

Ethan Edwards remains himself, a complex man full of bitterness, both a perpetrator and a victim of the racial strife which has torn America apart from its beginnings. Having returned Debbie to "white civilization," he slips away at the end into the Texas dust. His racism is located by Ford not only in Southern antebellum culture but in his first encounters with the Indians, which remain with him and which finally he, as he is, cannot wholly transcend. *The Searchers*, a brilliant film, belongs to the most serious trend of fifties filmmaking. Its nuanced characterization of the Wayne hero makes it one of the most disturbing fifties films, no less significant than the Brando and Dean portrayals for its glimpse of the male psyche as a symbol of American civilization itself.

VI

Though the repression of the McCarthy days produced a revolution in the male image in certain films, this was by no means the only influential trend in fifties filmmaking. There were many films endorsing the old

John Wayne in *The Searchers:* The legendary toughness of the masculine Wayne hero is fully exposed as maniacal, replete with the rot of racial hatred. The nature of frontier "masculinity," repressed, celibate, and brutalized, is revealed.

male stereotype, refusing as before to recognize the damage to the male personality produced by the demand that the screen male be tough, invulnerable, stoical, and superior, ever in command both of himself and of other lesser beings, male and female. The indefatigable Western hero, for whom any psychological glimpse into his motives and compulsions would be emasculating and irrelevant, still roamed the sound stages. For every film like *The Searchers* that cast a doubting eye on the myth of male invulnerability, there were several others urging that males must be strong and, above all, never admit to moments of weakness. Hollywood continued to sustain the status quo by producing as many unfeeling, one-dimensional heroes as it allowed male characters who were ambivalent, deeply feeling, and flawed.

At the head of the class of such fifties paeans to male strength was *High Noon* (1952), with Gary Cooper as the stoical marshal singlehandedly defending a town full of weaklings, hypocrites, and cowards. Three marauding outlaws come to town on a mission of revenge. No one will confront them but Cooper, in this elitist portrait and demonstration that we should be grateful for stern male leaders wherever we find them. The other men are too weak, incapable of the willed masculinity that is Cooper's trademark and is reinforced even in the title song sung by Tex Ritter, an old-time tough (if singing) cowboy himself: "If I'm a man, I must be brave . . . .else lie a coward in my grave." Collective action is presented as impossible as director Fred Zinnemann scorns those who failed to stand up to the bully of the day, Senator McCarthy. It is true that Zinnemann comments through *High Noon* on the collective paralysis and cowardice which permitted McCarthy to continue his reign of terror. In fairness also, Zinnemann's plea was that one man standing up would be enough to puncture the bully's invulnerability, showing to others that it could be done if only they would summon the nerve and take the risk. But with its assertion that only one man has the will to act, *High Noon* serves actually to legitimize the glorification of the single man of strength, rather than challenging the hold of that image on us. If *High Noon* was the work of men believing they were asking people to stand up to McCarthy, what they produced was a film suggesting that no such hope existed. Defeat is inherent in its plot, for only one individual, an unreal Gary Cooper superman at that, has the guts to face down the bullies. If it calls implicitly for radical defiance, the film reverts to the most conservative, traditional, and damaging norms of male behavior as well as to the most romantic myths of individual effectiveness and group futility.

Shy, sheepish, and lanky as ever, if no longer boyish, Cooper is about to turn in his marshal's badge for a private life when the safety of the town is threatened. A real man is needed, and in such circumstances a beautiful blond bride (Grace Kelly) is not enough for a man who has "never run from anybody before." Cooper chooses to fight because it is in his nature; he's "got to—that's the whole thing." Once again the melodrama of whether a male should commit himself to struggles which do not directly affect him is enacted on the American screen.

The bride, a weak and stupid woman, insists, "It's no concern of yours." Cooper won't deign to answer such a view, which fails to take into account a male's masculinity, what he needs if he is to approach his bride as a man. All he says is, "It seems to me I've got to stay." In this scene, evocative of the films of William S. Hart, words become gratuitous. With its montage sequences *High Noon* in fact approximates the silent Western. It is forced to rely upon visuals because the hero is a man not of ideas but of action whom, in some mystical sense, words would emasculate, undercutting his potency. He acts as if by reflex, and always with correct heroic responses: "I'm not trying to be a hero." He is such by instinct, one whose nature will not allow him to abandon the community unprotected and without a marshal.

High Noon looks back to the forties and ahead to the seventies in its insistence that personal violence is the only means by which a man can protect what is valuable to him: friends, community, or Quaker bride, a pacifist whose impulses are proven wrong by events. We are told, unequivocally, that the real man is one who fights. Cooper's former lover, Katy Jurado, dark-haired and tempestuous, understands this. She is a businesswoman and Cooper's emotional equal as well as a woman who appreciates a real man. But as a forceful woman with a mind of her own, she is also made Latin and hence slightly improper, with a touch of the whore. Cooper, of course, rejects her for prissy, colorless Grace Kelly, the "good" woman, unassertive and slightly cowardly. She is the kind of woman *High Noon* proposes to the masculine male, for she has no connection with the outside world other than through her man.

In a film which exalts a strong leader, it is not surprising that Zinnemann should include a cynical satire of the democratic process. The townspeople are vociferous in their rhetoric; each demands the right to speak, but none is brave enough to risk his life in defense of what he believes. Only the superhuman male can save the town. It is he who protects their civil liberties, as if our basic democratic rights would be destroyed by the majority and must be retrieved by a noble *Übermensch*.

Unlike Dirty Harry, Cooper is careful to grant his antagonists—Frank Miller, whom he had helped send to prison, and his two outlaw cronies —their rights, another leitmotif linking the murderers to the apathetic, cowardly townspeople. They can't be put in jail because they have yet to break the law, although it is clear that their mission is revenge, and Cooper their target. Yet in the confused ideology permeating *High Noon* the masses are to blame for having allowed Miller out of prison in the first place, jeopardizing thereby the lives of lawmen like Cooper, the very

Gary Cooper in *High Noon:* Only the superhuman male can save the town. It is he who protects their civil liberties, as if our basic democratic rights would be destroyed by the majority and must be retrieved by a noble *Übermensch.*

reason why he is resigning now in despair. The final lesson is that the iron-willed leader should determine when civil liberties are appropriate and when they stand in the way of law and order, a crypto-fascist note that is not surprising in a film made at the height of the McCarthy years it presumes to assail by parable.

Any penetrating psychological critique would emasculate the hero in this regression to earlier approaches to male sufficiency, which causes us to be left with scene after scene serving as tableaux of Cooper's maleness. When he is asked if he is scared, he does reply, "I guess so," and at one point he even puts down his head and cries in frustration at being so alone in the task of confronting the renegade killers. But these moments serve solely to glorify his solitary triumph, his Hemingwayesque moment of truth when later he tracks and kills each of the outlaws, the last with his wife's aid, as his example inspires her to function as his helpmate. A montage sequence of images of the town is punctuated by a shot of the clock face at high noon, synchronized with the sound of the whistle of the train bearing the released killer. Simultaneously, Cooper blots the last will and testament he has just composed. Separated from all the other people by his moral superiority, he is rendered one with the inanimate environment.

Shots presenting him at his crucial moment as small and vulnerable in the universe add suspense. Cooper's face is dirty. He sweats. A dolly high away to a boom shot pictures Cooper as a tiny figure on the town streets in the blinding sun. Yet he manages to outfox all the villains, aided by wife Kelly as the film anticipates the need to redeem her if they are to be reconciled. Having defended the town entirely by himself, he glances at the townspeople without expression and throws his marshal's star in the dust, as Dirty Harry will later toss his inspector's badge into a quarry pond.

The people don't deserve such men. The sole difference between Cooper and his successor Harry is that Cooper rides out of town with a woman who has shown enough grit to help him in his hour of stress, like the women in the films of Hawks who justify their existence by imitating the behavior of their men. The criminals in each era are sadists lacking any real motive, and in both fifties and seventies versions we are meant to experience a sense of loss at the end as we surrender our protectors when the lights come on.

Our heroes are about to be lost to us because we are too weak and unworthy of them. From the fifties on in the American film there is a threat of loss of the male as protector unless he is given unqualified support. We could always count on the return of Fairbanks or Mix; no matter how deeply we blundered in not appreciating them, they forgave us. The postwar film, with a startling amnesia about why the war was nominally fought in the first place, asks us to surrender our own autonomy as we place in command over our lives a male with unlimited powers. It is a demand which reveals that those in power in America saw World War II very differently from those who viewed it as a principled struggle against fascism, and that having won global hegemony through it, they now require some of the values of the defeated Axis.

The fifties films also had their share of Western heroes who preferred a buddy to a woman, from Hopalong Cassidy to the Lone Ranger forever being rescued tenderly by his lifetime buddy and companion, Tonto. Unlike Wayne in *The Searchers*, who rejected the Texas Rangers, the Lone Ranger has been separated from his troop and is forced to work alone for justice. These "B" Westerns were characterized by the same loss of trust in other men and their moral reliability that surfaced in more serious fifties films. But they were retrograde in their response to that alienation, repressing the experience and ignoring its existence. The result is the latently homosexual choice of the inseparable male sidekick who compensates for the essentially asexual life of the cowboy hero from Gene Autry and Hoppy to the Lone Ranger. All of them, including Roy Rogers, were both humorless and unsensual. In retrospect they resemble nothing so much as machines in their routine quest for justice and the righting of easy wrongs, robots in their compulsive response to calls for help from distressed men, women, and children.

The quintessential lone Western hero of the fifties, that nondomesticated protector of a besieged community, was Alan Ladd of *Shane* (1953), later mourned over in nostalgia for the fantasy he embodied in that film. The male who would retain his masculinity is here a drifter, unlike Wayne and Clift of *Red River* with their strong sense of family. Shane, in his wanderings, stops at a small ranch for food and stays to help out, earning his keep by doing odd jobs at the home of a family where the child (Brandon de Wilde) provides the film with a chorus endorsing Shane as the only person who can teach a boy how to be a man. It is Shane who instructs the boy in how to shoot. Van Heflin, as the boy's father, is a homesteader trying desperately to hang on to his claim. Without the help of Shane he couldn't do it, nor could Shane be man enough to help were he also encumbered with a woman and boy of his own.

Shane has been an overrated film, embodying as it does virtually every stock attitude and cliché of the "B" Western: wicked large ranchers hiring guns to terrorize small homesteaders, who are then defended by a cool superman with the fastest gun around. It offers an unabashed celebration of the most destructive emblems of maleness in the fifties, the very decade when these values were for the first time subjected to explicit challenge in the American film. The boy asks his pa if he is able to whip Shane. Heflin must admit that he cannot, director George Stevens shooting these embarrassing scenes exclusively from the boy's point of view as the film rabidly endorses these criteria of manhood. Shooting and killing, settling early who can beat up whom in the manner of disturbed nine-year-olds in a playground, provide the film's approved values. A male must remain solitary because accepting responsibility to another will weaken him, lessening both his willingness and his ability to do combat.

The homesteaders in *Shane* appear far less masculine than gunfighters like Shane and the black-garbed villain who is his adversary (Jack Palance). A real man, once again, can test his strength only in combat with another male, as if people were no better than animals squaring off in a limited natural space to claim territorial priority. Here we have a projection of that discredited social Darwinism which imputed to human beings enclosed in a society the behavior of animals competing for food in an area of limited supply. This pseudoscientific notion of human behavior, which would be enshrined in Robert Ardrey's *Territorial Imperative*, ignores that both male competition and human cooperation are learned responses.

"But Shane, there are so many," says boy de Wilde to his hero, who must confront an entire mob. Shane is a man who doesn't whimper over his wounds, "no matter how much it hurt," says de Wilde in awe, concluding, "I just love Shane, I love him almost as much as Pa." As in *High Noon* and *Dirty Harry* to come, the community is shown to be in need of a strong male like Shane, a cool hero in command of himself, expending no unnecessary emotions. Shane teaches the boy a form of controlled violence, the discipline a justification for slaughter. "The gun is as good as the man using it," says Shane, and since the use is related to holding society and the family together, it is lyrically approved. Later we perceive that these warriors are going out of style, a fact about which the film is nostalgically regretful; they are being replaced by the lesser domesticated variety.

Shane is accordingly called "Southern trash" at one point, a foil to Palance, who is dubbed "a no-good Yankee liar." The two gunslingers are refuse of the Civil War, their day done in a time of transition, and it remains for them slowly to kill each other off. Shane has nowhere to go. He knows a "man has to be what he is." He tried settling down and "it didn't work for me." He tells the boy to grow up "strong and straight," to be in these respects at least a man like himself. Shane climbs the hill at sunrise, a reversal of the traditional ride into the sunset for the obsolete cowboy. The final sunrise in *Shane* is a call for the resurrection of a style of masculinity which, according to this film, we can ill afford to lose if we are to continue, in whatever social setting we find ourselves. "Shane, come back," the boy yells into the morning, more the bearer of a seed implanted by Shane than the child of his father. We are left with—as our only hope—that he will grow up to be a man just like his idol.

Far more explicit in its reaction to the anxieties of the decade was

George Stevens' other saga of the day, *Giant* (1956). In the guise of a grand, sweeping adult Western, epic in its scope, Stevens repudiates the ferment of the late fifties and attempts to squelch the embryonic political movements already visible, if they were not to come to fruition until the sixties. Through its strong male hero, played by Rock Hudson, *Giant* romanticizes the racist South and insists that the slavocracy will redeem itself, moderating injustice without the interference of outside agitators, foremost among whom is the federal government itself. Even those reforms designed in Washington to stabilize the status quo are pilloried.

Brown versus *The Board of Education*, the classic desegregation decision handed down by the Supreme Court in 1954 to avoid black political mobilization, at once posed the question whether deeply entrenched Southern racism could be dismantled within the established order. If not, a broad disaffection among minority groups seemed certain to intensify. *Giant* was made, in part, to preclude racist obstruction of such reforms by the South, if only because such resistance might prevent a pacification of the black and Mexican population. Emmett Till had been lynched and the Montgomery bus boycott had begun in December of 1955, fortified by a Virginia court ruling stating that bus companies could not deny Negroes any seat whatsoever on their vehicles. The males of *Giant* are sketched in terms of official fear of the freedom rides, sit-ins, and boycotts to come. Its main point is to disparage such demonstrations as unwholesome responses to the South's subjugation of people of color. Intermarriage between Hudson's film son and a Mexican woman is offered as sentimental proof that the South will solve its problems by itself.

At the film's conclusion Texas rancher Bick Benedict (Hudson), muscular and grand if playing a man in his fifties, gets into a fist fight with the racist proprietor of "Sarge's Hamburger Joint" because Sarge has refused to serve Bick's Mexican daughter-in-law. The Southern male patriarch, *Giant* would have us believe, will himself fight for the rights of oppressed minorities. At the age of fifty, Bick at last becomes a hero to his wife, Leslie (Elizabeth Taylor). The virile male has been enlisted on the eve of the civil rights movement as a firm proponent of states' rights while acceding to a breach of the color line.

Old-fashioned and stubborn though he may be, Bick Benedict is presented by Stevens as the ideal male, patriotic toward Texas and the owner of no less than 595,000 acres of land. He begins as a racist objecting to his "foreign" Eastern wife's arranging medical attention for his ailing Mexican farmhands, who lack doctors and medication. Having learned (after three hours of film time) to accept the Mexicans as people, he ends by attending the funeral of Angel Obregón, the son of one of his hands, who has died as a hero in World War II. Bick has been convinced of the valuable contribution the Mexican population has made to America, and the audience should be equally satisfied that all right-minded land barons like himself are prepared to be likewise persuaded. Bick also begins by attempting to impose a John Wayne style of masculinity upon his son, but later comes grudgingly to respect the young man who hates riding, branding, and cattle, thus breaking three generations of male tradition. Unphysical and given to crying a great deal as a child, the son grows up wanting to be a doctor. But Stevens himself leaves us in little doubt that the tough, vital, raw outdoors male like Bick is infinitely preferable. The director is willing to bend sufficiently to the mood of the fifties to grant that his hero at least learn some degree of tolerance for the sake of law and order, accepting the existence of the weak, whether lesser breeds or effeminate sons, and thereby preventing uncontrollable upheaval should the system fail visibly to reform itself from within.

The only real challenge to Bick's aggressive style of masculinity occurs in the introduction, most incongruously, of the James Dean character, Jett Rink, the white-trash ranch hand to whom Bick's sister Luz leaves an oil-rich strip of land before her death. At first Jett seems the only sympathetic male in the film. It is he who initiates Leslie in the nature of the family into which she has married: "How did they get this land if they didn't take it off someone else? . . . They took it off Mexicans for five cents an acre." The scene in which Jett makes tea for Leslie in his tiny, pathetically shabby, yet spotless home is so touching that it almost allows Dean to steal the film. Jett seems an infinitely preferable style of male, one who can grow geraniums on his porch, who is disarmingly honest as he tells Leslie that she is "prettier than ever—or just as good, anyway." He makes an excellent cup of tea, and his gentleness is presented in sharp contrast to the behavior of Bick, who forces his screaming, terrified four-year-old son to ride a pony: "He's gonna stay in that saddle if I have to tie him on."

The Dean alternative is not sustained. Early on, the lonely Jett becomes both an alcoholic and a materialist. His uninhibited body language disappears, merged in greed as he spreads his arms and lets the oil from his first well flow over him like rain. The next moment he is punching Bick in the stomach: "I'm gonna have more money than you ever had." Thus we suddenly realize that our sympathy has been misplaced; that seemingly appealing rebels among the disadvantaged really hunger only for power and riches of their own, which, once achieved, will lead to even cruder abuses. Jett becomes utterly hard and belligerent, corrupted by his new wealth.

In contrast, the old landed South, represented by Bick, learns moderation and tolerance derived from its cultivated manner. Jett personifies the vulgar, boorish *nouveau riche* of the South, disdainfully opposed by the old aristocracy represented by Bick. Jett evolves into a multimillionaire and the most racist person in the film at a time when his aristocratic antagonists are mending their ways. At the grand banquet and celebration

Elizabeth Taylor and James Dean in *Giant:* The scene in which Jett makes tea for Leslie in his tiny, pathetically shabby, yet spotless home is so touching that it almost allows Dean to steal the film. Jett seems an infinitely preferable style of male, one who can grow geraniums on his porch, one who is disarmingly honest.

he throws in his own honor, having purchased the presence of all from the governor on down, Jett has given orders that no "wrong" people are to be admitted to the festivities. In this crude caricature, all the racism of the South is suddenly ascribed to the new upstarts while the old families are at last absolved and redeemed. Bick's genteel possessiveness toward his land and his stubborn refusal to drill for oil are treated as marks of breeding in the male, in contrast to the frantic Jett zealously pacing off the small piece of land granted him by Luz Benedict in her will.

Giant is even presciently aware of the coming demand for the liberation of women. Bick is criticized by wife Leslie (and director Stevens) for preventing her from discussing politics with their dinner guests on the ground that "this is men's stuff." Her confrontation with a husband who treats her like a child is thoroughly approved: "What is so masculine about a conversation that a woman can't enter into it?" Leslie objects in stridently rebellious terms to being demeaned, befitting the fifties film's confidence in the possibility of raising prickly issues only to put them to sleep once and for all. After her outburst, a guilt-stricken Leslie awaits Bick in their bed. The matter of her rights is dropped, and we learn that she now hopes to conceive their first child. Her demand that women be treated as the equals of men vanishes like a summer tantrum, as if it had been solved by this one fit of anger, something a woman must get off her chest, but in no sense an integral part of her life. Her "declarations" are now seen as the spirited excesses of a spoiled child. As she matures, her foremost concerns are taking care of her husband and having babies. Bick manages the ranch, the family finances, the political fate of Texas, and such matters. Like the issue of racism, the problem of the equality of women is to be solved by the patronizing indulgence of good-natured males who reform themselves by lending a tolerant ear.

It must be noted as well that Bick remains far from pleased at the prospect of having a Mexican grandchild. But when finally, in contrast to the corrupted Jett, he defends not his son but his son's wife and child at the diner, an orderly future is assured. The last scene offers in extreme close-up two babies side by side in their cribs. One is dark and obviously Mexican. The other is blond. Behind them are two lambs, black and white, in Christian imagery of the crudest sort. Conciliation has been reached and we are already on a benevolent course. Further political agitation would be utterly mistaken. The Benedict tradition, presided over by patriarch Rock Hudson and symbolized by his battle with "Sarge," has now accepted the responsibility of moderating any injustice within its midst. *Giant*, an unvarnished apologia refurbishing the old image of the indomitable male, expresses the most explicitly conservative political values, although it must be granted that before the fifties such issues were scarcely acknowledged at all on the screen. As in the late twenties, with social trouble again on the horizon old images are invoked to contain any coming challenge through the meager concession of openly admitting their existence. The physically strong male becomes the proponent of controlled progress and a firm if quiet sustenance of the status quo. Bick is powerful still, and so, we are to believe, are the old male values: "Oh, what a fight!" exclaims Leslie of the incident in the diner. "It was glorious!"

VII

Most "romances" of the fifties, unlike its dramas, were paeans to the magnificence of male sexuality, counter to the daring portrayal of sexual inadequacy in *Cat on a Hot Tin Roof* (1958), in which a physically splendid man will not or cannot perform. But despite the rear-guard action of the romantic film, sexual confusion and uneasiness remained on the fifties screen, not only to wean people away from their television sets at home by offering sexual explicitness unavailable on the tube, but also because this postwar decade of prosperity returned America to problems that had been temporarily pushed aside by the exigencies of the Depression and World War II. The camouflage of saccharine reassurance had worn thin. Tennessee Williams's dramas involving males who are homosexual, such as *Cat on a Hot Tin Roof*, were extreme examples, but not wholly atypical.

From Here to Eternity (1953), in its most honest moments, proposes three styles of masculinity: that of Burt Lancaster as the aggressive Warden, that of Montgomery Clift as the bugler, Prewitt, and that of Frank Sinatra as the loyal male comrade, Maggio. Good males bond and remain true to each other, a well-tested formula in the American film. But *From Here to Eternity* also reveals that the "bad" males, who are in the majority, enter more frequently into vicious forms of psychic and physical competition. Their violence toward each other is exacerbated in a peacetime situation, and it is with some relief that Pearl Harbor puts a finish to the internecine male strife permeating the film by sending these men off to inflict their brutal impulses elsewhere.

As in *Paths of Glory*, the men are haunted by a sense of unfulfillment. The army hierarchy subjects them to the will of their superiors, automatically depriving them of that male autonomy which had been the primary myth about masculinity cultivated in American films since the twenties. In *From Here to Eternity* no man can achieve unequivocal self-determination, least of all Lancaster, who chooses finally to remain in the army rather than become an officer and seek happiness with the woman he loves, the commander's unsatisfied wife, played by Deborah Kerr.

Montgomery Clift as Prewitt best exemplifies the fifties male, combining sensitivity and deep feeling with that male prowess which assures us that he is heterosexual and adequately masculine. His maleness is immediately verified when we learn that he blinded a man in the ring during his prizefighting days! His sensitivity, however, led him to the decision never to fight again, a choice that puts him in conflict with the crude company commander and his lackeys, who associate masculinity with brutality. They take it as their right to torture a male who will not conform to this standard, his very reluctance a threat to their ability to impose brutality on males as it also risks their own exposure to feelings they would rather die than face.

But even Lancaster's masculine prowess is limited because he is forced to do the dirty work of the commander. In particular, he is ordered to pressure Clift into joining the company boxing team. Lancaster as Warden respects Clift and wishes he could ignore his orders, but he cannot. Clift assures all that he is really OK, despite his principled quirk. He "can soldier with any man" and wants no more than to "go his own way." This the majority of conventional males will prevent.

Harassed and physically abused for his refusal to fight, he stands up to endless, sadistic punishment "like a man." "I can take anything you can dish out," he asserts, echoing Little Caesar. He anticipates Jimmy Dean in *Rebel Without a Cause*, who must prove his male credentials in the "chicken run." But in the more enlightened point of view of *From Here to Eternity*, Clift's manliness is perceived, not in the physical ability to prove his superiority to other males, but in the moral resolve that allows him to hold firm to his principles despite the most overwhelming intimidation from precisely those males who feel mortally threatened because he will not test his maleness and box for them. He will neither fight nor complain of their reign of terror. Because a man loves a thing, says Clift of the army, it doesn't mean it has to love him back.

Burt Lancaster and Deborah Kerr in *From Here to Eternity:* He has complete confidence in his sexuality, and consequently the lovemaking scenes on the beach with the surf breaking over their bodies are the most erotic of any fifties film.

Lancaster and Clift together embody components of the ideal male. Lancaster, "the best soldier," presses compromise upon Clift, all the while in awe of his extraordinary, quiet courage. But Lancaster's finest scenes are not his buddy moments with Clift but those with Deborah Kerr, in which he evokes pure male sensuality, desire, and considerable feeling for the commander's beautiful wife. "I hate to see a beautiful woman going to waste," says Lancaster, using words that usually denote a typical male come-on; here they are transmuted to simple appreciation, for it is entirely evident that they express precisely what he feels. He has complete confidence in his sexuality, and consequently the lovemaking scenes on the beach with the surf breaking over their bodies are the most erotic of any fifties film.

Here male passion is unalloyed by self-doubt and is heightened by the woman's responsiveness. Unlike most seventies films to come, however much flesh overwhelms the camera lens, we have no doubt that this man expresses his sexuality with a woman in preference to a man. His body is fully muscled and powerful, as traditional masculine standards demand, and the camera enhances his physique as the surf rolling in and washing over them reproduces the rhythms of their passion. In this film Lancaster plays a fully realized man through his expertise in making love, no saloon-talking male leering at women with ambivalence and apprehension expressed in every gesture.

The final male portrait is the least interesting. Frank Sinatra plays the spunky Maggio, small, physically weak, and pugnacious as a Pekinese, who out of male bravado stands up to a sadistic, two-hundred-and-fifty-pound army brute played to the vicious hilt by Ernest Borgnine. Sinatra even spits at his adversary when asked by "Fatso" (Borgnine) if it hurts as Fatso slams the billy club again into his guts. Sinatra, dying, is cradled in Clift's arms, and later Clift plays a moving taps on his bugle for his dead buddy, tears running down his face. A real man, we find, both feels and when pressed to the limit summons fighting skills, as Clift goes out to kill the monstrous Borgnine, enlisting the boxing prowess he has vowed to relinquish and which has led him to withstand precisely such Fatso-like bullying until now. It is as if the old male values win out because they do not permit the alternatives to survive. In this perverse sense, Fatso and his ilk triumph by finally forcing Clift to revert to their code. But the buddy relationship between Clift and Sinatra carries little of the erotic charge such friendships will in the seventies. It does not prevent Clift from loving a woman (Donna Reed). It provides him solely with an outlet for his compassion and his need to be a friend and a kind human being. The army becomes an appropriate emblem for the brutalization of the male, raising to explicit heights the masculine mystique in the culture. It would destroy all finer feelings and compassion in men. It is the need to humanize this masculine ideal that leads Lancaster to his decision not to marry Kerr; he refuses to become another officer perpetuating this de-based male standard.

The film's conclusion is a jarring capitulation, taking back much of what it has given as both Clift and Lancaster rise to the occasion of the Japanese attack, placing their loyalty to the army before their love for their women. Clift is eulogized accordingly by Lancaster in precisely those terms: "He loved the army more than any soldier I ever knew." Notwithstanding the sanction of patriotic duty in time of war which the film, like the society, uses to whip men back into line, the ending reverts, suggesting once again on the Hollywood screen, despite the brave moments of sensitivity within the film, that domesticity threatens male self-sufficiency. The heterosexuality of our heroes is assured by the compelling nature of the attack on Pearl Harbor, as the clear and distinct reason why they send their women back to the United States and go off among their male buddies to fight the good fight in the same army with the old values. But while the ending thus undermines the nuanced reassessment of male identity in *From Here to Eternity*, it cannot wholly eradicate it.

Most of the male-female relationships in films of the fifties ultimately restore the male to proper supremacy over women. In *Bus Stop* (1958) Don Murray as Bo must first agree to change his approach to women, for he regards them as recalcitrant cattle. He is taught to value Cherie (Marilyn Monroe) as a person and to abandon treating her like a cow. But once he apologizes for his insensitivity, she agrees with alacrity to give up her life to him, cooing, "I'd go anywhere in the world with you now."

The formula, as in *Giant*, is refined. Most fifties films which acknowledge sexual inequality and show at least ambivalence about male roles do so only to reinvoke the old solutions unimpaired. If Tom Ewell feels *The Seven-Year Itch* (1956), as the film acknowledges that monogamous sexuality is a difficult ideal to live up to, nothing has occurred between Ewell and Marilyn Monroe by the time the film concludes. The straying husband, a rotund cherub, should, we learn, have been glad to have a wife in the first place. Having failed in his abortive halfhearted effort to be unfaithful with "the Girl" upstairs (Monroe, who has no name in the film), he is restored to an exasperated spouse. If *Some Like It Hot* (1959) seems daring in its depiction of Tony Curtis and Jack Lemmon prancing through the film in drag as musicians on the lam, the disguise is so obvious that their masculinity is never seriously in question. This contrasts with the disguise, which makes him look very much like a woman, of Jeff Bridges as Lightfoot to Clint Eastwood's Thunderbolt in a latently homosexual buddy film of the seventies entitled, appropriately enough, *Thunderbolt and Lightfoot* (1974). And to counteract any doubt we may feel about the ease with which they assume the clothing and mannerisms of women, Curtis is provided a heavy, overelaborated seduction scene with

Monroe on a borrowed yacht. In the best fifties manner, Monroe's approach to Curtis is highly titillating as he challenges her to cure his nonexistent impotence. If anything, the musicians in drag are so virile that the effect is to poke fun at effeminate men who don't wear the clothing of women but who behave ordinarily with diffidence and an absence of sexual panache. If, therefore, sexual roles are the film's nominal subject, the question is posed for the purpose of refurbishing the old answers.

Neither here nor in the 1949 *I Was a Male War Bride* is the theme of transvestism treated seriously. As a typical fifties film, *Some Like It Hot* would dismiss any doubt about the feasibility either of women leaving behind their traditional roles or of men not living up to the norms concerning masculine prowess. That it came in the fifties is not surprising, given this decade's reactionary treatment of women. The transvestism serves to bestow contempt upon women, since the men imitate female behavior with mincing steps, high voices, narcissism, and self-indulgence, a grotesque caricature of the sex. Instead of emasculating these males or challenging macho stereotypes, the drag enforces the old values by pointing up the supposed absurdity of being female. These disguises thus work to disparage both women and "effeminate" men who do not live up to the womanizing, leering role Curtis and Lemmon assume when they are not wearing women's clothes. Their transvestism attacks men who are more like women than men, and women in general, and is only a ploy to set off "unwholesome" sexual deviations from the standard male norm. In contrast is Brando's use of transvestism in *The Missouri Breaks* (1976). Playing a vicious "regulator," or "enforcer," meant to behave exactly as Clint Eastwood does in his third Dirty Harry film, he dons a granny nightgown to deflate the current fanatic glorification of violence in both the Western and the police film. He even takes a bubble bath in one scene for the same reason.

Often male heterosexuality was celebrated, indeed exalted, as if it were under some mysterious challenge. In *The Quiet Man* (1952) John Wayne is more powerful than ever, precisely because he is pitted against a woman of spirit (Maureen O'Hara) whom he must conquer. As usual, Wayne plays himself, here a six-foot-four-inch Pittsburgh steel worker and former boxer (again) who once killed a man in the ring. He has retired to Ireland, where at predictable first sight he falls in love with Mary Kate (O'Hara), whom he wants almost as a horse breeder would a high-strung mare. He is thus a man who wants a woman, and no obstacle, whether Mary Kate's brother or Mary Kate herself, who won't sleep with him until he retrieves her dowry, will stand long in his way. He even breaks down her symbolic door: "There'll be no locks and bolts between us." By the end he has dragged her kicking and screaming to their home. On the way a woman offers him "a good stick to beat the lovely lady." It is a rather charming film, its lyricism concealing that at its heart lies some loss of confidence in the credibility of the supermale.

Such fifties romances recapitulate all the traditional expectations of masculinity. Their interest consists in the stridency with which they attempt an antidote to doubt and in the fact that such romances have virtually disappeared from the screen. Hollywood males since the fifties have ceased to find any value in pursuing women at all, for as women have become more autonomous and aware, Hollywood has immunized its men from the disease by eliminating women from the screen.

The passion of Lancaster for Kerr in *From Here to Eternity* never quite reappears in the American film. But it is also true that heterosexuality in fifties films came at a price: the women were almost invariably demeaned. In this *The Quiet Man* is an exception, for although the woman is conquered she does some conquering as well, and never is she a simpering fool or a weak, whining child. Ford would repeat the theme of a strong man taming a woman in *Mogambo* (1953), with its love triangle between great white hunter Clark Gable and two wholly different women, Ava Gardner and Grace Kelly. Gardner, the dark sultry woman, is an independent adventuress, the loose women of spirit who can never be a man's first choice, given the morality of the day. Kelly is first presented as the ideal woman to possess, the wife of a scientist who, as an intellectual, must inevitably leave her frustrated and longing for a real man. Gable is the sex object both women want. It is interesting that in the fifties, the triangle replaces competition between two men for a woman by two women waiting to be won by a single man. Gardner, the comradely, free-and-easy woman, is rejected at once by Gable. The sensual woman who makes no pretense of being demure cannot be trusted, and Gable dismisses her for not having "an honest feeling from her kneecap to her neck." The old fear that an independent woman will rob a man of his virility appears here as a cautionary note. Finally Gardner succeeds in extricating Gable from his uninspiring alliance with Kelly, whose dullness, consequent upon conforming to male requirements of docility, makes her not to his taste after all. Gable accepts Gardner, who at once jumps out of her departing boat into the water, so keen is she to reclaim him.

The infinitely desirable male stands at the center of all the fifties romances, which only appear to elevate woman as the sexual object. Despite the endless assessment of female attributes, the men are the real prize. In each of Marilyn Monroe's films a male is the central figure, from Robert Mitchum in *The River of No Return* (1954), Laurence Olivier in *The Prince and the Showgirl* (1957), and Yves Montand in *Let's Make Love* (1960) to Gable himself in *The Misfits* (1961). A notable exception is *Tea and Sympathy* (1956), which—if self-consciously—rejects the notion that a male who is frail and not good at sports is probably homosexual. However evasive the film, its insistence that the boy (Leif Erikson) initiated by Deborah Kerr is as much a man as any manifests fifties filmmaking in its most honest mode. And it turns out that the boy's persecutor, Kerr's husband, a superjock, is actually a repressed homosexual, a coach of athletes who releases his erotic impulses among young men and refuses to sleep with his wife.

The fifties evaluation of the appropriate relationship between a man and a woman is most clearly summed up in a comedy like *Dream Wife* (1953). Cary Grant plays the desirable male in search of a "perfect mate," bearing the heavy implication that he can win any woman whom he fancies. His choice narrows to a Middle Eastern princess trained in subservience ("I didn't know they still made them like this") and an independent career woman, Deborah Kerr in the role of a state department executive. The price of this woman's autonomy is posted: she will lose a prize male like Cary Grant unless she drops her career to return to home and hearth. Otherwise, he will indeed select the classical female alternative in feudal and slavish subservience.

Dream Wife fashions the male image of Cary Grant in a manner designed to convince the career woman that she had best return to the home. He is the romantic, arranging dinner to candlelight and soft music, living evidence that a strong man need not be immune to the finer things. He is even ready for the wedding without the usual male reluctance, as the fifties romance insisted that men had no qualms about marriage. It is Kerr who, in a satirical reversal, postpones the wedding because it interferes with her work, and Grant who argues slyly that the suffragettes "were probably lousy housekeepers," to the film's silent applause.

The ending provides a double reverse in that Grant rejects the princess, whom he compares (à la Paul Lynde) to his dog, Bruno. What he seeks is indeed a strong woman, but one who will devote her distinctive energies to the home, which is dressed up as a career in itself. In reality it is a role as subservient as its counterpart in the Middle East—and also veiled. She must retain the façade of strength and autonomy while fulfilling all the old functions. Her only real freedom is to serve a man. Such films provide a backlash to the decade's own re-examination on screen of male dominance. The princess proves to be a poor choice, since she mistakes her new freedom in the United States for license, opening charge accounts and picking up men in the streets.

The princess herself is a thinly disguised symbol of the traditional woman in America, slowly emerging in the fifties from the cloak of the male-protected home at the same time that the male's patina of invulnerable command is being chipped away on screen. But films of the decade sounded a cautionary note as well. Escape from servitude should not lead a woman to an unanchored life on her insufficient own. She should return to the home on different terms, less slavish and more spirited—rather like a salaried worker as opposed to a serf. But if the status and state of mind are different, the role is not. Men may become more aware and debonair and women more spirited and less servile, but the woman must stay at home.

The male sense of values, dissembling aside, totally pervades all fifties films about the relationship between men and women, no less in *Dream Wife* than in *Love in the Afternoon* (1957), in which director and male star conspire to celebrate the relationship between an aging Gary Cooper and an Audrey Hepburn of half his years. Were the male lead Hepburn's age and the female that of Cooper, it would hardly be as romantic.

The whole campaign for male superiority might be summed up for the fifties in Robert Wise's *Somebody Up There Likes Me* (1956), with Paul Newman playing boxer Rocky Graziano as a street kid who uses his fists to catapult him into fame and respectability. By the fifties, the industry felt that America was sufficiently beyond the Depression to allow working-class heroes in films. They reappeared in the fifties in order to reaffirm that upward mobility was still possible in America. It is a pollyanna motif which constitutes a clear regression from the more honest, if dark, days of the *film noir* when a hero like John Garfield in *Force of Evil* could not retain his integrity while working within the established order; by the end he has fallen back into the class from which he rose. In the boxing films of the forties, from *Body and Soul* to *The Set-up* to their fifties descendant, *The Harder They Fall*, the world of the prizefighter was a symbol of the degeneration and corruption of the society in general. *Somebody Up There Likes Me* is a saccharine example of the willed optimism of the fifties; dishonesty in boxing is presented as marginal and easily overcome.

Drawing on the Brando-Dean innovations for the male hero, the film presents Newman as a man rendered brutal by a father who "didn't like crybabies." Here such insight is reduced to a trite psychologism, for it is deployed to account for the protagonist's early hostility to authority, which is seen as unjustifiable. Psychology is invoked solely to deny a social basis for Graziano's anger, as if poverty would not reinforce and render appropriate his childhood hostility. The film goes on to applaud his toughness, physical brutality, and defiance, including his wildness in reform school and elsewhere. If it begins by perceiving these attributes as expressions of psychic damage, it later prefers to view them as admirable. Finally, we are meant to succumb to Newman, with his fists like a "lead pipe," bulging biceps, flat belly, and curly hair. If there are token moments of sensitivity, as when he learns of his mother's nervous breakdown and cries in frustration and pain, for the most part it is his raw "masculinity" that is exalted.

Somebody Up There Likes Me is a film in the service of the conformity of the fifties. It dictates to men that they should enlist all their strength in a quest for success within the established order. Graziano's are formula rewards, as he wins a "good" woman as well as the middleweight championship and, in an image borrowed from *Gone with the Wind,* becomes a proud poppa pushing a baby carriage. If in *Body and Soul* success was tainted because it required compromise with corruption, it is not so blemished here. Graziano will overcome blackmail, and his refusal to name those who approached him to throw a fight is a nice reversal of the glorification of informing in *On the Waterfront.* Even his stern, unloving father comes around: "Be a champ, like I never was!" The father now is seen, not as the jealous sexual rival of his son, but simply as himself, a frustrated fighter. Abandoning the psychological premise with which it begins, the film treats the hostility between father and son as superficial in origin and easily transcended.

Unlike those films which examined conventional notions of masculinity, this biography of the hero who began with no advantages only to become "champion of the world" is faithful to the spirit and the letter of the fifties' celebration of the established. True grit is all; success in the world is the only thing worth having, and it is attainable without the loss of one's soul. Marriage to a good woman, raising children, cherishing the nuclear family, making one's parents proud, and proving to the neighborhood that in America even a nobody, a former juvenile delinquent and ex-con, has "God on his side" compose the litany of values endorsed here. Only a heavenly choir and sun rays piercing the clouds are missing as we learn that any male who lives in keeping with these aspirations cannot help but be happy. The silver lining of American promise was refurbished in such fifties films as unquestionable and holy. Only in the 1960s would we finally be offered males whose manhood was inseparable from the will to challenge these values. This phenomenon arose not, as some have argued, because film audiences were composed primarily of alienated young people. Rather, it appeared because, emerging from the thrall of the fifties and aided in part by the more searching films of that decade, the culture itself was shaken by highly articulate and organized demands for change.

Paul Newman as Rocky Graziano (with Pier Angeli) in *Somebody Up There Likes Me:* True grit is all; success in the world is the only thing worth having, and it is attainable without the loss of one's soul.

The Sixties

In keeping with the harshness of America's policy abroad and spreading social ferment at home, the male hero in films of the 1960s predominantly became hard, ungenerous, threatened, and alone. As the decade wore on, those sensitive, introspective heroes of the fifties screen rapidly disappeared. Hollywood behaved as it had in the early forties, eliminating sensitivity in response to what it conceived to be the national interest. Psychological nuance in male behavior as depicted in the Brando films vanished as the Vietnam War progressed. Maleness itself appeared under siege and in need of defense. By the end of the decade, in such films as *Midnight Cowboy, The Wild Bunch,* and *Butch Cassidy and the Sundance Kid,* masculinity was treated as possible for men only through the exclusion of women from their lives.

One might have expected films of the early sixties to display optimism, reflecting the mood that attended the amelioration of the cold war after the death of Stalin. But Kennedy's rhetoric notwithstanding, the early sixties were rife with apprehension about nuclear annihilation and the powerlessness of individuals to affect matters of life and death. In contrast to such movies as *Pillow Talk,* many films of the early sixties revealed an inarticulate but prevalent despair. Some of the mannerisms of the fifties remained, but none of the optimism.

Historically, the early sixties were a prewar time, for the meaning of America's involvement in Vietnam had not yet penetrated the popular culture. The male hero gave up the possibility of success in a manner parallel to that of the postwar *film noir* of the late forties. When the American assault upon Vietnam surfaced in films, it did so through the arrogance and brutality of the secret-agent films peopled by James Bond and his imitators—self-confident and successful. But the anxiety at home is reflected in the early-sixties hero who has given up hope both in himself and in his society. Films like *The Hustler* and *The Cincinnati Kid* view life as a game fought by men within a society utterly hostile to their needs. In a revealing inversion, belief in the possibility of triumph and personal victory becomes unmanly because such pretensions expose the male as out of touch with reality. Whatever the causes, numerous films of the early sixties concern men who are losers.

The hero may survive and even score a minor moral victory, as in *The Hustler*, but he is marked above all by the tenuousness of his control over his life, whatever his physical capacities. The absence of psychological portraiture in these sixties films flows from the shocking discovery that physical strength and masculine bravado count for very little in an environment so unrelentingly hostile to any attempt by the individual to control his own destiny or to affect those in power. It is a social setting particularly vindictive toward the male arrogant enough still to believe that his personal qualities afford him some measure of superiority.

In the best films of the sixties, the financially successful as well as the minor ones, a dark mood governs the hero. The male image in so many sixties films reflects, not the enthusiasms of the civil rights movement, the antiwar struggle, or the counterculture, but the spirit accompanying the political assassinations which defined the decade: those of the Kennedy brothers, Medgar Evers, Martin Luther King, and Malcolm X, and the attempt on the life of George Wallace.

The economic prosperity of the fifties had induced Hollywood to give us a male on screen who roused himself from the despair of the *film noir* and regained a certain confidence in his own power to influence the world. The traumatic events of the sixties induced the Hollywood hero to tighten up, to reveal as little about himself as possible, and to find comfort in his own recalcitrance. Only with antagonism and on rare occasions would Hollywood at the end of the decade even admit into its films those young people who claimed that they were rebels *with* a cause, successfully devising new life-styles and articulating dissent against the established order. The important male stars admitted in their demeanor no disagreement with the sexual repressiveness of life in fifties America, whatever claims the young asserted about a sexual revolution. In films of the sixties there are vanishingly few examples of harmonious sexual relationships between men and women.

The most pervasive male image of the decade, that of James Bond as portrayed by Sean Connery, could relate to women only on a comic-book level by transferring to the screen the pubescent distaste for women disguised as lust for female objects like those flaunted by *Playboy* magazine. Bond may have performed ridiculous antics, but the Bond films appeared as parody only to the eye of the sophisticate. They were more in the image and spirit of Mickey Spillane of the fifties than of Robert Altman. Bond never doubted that women were sex objects eternally ready and grateful for his use; nor did he doubt his mission as a secret agent holding together the empire of the "free world."

Bond, however, could occasionally display wit and even direct it against himself. As Clint Eastwood began to take his place and became the most financially successful male star, even such marginal humor disappeared, first in the "spaghetti" Westerns Eastwood made in Italy and later in those shot in America. A morbid dread of feeling prevents Eastwood's voice from assuming any inflection and usually prevents him from speaking at all. He is estranged from everyone, and in his seeming "cool," his mannerisms, despite his service to authority, coalesce with the counterculture's own estrangement from nation, family, university—from authority in general—accounting ironically for his growing popularity with young men despite his contempt for them on screen. His impassive silence, while not on behalf of any political dissent—for he acts on behalf of the most violent and ruthless elements of the established order—duplicated nevertheless the spiritual mood of the sixties. Like the young so hostile to externally imposed standards of behavior, he has learned to distrust everything but his own effectiveness.

The sixties concluded with those paeans to male bonding and compulsive all-male relationships which would set the tone for a plethora of such films in the seventies. The male hero is so besieged by hostile forces that he rejects all open sexuality. Women disappear from his life because with them he would be expected to respond sexually. With other men he enters into relationships which are homosexual in feeling. Yet intimate relations between men, even though they are comfortable only with each other, are prevented. They are driven to participate in endless tests designed to demonstrate a strong heterosexual masculinity, and then to sublimate that feeling in distorted and one-sided male friendships. In unacknowledged need and a despair too frightening to ponder, the male hero finds that he can love and trust only another man.

The world had become doubly sinister since the days of the *film noir*. To accept failure, as John Garfield does in *Force of Evil*, was not even an option. As the sixties drew to a close the male increasingly found his very life on the line, his anxiety all-pervasive. In fifties films like *On the Waterfront*, *Rebel Without a Cause*, or *Somebody Up There Likes Me*, there seemed sufficient time for a male to find himself, to recover his identity through relationships with both women and other men. Time had run out for heroes of the sixties, for those played by Beatty in *Bonnie and Clyde*, or Fonda and Hopper in *Easy Rider*, for Peckinpah's *Wild Bunch*, and for the romantic male team of Newman and Redford in *Butch Cassidy and the Sundance Kid*. Women were now one more enemy threatening a man's dignity and self-sufficiency.

That James Bond and later the heroes played by Clint Eastwood should emerge as the most influential examples of the masculine male in films of the sixties both paralleled and reinforced macho values in American politics. Ushering in the decade as the most attractive political figure of the day was John F. Kennedy, affecting a style that was half (Henry) Fonda and half Wayne. The Kennedy charm barely concealed an authoritarian male image. With his perpetual wintertime suntan, his refusal to wear an overcoat or hat in freezing January and February, Kennedy also drew his style from Humphrey Bogart. He was an avid reader of the James Bond thrillers by Ian Fleming, and his love affairs have since become legend, but should have come as no surprise given the mode of masculinity he affected; Don Juanism perfectly suited Kennedy's devil-may-care attitudes, if not the office he held. Insisting on being represented in the press as more powerful than the ordinary man, he instructed newsmen never to call him "Jack" in print. In so many aspects Kennedy's style resembles that of Connery as James Bond. Like Bond, Kennedy had an almost inexhaustible supply of mistresses, and he and Lyndon Johnson after him proposed a Bond-style politics of confrontation with the Russians. During the Cuban missile crisis Kennedy became the aggressive supermale, and he sustained that posture in his obsession with Green Berets and Rangers—male commandos of counterinsurgency—as his first "solution" to trouble in Southeast Asia.

Politics was conceived in terms of two rival gangs squaring off with broken bottles and zip guns, with the American side led by the coolest, most stoical and domineering leader. In 1964 Stanley Kubrick would satirize this sick version of maleness in *Dr. Strangelove*, with Sterling Hayden as a Pentagon psychopath tormented over the depletion of his bodily juices. The bomb builder, modeled after Werner von Braun (an early Henry Kissinger), was viewed, appropriately enough, as a madman. The cold war, which was leading us to nuclear annihilation, was seen as the work of a ruling group manned by psychologically disturbed dominant males.

But *Dr. Strangelove* was an anomaly in the cinema of the sixties, which belonged to Bond and his imitators. Director Kubrick, like Orson Welles before him, found no space for his vision in the United States and emigrated to Great Britain. At a time when the continual talk was of "missile gaps," and it was believed only a strong leader could save us, the John Wayne approach to masculinity was revived as if the fifties and Brando and Dean had had no impact on the American film. One year after the release of *Dr. Strangelove*, Johnson began mercilessly to bomb the north of Vietnam. Terms such as "weak-kneed" and "jelly-backed" were attached to those who opposed the war, as if political belligerence and true masculinity were synonymous. A man who did not support the war was dubbed by Lyndon Johnson a "nervous Nellie," no better than a woman:

There will be some Nervous Nellies and some who will become frustrated
and bothered and break ranks under the strain. And some will turn on their
leaders and on their country and on our own fighting men.*

Movies of the sixties insisted that masculinity was equivalent to superhuman physical strength and sexual prowess, the model for which was
James Bond. And just as films expected of men sexual feats they had no
capacity to perform, derived as they were from fantasies of male power,
so the political life of the country, against which the young protested so
vigorously, was based upon one falsehood after another.

In contrast to World War II, which was a subject of the American film
from the moment of Pearl Harbor, the Vietnam War was virtually taboo
on screen. One of the few movies made about the war in the sixties was
The Green Berets (1968), which sanctioned as both manly and correct CIA
penetration of foreign governments and control of their internal affairs.
John Wayne produced, starred, and assisted in the direction of this film,
which exalts the courage of those men who put themselves in the line of
fire of those sly "Vietcong," portrayed in the racist mode of vintage
World War II "Japs." A reporter, skeptical about the war, appears in the
film as a foil. He becomes so indignant at the malevolence of America's
"enemies" that he does what any red-blooded American male would: he
picks up a gun and joins the fight.

At one point in *The Green Berets* a Vietnamese boy attached to a GI
named Peterson, who is killed in a raid, asks Colonel Wayne, "Was my
Peterson brave?" Wayne replies in character: "He was very brave. Are
you going to be brave?" The Vietnamese victims of American nerve gas,
electric torture, bacteriological weaponry, and the fragmentation bomb-
ing of both North and South are shown to prefer their tormentors, the
Americans, and to rise to the occasion of the example of masculinity set
by the invader. "I'll try," says the child. And having revealed his fiber like
Matthew in *Red River*, the boy is rewarded. Wayne places on his head
a green beret, a rite of passage marking his entrance into manhood,
identified here with American aggression in Vietnam. The Green Berets
were intelligence agents, an elite unit trained in the breaking of Vietnamese prisoners of war and even the village peasantry through "interro-
gation" and torture. A Vietnamese child is perverted into identifying his
own maturity as a man with such destroyers of his people, those callous
enemies of human life and dignity, the Green Berets.

Just as it took nearly fifteen years after Hiroshima and Nagasaki and
a world-wide "ban the bomb" movement to produce a film about the
danger of nuclear war *(Dr. Strangelove)*, we had to wait as long again for
a film that was honest about Vietnam. And only a director of proven
box-office pull, post-*Godfather* Francis Ford Coppola, could obtain back-

*Speech at a Democratic Party fund-raising dinner, May 17, 1966.

ing in 1976 for his *Apocalypse Now*. (Coppola in fact had to mortgage his personal assets as collateral to swing these loans.) Who among the corporations that finance films would pay for one challenging the masculinity of men like Lieutenant Calley and portray the massacre at My Lai as a travesty of maleness and a perversion of the human spirit?

During the sixties there were also some films which attempted to placate the disaffected, providing vicarious outlets for the pent-up energies of those frustrated by the absence of change. The most obvious of these was Arthur Penn's *Bonnie and Clyde* (1967), which concludes in a phantasmagoria of bloodshed designed both to numb and to intimidate. What was unique about *Bonnie and Clyde* was one facet which addressed the alienation of the young of the sixties from the dominant values of the culture. Openly avowing that the masculine mystique epitomized by John Wayne in decade after decade was a decreasingly viable lie, the film had Clyde share in the sexual impotence of his real-life counterpart.

Other escapist films to address the mood of the times included *The Graduate* (1967), which purported to offer a bona-fide counterculture hero rejecting the conformist and materialistic behavior of his parents, only to have him embrace many of these values by the film's conclusion. *Easy Rider* (1969) punished the male dropout who sought a life-style on his own terms with consequent annihilation at the hands of Southern crackers who stand for mainstream America. Nominally sympathetic to its protagonists, *Easy Rider* shows its heroes as not merely dissolute but adrift. They are lost souls in a menacing, ugly world, and if they represent disaffection, they are deployed to encourage despair.

I

The Hustler (1961), in bridging the fifties and sixties, reveals how tenuous it had already become for a male to retain manliness and also commit himself to a woman. The hero, Eddie, played by Paul Newman in a manner evoking the anguish characteristic of the male image on screen during the fifties, is brash, physically powerful, nonverbal, nonintellectual, and intensely competitive in the style of John Wayne. Yet equally derived from the fifties is the fact that Eddie lacks any real social outlet for that competitiveness, no arena which would allow him to be a man. A salesman, Eddie is a man only when he plays pool. The game becomes a vehicle for the expression of his male identity, thwarted in his normal work and the sole means by which he can progress toward that "cool" which has been the emblem of masculinity in the American film since Gary Cooper in *The Virginian*. *The Hustler* thus spans the two decades:

the male is tormented and forced to the periphery of a society in which he fails to find a satisfying role. Yet he is returned to the late forties in his stoicism, fierce competitiveness, and devotion to proving himself a man.

As he plays pool, Eddie guzzles bourbon straight from the bottle, affecting a "masculine" posture. A cigarette dangles from his lips in the manner of Bogart. He has learned never to walk away from an encounter. Eddie plays pool until his money runs out, risking all because his drive to succeed is so overwhelming. A man must test himself against his superiors, and Eddie challenges "Minnesota Fats" (Jackie Gleason), the best pool.player in the country. No one has beaten Minnesota Fats for fifteen years, but Eddie as a man in America in the pre-counterculture years of the sixties cannot rest until he has become "the best."

By the close of *The Hustler* Eddie has betrayed the woman who was devoted to him: "I loved her. I traded her in on a pool game," he comments, having acquiesced in her humiliation by Burt, a pool sharpie played by George C. Scott. Eddie failed to be available to her when she needed him, for the game and winning are all and a man makes his first commitment to success. If his woman is too insecure to survive in second place, she will have to risk destruction. Lame, alcoholic Sarah (Piper Laurie), wholly dependent, kills herself upon being so abandoned.

The sexuality of Eddie joins the fifties and sixties. The gaze of his light eyes is direct and bold, offering more honesty than the gruffness of John Wayne or the shyness of Jimmy Stewart and Gary Cooper. His biceps bulge as he parades about in an undershirt similar to that which Brando made an emblem of masculinity in *Streetcar*. Like many fifties heroes, Eddie can be gentle, as when he bandages Sarah's cut finger. And throughout he carries a little boy's vulnerability, which allows him to accept a woman's help. Yet like Cooper he is too alienated from his feelings to speak the words "I love you," assuring that distance between man and woman typical of the American film. The melodramatic ending in which Sarah is raped by Burt (Scott) and Eddie retaliates by refusing to pay Burt off evades entirely the issue of how a relationship between a man and woman could work in the early years of this tumultuous decade.

But despite the downbeat ending, *The Hustler* is far from critical of the style of masculinity that leads to Eddie's destruction. His flaw lies, not in his heartlessness, but in his lack of sufficient cool. If he is guilty of allowing Sarah to die through suicide, the film would redeem him because he stands up to Burt: "You don't know what's living . . . you're dead . . . you're a loser." Morally restored, Eddie can cry, Newman at this point drawing upon the release allowed men portrayed in the fifties by Brando, Dean, and himself. Eddie repudiates the rackets and refuses to pay up, although the price of his defiance will be his right to enter pool competition again. He compliments Minnesota Fats on the great game of pool he plays and is rewarded in turn with homage to the masculinity of which he has spent his life in search: "So do you, fast Eddie." The offhand style of the compliment establishes the bond between them as much as the tribute itself.

Thus, far from challenging this assertive style of masculinity, *The Hustler* enshrines it, chastising Eddie for failing to learn the male rituals soon enough. His frantic competitiveness turns out to have been to his credit. It was entirely correct that he seek to be the best and aspire to challenge the champion. For who could blame Eddie for his escape from the emasculating role of salesman, a role no hero in an American film could accept without shame or emerge from with his masculine identity still intact? Eddie's error consisted in his being so overwhelmed by the game that he permitted himself to be edgy. *The Hustler* finally celebrates insensitivity and repression, positing these as touchstones of male effectiveness. It is Eddie's keenness for pool that undoes him, for any enthusiasm betrays desire. "He can't quit ... he's a loser" someone says. Inadvertently, *The Hustler* exposes what the need to "win" has done to the male in America.

The mood of disorientation and uneasiness which characterized *The Hustler* in its approach to maleness is further expressed in *The Cincinnati Kid* (1965). Like *The Hustler,* it attempts a spurious association of masculinity with gambling, as we shall find in the seventies with *The Gambler* (1975) and *California Split* (1974). In earlier Westerns like *My Darling Clementine,* the hero played and won at poker as a casual pastime. In the sixties, the male has been so deprived of something to which he can commit his passion and of a significant vocation that only in a compulsive fantasy world like gambling can he restore to himself the sense of free choice and the illusion of having some control over his own destiny, always indispensable for the male's sense of self.

As late as 1965 the masculine male in American films can still be called by that paradoxical nickname "the Kid," at once a code and a testament to the hero's toughness and fear of age as he yearns to be forever seventeen, eager, and potent. Only unconsciously does it carry the infantile nature of the grown man's frantic need to escape self-doubt with a six-gun or at the gambling table. When applied to a real youngster, the appellation announces that the hero, if a youth, is already a man. Billy the Kid was reputed to have killed his first adversary at the age of eleven, a fact included by director Arthur Penn in *The Left-Handed Gun.* Sometimes an older man retains "the Kid" as a nickname, insisting overly that age cannot undermine that masculinity embodied in the energy of a stripling. Cary Grant's aging sidekick in *Only Angels Have Wings* is called "the Kid," absurdly, the character being played by a Thomas Mitchell well along in years, with director Howard Hawks failing to make use of the irony. John Wayne was called "the Ringo Kid" in *Stagecoach*, leaving none of us in doubt that if he committed wrongs, he was as much a man as any who lived.

In *The Cincinnati Kid* we have Steve McQueen again as a "kid," a cool young man on the make if the second-best poker player, as Eddie was number two at pool in *The Hustler*. McQueen's adversary is portrayed by Edward G. Robinson, the older man against whose skill he must test his own masculinity. As Eddie consecrated his emotional life to defeating Minnesota Fats, the Cincinnati Kid re-creates the syndrome with Lancey Howard (Robinson).

There is a fierceness and desperation about the competition between males in these sixties films; with their world falling apart, males must win games, if only to locate purpose, discover goals in which to invest real emotion and through which to find surrogate reasons to continue living. Relationships with women recede and are renounced. "Women are no good for this life," counsels Lancey Howard, the canny sage. "Just tie into someone nice while it lasts." As in the Wayne cavalry Westerns, which so deeply influenced the characterization of maleness in the American film, an older, more experienced male initiates those younger into what it means to be a man.

A mood of nihilism pervades *The Cincinnati Kid*, the inexorable consequence of men forever in combat. The heavy-lidded McQueen does his best to be an adequate male by being wooden, expressing no feeling for anyone; he largely succeeds. He who is concerned least with life is the winner in this world, for caring is the prerogative of losers. Only one guideline remains for the foundering male: he must win without cheating, the last absurd vestige of a moral code as anachronistic as the honor of a hidalgo in a valueless world.

McQueen loses the big game with three aces in his hand, a defeat anticipated by a previous scene in which his "girl" discovered him in bed with another woman. That he had not a particle of feeling for the woman only adds to the sense of futility and moral decay. In the last scene the "kid" is even beaten when pitching coins with a shoeshine boy. "You tried too hard, man," he is told, echoing the code of *The Hustler;* "you just ain't ready for me yet." A male must learn actively to desire nothing, not even winning itself, for only when he is cynical about its value can he pursue the game. Such scorn for feeling leads with psychic inevitability to the slow death of sensation as this film, itself a paean to empty decadence, bemoans with crocodile tears the valueless world of the time. McQueen's naked chest and flaunted biceps are of depleted utility, given the film's theme that the world is now so depleted that no arena remains worthy even of masculine display.

II

The Westerns of the sixties treat the male hero in a mood of nostalgia, as if in remembrance of things lost. Implicitly they avow that the world in which the audience lives precludes belief in a frontier-era ethic. Such a mood pervades *The Magnificent Seven* (1960), an adaptation of that Japanese classic *Seven Samurai,* itself permeated by nostalgia for the passing from history of the warrior samurai class. Kurosawa's masterpiece depicts a time of transition in Japanese history with the feudal world of the warrior in early decay. The American version follows the original rather closely. Steve McQueen and Yul Brynner play male buddies, gunslingers in a world where individual hired guns have become obsolete. Knowing their way of life to be doomed, the two, more out of futility than conviction, agree to aid an impoverished Mexican village harassed by marauding bandits. Their commitment is at once gratuitous and sad because such warfare can only result in the depletion of their ranks, and the good deed serves finally to hasten the obsolescence of the masculine man of the West.

Before these rough, animal-like males, led by a cigar-smoking Brynner, men idealized by the film for their ability to maintain the legendary masculine toughness which "settled" the West, the peasants cower. These peasants are "afraid of everything," and as such are something less than men. They have had to hire gunmen because of their inability to rouse themselves to the violence necessary to defend their village, a brutality thoroughly endorsed by this film. Salesmen from the East, effete city-dwellers, are dubbed "dudes," passive men whose failure to call the necessary physical violence into play renders them decidedly unmasculine. The theme of tragedy in the film is attached to the insight that physical prowess and the ethic of John Wayne now, to our detriment, count for little, a thesis which, though set in the past, speaks directly to the beginning of the sixties.

Nor does the sensitivity of films of the fifties touch *The Magnificent Seven,* a film made in reaction to earlier portraits of sensitive males. Between Brynner and McQueen as gunslingers not a word of feeling passes as they communicate in gruff tones and one-word sentences. The most they will reveal about their sense of the world is an acknowledgment of the dead end to which their kind have come. The atmosphere is parallel to that closing *The Cincinnati Kid.* Male prowess suddenly is no longer enough: this is the source of their despair about the world. Sufficiently secure in his masculine persona that, like Bogart in *The Maltese Falcon,* he can admit his hands sweat "every time" before a fight, McQueen has for a long time ceased to find a conflict worth the risk of life. And since these men find their way of life in danger of extinction, they and their code are all the more glorified. Their word is their bond. The contract they effect with the peasants is not, says McQueen, "the kind that would hold up in court," but, Brynner responds, "just the kind you keep." Useless law, a vapid society, a civilization gone soft, and weak social institutions all conspire to thwart male identity. It is a sensibility akin to fascism in its *Weltschmerz*, the ripening of all that has been implicit in the myth of the powerful male. In contrast to *Red River*, the struggles of life now far outweigh its joys, a good measure of the distance we have traveled in psychic decay, notwithstanding the aesthetic disparity between these two films. McQueen once thought of settling down and raising cattle, as Wayne did in *Red River*, but this prospect has ceased to be available. Open land no longer exists, and men who once roamed (and plundered) it suffer most from the closing of the frontier.

That *The Magnificent Seven* finds the attempt to resurrect the most outworn worship of the male body, masculine strength, and manly fortitude no longer possible, while continuing to insist that these alone make life worth living, is a measure both of despair and desperation in the Hollywood of the sixties over the profound disaffection with these very values in the nation.

In *The Man Who Shot Liberty Valance* (1962), one of his finest films, John Ford participates in the nostalgia of sixties cinema for a lost machismo as he mourns the high price paid by this vanishing breed of men who try to remain true to the male ethic of the West. Once men like John Wayne —both the film's hero and the subject of its title—ensured our survival in the American wilderness. They have since been lost as a spurious consequence of "progress." Nostalgia here is not yet the formula it would become in the seventies, but it already reflects a deeply felt longing for a pure maleness whose absence even the Hollywood of the sixties celebrated in mourning.

Three styles of maleness are pitted against each other. Liberty Valance (Lee Marvin) is the male as outlaw, unrestrained and brutish, living by the ethic of a predatory *laissez-faire* as he takes whatever he wants, preying upon the weak and flourishing in the absence of law and order on the frontier. If his homicidal viciousness was once implicitly glorified when Indians were its object, now it is pilloried because settlers are his victims. If civilized life is to be sustained in the territory, families live in peace and educate their children, and the territory join the union, men like Liberty Valance must now be eliminated.

But who is to accomplish this? Ransom Stoddard (James Stewart) is a young lawyer come from the East to Shinbone, the town in which the film is set. He would defeat the Liberty Valances through reason, intellect, and common decency. He hangs out his shingle to invoke "the law." But the term is empty unless it can be enforced, and Stewart's indignation cannot make the slightest inroad in the power of the vicious Liberty, whose name carries the unsubtle statement that liberty unrestrained means license. He can be defeated, we learn, only by a man able to meet him on his own terms, strong enough to be his match in combat. John Wayne as Tom Doniphon is such a figure, the one person masculine enough to shoot Liberty Valance, and hence, by the film's set of values, the only male who has earned the right to call himself a man.

In films of the sixties to be such a man, even in a past setting, is no longer enough. The effeminate Stoddard, who in several scenes wears an apron, his logic and reason associated by Ford with domesticity, will falsely be given credit for having shot Liberty Valance. On the basis of this fraud he becomes the new state's first senator, and by claiming the male accomplishment of physical action against villainy, wins Doniphon's girl, Hallie (Vera Miles). In the hangdog sixties the world conspires against and betrays its authentic males.

Our world is now one represented by those newspaper reporters at the conclusion of the film who discover the true story of who shot Liberty Valance and suppress it; they represent the new social order based upon the perpetuation of lies. "When the legend becomes fact," one declares in a now classic line, "print the legend!" Manliness goes unrewarded; Doniphon is left to live out the remainder of his life alone and in obscurity, kept company only by Pompey (Woody Strode), his loyal black servant. Stoddard, on the strength of being thought to have killed Liberty Valance, gets the recognition, power, and dignity which are the prerogatives of the masculine male. The values remain, but the men who profess them are no longer worthy. It is a film like *The Magnificent Seven* in its regret for the passing of the man of action, but it goes beyond nostalgia to suggest that society has built its law and order on a lie. The weakness of Ford's conception lies in its false association of justice with the ability to enforce it and the further implication that unless we recover the male skills of a Doniphon, the legend will cease to suffice.

Framing scenes at the opening and closing of the film depict an aging couple, Mr. and Mrs. Ransom Stoddard, come home to Shinbone for the funeral of Tom Doniphon, a man no one else seems to know. Hallie Stoddard places a cactus rose on Tom's coffin. The years in Washington as the wife of Senator Stoddard seem to have brought her little happiness or contentment; she is eager to return permanently to Shinbone, still an authentic place, where her roots lie. Now she must attend the funeral of the man she would have done better to have chosen. "My heart is here," says Hallie.

We who have derived our community from both the prowess and the sacrifice of such men as Tom Doniphon will reap the whirlwind of incapacity and deceit. We have gone soft and lost our way. Doniphon dies alone and forgotten, to be buried by the county. Although it was he who brought the possibility of civilization to Shinbone, there is no mention of him in the records of this now flourishing town.

Sixties films about the absence of strong males to solve our problems would have us longing for a redeemer who is dangerously late, perhaps lost to us forever because we have not been worthy of him. We must as a consequence suffer our emptiness. Since neither the American film nor American culture has produced an alternative to the patriarchal Wayne, we keep returning to an adulation of his physical person. A decade before the women's liberation movement, films could still idealize Wayne's Tom Doniphon, a man who could never admit to a woman that he loved her and whose emotional depth is plumbed by such condescending clichés as "You're awful pretty when you get mad." To John Ford, Wayne's inarticulateness remains an emblem of his purity. If a woman neither perceives his virtue nor values his honest stolidity, she, like Hallie who marries the wrong man, is no better than a fool.

Thus *The Man Who Shot Liberty Valance* constantly contrasts the manliness of Wayne with the effeminacy of Stewart. Stewart drinks coffee; Wayne, whiskey. Stewart plays a man of the community, incapable of decisive action on his own and drawing others to his cause. Wayne proclaims, "Out here a man solves his own problems." Stewart seems sensible in allowing Liberty Valance to humiliate him when he picks up the steak Valance has thrown on the ground. It appears rational to avoid death by not getting provoked over a steak.

But the occasion of abuse begs the question, and such reasoning is the path to enslavement. Appeasement never works. Since willful malevolence is not amenable to rational appeal, Stewart's is the logic of capitulation. Hallie carries Ford's purpose when she cries out, "What good has readin' and writin' done you? Look at you—in an apron!"

Stewart's Ransom Stoddard offers Hallie the chance to see "a real rose," but it is only when she believes that he has at last summoned himself to manhood by shooting Liberty Valance that she accepts him. The rough, phallic cactus rose proves more appropriate and of more durable value than the "real" or cultivated substitute Stoddard offers. The progress for which Doniphon sacrificed all his hopes of happiness turns out to have been a sham. Someone is about to rob Doniphon's dead body of his very boots; materialism and greed prove to be the fruit of the new "civilization," on behalf of which he shot Liberty Valance.

When Senator Stoddard, the people's representative, descends from the train, no one recognizes him, for alienation of people from their leaders is another consequence of the taming of the West. Something precious has been lost in a culture that lacks a place for authentic men like Tom Doniphon. Representing the oldest and truest impulses of male America, Doniphon even lived with his black attendant Pompey, condescending proof that America was not really racist but protectively paternal. Pompey alone of all of Stoddard's literacy pupils remembers the line from the Declaration of Independence, "all men are created equal," as Ford suggests that America's victims really share its values. The devotion of Pompey to Doniphon proves his virtue. It is also part of Hollywood's consistent portrayal of blacks as basically loyal, as if the danger of black disaffection could be thus aborted, especially during the civil rights movement when this film was made.

Nostalgia alone accompanies the portrayal of the masculine human being, now an endangered species. Tom Doniphon was only capable of life as an individual; his "personal plans" prevented him from accepting a nomination as delegate to the territorial convention, for even as he was not a man to prowl legislative corridors making deals, his way of life was obsolete. Yet without his rugged individualism, his solitary male stance, there would have been no statehood for the lawless territory. He should have been a symbol, the beacon guiding future society; that he was not condemns us to the mediocrity of living a lie, of which we are reminded in the last moments of the film when an obsequious train conductor bows and scrapes to Senator Ransom Stoddard, to whom he proffers a brand-new cuspidor because "nothing's too good for the man who shot Liberty Valance."

III

The sixties was the decade of the glorification of the unprecedented power of the secret agent and the intelligence agencies. The Green Berets openly made their presence felt in Vietnam. The assassinations of Diem in Vietnam and Lumumba in the Congo have since been exposed as Central Intelligence Agency actions, as was the coup against Sukarno in Indonesia with its attendant slaughter of nearly one million people. Juan Bosch in the Dominican Republic was joined by Ben Bella in Algeria, Nkrumah in Ghana, and Goulart in Brazil, among so many. Within the United States, Malcolm X and Martin Luther King may have fallen in the same way. In film the American hero took lessons from the most popular male figure of the decade, Sean Connery as James Bond. Only in retrospect is it clear how crudely deliberate was the propaganda of the Bond films and how obviously they sanctioned what real-life 007's were doing all over the globe. In James Bond the cinema glorified the secret agent.

If ever there were a willed screen ideal, it was Bond, a loyal toiler in "Her Majesty's secret service," never questioning the cold-war premises behind his assignments. SPECTRE, Bond's ubiquitous adversary, was not merely the Soviet Union but any social challenge to Western capitalism. The veil concealing the social basis for male belligerence and domination was lifted. One Bond film, *From Russia with Love* (1963), makes explicit what had previously been implied. And the cold-war myth that unless we armed ourselves to the teeth the Russians—and as the decade produced détente, the Chinese—would camp on our very doorsteps is reflected in the Bond thriller *Goldfinger* (1964), in which SPECTRE's target is Fort Knox itself.

But Connery as Bond is no John Wayne. Where Wayne is always flesh and blood, Bond is plastic, a bionic man whose agility occurs at the whim of a concealed puppeteer. Where Wayne is meant to seem real, Bond is a cardboard figure, an obvious fabrication. There is a superficiality about the Bond characterization, almost an acknowledgment that despite the straight adventure-realism of these films, the woman-consuming male hero is but a fantasy. Bond can appear so inventive and physically inde-structible as he extricates himself from one certain death after another because he is not real. He is endlessly potent sexually because we are witnessing, not sexuality, but the use of the male sexual organ as a weapon of demolition. To many at the time, newly introduced to the foreign films of the decade, those works of Antonioni, Truffaut, Bergman, Buñuel, and Fellini which many felt were the only films worth seeing, Bond was grotesque, a cartoon parody of maleness. He could be enjoyed as camp. But that his exploits evoked approval in many, despite their dismissing these films as jokes, is revealed in their enormous box-office success. So enjoyable did both the innocent and the jaded find him that he occupied much of the space allocated to male personalities in the cinema, and this despite the fact that he originated in England. There was no Humphrey Bogart, Marlon Brando, or James Dean of the sixties, and the Bond films were more popular than far better films such as Paul Newman's *Hud* (1963) or *Cool Hand Luke* (1967).

The appeal of the Bond films may in the last analysis have been that beneath his exploits we sensed that he, like us, was powerless.

Wayne was always the engineer of his actions, a free man who made his own decisions, set his own goals, and chose his own course, as at the beginning of *Red River* when he alone decides to leave the wagon train. Bond, lacking any spiritual or moral sense of his own, always followed orders like a robot, mechanically fulfilling his assignments. What was meant to engross us in Bond was the manner of implementation, the technology availed him by the state to overcome his adversaries, never the value or purpose of the assignments themselves, which were deter-mined by others on the basis of considerations of which Bond himself was ignorant. His power flowed from the established order and his obeisance before it.

Thus, despite his sexual virtuosity, Bond was essentially a powerless

Sean Connery in *You Only Live Twice:* Bond's crude sexual exhibitionism shows only the need endlessly to prove a capacity which the more secure Wayne always took for granted.

male. His sexual bravado and the incredible vulgarity of such male fantasy figures as "Pussy Galore," the "heroine" of *Goldfinger,* only confirm this fact. John Wayne never had to display sexual prowess. Bond's crude sexual exhibitionism shows the need endlessly to prove a capacity the more secure Wayne always took for granted. The Bond image was thus not an updated version of the old-style masculine codes embodied by John Wayne and Gary Cooper. It offered a very different premise, in which the audience was drilled: in our complex age a potent man is someone who accepts direction from those who are powerful and above him. Equally, he accepts another's definition of what it means to be a man and acts upon this without reservation.

Maleness was thus preserved in the Bond films by the willing *sacrifice* of the hero's autonomy. It was his personal feeling that what he did was valuable and freely chosen which made the John Wayne image credible to many. He, like Cooper and Fairbanks Senior, cared about what he was doing; he had a decisive hand in shaping the future of his small universe. Bond cared only about winning, and if he, like Wayne and Cooper, was also indestructible, he was an alloy manufactured by the powerful as their tool.

Because their hero was so obedient to orders imposed from above by superiors far more knowledgeable and wise than he, the Bond films were antidemocratic to a degree never reached in those of Wayne. With their superhuman hero, they demanded that we place ourselves in the hands of an elite of strong leaders who alone had enough information to make political decisions and who alone could save us, since the fate of civilization itself was now at stake, a theme which entered the film with a vengeance in the sixties and seventies. The strong male overtly substituted himself for concerted action by the many, significantly in the same decade when mass movements arose protesting the very activities celebrated in the Bond series.

However obvious their message, and however outrageously unbelievable the hero's stunts, the Bond films were not without a certain significance. They attempted to undermine disaffection by insisting that only the supermale hero could save us. In *Thunderball* (1965), the Ban The Bomb movement (1958–1962) is ridiculed. Bond alone, a man of incalculable power, is able to locate the two stolen atom bombs which SPECTRE plans to detonate. With his open shirt displaying a chest of matted hair offered as the epitome of virility, Bond might be viewed as the response of the status quo to the ferment of the sixties. To the large numbers of people making their voices heard in this decade, attempting to influence the political issues of the day, the Bond films counterposed one individual who could do it all—but always on behalf of the ruling order.

Since Bond obviously appealed most immediately to male adolescents, the films offered its young audience vicarious identification with a *Play-*

boy-style adventurer and superman. They were made in rapid succession, one a year, from *Dr. No* in 1962 to *Thunderball* in 1965; 1967 and 1971 saw *You Only Live Twice* and *Diamonds Are Forever,* an effort to sustain the fantasy. If Roger Moore had replaced an aging Connery, *Live and Let Die* (1973) lived up to its title. By 1977 there would be ten Bond sagas.

The protest movements had numbers; Bond offered to young men involved neither in the counterculture nor antiwar activity not only the image of a man with iron fists in the manner of John Wayne, but trick vehicles and weird devices that each Bond film would pause to examine, catalogue, and demonstrate—toys to divert the young. Tom Mix's helper was a living creature and his best friend, Tony the Wonder Horse. Bond, the plastic human being, had as companions only inanimate objects, such technological contraptions as flame throwers, trick cars, fancy parachutes, and walkie-talkies—gadgets clearly intended to make us see how inadequate are our own resources, how futile it is to oppose such power, and how nice it would be to gain access to such delights by serving such a master.

The message is clear: Vicarious identification with the power of a male superior to ourselves is preferable to our own ineffectual efforts to change the course of events. And from the frustration of our inability to prevent such dangers as the mad stockpiling of nuclear weapons, the Bond films create a dream world in which everything turns out all right. We are thus urged to place ourselves in the hands of secret agents like Bond; it is as if the producers of these films had taken instruction from the Central Intelligence Agency itself, so blatant is the rationale for the spy and the intelligence killer "protecting" us by doing their worst in endless foreign lands. And Bond himself, of course, always travels the globe.

The male we are subjected to on screen is infinitely boring, a predictable figure with no personal range. It is his personality as well as his arsenal that is mechanical, ever dependent on cheap surprises to keep us watching, as in the first sequence of *Thunderball* when Bond slugs a woman in widow's weeds. "She" proves to be a man. Even if this had not been the case, so dedicated is Bond to his cause that he would not hesitate to smash a woman if she were working for the sinister other side, like the vicious character played by Lotte Lenya in *From Russia with Love,* who carries her own virulent weapons.

Beyond his secret agentry, Bond acts for NATO and the United States, as in *Goldfinger. Dr. No* shows us that he is on the side as well of *white* civilization, for here the villain is an insidious Oriental. With *You Only Live Twice* we enter the mood of détente with the Soviet Union. The villain is now intercepting both United States and Soviet space capsules, hoping to trigger a nuclear confrontation between these two powers. The threat to world security has become the "Red Chinese" in this film set in Japan but taking place partly on "Matsu," one of the offshore islands that became an issue in the Kennedy-Nixon debates of the 1960 presidential election. The Chinese have teamed up with former Nazis and, like their predecessor and model, they are out to dominate the world. A subplot casts a doubtful eye on the resurgence of Japanese militarism, with the clear implication that no Orientals are to be trusted and that the Japanese may well rise again, this time on the side of the Chinese. Other Japanese who support us are Westernized enough to be tolerated.

The Bond films are intensely racist, in obvious defiance of the growing conviction in the United States that racism was a blight upon the land. Invariably the films pit white against yellow. Oriental *women*, always potentially treacherous, must be watched with special care. Even the humor of the Bond films is racist. In *You Only Live Twice* Bond asserts that the "white" manner of lovemaking is superior. He must, even in sex, remain on top, refusing to taint his sexual life "Japanese style."

In appearance Bond is a person of the fifties, not the sixties. His dark hair is cut short; the roughness of his accent revives the myth of working-class virility. His wit is that of a schoolboy: when told that in Japan men always come first, he declares, "I may retire here." Bond also suggests a pre-fifties ideal in that he has no need finally of money, cars, or clothes —all the material things for which the male of his time must sell himself into grey-flannel bondage. These are supplied him by his superior, as is his travel to exotic places.

Never is Bond domesticated by commitment to one woman—certainly not beyond the length of a single picture—and he recapitulates the myth that the male who has neither family, children, nor mortgages is the most potent. But in contrast to Gable in *It Happened One Night*, Wayne in *Stagecoach*, Cooper in *The Virginian*, Clift in *Red River*, or Brando in *On the Waterfront*, there is no prospect of his ever being tied down, no disparate conclusion that presages an end to his adventures. Bond keeps on going through the alarming sixties until Connery is replaced in the seventies by other faces. The male body sustains its role as sex object; the women in the Bond films may be scantily clad, large-breasted, and in heat, but they remain faceless.

IV

Bond's American counterpart in the sixties and seventies was Clint Eastwood. In times far more threatening than those described in *The Man Who Shot Liberty Valance*, Bond and Eastwood instruct us in what is necessary to revive the male image. The individual has long since lost his capacity to right the community's wrongs. Eastwood arrives, a male determined to do whatever is necessary to survive, and as amoral as Little Caesar.

Where Cooper in *High Noon* was angry and appalled that the community should refuse to fight back and arm itself against the bullies threatening its peace and security, Eastwood impassively takes it for granted that he can rely on no one but himself. With consummate inexpressiveness he assumes the role of supermale, immune to either the praise or the gratitude of others, living by his own code in a world where men like himself have long since become obsolete. The theme begins in Eastwood's spaghetti Westerns, from *A Fistful of Dollars* (1964) to *The Good, the Bad, and the Ugly* (1966), directed in Italy by Sergio Leone, through their American imitations like *Hang 'em High* (1968). *A Fistful of Dollars* stands as a typical example of Eastwood's work in the sixties.

Modeled after *Yojimbo*, another Japanese film by Akira Kurosawa, *A Fistful of Dollars* focuses on a penniless, down-and-out warrior lacking an outlet for his superior skills in a society in disarray, having failed to preserve order and the manly code it once embodied. Even a spaghetti Western made in the sixties cannot fail to perceive that the old social order is deeply in trouble. Eastwood, far from being appreciated for his manly skills, is in prison when the film opens. He is pardoned on the condition that he will clean up the corrupt town of San Miguel. With times so menacing, Eastwood has no time even for the wisecracks of a Bond, who knew that the evil he opposed would be ultimately subdued. Eastwood is himself besieged. There is virtually no conversation at all in this or his other films. His beady blue eyes survey a world in which potential danger lurks everywhere. Like Bond, he must kill without feeling. Having polished off several no-goods before the film has barely begun, he instructs lesser men in the elements of survival: "If you're the sheriff, you'd better get these men underground."

In all his films Eastwood appears as a man who cares for nothing. The fear of feeling has determined his very nature; his every gesture and bodily movement betray it. He is ever on the lookout for any expression of vulnerability, since for such a lapse he would be punished with instant failure. No matter what happens, he is impassive. He speaks in a low, indistinct monotone, the threat of violence creeping into his very voice. The Eastwood male knows better than to attempt to reform a decadent world. In *A Fistful of Dollars*, in order to rid San Miguel of its "evil," he must murder a townful of people. For even to describe evil is pointless since it is an undefined, mysteriously present force. To define it might lead to an examination of poverty, social distress, and the structure of power which creates lawlessness. The Eastwood film evades this consequence by simply refusing to sympathize with those who do not shape up, who fail to be successful. Anyone who breaks the law is immediately marked for swift liquidation.

To young men of the sixties who remained unaffected by any of the protest movements, yet felt anxious about their maleness, the authoritarian Eastwood hero suggested that the traditional superiority of the strong, silent male could be recovered. Were he only to retap those hidden founts of male capacity, a man could once again assume control over his life. Quick, decisive action unhampered by introspection is best. Eastwood became especially popular with young working-class men, who were hardly able to feel masculine and in command at work when layoffs could render them powerless at any moment.

Yet one of the most interesting aspects of the Eastwood screen personality is that it also appealed to the disenchanted student young—not perhaps the more conscious, but those alienated politically from America's social institutions. The Eastwood hero also was alienated from the established culture. And in this sense he even appealed to some young women before the women's movement exposed the neurosis of the male so incapable of seeing anyone female as equal to himself or as a human being at all.

In *A Fistful of Dollars* someone proposes to make Eastwood feel at home. He replies that he never found home that great. His "cool" complemented the counterculture's own estrangement from authority, home, family, and all externally imposed standards of behavior, all the moralism which people preach but do not practice. The John Wayne–style male lost his relevance in the sixties because he would never permit criticism of mother, home, or hearth or—in the John Ford Westerns—country. To Wayne, the suggestion of corruption being inherent in the social order was sacrilege; in all this, tough or not, he was essentially "square."

In an unavowed manner Eastwood even responded to that alienation of the sixties in which the most radical among the young refused on principle to accept any established values as sacred. Like Eastwood, they distrusted everything but their own effectiveness. The anger masked by Eastwood's face in dissociated impassiveness found in the deeply alienated a perverse echo. Eastwood too felt that the world had betrayed him, and was outraged. He, however, handled his fear of weakness by suppressing rather than expressing all feeling. Hence, he held that weakness deep within him; and this is why he served the strong, particularly in his films of the seventies, directing his rage against the weak now presented as a menace to the established order. Eastwood's alienation leads finally to concealed submission. Those remnants of the counterculture, much fewer in number than their press coverage suggested, still respond to the anger conveyed by Eastwood.

Eastwood's silence itself duplicated the spiritual mood of the sixties. It even imitated the silence of Zen, as the counterculture defined it. Having heard so many meaningless slogans, some young people began to see words as lies by definition, serving only to obfuscate, as the American government coined new terms to conceal its behavior in East Asia. Describing the generation of the sixties in *The Greening of America*, Charles A. Reich claims for those he knew a spiritual transcendence based upon the freedom from language: "They are all the closer to each other because their being together is not mediated or separated by words." This willed inarticulateness describes no one so well as Eastwood. This was also the style of the more militant members of the antiwar movement, who substituted action, however futilely terrorist, for the "effeminate" words deployed as substitutes for deeds by "cowards" afraid to take risks. Thus does Jane Alpert describe the personal style of Sam Melville, who died in the Attica uprising after having been imprisoned for terrorist bombings of corporations and public utilities: "I rarely heard him contribute to the discussions except for occasional outbursts that talk was bullshit, and why didn't we *do* something." Eastwood's manner perfectly reflected the mood of these young dissidents, despite his alignment with official forces of repression, a relationship to emerge fully only in the 1970s with *Dirty Harry*.

In the sixties, Eastwood functioned best as a nihilist, standing for nothing in *A Fistful of Dollars*, pitting both factions in the town against each other since they are equally corrupt. If Leone includes the episode from the Japanese original in which the warrior shows sympathy for the weak and helps one family, his hero remains as cool as ever. He comes to their aid because "I knew someone like you once. There was no one to help." There is a bare hint that he would like to ally himself with something positive. Like those in the student movement, he too calls the government "dangerous." He is the alienated sixties male, both working-class and middle-class protester, confronting a world he fears and despises. And his violence can be justified as self-protection; in his sixties films it does not even seem excessive given the pervasive corruption facing him. "The kind of thing I do is to glorify competence," Eastwood has said of his films. The young men who have made him a cult figure transcending class origins and who account for the increasing financial success of his films are starved for just that sense of self-command.

Eastwood sustained this personality type through the sixties, in such films as *Coogan's Bluff* (1968) and *Hang 'em High*, before evolving into a vigilante in the seventies. In *Hang 'em High* the seventies Eastwood can be clearly discerned. He begins as an innocent rancher unjustly hanged by a mob, a motif borrowed from *The Ox-Bow Incident*. But this time the hero is a supermale who survives the hanging to become a marshal, legally to pursue his "killers." If he is icy and impassive, such rigid constraint seems appropriate in a world where the innocent can be hanged at any moment. A black scarf wrapped around his neck conceals the hideous scar that is a souvenir of the hanging. He is "the best there is," his skill fortified by anger as he brings in killers and degenerates singlehanded in this early study for *Dirty Harry*. He is not yet as besieged as Harry because he can still be a gentle and tender lover to the woman Rachel, a widow searching for the two men who raped her and killed her husband. She is his moral counterpart and can understand the way he feels. Yet at the end he sacrifices a full personal life with this woman for a lawman's badge. Unlike the besieged Harry Callahan, restrained and prevented from doing his job by a set of laws which allow criminals to go free, Eastwood here can still aid the community as its appointed guardian.

V

The despair of the age, the pain of living in a world without value, is made easier in the Eastwood films because the hero at least is fair-minded and virile, competent and undaunted by the atrocities which daily come into view. The male in the films of Sam Peckinpah, of which *The Wild Bunch* (1969) is a typically virulent example, is no better than the decaying corrupt world that is squeezing him out. Equating masculinity with sheer barbarism, Peckinpah justifies his cynicism by mythologizing the obsolescence of manliness in civilized America. For Peckinpah a man is someone violent because he possesses male genitals. His world is one in which violence has no direct, individual outlet and thus turns back upon the man himself, compelling him to orgies of self-destruction. If Jesse James fought against the corrupt railroad companies in a late-thirties film because they robbed the poor of their land, the Peckinpah hero fights because it is in his genes. In an early shot of *The Wild Bunch* we observe children torturing a scorpion by afflicting it with insects. Fascinated, they watch it slowly dismembered and devoured. Since we are sadistic from childhood, feeling an erotic fascination with the power to destroy life (the female no less than the male), it is better that the world accommodate itself to our need to be bloody. Periodic and ample release of violence will distort us less than self-denial.

By the time the "wild bunch" ride into town, we have been prepared to view their brutality as heroically male. "If they move, kill 'em" is their attitude toward innocent hostages during a holdup. Blood splashes in slow motion, another plagiarism from Japanese samurai films in these Peckinpah hymns to male violence. If his heroes grow desperate and edgy, it is because their maleness has been thwarted and they lack sufficient opportunity to rampage and kill.

Toward these men, portrayed by William Holden, Ernest Borgnine, and company, Peckinpah feels both admiration and a deep nostalgia, since they are passing from the scene, as were the gunslingers in *The Magnificent Seven*. By the time they have ridden out of town, the insects have thoroughly demolished the scorpion, and the children, surrogates for the male heroes, now set the remains on fire in a primitive ritual intended to locate adult behavior in the collective unconscious of our species. The streets of the town, which had been hosting a temperance meeting—always a symbol in the Western of the overwhelming of masculinity by churches and their repressed women—are now filled with bodies. Restraint, symbolized by the prohibition against the drinking of alcohol, is blamed for the disaster, and not the very bullies who had never shown a qualm about killing anyone in their path. If only unnatural restrictions on his impulses were not forced upon the male, says *The Wild Bunch*, he could fulfill his needs in organized rather than random slaughter.

In a way the members of the wild bunch evoke John Wayne's Tom Doniphon in *The Man Who Shot Liberty Valance*. Once Shinbone becomes civilized, Doniphon is forced to spend the remainder of his life in isolation and loneliness, but Doniphon was too good a man ever to vent his frustration in violence against the innocent. Peckinpah's males, faced with the same frustration, go mad with rage and hostility, killing easily because they are incapable of seeing other people as human. Ford valued Tom Doniphon too much to undermine his importance in so infantile a manner; Peckinpah makes us long in fact for the steady rationality of Jimmy Stewart as Ransom Stoddard.

Thus, where John Ford recognized the value as well as the limitations of progress, Peckinpah petulantly finds the social order only hypocritical and unfair. He stacks the cards, lacing *The Wild Bunch* with bounty hunters who track his heroes and prove far more venomous than they. It is Peckinpah much more than Ford who responds to the strains of the sixties and that despair consequent upon having nothing to believe in which was the legacy of the McCarthyite fifties, especially for those too tired and jaded to respond to youthful activism. Where the young showed vitality and moral fervor in their defiance, Peckinpah's violent despair is the disguised futility of sour middle age.

Peckinpah is left only with solitary gestures of manliness. He sees grandeur in an act like William Holden's, when he kills one of his own group who is wounded and too weak to ride. He finds nothing unmanly about Holden's refusal even to stop and bury his friend, a companion who had ridden with him day after day. Survival and energy are all, according to this male ethic which Peckinpah will continue into the seventies. The only reason that a former member of the wild bunch, Robert Ryan, joins the bounty hunters is that he is threatened by prison. It is he, admiring his old besieged cronies, who speaks for Peckinpah: "We're after *men*," says Ryan, "and I wish I were with them." To be a man in a Peckinpah film is to be a precious, superior, sanctified being.

Peckinpah attempts to elicit sympathy for his pack of mad-dog male warriors by placing them in danger and on the run, by making them underdogs, if curs nonetheless. All they find in the sacks they loot from the town they shoot up in that first sequence is a passel of hardware-store nuts and bolts. The town *has* no treasure to pillage. Growing old—a tragic occurrence for this hero-worshipping director—Holden and Borgnine have nothing to show for the rampaging life they have led. All that remains to them is the male ethic of fighting for whatever they get and loyalty toward their own. Peckinpah actually expects us to mourn the diminution of the vital force, the "masculine" power of these brutish people. Pike (Holden) falls off his horse. A Mexican elder, another Peckinpah spokesman, says, "We all dream of being a child again—even the worst of us—perhaps the worst most of all." That "worst" indicates no moral judgment, however, only a form of admiration. Viciousness is all in this Peckinpah Western, and male virility finds its purest expression in violence and in the blazing forth of primitive instinct.

Meanwhile, erotic energy throbs between these men. They take baths together. Borgnine and Holden, as the strongest and most mature members of the group, neither need nor want women at all. Holden does make love to a Mexican woman in one scene, tossing her a handful of coins when it is over. Women are objects to be taken and paid off, as easily replenishable as fresh horses. After this sexual encounter, Holden's eyes meet those of Borgnine and they exchange a smile. Their code of manhood demands a perfunctory heterosexuality (although Borgnine remains chaste throughout), but they use women solely for the sake of sharing these sexual experiences with each other.

Finally Borgnine and Holden are killed, yelling each other's names with such feeling that we see they long only to be together, on the other side as well. Buzzards sitting on their corpses symbolize the evil bounty hunters, who take even the gold from their teeth. Ryan survives, a woebegone man cut off from his comrades who now hears the sound of shots in his head, longing for the days when men could ride together wild and free, doing what they would. He and another survivor, the old man Sikes (Edmund O'Brien), will now bond together: "It ain't what it used to be, but it'll do." With a dissolve we are returned to the past, to Holden and Borgnine convulsed in laughter, sharing great joy and abandon in what, when all is said and done, is a homosexual *Love Story*. Theirs is the laughter of men true to their gut responses, living by an authenticity which alone makes life worth living. A Mexican guitar adds an elegiac note, as this loathsome spectacle equating masculinity with brute force comes to its welcome finish.

VI

The comedies of the early sixties belong to the tradition of *How to Marry a Millionaire*. In attempting to resurrect the virile image of Clark Gable, they pretend that Brando, Dean, and Newman had not revolutionized the male image in the American film. The pattern of the Gable films, in which a playboy finds the right woman and settles down to uneventful domesticity, was resurrected in *Pillow Talk* (1962), a Doris Day vehicle with the prudish, prurient view of sex characteristic of the American film before the sexual revolution. Rock Hudson is the model male as Hollywood would have maintained him throughout the sixties had it not been forced by the middle of the decade to respond to a moral challenge to official culture. Hudson plays a womanizing songwriter. Beautiful women telephone him constantly, as once again in the American film the male coyly allows himself to be pursued while he affects cool indifference. An unending supply of mistresses parade through Hudson's pad, flaunted before the audience in the latest *Playboy* decor. He cares for none of them, settling down finally with the virginal Day for whom sex and marriage are still inseparable.

Pillow Talk, easily forgettable though it is, reveals the masculine ideal of the day. A male is encouraged to sow many wild oats before marriage as a primitive safeguard against postmarital infidelity, while truly eligible women remain virgins. Hudson's sexual adventures are treated in *Pillow Talk* as an anthropological rite designed to test his potency and ensure that he will not fail in bed as a husband. It remains only for his sensuality to be domesticated.

In the early sixties Hollywood was still perpetuating the myth that a real man is ever ready sexually, his record of performance unblemished by a single failure, moment of ambivalence, or fatigue. Woe to the real-life male whose experience is not quite so unflawed. A woman sent by the telephone company at Day's request to check on Hudson's abuse of their mutual party line falls for him at first sight. She reports at once that the complaint—that any complaint—is "unjustified." Double-entendres are not merely sounded but clanged. All women are for the having by the virile male, in defiance of which Mae West's declaration to Cary Grant, in *She Done Him Wrong*, that *he* could be had was so refreshing.

The other males in *Pillow Talk* are foils for Hudson. Nick Adams plays an effete rich boy replete with neuroses and a history of psychiatric treatments, a mama's boy to boot. Tony Randall is also mother-dominated. The ideal is the fabricated Hudson, a bionic, plastic toy no less than his contemporary Sean Connery as James Bond, that mini–Hugh Hefner. Through sexuality the male can even be upwardly mobile, and

Hudson is a person who worked his way through college, as a real man would.

At the end marriage unites Hudson and Day—she never having had a sexual experience, he having enjoyed an infinite variety of the same. Each has pretended to be inaccessible and so has caught the other. Day holds out the longest to allow Hudson to fulfill literally that other concomitant of the masculine mystique by playing the conquering cave man. So he must march into her apartment, wrap her in her baby-blue blanket, fling her over his shoulder, and carry her kicking and screaming to his pad. Passers-by do not intervene because male dominance is so acceptable in our culture that it is applauded whenever it comes into view (a motif almost identically employed in *The Quiet Man*). The police even comply. A real man seizes the female of his choice and carries her to his lair. And she loves it.

A coda informs us that playboy Hudson has already passed along the male cycle from playboy to proud poppa, enshrined in a properly upper-middle-class style of life. The formula for perfect happiness is packaged as dishonestly as it was in all those Gable films in which we were expected to believe that the man about town was secretly waiting to settle down with pipe and slippers.

By the mid-sixties not only the counterculture but the film audience as a whole would challenge these premises about masculinity. *Pillow Talk*, a 1962 film with a fifties vision of the world, could never have been made after 1965 when many of the film audience composed of the disenchanted young had declared war on conformity to plastic values. What was important to this new generation was integrity and the search for a life-style in keeping with these principles. Hollywood proceeded differently in consequence, suddenly appearing to embrace the new sensibility while preparing to refurbish the old. By 1967 the male hero of the highly successful film *The Graduate* is appalled when one of his parents' friends advises him to "go into plastics."

Hudson in *Pillow Talk* is a vain, egocentric, selfish male who cares for nothing but himself and his own pleasures and comforts. His entire life is organized around the accumulation of useless commodities and the pursuit and conquest of women. With the new radical ideas of the sixties, young people sought to return to their feelings. Rejecting what was perceived as a craven embrace of Madison Avenue consumerism and the shabby individualistic ways of a Rock Hudson in *Pillow Talk*, many of the youth believed in the dream of a communal life-style, sharing possessions with others and rejecting the obsession with acquisition because it alienated people from themselves. Whatever the success of these experiments, they reflected a new sensibility. Psychedelic experiences with drugs reflected equally the desire, in a profit-centered culture, to restore oneself to a more authentic humanity. The young male affected by these ideas admitted to the emptiness of his life. "Loneliness, estrangement, and isolation separate human beings from each other," read the Port Huron Statement which launched the Students for a Democratic Society (SDS). Life-styles based upon competition and the accumulation of wealth were challenged if not replaced, particularly by the student, and hence middle-class, members of the movement, who had never known want and thus minimized the difficulties of living a life utterly free of what they termed "bourgeois values." But it would take the 1970s to raise the issue of the equality of women, and only the women's movement would perceive the direct connection between the emptiness of the culture, materialism, and the nature of male identity. Throughout the sixties, a sexism as pervasive as that of the 1950s prevailed on screen, among blue-collar men, within the student movement, and within the counterculture. Thus would Jane Alpert recount the terms of her relationship with "radical" Sam Melville: he as "a sultan and me his odalisque." Stokely Carmichael announced that the proper position of women in the movement was "prone."

VII

Hollywood had always praised the dominant values of the day, yet it had to take into account the new mores of the counterculture if movies were to remain credible at all in their representation of life in the society. The problem was solved by Hollywood in a predictable manner. The values of the counterculture were invoked in caricature, and considerable film energy was focused on the most unappealing facets of the youthful disaffection. Films were made characterizing all radical youths as drug addicts; the life-style that rejected material values was presented as dirty and repellent. Protest marches were shown to be violent, ridiculed in no small measure because the exhibitionist wing of the movement provided Hollywood with the ammunition to make them a joke, as in the Yippies' ambition in the 1967 march on Washington to "levitate the Pentagon." As long as the movement failed to create support for itself from the majority of ordinary Americans, who nevertheless wished the war were over, Hollywood could find a ready audience for these films of ridicule. *Easy Rider* and *The Panic in Needle Park* (1971) saw the young as dope-pushers or as aimless drop-outs like their predecessor, the sanitized Benjamin of *The Graduate*.

Yet for the first half of *The Graduate*, Benjamin (Dustin Hoffman), its alienated hero, appears to be a man of his decade. The words of Herbert Marcuse, one of the gurus of the day, resonate through his confusion in adjusting to a materialistic world he despises. "This society is irrational as a whole," Marcuse preached in *One-Dimensional Man,* one of the most influential books of the sixties; "its productivity is destructive of the free development of human needs and faculties, its peace maintained by the constant threat of war." Freedom, Marcuse urged, should mean not free enterprise but freedom from the economy as it exists and from politics over which the individual has no control. Intellectual freedom requires above all wresting oneself from the influence of the mass media in the control and pay of authority, the primary purpose of which is to reinforce established values.

The quest of young men of the day and of Benjamin in *The Graduate* was to rediscover and create an autonomous personality and way of life; they sought a means for the individual to be true to himself, no matter the cost. The implication (at last) was that previous male personalities on the American screen were slaves to values that demeaned them, however insistently they pretended to be free.

By the end of *The Graduate,* Benjamin's struggle has degenerated. His "triumph" consists finally in a conventional pursuit and conquest of Mrs. Robinson's daughter, Elaine, affirming the long-ascendant values of marriage, the family, and a style of life essentially similar to that of his parents. Only in passing has he recognized real needs rather than false ones. The preoccupation with the self and the male as bold pursuer go unaltered.

But in those segments of the film in which Benjamin attempts to overcome his dehumanization, he becomes one of the most attractive male personalities on the sixties screen. No matter that he is small and dark, with a prominent nose. Nor is his masculinity impaired because he is insecure and virginal. He emerges as a real male of his time. The first image of Benjamin as a victim of values not his own appears under the credits, as he travels along a conveyor belt at the airport, having arrived home from college. He does not yet move on his own. In the manner of the fifties he wears a suit. Launched as he appears to be on the treadmill of conventional success, it seems likely that he will merge with the established order. A full shot of his suitcase suggests he is about to be turned into an object, while an automated voice calls out instructions for safety on the conveyor belt. He does not yet have the courage to substitute his inner voice for those from outside which shape his life.

As soon as he arrives in the lavish suburbia of his parents, Benjamin shows himself to be a youth of the sixties, rejecting the life-style of the organization man to which affluent Americans of the older generation still cling. Benjamin admits to being "worried" about his future, but of one thing he is certain: he does not want a life like that of his parents, who attempt to usher him into consumerism by giving him a graduation present of a bright red sports car.

Yet Benjamin's discontent—or what it is that bothers him about the world of his parents—is never made clear. Unlike the best young people of the counterculture, he remains a rebel *without* a cause, a cousin of James Dean. *The Graduate*, cowardly and hypocritical at its root, fails to allow Benjamin the intelligence or imagination to define his discontent or articulate how he perceives the society he rejects, let alone how he would alter it. Vietnam is never once mentioned in the film, nor does Benjamin have *any* positive ideas about what he wants to do. "I'm sorta disturbed about things in general," he weakly informs Mrs. Robinson, whose mind races frantically to figure out how most opportunely to seduce him.

Yet the affair with Mrs. Robinson brilliantly deflates the male image as it came to us in films like *Pillow Talk*. The role reversal, in which the woman is superior, calling the shots with the male as initiate, belongs to the late sixties and distinguishes this film, despite the fact that Mrs. Robinson is represented as a neurotic bitch reduced to preying upon the sons of her friends. Later Benjamin will become the masculine male superior to his conquest as he retrieves her daughter, the passive Elaine. The first half of the film is finer by far than the second, in no small part because we are offered the unusual spectacle of a male in his first sexual encounter exposing all his anxiety and inexperience. For Benjamin is an inept virgin who must be instructed in his every move, too shy even to reserve their hotel room until Mrs. Robinson bullies him into it.

Small and insecure, Benjamin quickly brushes his teeth before the predatory Mrs. Robinson arrives. Timidly he turns out the light, as modest *women* have done in the American film. Finally he verbalizes his dilemma: "I don't know what you want me to do." When he plunks his hand down on her breast, so lacking in sensuality is the gesture that Mrs. Robinson doesn't find it worthwhile to notice. Only when she taunts him with being "inadequate" does Benjamin manage to perform. We are a long way from protestations of male prowess. Mrs. Robinson, his instructress, suggests that Benjamin sow a few wild oats. Unlike Rock Hudson in *Pillow Talk*, Benjamin doesn't know how.

The pressure on Benjamin, a "Frank Hoppingham scholar" at school, is to do something. "What was the point of all that hard work?" his father asks. "You got me!" rejoins Benjamin—to the delight of his audience. The sixties male already knew that there is no glory in conforming. But where does Benjamin go from here? The affair with the emasculating, frustrated Mrs. Robinson begins to disgust him, for at heart he is a good, pure boy, his fifties mentality basically intact. As a project which becomes virtually a *raison d être*, Benjamin sets out to win Mrs. Robinson's daughter, Elaine. No liberated man exploring sensuality, Benjamin finds sex without "conversation" unappealing. Like Doris Day herself, he shuns sex without "love."

And so he settles on Elaine, a clean-cut, ideal American girl, the "right" match, as the delight of his parents reveals. *They* communicate. Both feel a malaise, which is treated, however, not in terms of the political ferment

Dustin Hoffman with Katharine Ross in *The Graduate:* It is up to Benjamin to assume command, as males of old have always done. "Why don't you drag me off?" pleads Elaine. By the end of the film, he has.

of the sixties, but as the inevitable alienation of young people who will shortly settle down to lives not very different from those of their parents.

Refusing to take a conventional job (and thereby retaining the sympathy of the young in the audience), Benjamin pursues Elaine to Berkeley where she is a student. If the Free Speech Movement was still alive, we wouldn't know it from this film. It wouldn't interest Benjamin anyway, since his concern is solely with winning the elusive Elaine and rescuing her from marriage to a square medical student. He couldn't care less about the fate of the university or the society. By this point in the film he has become a caricature of Douglas Fairbanks surmounting superhuman odds, rather than an anti-hero.

More and more we are treated to shots of Benjamin unclothed. If he is a small man, his biceps are respectably prominent, as they will be in *The Marathon Man* (1976). He is clearly virile; his strength of character and determination also assimilate him to the most old-fashioned notions of the ideal male. When his landlord suspects him of being one of those "outside agitators," we laugh, knowing that this couldn't be further from the truth. Highly conventional, Benjamin, as did Fairbanks, devotes all to love. And in keeping with the twenties film pattern *The Graduate* has now adopted, Elaine finds him irresistible. She comes to his room and asks him to kiss her. Weak and passive, she is railroaded by her mother into marrying the jock. It is up to Benjamin to assume command, as males of old have always done. "Why don't you drag me off?" pleads Elaine. By the end of the film, he has.

The suspense of the ending consists finally in whether Benjamin will get to the church on time to stop the wedding; the spurious race to find where the church is located, with beautifully photographed shots of his frenzied drive to Santa Barbara, disguises the conservatism of Benjamin and his goal. As Tom Mix's horse expires in *Dick Turpin*, forcing him to rescue the heroine on foot, so Benjamin's car runs out of gas at the penultimate moment. On the run he approaches the huge white edifice of the church where Elaine is about to be married. She is just being married as he bangs frantically on the glass door shutting him out in a twist that returns *The Graduate* to the sixties; it is a spoof of all those unlikely endings where the hero arrived on time. But Benjamin's triumph is no better than that of any preceding strong-arm hero; he delivers a karate chop to Elaine's father and sends the rest of the crowd of angry guests reeling by hitting them with a weighty cross—as heavy as the symbolism. Using the cross now as a bar, he locks the unfeeling parents and relatives into the church, and he and Elaine escape. The symbol conveys sacrilege, a transcendence at last of traditional morality as Benjamin indeed runs off with a *married* Elaine. But the implied object of their defiance is that very sanctioned relationship they have just successfully defied. Nothing so well sums up Hollywood's handling of radicalization. If the code words and style are allowed, the substance not only goes unaltered but is strengthened because the old values surmount the nominal reference to the new.

Benjamin and Elaine are hardly rebels, although the film attempts to have it both ways by picturing them in defiant violation of convention, escaping on a city bus with Elaine still in her wedding gown and Benjamin wearing filthy blue jeans. Elaine glances sidelong at Benjamin, her male protector. He, now confident and in full command, doesn't return her gaze, but stares straight ahead, already the male fulfilling his proper role. What is to follow? The future for Benjamin and Elaine is in no particular different from that of Hudson and Day in *Pillow Talk*. Marriage, babies, and a conventional job are all on the agenda.

Despite its having pleased its young audience, in retrospect *The Graduate* emerges quite clearly as a rejoinder to rather than an endorsement of the counterculture; in fact, it challenges the assumption among the young that they had forged new life-styles. Mike Nichols's film does reflect, if with malice aforethought, that the youth movement did not really produce an alternative male model or a new approach to relationships between men and women. Out of a failure of nerve, born of its inability to create an ongoing movement to struggle for new values, the counterculture indeed relied on outworn male models. *The Graduate* reveals that the absence of new goals and new models of behavior in turn contributed to this movement's failure to sustain itself.

The most refreshing, if inadvertent, truth brought out in *Easy Rider* (1969), a film made for this very audience by two supporters of the counterculture, Dennis Hopper and Peter Fonda, is that the counterculture indeed perpetuated the same notions of masculinity that had always been current in American culture and glorified in the American film. If clothes and hair length were to become unisexual and the rigid male pattern of behavior was assailed, the attitude of men to women was not.

Easy Rider proposed to depict at last the alienated male of the sixties as he was. But like *The Graduate*, it aimed to please all the hippies themselves as well as those who dreaded and despised them; and also like *The Graduate*, it attempted to salvage both audiences by perpetuating the oldest clichés about the masculine male. The heroes ride motorcycles in a fifties association of male virility with the machine. They also sell narcotics, as if every young man of the sixties who rejected conformity and a grey flannel suit was really a drug-pusher. Having retained this undermining cliché about drugs and dissidence, Hopper then openly defended it: "They peddle dope because that seems no worse to them than the Wall Street tycoon spending eighty percent of his time cheating the government." No one in the film actually raises this spurious argument, but nothing in the plot can retrieve the film from its own premises.

Yet despite our knowledge of the destructiveness of drugs and of how they afflict no one so much as the ghetto young, Hopper and Fonda appeared to expect us to sympathize with their dissolute dealers. Like Peckinpah, they attempted to manipulate audience identification by having their heroes besieged by lowlives far worse than themselves. Hopper and Fonda are called "Commies" and "queers" by the rednecks they meet out on the road and by whom they are eventually murdered. But to offer the drug-pusher as a hero and at the same time ask us to view that hero as the best of his generation, confused but searching for authenticity, is to sound the death knell of the youth culture itself as a viable alternative. The film remains incapable of creating any real distance for us from these youths. They are seen as exciting, prophets of something new, as they endorse the spirit of the ragged commune they visit: "They're gonna make it."

Beset by such confusion, *Easy Rider* returns to resurrecting the old masculine myths which form so vital a part of the culture its heroes are presumed to be rejecting. It is finally no more than an old-fashioned buddy film in which two male heroes pit themselves against the rest of the world. The only difference between this and *Only Angels Have Wings,*

apart from *Easy Rider's* absence of style, is that in homage to the decade
our heroes smoke pot, as did the actors during the filming. The civil rights
and antiwar movements coalesce in the image of a hero taking to the open
road, sans commitment or ideas of any kind. If *The Graduate* was a remake
of *Rebel Without a Cause*, *Easy Rider* recapitulated *The Wild One*, complete
with motorcycle and alienated, inarticulate males at its center. Like
Brando in *The Wild One*, the heroes of *Easy Rider* are dropouts, doing
their own thing, making a religion of sexual freedom, letting their hair
grow long as they deck themselves out in absurd regalia. Fonda's black
leather jacket, right out of the fifties, adds but one note of defiance: it
has an American flag sewn on it.

That these two young men are so tormented awakens our sympathies
even if we are repelled by them in all other aspects. By the end they are
rendered martyrs to American intolerance, a fate meant to evoke the
decimation of human life in Vietnam, a war fought by rednecks like those
who kill Fonda and Hopper. But it also proposes as fashionable both
hopelessness and despair. Like the gunslingers of *The Magnificent Seven*
and *The Man Who Shot Liberty Valance*, these dissidents are doomed by an
overwhelmingly hostile society essentially impervious to change. *Easy
Rider* does mark a step forward in honesty from *The Graduate* in that it
actually allows its heroes to drop out, whereas Benjamin, finally, pursues
a traditional male role. But *Easy Rider* allows us to dismiss the dropout
as a lunatic, rendering him utterly repellent. The film seeks to retrieve our
sympathy for their ways by enjoining us to pity dead protagonists we
could barely tolerate alive.

Unlike *The Graduate*, which did offer a hero outside the mold, *Easy
Rider* reeks of male contempt for women. Alcoholic dropout Jack Nicholson, an ACLU lawyer who defends long-hairs, directs our eager
heroes to the "finest whorehouse in the South," where they can buy and
abuse women to their heart's content: "These ain't no pork chops. These
are U. S. Prime." Women are not merely objects but carcasses, deperson-
alized by the imagery of the slaughterhouse.

The motorcycles that propel our buddy heroes to their doom are
rendered phallic by the worshipping camera, emblematic of an idealized
masculine force, as in Kenneth Anger's paean to male sexuality, *Scorpio
Rising*. An inordinate number of shots are devoted to picturing our
heroes out riding, as if in so doing they best exhibit their male sexuality.
If they pretend disaffection, they appear little different from the buddy
gangs of Hell's Angels. Only the peripheral character played by Nicholson—who, his misogyny apart, steals the film—has a vision of a different
world. He thus describes UFO visitors from outer space:

> They don't have no wars, they got no monetary system, they don't have
> any leaders, because, I mean, each man is a leader. I mean, each man—
> because of their technology, they are able to feed, clothe, house, and trans-
> port themselves equally—and with no effort.

Easy Rider reeks of male contempt for women. Alcoholic dropout Jack Nicholson directs our eager heroes (Dennis Hopper and Peter Fonda) to the "finest whorehouse in the South," where they can buy and abuse women to their hearts' content: "These ain't no pork chops. These are U.S. Prime."

Only through Nicholson are we given any attempt to grant some substance to this rebellion, some vision of an alternative society. It doesn't work because it is imposed by an outside, extraneous figure and is thoroughly unintegrated in the lives of Hopper and Fonda. Nicholson informs them, on behalf of the filmmakers, that they represent "freedom," and the film attempts to make this credible by contrasting the two with an assortment of scoundrels.

If anything, *Easy Rider* functions as a warning *against* the kind of freedom it pretends to idealize through its unrestricted young men out on the open road. Besieged everywhere, they are forced to bond together virtually to fight for survival, as the audience, too, implicitly is warned to conform lest it also meet disaster. When the three are beaten in their sleep, Nicholson is killed. Hopper cradles an unconscious Fonda in his arms in affection and fear. Sex with the women in the whorehouse-and-cemetery sequence is accomplished only under the influence of LSD and without particular enthusiasm for the partner. They do it for "George" (Nicholson), not because heterosexual relations particularly appeal to them. And during the orgy we actually hear Fonda calling out for his mother: "Oh, Mother, Mother, why didn't you tell me? Why didn't anybody tell me anything?"

Passing judgment on the whole escapade, Fonda concludes, "We blew it." But could they have done otherwise? In the apotheosis of an aerial shot Fonda flies through the air on his motorcycle, which then bursts into flames, the victim of two crackers who decide to blast these hippies off the road. But the vulnerability of Fonda and Hopper resides in nothing so much as their own emptiness. We are left with an ambivalent film that has at its core a macho sensibility and a belief, too infantile to carry any conviction, that a real man enacts his masculine defiance by racing down highways on a revved-up motorcycle accompanied by a buddy who understands him.

Far more negative yet were the portraits of the student dissenter and counterculture male in films of the early seventies. Designed to discredit every aspect of the youth rebellion, these films depict the nonconforming male as so physically repulsive as to inspire instant rejection. In *Joe* (1970), the hippie protagonist is ensconced in a filthy New York Lower East Side tenement room, which serves as the headquarters for his dope-pushing. As in *Easy Rider*, the refusal to live by traditional norms is made synonymous with the selling of narcotics. A poster of Che Guevara adorns this hippie's abode, as if Guevara had favored drug abuse and hustling. No Guevara, this "hero" is lazy, and when he is not involved in the drug trade, he abandons himself to sexual license. At the end of the film an outraged middle-class advertising executive, appalled by his daughter's flight, massacres her inadvertently as he hysterically attacks a disgusting flock of screaming hippies. Seeking to appeal to students as well as to their elders, the film presents workingman Joe as no better than the young, a fascist and a bigot. "The white kids," he declaims, "are worse than the niggers." Unable to respond except negatively to the new ideas in the air, yet unable to ignore what is happening in the culture, *Joe* can locate no male model to approve. Instead, it devotes itself to reinforcing the alienation between different groups.

In *Drive, He Said* (1971), the student rebel is even more repulsive and deranged. He parades in fatigues with a gun, a make-believe jungle guerrilla psychotic in his infantile tantrums. His political ideas are not worth listening to, his aim no more significant than the disruption of a college basketball game. His slogan is "The country is going to seed because no one is humping any more."

Drive, He Said, directed by a man with the most unrelieved macho sensibility himself, actor Jack Nicholson, insists that the counterculture male's refusal to join the establishment is dangerous when it is not laughable. His student rebel is a psychopath, considerably worse than the drug-pusher; the film demonstrates his viciousness when he attempts to rape the whorish wife of a professor. At the draft board, confronted by a paternal army psychiatrist, this youth thrusts two fingers down his own throat, threatening, "I'd like to puke in your face." He is made to fear the army rather than oppose the war. The rebels of *Drive, He Said* are infantile weaklings without ideas or the slightest compassion for others. Antiwar rebel Gabriel's final act is to enter the college laboratory stark naked and set free the snakes, frogs, rats, and insects kept there, an act symbolic of the nightmarish, savage impulses he would unleash on society in the name of a rebellion reduced by the film to psychosis.

A further attempt to discredit and render repellent the attempt on the part of many young people to locate a more authentic male identity during the sixties occurred in *The Panic in Needle Park* (1971). Protagonist Bobby (Al Pacino) is once again, ad nauseam, a drug-pusher. As in *Drive, He Said,* the hero's disaffection is nothing more than a ruse to avoid the normal responsibilities of adulthood, and the character lacks any genuine response to injustice or disaffection with the social order. Rebellion and moral degeneration are again equated.

An opposite tack is taken by *Billy Jack* (1971), which argues that for the youth culture and the radical movement to survive, it must emulate the most ruthlessly masculine behavior of John Wayne himself. A freedom school, run on the principle of nonviolence, cannot survive without the protection of our hero, Billy Jack; he is half Indian, a karate master and Vietnam veteran who uses brute physical force to devastate types like those who blew Hopper and Fonda off the road in *Easy Rider.*

The pacifist teacher, Jean, is raped. What is Tom Laughlin as Billy Jack to do but assume that traditional male role of lone ranger, avenger of injustice? A strong, silent male, furiously inarticulate and forced to resolve his dilemma with his fists (and feet) alone, Laughlin typifies the Gary Cooper mode of masculinity in the trappings of the sixties. Mobilizing no one else, Billy Jack, like a good Hollywood hero of old, protects the weak singlehandedly. When pressed by the superior force on the other side, he relies on "Washington" to be kind. He had "turned his back on society" only because it had been deaf to the needs of his people. For all the sixties jargon and style of dress, the director (Laughlin himself) is expressing ideas of the thirties, as the film ends on the illusion that once Billy Jack makes the needs of his people known, they will at once be met by good-hearted individuals. Pacifism and nonviolence are the film's ostensible values, while physical violence and an aggressive hero are alone shown to be effective and authentic. *Billy Jack* was Laughlin's first remake of *Mr. Smith Goes to Washington;* he has since filmed another, more literal version.

Thus in the sixties and seventies, when the young people of the counterculture and the antiwar movement surface on the Hollywood screen, they appear only in order to be degraded. Generally they fail to survive, and most often they are physically repulsive. Virtually always they are hypocrites who are revealed to believe in the very values they purport to reject. With rare exceptions, when the question of male identity is at issue during the sixties and seventies, the American film returns to the male styles of Wayne and Cooper in the course of a vigorous denial that there was anything unappealing or lacking in the masculine code they proposed. The Wayne persona had been criticized for harshness both by Hawks in *Red River* and Ford in *The Searchers*. In the sixties and the seventies the bravura machismo of Eastwood, of an arrested adolescent like Burt Reynolds, or of Charles Bronson is sanctified. Black films like *Sweet Sweetback's Baadasssss Song* (1971) square the circle by marrying their criticism of racial injustice in America to the myth of the inexhaustible sexuality of the black male, refurbishing the old racist stereotype of the "buck," the black stud.

VIII

Marking the transition into the seventies were *Butch Cassidy and the Sundance Kid* (1969) and *Midnight Cowboy* (1969), both of which were forerunners in chronicling love relationships between two men and in flaunting the emotional exclusion of women. Following upon the sexual revolution ushered in with the radicalization in the sixties, the women's liberation movement began to demand on film independent women comparable to the male star and sharing that strength of character hitherto his alone. The fear that if a woman were presented as equal to men the hero would lose his virility resulted in the virtual elimination of women from films. Indeed, the prospect of women competing for jobs in a declining economy and no longer nurturing the young in approved values led Hollywood to look on the female sex itself as too dangerous to allow on screen. Dominance over women and masculinity had been made synonymous by virtue of their long association in this culture. Women, in demanding equality at work, were believed to threaten men, who might at worst be replaced and at best be forced to compete with women brandishing skills equal to their own. By the end of the 1960s, images of male superiority fill the screen, asserting that men do not need women after all.

Poorly directed and tiredly resurrecting old stereotypes buried with the Western of the forties, *Butch Cassidy and the Sundance Kid* would have us look once again with nostalgia upon a male image in danger of extinction. Yet despite its amateurishness and banality, it set the tone for buddy films to come in the seventies. Newman and Redford, bank robbers on the run, are presented as two more heroes of old. Redford plays the Sundance Kid, fastest gun in a now-dying West; Newman is Butch Cassidy, the brainier and hence less virile of the two. For the sake of his wisdom he is deprived entirely of women, while Redford is allowed a perfunctory relationship with Katharine Ross. These two men love each other, understand each other, and die together. Ross leaves the film in time for the heroes to spend their last moments in yet one more hopeless if heroic encounter.

The demands of their partnership provide the emotional core of the film. Under the bedroom window of Redford and Ross after the film's one love scene, Newman rides his new-found bicycle. "What are you doing?" asks a barely awake Redford. "Stealing your woman," is the reply. "Take her, take her," answers Redford, scratching himself and turning away from the window. Only half meant as a joke, the line comes off as serious. Meanwhile, enduring cliché after cliché (the bicycle as emblem of the new, post-cowboy era), we are meant to eulogize these two men who live on in an epoch where they no longer have a place. Their relationship becomes all the more essential as they are besieged, replicating the themes of *The Wild Bunch*.

If Newman and Redford take Ross with them as they escape to Bolivia, it is because traveling with a woman provides a good cover. If she whines, they warn, she'll be dumped. Ross remains outside the emotional high points of the film. Finally, superfluous in every way, she leaves Bolivia of her own volition. We are left to view the last days of two powerfully bonded males; as emotionally tied as any heterosexual couple, Newman and Redford seem united in a virtual marriage.

Like other couples, they engage in petty quarrels, exacerbated by their being on the run. If they get on each other's nerves, even to the end when they are finally surrounded, their banter is the stuff of romance. "Is that what you call giving cover?" demands Redford, half-affectionately. "Is that what you call running?" replies Newman, always ready with a barb of his own. Each must pretend, heroically, that his wounds are slight: neither would distress the other. They are, in fact, in love. At the end they emerge courageously from the shack where they have holed up, poignantly unaware that what appears to be the entire Bolivian army is lined up waiting for them in ambush. At the moment they are about to be gunned down for good, director George Roy Hill freezes the frame, sparing us the view of his two heroes as anything but upright, fearlessly braving the odds in this last impossible stand.

Midnight Cowboy, with more honesty and openness, seems to examine the relative merits of heterosexual and homosexual love. Jon Voigt as a dishwasher from the provinces, appropriately named Joe Buck, has modeled himself on the male heroes of the Western, dressing, however, in cowboy boots and shirt more in the manner of Roy Rogers and Gene Autry than of John Wayne. He comes to New York prepared to sell his body to women; his experiences with that sex are so unpleasant that he becomes convinced he can find love and understanding only with another man. Thus his attachment to the scruffy, tubercular Ratso (Dustin Hoffman) is not a truly natural homosexual relationship but a defensive response to the unsavory women with whom he comes into contact. The bonding between Joe and Ratso is a defensive reaction to a hostile environment peopled by predatory members of the opposite sex, and because it does not depict homosexuality as a natural preference, *Midnight Cowboy* suggests that male bonding, never first choice, is the coming together of losers. Yet Joe and Ratso genuinely love each other and do find in male friendship a happiness neither has known before. But that their friendship is presented as a consequence of Joe's dehumanizing encounters with corrupt women seems to have made it impossible for director John Schlesinger to depict any sexual experience between Ratso and Joe.

The close of the film finds Joe Buck journeying by bus to Florida, fulfilling the dream of his buddy Ratso. In nurturing his dying friend and assuming responsibility for his needs, Joe becomes a man. On that alienating bus full of hostile, disapproving strangers, Ratso dies in Joe Buck's comforting arms.

According to Dustin Hoffman, there was some discussion during the filming of *Midnight Cowboy* concerning an actual sexual encounter between Ratso and Joe Buck. No such scene appears in the final cut, and Ratso is never explicitly labeled homosexual, although Hoffman speaks of the character as if he were. It hardly matters, for enough erotic energy passes between the two men for the film to make its point that men are better off with each other. Had *Midnight Cowboy* been as honest as *Dog Day Afternoon* toward the theme of homosexuality, it would not have made the erotic or sexual preference of Joe and Ratso for each other dependent upon Joe's being humiliated by women.

Thus what we have is not true homosexuality but a male friendship based too much upon the distrust of women to allow for any real sexual fulfillment. The men seem to reach out for each other but are not allowed to touch, as if the homosexual relationship they seem in all respects but the physical to have chosen were still taboo. In avoiding the depiction of homosexuality to escape an "X" rating or to save the reputation of male stars not wishing to be so characterized, Schlesinger sets the tone for many buddy films to come. Allowing their heroes a sexual life with neither men nor women, these films become more hostile to the male than any film that was open about the sexuality of its characters could ever be.

Joe Buck begins as a victim of the culture's advertisement of Cooper and Wayne as models. On his trip to New York he hears a radio program in which a woman calls Gary Cooper her ideal man. He himself carries a picture of Paul Newman in his suitcase. Yet his teen-age experience, dramatized for us in flashback, in which his girlfriend had been gang-raped, bears no resemblance to the kind of problem faced by Hollywood's male heroes. The reality of heterosexual life is light-years away from the screen experiences of a Gary Cooper.

In each of Joe Buck's encounters with women he is humiliated, beginning with the first when he was unable to save his girl from being brutalized. In his New York experiences the women actually use him and are far more unfeeling than he, despite his aim of selling himself to them as a stud. Street-smart Sylvia Miles, impatient with his innocence, unzips his fly as she talks on the telephone. Manipulating him with a flood of tears in a caricature of the predatory woman, she takes money from *him*, despite the astonished Joe Buck's intention of its being the other way around.

At a swinging party he is picked up by an independent woman, played by Brenda Vaccaro, for whom he is also just a body. She passes on his name to a friend. These women have fully assumed roles hitherto enacted by men, viewing men purely as objects of their lust. Director Schlesinger is oblivious to the poetic justice of this distortion, perceiving solely that independent women emulate exploitative male patterns. He is incapable of sympathizing in any manner with the women in his film. His camera is concerned solely with the travails of a male venturing into the jungle of predatory independent women, who know no restraints and prove more cruel than men have ever been to women. Nor does the film blame Joe Buck in the slightest for failing to obtain an erection for the harridan Vaccaro. Joe is puzzled—"It never happened to me before"—another device used by Schlesinger to place the blame for male impotence on castrating women. Only when she taunts him with being "gay" is Joe, who would never admit to homosexual feelings despite the growing exclusivity of his relationship with Ratso, inspired to mount her with effort, and the tearing and rending of his performance prove adequate enough for her to recommend him to her friend the next morning. Unlike Miles, she at least pays his fee, money he will use to purchase medicine for the dying Ratso. Unfortunately uneasy himself about depicting his heroes as homosexuals, Schlesinger devotes considerable time to justifying this sexual preference by denigrating women. And by so doing he implies that homosexuality is a perversion which all men would avoid were women more worthy of them, a reactionary view that runs counter to the many interesting moments in *Midnight Cowboy* when either Schlesinger or his characters challenge outmoded sexual stereotypes.

Yet despite its retrograde elimination of women from the lives of men, *Midnight Cowboy* manages at times to revolutionize the male image in film. It is unique in its honesty about male anxiety over sexual performance, and it admits that a strong, vital young male may occasionally find himself impotent and even homosexually involved, themes never before so openly discussed in an American film. A comparable moment would occur in 1976 in Robert Altman's *Buffalo Bill and the Indians* where Paul Newman, as the aging Wild West star, suffers a night when he is sexually inadequate and must apologize the next day, fooling nobody with the excuse that he is a "morning man."

Equally daring is *Midnight Cowboy*'s favorable treatment of the apparent homosexual in Ratso. Sweating with fever, lame, filthy and unappealing, full of the cheap tricks of a hustler, Ratso by the end of the film has sufficiently endeared himself to us so that we mourn his pitiable death. He has offered Joe Buck something of which the women, as dangerous and unsettling as they are predatory, are incapable. "You don't look like a fag," Joe tells Ratso at one point. The stereotype of the effeminate homosexual is at once transcended. The affection between men is presented as neither sick nor destructive, another important departure. Its contradictory approaches to the attachment between Joe and Ratso notwithstanding, *Midnight Cowboy* nonetheless paved the way for films about bisexuality which were even more open, such as *Dog Day Afternoon.*

Ratso is particularly appealing when he initiates Joe Buck, the supposedly macho male, into what it means to be a man. Joe, with his Western shirt, suede cowboy jacket, black hat, and boots, is informed that "cowboy stuff" is "strictly for fags," a dishonest moment because Schlesinger here seems to wish to have it both ways, suggesting that his heroes do have sexual feelings for each other after all even though they use the pejorative term "fags" as if it didn't apply to them. Yet in separating sensitive homosexual feeling from the stereotype and in exposing the repressed and latent homosexuality in male bravado, the film remains courageous.

What Ratso says is true. Only a male insecure in his masculinity would need to deck himself out in the manner of the old West, a packaged formula historically assumed by males in doubt of their male identity. Joe is told that the more a man strives to prove maleness, the more doubt is thrown on his actual capacities. The implication is as clear as it is true. Nearly all the heroes of American films were, in their stoical manner, actually concealing sexual ambivalence and uneasiness with the outward display of heterosexuality. Ratso observes, quite correctly, that the tough male in the manner of Eastwood really does not like women, the one terrifying fact his silence is designed to conceal.

Joe Buck, raised on the definition of masculinity offered in Hollywood films, is incredulous: "John Wayne—you want to tell me *he's* a fag?" Joe Buck, the on-screen victim of the mass media, is frantically trying to live by a style of maleness which has no basis in reality or psychological health. He is set straight by an outsider to that world, the scruffy Ratso,

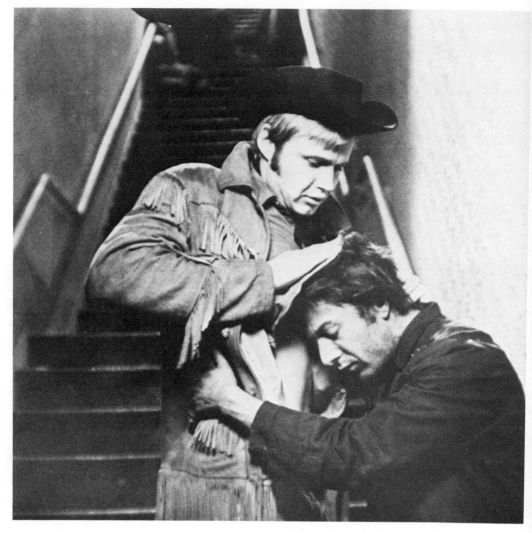

Jon Voigt and Dustin Hoffman in *Midnight Cowboy:* Ratso is particularly appealing when he initiates Joe Buck, the supposedly macho male, into what it means to be a man. Joe, with his Western shirt, suede cowboy jacket, black hat, and boots, is informed that "cowboy stuff" is "strictly for fags."

who speaks for men who would protest a male ideal none can hope to approximate in their real lives. That ideal has produced anxiety, self-hatred, and fear of women. Ratso's lesson is hence liberating, one of the reasons *Midnight Cowboy* has become a classic with the young. The ideal, says Ratso, is a sham. The John Waynes, Clint Eastwoods, and Charles Bronsons are "fags" to the very extent that they must so aggressively flaunt a masculinity of which they can only be secretly in doubt. They simply protest too much.

Meanwhile, a "marriage" between Ratso and Joe Buck begins, as Joe moves into the condemned building that is Ratso's home. "I don't go nowhere without my buddy here," says Joe Buck loyally. He wipes Ratso's sweating brow. Ratso holds him around the middle, tucking in Joe's shirttails. Their short time together is touchingly depicted. And for a film so honest about maleness, a "happy" ending is unthinkable. For these men live from hand to mouth on the periphery of a society which flagrantly ignores the weak and the needy. The homosexual whom Joe brutalizes is a victim's victim, as Joe allows himself to be picked up in order to get the money for the journey to Florida of which Ratso has dreamed. So men have victimized homosexuals, who remind them of feelings they repress as they too are victimized by the codes they embrace.

Midnight Cowboy: Even the perfunctory women of *Only Angels Have Wings* and *Red River* are gone. Yet in a world where women are rejected as a destructive element, men are shown as loving each other with real tenderness.

On the bus, Ratso, in fever, wets his pants. Joe is tactful and accepting: "You just took a rest stop that wasn't on the schedule." When in the entire history of the American film has a principal male character done such a thing? Joe Buck dresses Ratso in clean clothes, zipping up his fly. When Ratso dies, Joe closes his eyes and holds the body in his arms until he can get off the bus. The film ends with Joe's arm still around his dead friend. The last music occurs over a black screen, as if in homage to their love.

In the tawdry, manipulative world in which we live, symbolized here, as in *Taxi Driver* and *Death Wish* to come, by New York City, only two men can nurture each other, in an emotional homosexuality forced as a result of the alienating presence of women. Even the perfunctory women of *Only Angels Have Wings* and *Red River* are gone. Yet in a world where women are rejected as a destructive element, men are shown as loving each other with real tenderness, even if the price they pay is the renunciation of any sexual life at all. In this sense Schlesinger has produced a liberating love story and an attack on the false and destructive stereotypes of what it means to be a man.

Midnight Cowboy and *Butch Cassidy and the Sundance Kid* shaped the pattern for the treatment of love in films of the seventies. In these quiet years when the radical movements had dissipated, the violent, insensitive male has been resurrected on the Hollywood screen, now in open service to authority. The rebel has been supplanted by the cop. And in reaction to the demands of women no longer to be subservient to dominant, superior, authoritarian men, women have been eliminated from American films, with the occasional exceptions of Liza Minnelli, Barbra Streisand, and by 1977 once again, Jane Fonda.

The Seventies

In response to the mood of the sixties, American films of the seventies frequently insist that changes in the social order are beyond our control. The dissolution of the movements of the sixties serves as the implicit excuse for that hopeless, dog-eat-dog view of our society taken by the seventies film. Injustice is ubiquitous, but frequently in these distorted films it is the victim who is represented as the oppressor. The poor and the minorities are treated as malevolent forces, wreaking havoc on the community and jeopardizing the safety of the ordinary citizen for no reason other than their own inherent evil; the disaffected are openly treated as vermin to be exterminated. A violent, equally ferocious male hero is acclaimed by so many seventies films as the sole defender against the bestial criminals who mindlessly attempt to destroy all that is sacred. The quiescence of the American public after the revelations of Watergate exposed the corruption pervading our government has encouraged filmmakers in their insistence that the evil really stems from the poor. In its entire history Hollywood, of course, has never examined the causes of the jungle brutality into which disadvantaged people are pressed, for such an exploration would lead directly to a challenge of the wealth and power of the few. And these few continue to control the financing of American films.

In earlier films official injustice could be challenged because it was believed that once the callousness and selfishness of a few bad seeds were exposed, order and the good life would be restored to all. This is the theme of both *Mr. Smith Goes To Washington* and *On the Waterfront*. Reforms from within would make America once more a land of plenty. Both the Capra and the Kazan films conceal the remoteness of government from the people as a whole by making the power structure so willingly accede to the individual. The history of the American cinema is dotted with such films, which create the illusion that government is truly responsive to the people. Watergate, the Vietnam War, domestic spying, and political assassinations have shown that injustice goes much deeper. And since the concept of reform itself has lost much of its credibility, Hollywood has turned to a virtually fascist endorsement of the tough cop who will solve all our problems and whose flagrant violation of the civil liberties of those he hunts is glorified as necessary for the survival of the community. The male embodiment of this neofascist approach to the social unrest that has deepened in the cities as the seventies have progressed is Clint Eastwood.

Eastwood himself has remarked that because people feel such guilt and impotence over Vietnam and Watergate, "the need for a heroic kind of thing is more necessary than the need to play away from it." Hollywood has attempted to deny how little control we have over our government —and our lives—by treating us to brutally unfeeling, impassive heroes in the service of that very social order so inimical to our well-being.

I

The Eastwood films, whether those in which he stars or those he directs, are a response to the growing loss of confidence on the part of American males in the old symbols of virility, which itself results from the political failure to demand a decent society amenable to human need. The supermale Eastwood hero would, in the manner of the thirties, provide the audience male with a vicarious sense of personal potency. Eastwood also propounds a clear political message in films like *Dirty Harry, Magnum Force, The Outlaw Josey Wales,* and *The Enforcer.* Student-type dissenters are transmuted into vicious terrorists, snipers, whiners, and bullies, a species of sub-being. Blacks are either pimps, bank robbers, or cops. The world has becomes so treacherous that it is unsafe for us even to swim in our own pools. Both *Dirty Harry* and *Magnum Force* contain scenes in which joyful young swimmers, blondes in bikinis always among them, are slaughtered by lurking snipers.

The strong arm of the old-fashioned individualist hero, aided by the cannonlike devastation of the .357 Magnum revolver, is now necessary to protect us all because we are politically impotent and unable to take care of ourselves. That we could survive without Inspector Harry Callahan appears inconceivable. Later films like *Lipstick* (1976) are also structured around the concept of a vigilante out to avenge violent crime. Had Harry been on the scene in *Lipstick*, we feel, he could have prevented much pain. As it is, the rape victim played by Margaux Hemingway must, like Charles Bronson in *Death Wish*, enact her own revenge. The persona of Dirty Harry thus guides even those vigilante films of the seventies in which he does not appear. The clarion call is unmistakable. What we need in a world where, as in *Lipstick*, a gentle music teacher is really a degenerate rapist is more men like Harry, who never hesitates to use his Magnum, who doesn't wait for search warrants before ferreting out the criminals who prey on us all, and who won't bother to tell them of their rights. Harry rejects all these legalities behind which the vicious hide as they continue to wreak havoc.

The glorification of this vigilante male has become the dominant masculine myth of the seventies. *Dirty Harry* created the image, to be followed by *Straw Dogs*, *Walking Tall*, *Death Wish*, *Taxi Driver*, and others, not to mention the sequels to *Dirty Harry* and to *Walking Tall*.

Harry Callahan seems an unlikely male image to appeal so deeply to young men of the seventies, who retain many of the values of the counterculture even if they no longer take part in politics. He is the opposite of small, dark Dustin Hoffman in *The Graduate*, so justifiably suspicious of the world of uniformed force. Harry embodies this authority, a man even more firm and rigid than the typical policeman, who is too weak really to be effective, so enmeshed has he become in red tape. At the end of *Dirty Harry*, Eastwood, thwarted by official interference which has prevented him from effectively, if unconstitutionally, trapping his prey, a vicious young sniper, throws his inspector's badge into a quarry pond in disgust; already floating there is the bloody corpse of the evil sniper, at last exterminated.

Harry's heroism recapitulates elements of the male image as Hollywood has presented it. Like Fairbanks and Mix, he is capable of athletic feats; Eastwood does his own stunts in two key scenes. In one he ascends a fireman's ladder to save a potential suicide. In the other, he jumps off a railroad bridge onto a moving schoolbus driven by the maniacal sniper, who is holding hostage a busload of children. Like his predecessors, Eastwood as Harry is utterly fearless, never missing a beat, as in *Magnum Force* where, having retrieved his badge, he ventures calmly, disguised as a pilot, onto a plane held by highjackers.

Tall and slim with thick brown hair adding sensuality to his otherwise ascetic appearance, at once muscular and taut, Harry is like a panther always ready to leap upon his prey. Behind his ever-present sunglasses he conceals all feeling. It is not that he is incapable of emotion, but that "bleeding heart" sentimentalism, pity for the villain whom poverty has turned to a life of crime, might affect his timing and cause him to lose the firing accuracy so desperately needed against the unruly in these degenerate times.

Harry remains silent except for occasional cutting remarks directed at those less zealous than he. Harry, in fact, hates to talk. His mode is that of Little Caesar, who set the tone for so many heroes of the American film by announcing that he would shoot first and do any necessary talking afterwards. Harry's job constitutes his whole life, and his superiors, who are portrayed as weak or stupid, fear a "bloodbath" when Harry is put on a case. But none can resist Harry's logic. When an adult male has "a butcher knife and a hard-on," Harry explains, he'll gun him down and ask questions later: "I don't figure he's out collecting for the Red Cross." Trust Harry, in this verbally permissive film of the seventies, to tell it like it is.

The .357 Magnum Harry carries is a surrogate penis, gigantic and under his complete control, a fantasy of the terrified and the impotent. Harry is also the best marksman on the force until he is replaced in *Magnum Force* by one of the rookie vigilantes who must learn their "limitations." The twist of the sequel is that Harry now stands for the authority of the police force and the law as a limit the cop must place on his own zeal.

"My, that's a big one," says one of the killer maniacs, ostensibly speaking of the Magnum .357. Harry is admired even by his victims for a sexuality too urgently needed elsewhere to express itself in intercourse. Violent activity suffices, as if women are no longer required for men to be virile or physically fulfilled—a variation on the elimination of women from the buddy films. Men band together in the vigilante pictures as well, nor is this ever perceived as an unpleasant restriction. In *Magnum Force* the Special Forces rookies who have taken to killing lowlives on the street without regard for their rights, or innocence, are accused by fellow cops, revealingly, of homosexuality because they stick so close together. "If the rest of you could shoot like them," says Harry, "I wouldn't care if the whole damn department was queer."

Harry has yet to discover that these cops stay so intimately together because they are carrying out clandestine vigilante assassinations of "criminals" on their own. Made at the height of the revelations about the Central Intelligence Agency's role in both foreign and domestic political assassination and its association with organized crime, *Magnum Force* and *Three Days of the Condor* (1975) ascribe such assassinations to rogue operations within the CIA and the police force unknown to the official leadership. Thus, Hollywood can concede the unthinkable for the purpose of resurrecting those same official bodies as the protectors of us all. In *Three Days of the Condor* the "gone-berserk" CIA unit that branches out on its murderous own is finally brought to heel by the agency's official leadership. And in *Magnum Force*, loyal Harry, turned respecter of the law, admonishes the unit of killer veterans who would bring My Lai home. This *volte-face* is designed to head off public outcry and shock attendant

Clint Eastwood as Dirty Harry Callahan: The .357 Magnum is a surrogate penis, gigantic and under his complete control, a fantasy of the terrified and the impotent.

upon the realization that the CIA and like agencies may be assassins on the loose. Hollywood regroups to exonerate the power structure and to throw the hired hands to the public, as Lieutenant Calley was served up to save those who had given him his orders.

Harry, although himself a loner, recognizes the life-giving qualities of male camaraderie. He never needs a woman in *Dirty Harry* and as a widower remains loyal to the memory of his wife. In *Magnum Force*, because it liberalizes the original character and rehabilitates the police as a viable institution, Harry has an affair with an Oriental woman, the *Playboy* attitude toward sex always the alternative in the seventies to eliminating women entirely.

Harry appeals because he is "cool," as he reveals in the trick wherein he corners a victim and offers him a chance to escape, the target's risk being based on whether he can remember if Harry has spent all six or only five of the shots in his Magnum clip. It is a game as adolescent as it is sadistic, reminiscent of the "chicken run" of *Rebel Without a Cause*, only here the player is not a disturbed, rebellious adolescent but society's official representative, a measure of the drift toward authoritarianism in America. The black bank robber in *Dirty Harry* could have killed Harry, but foolishly chose not to take the chance; the white man is always the intellectual superior of the black in these films. The vicious hippie sniper does take the chance. Harry, knowing his adversary well, has preserved one shot.

Harry is always stoical, another absolute value in these films. In *Dirty Harry* he asks a doctor to attend his wounds without cutting the pants leg on his $29.50 trousers; in *Magnum Force* he takes seven stitches without an anaesthetic. Never does Harry let down his guard or allow others to make decisions for him: "Do things someone else's way and you take your life in your hands." He is a saint, no cop on the take, but poor, living in a shabby if clean tenement apartment that we visit in *Magnum Force*. He is more pure than we, more tough than his enemies. Above all, as Eastwood has proudly spoken of Harry, he is "competent" at a time when all others feel impotent.

In the best male tradition of the American film, Harry is intensely anti-intellectual and sarcastic toward learning, which he equates with impotence. In *Dirty Harry* he greets his Mexican partner with an insult: "Just what I needed, a college boy." He much prefers those Special Forces rookies of *Magnum Force*. Only a physical male as opposed to a prevaricating intellectual can be as skillful with a switchblade knife as Harry is; no one but a fool would go out to meet the evil sniper without one.

All the elements of this male picture coalesce in the central scene of *Dirty Harry*. Harry has at last discovered the hovel of the hippie sniper, and as he closes in on his enemy, the sniper begins to gurgle and whine.

He is a coward after all as he begs Harry not to kill him and yells into the night for the right to call his lawyer. Only a weak buffoon would grant such a scoundrel any rights; Harry kicks and crushes him as he would a bug. But having lacked a search warrant to enter the killer's den, Harry must watch the sniper be subsequently released by the police, hamstrung by an effete society that coddles cutthroats. The intractable Harry can but reply in disgust: "Well, I'm all broken up about that man's rights." The mood might be equated with that of fascist rage at the vacillations of a Weimar Republic where "anarchists" and "disruptive elements" are concerned. They are like germs and should be wiped out totally to preserve the purity of the organism—the body politic. All depends on stability, order, and established power: those who hesitate are lost.

With such insipid civil libertarianism rampant, why does Harry remain on the force? He himself doesn't know. "I really don't," says Harry. He is so much the man that he doesn't have to inflict all this violence to demonstrate his masculinity. His motives transcend the personal. His wife died in a car accident, having been hit by a drunk. Life is absurd and senseless and Harry has one devotion left, to do what he can for order. "Some days I wake up and wonder where the world's going to," he says in *Magnum Force*. Apart from his male prowess, he has a following because his mood echoes what is felt by many in the seventies. There is no point in looking too deeply into things. All is awry; only power has a chance of protecting. Effective action is all. If we remember any image from *Dirty Harry*, it is that of our hero standing expectant and alone on that railroad bridge, quietly poised to leap as he awaits the schoolbus soon to pass beneath him. The compelling quality of the portrait is enhanced because Eastwood in life emulates the fantasy he enacts on screen as the loner. Eastwood and his wife have stressed this in explaining him as "just a backwoods type."

This "backwoods" aspect emerges in such Eastwood Westerns of the seventies as *High Plains Drifter* (1973) and *The Outlaw Josey Wales* (1976). *High Plains Drifter* recapitulates *A Fistful of Dollars* with its hero of no name and the town that does not deserve him. Silent and fierce, the just man returned to this world, he hates all the cowardly males incapable of defending themselves. His recurrent dream is of himself when he was alive as a marshal being horsewhipped to death by villains, finally begging for help that fails to come. The image consciously evokes all those urban rapes and killings in which passers-by refuse to intervene.

High Plains Drifter is nothing so much as an angry remake of *High Noon*. It too has its villains prematurely let out of jail and planning to burn the town. Like Gary Cooper, Eastwood must face a town of craven people who refuse to fight for their own lives. But if *High Noon* in the fifties suggested sheriff Cooper as a model people would do well to emulate, *High Plains Drifter* in the seventies sees a world where reform is impossible. Cynicism now pervades the American film with the view that people are no better than they have been, and never will be. They did not deserve this Western "Harry" when he was alive, and they warrant his punishment now.

In contempt of dissolute times, Eastwood has the buildings of the town painted red and its name changed from "Lago" to "Hell." It is the world of *Dirty Harry* and *Magnum Force,* no different in the nineteenth century than today. Our protector befriends ragged, brutalized Indians and the town dwarf, whom he dubs mayor and sheriff combined, in utter scorn of the real men, whose moral dimension is truly minuscule despite their seemingly normal size and appearance. The town burns as weaklings and cowards are contrasted with the one valuable man, just as the *Dirty Harry* trilogy pits madmen against saintly cops. And the hero leaves the world once more, drifting beyond the morally higher "plains" in a beautiful mirage, this time for good.

The Outlaw Josey Wales attempts to resurrect male individualism through a folk hero of the slavocracy who resembles Pretty Boy Floyd far more than the Bronson of *Death Wish* or Harry himself. Josey is a farmer who, during the last days of the Civil War, is forced helplessly to watch the slaughter of his wife and son by Union marauders. He joins a band of renegades out for vengeance, modeled on Quantrill's Raiders. When the war is over, Josey alone refuses to disarm and swear loyalty to the Union.

Because his supermale skill and flawless violence are so awesome, Eastwood can allow a populist softening and ambiguity to color his usual image. His endless spitting of tobacco juice identifies him as plain folks. But his impassive stoicism notwithstanding, Eastwood as Josey Wales is also a tenderly solicitous father, in silent agony as the charred hand of his son's corpse slips accidentally out of its burlap sack as he drags it to its final rest. It is the most understated and powerful image in the film, as opposed to the endless violence which, because it cannot suffice, betrays weakness.

The friends Josey accepts in his travail are all weak: a boy dying of gunshot wounds whom he gently nurses with poultices made by an Indian woman, an old Indian dispossessed of his land, an Indian woman exiled by her tribe for not having resisted a rape fiercely enough, and finally, an old woman and her granddaughter about to be sold to the Comanches for horses. In a fine moment the dying boy chuckles over how, in the absence of a mother, his father actually did the Confederate embroidery on his grey linsey-woolsey shirt. Nor is Josey a sexual athlete; seventy-year-old Chief Dan George beats him to it before he can make love to the Indian girl. In a romanticized scene Josey communicates with Will Sampson, playing an Indian warrior, about how both will approach life by taking only what they need and living in harmony. At the end we see Josey could not have survived had he not been aided by the canny, ironic old Indian and the three women who came to his rescue.

The battles are routine, owing much to the Japanese samurai film, which influenced so deeply those Sergio Leone spaghetti Westerns in which Eastwood starred in the sixties. What redeems this film is the softening evident in the suggestion that even a supermale must accept the help of others. Unlike Bronson in *Death Wish*, Josey hates the role of vengeful renegade. He would, if he could, be free of his tragedy and become absorbed into ordinary life with planting, harvesting, dancing, and gentle joys. "What do you say to the war being over, Mr. Wilson?" Josey's nemesis, Mr. Fletcher, asks him at the end. "I reckon so," says Josey, the reply not so much that of the repressed automaton as of a man who has suffered and yet survived.

One reason for this humanizing of the Eastwood character, designed to reveal him as martyred and underneath his rage a generous, humane person, is the overriding desire in this film to attach these qualities to the Confederate cause and its defenders. The author of the novel upon which the film was based, Forrest Carter, is said to be Asa Carter, a former speechwriter for George Wallace and the very person who drafted Wallace's inaugural address in 1963 in which he uttered: "Segregation now! Segregation tomorrow! Segregation forever!" Asa Carter left Wallace because Wallace had become too liberal! The romanticism attached to the renegade Southerner battling the brutal Yankees who kill women and children is pure Confederate propaganda. *The New York Times* has in fact noted that Asa Carter's particular hero was the Confederate general Bedford Forrest, the first Imperial Wizard of the Ku Klux Klan, and Forrest Carter's first copyright was appropriately enough recorded in the name of Bedford Forrest Carter. Southern populism and nostalgia for the racist, feudal past fuel this softening of the Eastwood male persona, freeing it (if for this sentimental purpose alone) from a measure of Eastwood's usual impassivity.

II

Film after film of the 1970s returns to the model of *Dirty Harry*. Male sexual survival itself becomes dependent upon a man's becoming a violent vigilante, taking the law into his own hands to rid his community of a ubiquitous and unendingly marauding criminal element. In the trying times of the seventies, physical brutality alone and an outsize weapon to reinforce it offer sufficient proof of a penis in good working order. Only violence against other men can prepare a male to be a lover skillful enough to satisfy a sexually alive woman. These themes coalesce in *Straw Dogs* (1971), Sam Peckinpah's most important statement on the nature of masculinity.

David (Dustin Hoffman), an intellectual, is a slow-moving, passive man. Effeminate in appearance, he wears glasses. A mathematician by profession, he spends his time indoors before a blackboard filled with equations, no place for a real man. He seems thwarted, whining, and inept. Peckinpah insists that only men who spend their days hunting or in demanding physical activity are worthy of the name. In this neofascist ethos, the strong are graceful and measure their power against the weak, the very presence of whom is an outrage and an incitement to violence.

The "real" men of Cornwall, the film's setting, are the village rowdies who torment David and his wife, Amy (Susan George). Ripe, full-fleshed men, they lust after sexy Amy, who came originally from this village and is their female counterpart. In this sense she already belonged to them before she and her distracted husband arrive. She is returning to them before they claim her, an act which flows from what Peckinpah presents as a blood entitlement, a repossession of what nature has granted. David is the alien corrupting her. Unlike her brutish male clansmen, he is unable to stir the coursing of her blood. It is blood, whether spilled or stirred, which forms the driving metaphor of the film. In this sense, Peckinpah imagines himself a latter-day D. H. Lawrence—a man contemptuous of those whose animal vitality is sicklied o'er with the pale cast of thought. Real, physical, vital men "think," *pace* Lawrence, with their blood.

David belongs to another world. He is a male who sees no reason to disguise his weaknesses—or his humanity. He blows his nose, something rare for a hero in an American film because even so normal and natural an act bespeaks vulnerability. And like a mouse fascinated by the encircling rattler, he is weakly drawn to his predators, hiring them to do odd jobs about his farm, a suppliant posture Dirty Harry Callahan, ever on his guard, would find inconceivable. Harry, too attuned to the unstated code of violence and savagery, would never enter into relations with anyone except on terms of mastery and self-command. David, who has kept his nose in his books far too long and whose instincts are submerged and overlaid with abstraction, is not even aware, as Peckinpah's ideology demands, that the world is a jungle. To complete the stereotype of David as the unmanned, effete intellectual, Peckinpah even has Amy drive their car, surging along with the power belonging properly to the male. Her discontent at this very moment is written all over her face, for what a woman craves is literally to be driven, blood racing, by a male of dangerous power. Harry could not sit passively as his woman took the curves, propelling *him* with a touch of the symbolic wheel. Intellectuality and cultivation of the mind are insidious and repellent to Peckinpah, depriving modern man of the full completion promised by his male hormones. Masculinity is now in danger of extinction unless men take drastic steps to redress the balance.

Straw Dogs is thus conceived as a primer on how to be a man. It is also essential to this perspective that those against whom we must salvage our capacity to survive are the masses—the poor, the outcast—all those groups implicitly represented by the gang of out-of-work roughnecks who torment David and Amy. We must recapture their earthy vitality for different social ends. The call is for fascist brutality in the spirit of Conrad's Mr. Kurtz, the insane imperialist: "Exterminate the brutes!" Recovery is essential, even as Harry Callahan stood beneath a sign for a salvage company, a rather heavy-handed summons, at the end of *Magnum Force*. A real man, says Peckinpah, is one who knows how to handle the jungle world, does so proficiently, and above all takes care of his own.

Meanwhile David has on his hands a bored, frustrated wife, reduced by her dismay at his unawareness of her needs to erasing or altering his blackboard equations when he is out of the room. The camera enjoys, as if in slapstick, David's perplexity when he returns to his formulae, unaware that Amy has changed a plus sign to a minus. Her disrespect for the world of absorbed intelligence matches that of Peckinpah. The wife, like all women, is fixated on her father: "*Every* chair's my daddy's chair," she tells David. What every woman craves is a powerful, overwhelming male figure to take her father's place. Her husband must assume command over her life as an authority before whom she can psychically kneel, worship, and inwardly tremble, not solely in fear but in arousal as well. He, in turn, will protect her and their lair from the savage world. It is a metaphor for the cave life, a Hobbesian projection of life as brutish and short. "Rats is life," says one of the lowlives, speaking for Peckinpah. If a male does not naturally possess the requisite capacity for authoritarian control won through violence, he must either rapidly learn it or, as a eunuch, lose his child-woman.

Peckinpah reinforces this thesis by demonstrating that men must be violent, not simply because it is mapped in their genes to be so, but because, even if they would, the world will not allow them to live in peace without imposing personal power. Parallel montage and alternate cutting between scenes of the rowdy youths and those of David and Amy together establish structurally that this couple will not survive unless they come to terms with the reality of these aggressors. That David is physically insufficient and not yet in self-command is considered by Amy to be the original cause of all the trouble. If, for example, he could have done the repairs and odd jobs by himself, the bullies would be gone. She accuses him of having come to England to hide, not being man enough to compete in the world and carve out his own turf. Peckinpah scorns his hero as boring and weak, granting David his patriarchal approval only when David slaughters his tormentors at the end. It takes the murder of their cat and the rape of Amy, which arouses her at the deepest level, before David can sufficiently rouse himself to become a man.

The rape, to which Amy, a feline tease, responds in whimpering relief, occurs because David can neither protect nor command her. He is lured out of the house by the lowlives on a pretext of going hunting with them. While he waits in the bush for prey, their leader goes off to hunt the woman David should be defending. Parallel action again characterizes this sequence. As we watch David patiently waiting for the game to emerge, the roughnecks enter the house and one of them rapes Amy. The violence of the attack itself excites her, decisive evidence that women respond most deeply to being taken; male violence becomes essential to female need. Her heavy breathing overlaps with an image of David patiently waiting with his rifle. As David finally shoots a duck, she is in raptures. When a second rapist arrives to take her, she calls the first rapist a coward for allowing it. He, a former lover when she was a schoolgirl in the village, should have protected her. The world divides into those who will commit any act of violence, however heinous, to possess what they crave and those who, for whatever reason, fail the test. There is no middle ground, only aggression or cowardice.

In the gory final sequence David redeems himself. A humane person, he shields a retarded man named Henry from the village bullies, out to kill Henry for his accidental strangling of a provocative, taunting Lolita who had lured him and seduced him in a dark place—recalling *Of Mice and Men.* Women are vicious teases by nature and from birth. It is in these hysterically violent scenes that David becomes a man, finally driven to do anything to defend what is his.

"This is my home," David proclaims, savoring this truth as if for the first time. In keeping with his new sense of himself, he is able at last to treat his wife in the appropriately imperious manner and to assume command by ordering her about: "Why don't you make some coffee!" Coyly pleased, she obeys. Dominant males are the only mates who can satisfy their wives. David will ultimately slaughter each of the ruffians in turn: "This is where I live. This is me. I will not allow violence against this house." It is an affirmation of self and of life. Sexual identity flows from the assertion of these primitive, primal feelings. The law arrives in the person of the constable, but he is easily murdered by one of the villagers. As in *Dirty Harry,* the legal procedures are too ineffectual to deal with the savage menace. The individual must protect himself with cunning and animal instinct. David devises a wire noose, boils oil, and maneuvers an animal trap to kill off his enemies. The angle for the shots of David in action is slanted and surreal; he is transcendent, having become something beyond what he has hitherto been: a natural man. Amy's second rapist is literally guillotined, the jaws of the trap snapping around his throat and neck. David has now discarded his glasses. Finally in the last encounter he needs Amy's help, having proven himself man enough to deserve it. She fires the gun. Full of feeling, she watches as David departs with Henry. "I don't know my way home," says the retarded man simply. "That's OK. I don't either," says David. As he moves off into the darkness, he is smiling. A man who has so completely found himself could hardly become lost.

In *The Marathon Man* (1976) Hoffman re-creates the role of David. He begins as another effete intellectual, a Ph.D. candidate at Columbia University and a sham of a man, writing a dissertation on fifties repression in America. John Schlesinger, regrettably assuming the mantle of Peckinpah, contends that masculine men act, unlike Hoffman's pathetic father who killed himself after being hounded and professionally destroyed by the investigating committees of the fifties. David cannot redeem his father's martyrdom by writing about it; he will have to become a man unafraid of risking all to destroy his enemies. That the foes are made sadistic Nazis, epitomized by an absurd former concentration camp torturer, Szell (Laurence Olivier), is meant to sanction and render tolerable this view of masculinity.

Hoffman begins as a man incompetent with women, as we see when he approaches a girl (Marthe Keller) in the library. She asks him if he is always so awkward. His reply is self-deprecatory and lacks all confidence: "Yes, today is way above average." His Puerto Rican neighbors ridicule him as a nonmale, calling him "creepy." Even his long-distance marathon running is perceived as the athletic choice of a weakling. By the end, having engineered the death of the vicious Szell, Hoffman has become a man in the Peckinpah sense—a person capable of physical brutality, for by then he has shot three other Nazi henchmen. In an earlier version of this conclusion, Hoffman shot Szell. This was rewritten to show lingering incapacity on Hoffman's part as Szell falls to his death, one small vestige of realism.

His brother is all Hoffman is not. Tough, virile, a superbly competent killer in hand-to-hand combat, he is a man of the world with supreme *savoir-faire*. It strikes us as odd that the son of an academic father persecuted because of his communist sympathies should be not only in the CIA but in special operations, performing those tasks too nasty to be subsumed even under CIA or like agencies. He is an expert in elimination and devious double-agentry. But we learn that both he and his CIA sidekick have become free-lancers to facilitate the retrieval of the diamonds of the Nazi Szell. If the CIA operatives are now one with a mass murderer, they are so on their own without agency sanction.

Only one person, the gentle, ineffectual, and grubby Hoffman, who keeps the suicide weapon of his father, can eliminate Szell. But first he must learn to be a man by overcoming his father's suicidal cowardice and its traumatic effects. Hoffman, surviving torture by Szell's dentist drill, his brother's gory death in his arms, and the pursuit of Nazis and CIA operatives alike, does so when he kills all his pursuers. Thus he avenges his weak father and the brother whose corruption, his male competence notwithstanding, was also the debilitated product of his father's failure of nerve.

The irony is that director Schlesinger fully assimilates a Nazi view of masculinity, replete à la Riefenstahl with the camera's glorification of Hoffman's manly body. The Jews who sell diamonds on New York's Forty-seventh Street are perceived as weak and grasping, as if the camera sees with the editorial eye of Szell himself. Szell is equally caricatured, not merely as a Nazi but as a German national, the film managing to be simultaneously anti-Semitic and anti-German. Schlesinger and screen-writer William Goldman attempt to conceal the essentially corrupt nature of this film by adding a thin veneer of anti-McCarthyism and an equally superficial though accurate claim that one wing of the American CIA actually supports and shields Nazi war criminals. The whole is dishonest, a hypocrisy nowhere more evident than in its glorification of the warrior male, a far cry indeed from Schlesinger's Midnight Cowboy.

The same advocacy of violence and association of masculinity with brutality appear in Walking Tall (1973) and Death Wish. That the real-life hero of Walking Tall, sheriff Buford Pusser, was murdered in 1974 after the completion of this film, lends credibility to the concept of masculinity at its heart. Buford begins as a tough outdoorsman, even as Eastwood dubs himself a "backwoods type." He hates guns, a flaw obvious to an audience initiated into the appropriate male demeanor of the seventies.

Buford returns to discover that his home town has been taken over by thugs. The vigilante films all share the same tired imagery. Women are divided into the "good," such as Buford's wife, and whores, with Peckin-pah's cynical variation that good women are secretly whores because beneath the domesticated veneer lies the need to be mastered and to invite fierce combat among males for their possession. The presence of "good" women in most of these films functions as a pretext for male violence, since as possessions and dependents they must be protected from being seized or spoiled. Most men, borrowing from High Noon, are cowards, weak and useless, who need strong, violent leaders to protect them and to instruct them by example, a formula that prepares so patently for the submissiveness and brutality of fascism that it might have come out of a textbook of the Nazi era.

All the heroes of the vigilante film must be initiated in an ordeal, a trial by fire which sufficiently arouses and steels them. Buford is savagely beaten by bullies. His shirt drenched red with blood, he crawls out onto a highway for help. As in Eastwood's far superior High Plains Drifter, no one stops. The callous timidity of the many is also used as a rationale for the hero's subsequent assertion of animal force. Buford confronts the sheriff to demand that he take on the gamblers and clip joints, that he do so as a man who who would "walk tall." Soon Buford becomes a citizen vigilante, who must act alone. He first arms himself with a phallic baseball bat, using his large size to lay low everyone present at the gambling den which is the hangout for the local hoods.

In the seventies film, people are allowed no option: they must meet force with force. Arrested for breaking the law and for acting unilaterally, Buford refuses to plead guilty. He will neither compromise on his plea nor accept a lesser sentence. He acts as his own lawyer because a real man relies on no one but himself, even as Clint Eastwood is described in the advertisements for *The Outlaw Josey Wales* as "an army of one." The jury finds Buford not guilty, a particularly significant moment. The people, craving the strength of decisive authority, are shown to want strong, tough men to protect them, a decision that justifies the ascendancy of the leader with *carte blanche* to save the community in any manner he sees fit.

Buford now runs for sheriff, as a figure who will "walk tall" and win; the film does not yet find it necessary to insist that the vigilante avenger work completely outside the law. But, like Harry Callahan, he suffers frustration owing to the corruptibility of institutional life by the criminals themselves; they have invaded the law courts and bribed judges, all the while invoking civil liberties and the Bill of Rights, which function as a blind allowing murderers to get off at will. In the world of the seventies, vigilante films represent that our civil liberties are a threat to our safety instead of a safeguard against governmental tyranny and injustice. Neofascist to the core, these films would substitute for the Bill of Rights a strong leader with absolute authority, making it clear that rights consist in allowing the strong leader to work his will against the unruly. It is thus for us to choose—and our survival is at stake. Nor is there ever any ambiguity about criminality. Guilt is instantly apparent to all; hence legal rights are but a pretext for tying the hands of the defenders of the good.

Death Wish is virtually the same film transported to an urban setting, the better to play upon existing fears of mugging and rape on the part of city-dwellers living on the edge of ghettos crammed with the unemployed and the hopeless. As the American economy nosedived in the seventies, and inflation made life a precarious struggle, the unemployment rate among the black and Puerto Rican poor was quadruple that of the white population. These are the very people represented as a menace to the society which so victimizes them, a neat reversal of the social reality born at once of guilt, fear, and projected hatred. The poor are characterized as wild, maniacal beasts motivated to rampage and kill, not because they are starving or desperate, but because they are insane and subhuman, one step down on the evolutionary scale.

In a phantasmagoria of violence and sex, hero Charles Bronson's wife is killed and his daughter sodomized and reduced to a catatonic vegetable. Enraged that the police either do nothing or release such brutes to roam the streets and prey upon innocent citizens, while they round up lost dogs and arrest prostitutes, Bronson, an individualistic and hence virile male, takes it upon himself to clean up the city. In the beginning we see Bronson as an architect actually labeled a "bleeding-heart liberal," presumably one of Lyndon Johnson's "Nervous Nellies," not to mention Spiro Agnew's "effete snobs." He visits the West, where real men defend what is theirs. Everyone owns a gun and it is safe to walk the streets at night. An idea is born.

It is not long before Bronson becomes the leading vigilante of New York. If he vomits after shooting his first mugger, he soon gains control over himself and never reacts in so unmanly a fashion again. The act of gunning down others before they have a chance to defend themselves transforms this architect into a real man; his very appearance changes. After he has killed an ex-con and drug addict and three thugs who have just mugged a victim, people remark on how well he looks. Meanwhile, the film takes time to articulate Bronson's disgust with the press and the government and with the law, which now devotes itself to tracking down our hero-vigilante, who has shouldered its (and our) burden, instead of cleaning up the streets. But Bronson, a new man, remains happy. He has his apartment painted orange and plays loud music on the hi-fi. Muggings in New York have been reduced by him to one-half, to the district attorney's secret delight.

There is the faintest suggestion from the original novel by Brian Garfield that our hero has become demented, unable to desist from killing one more "mugger." (Actually, he kills stray youths before they have committed any crime. If they are of the streets, they qualify for elimination.) The last sequence finds Bronson in exile in Chicago, pointing his finger in mock gunplay at a group of assembled youths. Yet if he seems possessed, his is the single-mindedness of dedication. This lone superman and avenger is justified in carrying on where he left off, in a new city.

Like fascism, *Death Wish* makes its appeal to the powerless little man trapped in big cities where he feels assaulted by forces outside his control against which he is unable to defend himself. He achieves a vicarious sense of power by identifying with the male image proposed by an unflinching Bronson. Behind such a leader the susceptible audience male would hide, recovering the sense of his own safety at whatever cost. In this glorification of the self-styled avenger lies an appeal to bring fascist Argentina or Chile to the United States.

Death Wish makes its appeal to the powerless little man trapped in big cities who feels assaulted by forces outside his control against which he is unable to defend himself. He achieves a vicarious sense of power by identifying with the male image proposed by an unflinching Bronson.

Taxi Driver (1976) was another vigilante film, viewing New York with unbridled hatred and disgust through the eyes of a former Vietnam veteran, played by Robert De Niro. Taxi driver De Niro is so sickened by the pimps and whores with which the ghetto poverty of New York is shamelessly defined that he decides upon an orgy of violence. The ostensible justification of his sick behavior is his desire to rescue a twelve-year-old whore from her pimp, permitting director Martin Scorsese and screenwriter Paul Schrader to wallow in one more neofascist depiction of the poor and disadvantaged as vermin. If *Dirty Harry* and *Walking Tall* attacked the Bill of Rights, *Taxi Driver* glorifies its vigilante avenger by giving us a hypocritical politician named Palantine, a McCarthy-McGovern composite who won't clean up the "mess" of New York. It remains for our Vietnam veteran to do the job with his .44 Magnum, a lone assassin practicing with guns in the mirror in a scene that is barely satiric. No matter how psychopathic De Niro is allowed to seem, the film will not dissociate itself from him. Like Bronson in *Death Wish*, he is a hero deserving the gaudiest badge of masculinity, "a man who would not take it any more," the identical cry elicited by news commentator Peter Finch in *Network* (1976). Instead of examining how the misery of slum poverty, the gang-run drug business, and police repression force people driven to despair to lash out in crime, the film directs this understanding toward a soldier who killed in Vietnam and, returning home unable to do more than drive a cab, is moved by disgust to kill anew, targeting social victims at home as he had abroad. Only *he* has concern for life among the impoverished, but only to destroy, never to redeem.

Finally, violence fuels the 1976 film *Jaws* (based upon Peter Benchley's potboiler), with its three standard male types: the egotistic, self-assertive loner (Robert Shaw), the policeman who must be initiated into the need for greater violence (Roy Scheider), and the intellectual, who is ineffectual without stronger men by his side (Richard Dreyfus). Vigilantism on behalf of the community is, in this variation, directed against an animal predator, but the formula remains otherwise intact.

However, this film of the mid-seventies proposes a reversal of power from that typical of the American film. The loner, Shaw, an emblem of the solitary frontiersman of consummate skill and raw physical courage, nevertheless lacks sufficient force to defeat the overwhelming menace and is swallowed alive. It is the lawman, Scheider, as settler and beneficiary of civilization, who, with his patience and violence, combined with the aid of the intellectual, Dreyfus (sneered at by real man Shaw), defeats the seemingly omnipotent force of disorder threatening society. Only these two, working side by side, can defeat the shark. And so once more in a seventies film does the cop emerge as our hero and protector, here rational, self-sacrificing, and eminently worthy of our most unqualified confidence.

Hollywood offers us no repulsive Adolf Hitler as the specific male leader who would guide the authoritarian police state being proposed to us. Instead, we are offered the irresistible, finely wrought maleness of a Clint Eastwood or the animal power, combined with latent tenderness toward those who deserve it, of a Charles Bronson. Robert De Niro's nervous intensity might also do. If we know what is good for us, argues one vigilante film after another, we will place our trust, and our very selves, in the hands of the angry avenger, the authoritarian, ever-violent male.

III

Friendships among men dot the history of the American films: the cowboy and his sidekick, the gangster and his partner, the comedy team of savvy fellow and buffoon. But only for psychopathic personalities like Little Caesar, glaring in pain at the moment of the Depression, did this male companionship entail the complete exclusion of women from their lives. Yet the dominant sexual motif in filmmaking of the seventies has been the male friendship. A dread of powerful women has entered the mass media, personified by television's redoubtable Maude, whose wit and panache are joined to physical formidability.

Such books as *The Male Dilemma: How to Survive the Sexual Revolution* are now commonplace. In the American film masculine dominance has always accompanied expressions of male virility. The belief that a relationship of equals would lead to male impotence would be sufficient cause for the disappearance of women from the seventies film. That women in real life are competing with men for jobs may have led to the unprecedented punishment of women in films, and to what appears to be a willed decision to represent the good life as excluding the female sex entirely. But beyond this, women in the nuclear family, tied to child-rearing and homemaking, had, like all subordinated groups, internalized dominant values. They were thus decisive in perpetuating male and female roles through the nurturing of the young. From the moment women ceased to accept their role and their suppression, the consequences for all established values, including that demanding the dominance and superiority of the male, were dire.

The history of the American film and its influence upon its audience, generation after generation, has contributed to this virtual elimination of women from films of the seventies. The cruel and impossible demand that real-life men live up to a supermacho image or fail to be considered masculine has fostered misogyny in our culture. Hostility toward women is the inevitable result of the pressure upon men to conceal feelings of vulnerability if they are to be perceived as adequately heterosexual. The characterization of the women's movement in the mass media as shrill and peopled by hysterics crying for orgasm on demand has paved the way for the acceptance by men of films in which women have no part. Buddy bonding on screen is a reflection of the damage done the American male by the national cinema.

To spend one's waking hours and intimate moments with another male of masculine demeanor becomes less threatening to the basically hetero-sexual male than to be paired with a woman of strength with whom a man is constantly forced to measure his adequacy. Jon Voigt establishes this in *Midnight Cowboy*. Seventies films frequently transport their male part-ners to remote environments free of women, as in *Deliverance* (1973), *Papillon* (1973), *The Longest Yard* (1974), and *The Sorcerer* (1977). Other safe havens are those settings where women must be peripheral, circum-stances described in *Mash* (1970), *Husbands* (1971), *The Sting* (1974), and *California Split* (1974). That male superiority has been placed in real jeopardy by the woman's movement has filled the film industry with such dread that it rarely risks and can scarcely imagine the depiction of tender heterosexual love, and certainly not without the male's first having proven himself with some variation of the symbolic Magnum. Only the absence of women will permit peace and harmony to reign on screen, as they cannot in real life because women have begun to expect autonomy and an equal voice in their relations with men.

The seventies have become with a vengeance the decade of the "buddy" film, a term that has passed into cultural analysis in America, so aptly does it describe the most popular and pervasive sexual pattern in our movies. Love, though just as sentimentally and tenderly portrayed as that between men and women in films of the thirties, is now reserved for males alone. This essentially homosexual feeling is best epitomized by that glance shared by Redford and Newman across a crowded room in *The Sting*. Newman's blue eyes fill with tears of relief as he spies Redford safe and sound after an attempted ambush from which Newman has saved his protégé. What the buddy film finally reveals is the dark, terrible, and closeted secret of American culture. The most masculine man, rigid, stoical, repressed, and hence thought to be powerful, has carried all along an essentially homosexual sensibility, as a person who can express his manhood fully and uninhibitedly solely through interaction with other men. Only "weak" men allow themselves to become entangled with women in these films; heterosexual interaction feminizes, as if women and their ways were like a virus. Same-sex exclusivity reinforces male identity.

The preference of males for each other is frequently grotesque in its stridency, as in *Mash*, where the cool butcher-surgeons Donald Suther-land and Elliott Gould are pitted against a demeaned female adversary named "Hot Lips" Houlihan (Sally Kellerman). As the only female lead —if such she can be called—"Hot Lips" is stupid enough, in the view of this nihilist film, to take the army and its rules seriously. She is so unattrac-tive sexually that one male inquires of another who has sampled her charms if they were in fact "any better than self-abuse."

Women are the "other," while the men enjoy the close camaraderie that only life at the front can provide, a motif of the buddy film which dates from *What Price Glory* in the twenties. Sutherland communicates with his pals via a little whistle he utters under his breath, an unspoken visceral code for reactions to emotionally charged moments. Swinger Gould carries a bottle of olives, ever ready for martinis in the bloody theater of war. They are three miles from the front lines in Korea, but it could just as well be the Wars of the Roses for any interest the film takes in its historical background. What counts is the relationship between the men, and that alone.

Director Altman is interested only in depicting the cool machismo of his heroes, toward which he demonstrates not the slightest irony. Altman considers that nothing could be more appropriate during an unjust and senseless war than for real men to settle down to a game of touch football outside the operating room. *Mash* gets its share of laughs, but these are juvenile in spirit, even as Altman's heroes are overgrown, arrested adolescents. Despite the film's ostensible pacifism, it employs a male style right out of the most flagrantly macho war films. No matter how many deaths they witness, our male heroes show no emotion. The worst thing that can happen to a man is the loss of his virility, as in one episode a temporarily impotent dentist declares himself "a victim of latent homosexuality" and decides to commit suicide.

His buddies will save him because everyone knows that impotence is only a result of having been with the wrong woman; real men are never sexually lacking, let alone homosexual. A nurse and an aphrodisiac are enlisted to restore the dentist to sexual potency (the remedies work). Other antics include exposing "Hot Lips" in the shower to determine whether or not she is a real blonde. The films which purport to satirize war prove to be even more misogynist than those applauding combat against the enemy. Grant, Wayne, and Bogart were, after all is said and done, chivalrous to women. In *Mash* women are present to be humiliated, further evidence that these buddy films were made in conscious hostility to the women's movement. As in *Midnight Cowboy*, women appear solely to be labeled, abused, and cast aside as a threat to male integrity and male sexuality.

Mash ends on an obligatory football game, which turns up in more than one seventies film as an arena for the demonstration of male prowess. A black jock named "Speerchucker" Jones (Fred Williamson) saves the day for our side, as *Mash* attempts to conceal its contemptuous attitude toward women with token liberal concessions to blacks. In a parody of the field of battle, player after player is carried wounded from the football field. But here the film fails as a denunciation of war to the degree that it endorses male dominance. The machismo of football is celebrated to the full, along with the male touching, the embrace of the tackle, and the pile-up, evocative of nothing so much as a disguised male orgy. Thus Altman's analogy between the game and the war establishes unwittingly that combat too is a pleasing arena for male self-expression. The theme of the senselessness of war, central to the film until this point, loses its thrust as *Mash* degenerates finally into one more male chauvinist joke. At the end poor Hawkeye (Sutherland) receives his orders to go home. So sorry is he to leave his male companions behind that he hesitates. The sense of comradeship with his buddies has been so heightened by the near presence of war and disaster that he must speed away before he changes his mind.

Husbands (1971) brings the same theme home and treats its women identically. Three men, their fourth buddy having died before the film opens, go on a bender, first at home and then in London. Wives—and all women—are alien, irrational beings; Ben Gazzara's wife actually tries to stab him with a knife at one point. But brief sexual encounters with cheap pickups in London afford no more satisfaction.

Husbands glorifies the love between men. Although it does not culminate in openly sexual acts, there are moments when the male contact does become highly physical. In a highly emotional scene in a bar toilet between Peter Falk and John Cassavetes, and at other moments when the buddies kiss, they approach some consummation of their affection. Like so many seventies films, *Husbands* finds everything hopeless and meaningless, with death as our only destiny—the film opens with a funeral scene —and concludes that in such a world males can find affection and peace of mind only with other men. If the title is ironic, there is no irony toward the precept that only the love between two men is dignified and worth having.

The essence of a buddy film emerges through the director's, and hence the film's, view of male bonding, which can be approved, satirized, depicted neutrally, or deployed to expose the emptiness of the characters' lives. In *Midnight Cowboy, Butch Cassidy and the Sundance Kid,* and *Mash* there is no doubt that the director wholly identifies with his male heroes, applauding their choice of each other to the exclusion of women and approving their liberation from the heterosexuality by which they had lived. If director Cassavetes, however, portrays his three husbands as pathetic, lonely, and unfulfilled men, he still does not suggest that the camaraderie and love they seek and find together would be possible with women as their partners. The reverse is the case, as the film becomes an implicit argument against heterosexual relationships, while not allowing these men the choice of homosexual relations either. The women in the film, perceived solely through the eyes of jaded male characters, emerge as absurd, grotesque, and subhuman. Had the director wished to offer a view in opposition to that of his heroes, he would have been obliged to depict at least one woman whose qualities conflicted in some measure with the diminished view held by the males at the center of the film. And had the men been acceptable to the director as homosexuals, his characters would not have felt the need to be so hostile to women.

Carnal Knowledge (1972), despite the protestations of screenwriter Jules Feiffer, falls clearly into this category. Feiffer has argued that when he wrote the script for this highly influential buddy film of the early seventies he was distancing himself from his protagonists Jonathan (Jack Nicholson) and Sandy (Art Garfunkel). His avowed aim was "to show that heterosexual men can hate women just as much as homosexual men"; the film, he pleaded, might be seen as "an army training film—it describes the symptoms of a disease." Indeed the ending of *Carnal Knowledge* pictures our heroes in a sorry state. Jonathan, sexually impotent, can only achieve his climax through manual manipulations by a seedy prostitute (Rita Moreno). Sandy has taken up with a flower-child of the sixties, a ragged hippie who, he deludes himself into believing, holds the "secret" of love.

That the film criticizes its heroes does not automatically mean that it dissociates itself from the premise that men are superior to women or that the sturdy macho attitudes of its heroes are not inevitable aspects of their masculinity. When Jonathan refers to women as "big tits," laughter rises from the audience, but it is delighted laughter, in recognition of a shorthand device for evaluating sexual partners. It rises because the film jokes good-humoredly along with Jonathan in his refusal to treat women as human beings.

The buddy aspects of *Carnal Knowledge* are so felt and immediate because they are woven into the lives of men who pursue *women*. Their love for each other emerges in the mutuality of sharing and recounting sexual experiences. The homosexual feeling hovers beneath the surface. Theirs, after all, is the abiding relationship in the film, outlasting all their encounters with the women they live with and leave. In one exchange Sandy has just told Jonathan that he can really talk to Susan (Candice Bergen), the girl who will be the "first" for both. Jonathan replies, "You can talk to me too. Are you in love with me?" It is not that these men are explicitly homosexual, but that in a culture which encourages distrust of and hostility toward women, erotic trust becomes possible only between men. *Carnal Knowledge* acutely chronicles that sexual tension which grows up between men as an inevitable result of their treating women as the alien "other."

Finally, *Carnal Knowledge* unfolds too long from the viewpoint of hero Jonathan, for whom all women are "ball-busters." Since the women drop from view one by one, including Susan, filmmakers Mike Nichols and Jules Feiffer elect to avoid any suggestion that Jonathan's view may be distorted. "You think a girl really goes for you and you find out she's out for your money or your balls or your money and your balls," Jonathan reflects; "the women today are better hung than the men." Nothing in the

Jack Nicholson and Art Garfunkel in *Carnal Knowledge:* Their love for each other emerges in the mutuality of sharing and recounting sexual experiences. The homosexual feeling hovers beneath the surface. Theirs, after all, is the abiding relationship in the film, outlasting all the encounters with the women they live with and leave.

action of *Carnal Knowledge* suggests that this is not true. Jonathan speaks these words facing full front, talking into the camera, as if telling the audience a received truth, a technique which in itself precludes distance by the film from this spurious message.

For to dissociate itself from this point of view, *Carnal Knowledge,* like *Husbands,* would have had to depict some women who were not "ball-busters." Instead we remain in the insulated world of the two buddies sharing their little confidences as they exchange women. It is only to Sandy that Jonathan confesses, in a moment of startling honesty, that for the past year or so he has had trouble "getting hard." "Girls today," he confides, "they judge you, they judge you very quickly." Such a confession functions as a transparent surrogate for explicit sexual contact with Sandy. It also demands audience sympathy with Jonathan against the castrating shrews, those products of the sexual revolution who are causing men such pain. In one of his fights with sexy Bobbie (Ann-Margret), she actually accuses Jonathan of preferring Sandy and loving *him* best: "You wouldn't want to cheat on Sandy," she taunts. "He spends half his life over here." Jonathan rises to this ultimate accusation that he is not quite as heterosexual as he pretends: "Wait a minute—a second ago you had me screwing Cindy"—Sandy's current woman—"Who'm I screwing now? Sandy?" Significantly, it is this particular exchange which gets Jonathan "hot" and enables him to screw once more. The mention of a sexual relationship with his best male friend turns him on, a revealing moment over which the film slides, blurring its meaning.

The most grotesque woman in the film is this same Cindy, because she "wants balls ... she's a little masculine ... in bed it's like a close-order drill." Cindy (Cynthia O'Neal) is the "new woman," sexually free and in command; that she is so truly a ball-buster enables the film to remain with Jonathan, viewing matters through his eyes. With Susan, who is not so satirized, repeated sex proves not to be enjoyable. And if sex even with a woman you love becomes boring and mechanical, avers *Carnal Knowledge,* why not indeed settle in with a male buddy to whom one can at least openly confide one's problems without being emasculated?

Deliverance (1973) pictures four male friends on a camping trip, which affords them a precious respite from the obligation to pursue women. The trip becomes so fraught with trauma that the men draw together. The nightmares evoked express the unresolved and frightening sexual feeling that hovers between these males. The two central characters, Ed (Jon Voigt) and Louis (Burt Reynolds), seal by the end a communion and bond rarely possible for the alienated beings of the seventies film, and possible if at all between men alone.

The four men set out on a weekend, their plan to navigate by canoe "the last unpolluted river." "Pollution" describes the repressed and unrealized feelings shared by these characters as much as it does the world from

which they are escaping. The ecological metaphor is particularly appropriate to the feelings filmmakers bring to their films in the seventies. Most
see their culture as so corrupt that men must journey into the very
wilderness to recover something of value.

At first director John Boorman keeps his men in long or middle shot
to distance us from them, even as *Carnal Knowledge* sacrificed objectivity
toward its male heroes with a succession of close-ups of Jonathan and
Sandy. Louis is the male obviously in doubt of his virility, dressed as he
is in tight jeans, flexing his bare arms. He loves the rapids, which he
openly equates with sex: "Best . . . second best sensation I ever felt."
Unattractive in his adolescent brashness and bravado, and in Burt Reynolds perfectly cast, Louis is a figure of irony for the first part of the film.
There is no endorsement of his strident schoolboy masculinity.

But as the trip continues, Boorman suggests that a potential for emotional closeness between men has been held within and, in the absence of
social restraint, should be cultivated. If in the fifties shooting the rapids
evoked heterosexual experience, as Katharine Hepburn was awakened to
her sexual attraction to Bogart in a similar scene in *The African Queen*, here
the same event unleashes homosexual feelings. It allows the full import
of male bonding to surface. All the events of *Deliverance* lead cumula-
tively to the unacknowledged sexual search of the men for each other.
And because these homosexual feelings are taboo in our culture, they are
even more powerful for being fully repressed instead of naturally released in open affection and touching, as in cultures where male physical
feeling does not impair masculine identity.

Deliverance begins to crackle with terror. The men first play at being
competitors, each pitting his masculine bravery and capacity for survival
against those of the others. These attempts to advertise their male prowess
are preludes to seduction. Screenwriter James Dickey, author of the
original novel, nearly allows these feelings to emerge. Reynolds confronts
Voigt with a question reflecting inner doubt: "Why do you go on these
trips with me?"

In the primal event of the film Ed (Voigt) and Bobby, but not Louis
(Reynolds), are captured by two rural degenerates, men primitive enough
to act out those forbidden sexual impulses "civilized" men like our heroes
repress and deflect into more acceptable manifestations such as hunting
animals or contact sports. Ed is tied to a tree. Bobby, a fat, ineffectual man,
is ordered to drop his pants and is raped. Both men are threatened with
having their "balls cut off," whether or not they cooperate. The terror
evoked is not just that of being violently mutilated by degenerates but
of being forced to express latent homosexual feelings, and in a passive,
vulnerable, receiving manner at that.

The violence of these strangers allows the sexuality trembling between
the men to surface. The film neither applauds nor is distressed by what

is revealed about the men; it simply suggests that were these male friends honest enough, they would admit to such feelings for each other, accept them without shame, and feel released from the need to shoot rapids or endlessly test their male credentials. Just as Ed is about to be forced to perform oral sex on one of the hillbillies, Louis shoots the man with his bow and arrow. He is defending his friend and rescuing his lover, if hardly in a romantic situation.

As if in shuddering reaction to what has been seen, the film now turns to an advocacy of male force, in contradiction of its earlier irony toward Louis's macho flaunting of his strength. Now homosexual need and male eroticism for other males are associated with dark, savage, and primitive needs *properly* repressed by civilization. If civilization limits us, going native means that the dark forces of the id, symbolized by the ghoulish hillbillies, as malevolent as gargoyles, will overtake us. *Deliverance* is, in sum, a Freudian fable of the dangers of our instinctual life. If the price of civilization is the curbing of male vitality and release, the consequences of going back are surrender to the savage animal world of rape and violation of the weak by the strong. Thus *Deliverance* finally endorses the very impulses which are still associated with virility, but prefers them sublimated in football, burlesque shows, *Penthouse* magazine—or shooting the rapids.

In this world without social restraint a male must personally be ready and able to kill, for such self-defense, like that of Dirty Harry, is needed against the human beasts lurking in the jungles of our minds and our society with its seemingly peaceful rural byways. (Similarly, the peaceful tourist village in *Jaws* (1976) is surrounded by an ocean of unspeakable menace.) "Where's the law?" screams Louis, justifying his act of murder. The film wholly applauds him, as the buddy film merges with the vigilante saga, the two dominant strains of the American film in the seventies. The obligatory rescue now involves one man guarding the chastity of another, so deeply has the buddy film unwittingly renounced heterosexuality in the course of preserving the masculine mystique.

This moment of shared love will be sanctified by a pledge of secrecy the men will share for life, not only because any local jury would side with the hillbillies and, therefore, they remain in danger, but also for darker reasons. The event has touched upon the sexual feelings throbbing between the men. It has partly answered Louis's question why they continually venture on these seemingly pointless trips: they go because they need to spend time alone together. The four men dig the grave of the murdered degenerate with their bare hands, as if performing an ancient fertility ritual, burying the corpse as they do their own instinctual life so that the land will be productive the following spring. Their secret involves their arousal by the forced rape, so exciting because it evoked an act they would willingly perform on each other were they not so

Deliverance: If the price of civilization is the curbing of male vitality and release, the consequences of going back are surrender to the savage animal world of rape and violation of the weak by the strong.

repressed and alienated from their real feelings by the false accouterments of civilization. Many audience men have reported on how disturbed they were by the rape sequence, aroused and alarmed, their reaction offering them an insight into what women fear and feel about being forcibly taken.

With this sexual secret in the air, the men become disoriented. One is shot by a mysterious sniper and drowns. Ed now explicitly needs to be close to his best friend, crying out, "Louis, Louis," and abandoning any furtiveness about his concern for the person he loves most. Louis has been injured by another shot, his leg torn open with the bone poking through. The sniper they fear turns out to be actual, the degenerate's own best friend and a living expression of the feelings for each other that have slowly if relentlessly escaped during the trip, emotions they fear as much as physical death itself. Disoriented by these distressing revelations, all of them become weak, bumbling, and unsure. Ed impales himself upon his own arrow, having just barely hit the sniper. He and Louis embrace.

They have survived the terrain, the hostile elements, natural and human, and their own feelings. Bobby, who was raped, tells Ed they won't see each other for a while; his shame at having been the actual object of homosexual lust is too overwhelming.

In the final sequence, a coda to the action, Ed, "delivered" to his wife and son, wakes up screaming "No!" He is plagued by nightmares. The dueling banjos played in frenzy by a retarded boy, the sound which accompanied the men on their trip, twang in the background. Of what outrage has Ed in terror dreamt? And for what repressed sexual release is he longing? At those moments which touch upon the forbidden sexual feelings between men, *Deliverance* becomes one of the finest of the buddy films, locating honestly the emotional mood of the male in the seventies, on and off screen. Notwithstanding its conservative call for social restraints and its presentation of unconscious needs as savage, it reaches an understanding of what male dominance does to men, fixating them on each other in the process of demeaning women.

Rites of passage to manhood are frequently part of the buddy film and nowhere more so than in *The Last Detail* (1973), which chronicles far more superficially the feelings expressed in *Deliverance*. Navy lifers Buddusky (Jack Nicholson) and Mulhall (Otis Young) set out to deliver a frightened young sailor to a Portsmouth, New Hampshire, prison. En route the boy becomes a "man," having shared those experiences which the seventies film feels sufficient to confer manliness. He now drinks beer, is introduced to a prostitute, and even attempts to escape. In all these male initiations, his buddy guards enjoy him vicariously. The military service and prison, as in *Papillon*, which was made the same year, are perfectly tailored arenas for male heroism, inhabited as they are exclusively by men. Only in such exalted sanctuaries do men still achieve small moments of triumph, as when Steve McQueen as Papillon dives from a towering cliff into the sea and freedom before the amazed eyes of buddy Dustin Hoffman.

Peckinpah, predictably, has also contributed a buddy film, *Pat Garrett and Billy the Kid* (1973), which explodes with unavowed sexual tension between two male pseudo-antagonists. Like Butch Cassidy and Sundance, Billy is another hero who has outlived his time. Pat Garrett tells Billy that times have changed, that he, for one, is no longer an outlaw and, as a lawman, will have to pursue his old friend. "Times, maybe, not *me*," says Billy (Kris Kristofferson) softly in what we are meant to experience as heroic resilience. Billy's friends ask why *he* doesn't kill Pat Garrett (James Coburn): "He's my friend," is the response. Billy is the better man, for Garrett, now serving a social master, does kill *him*. Yet throughout they remain male lovers who touch without touching, cool in the face of death.

Meanwhile, we are treated to no small sampling of Peckinpah's usual gore. Violence is, in fact, inseparable from male bonding in the Peckinpah films, as if extreme brutality mitigates self-hatred; it is the distorted, ambivalent embrace of male antagonists in a homosexual fulfillment denied open expression by the masculine mystique and the need to maintain their posture as "men." Garrett has married a Mexican woman toward whom he feels nothing, and he escapes from her to a saloon whenever he can. "You might say you're glad to see me," she accuses. "It's a week since you've gone." But all of Pat Garrett's energy flows toward Billy the Kid, a pursuit of pathos and passion: "Us old boys," Garrett admits, "shouldn't be doing this to one another."

With *The Sting*, the buddy film reaches its apogee as the most bankable formula of the seventies. Newman and Redford return to each other's arms; this time the women in the film are completely faceless and peripheral, no threat whatsoever to the relationship of the men. Like many buddy films, *The Sting* utilizes the tired plot of an older, sophisticated male (Newman) initiating one younger and less experienced into the ways of the world. Sexuality lurks just below the threshold of their camaraderie. Interestingly enough, when they first meet, Newman is in the shower and Redford addresses him from a toilet seat!

The Sting is an infinitely more paltry and facile film than *Deliverance* because director George Roy Hill seems blind to the erotic implications of this exclusively male relationship. In *Deliverance* we are always aware of a sexuality which the characters themselves have not yet recognized. *The Sting* attempts, disingenuously, to remain as innocently naïve as its heroes, who, as a result, are cardboard caricatures not only with respect to their sexuality but as human beings. Newman attempts erotically to win the esteem of Redford by showing off his biceps and by displays of bravado. He can round up two, three hundred guys to pull off "the sting." Redford, as he will be in *The Way We Were*, is the sex object, all manicured and prettied up.

The blue eyes of Newman meet those of Redford across crowded rooms as if by clockwork. He winks at Redford as he fools with a deck of cards, blinks back tears when Redford returns from the ambush. There is much secret signaling as Doyle (Robert Shaw), the patsy, is led up to the appropriate window to bet on the horse he has been told, at the fake gambling establishment, is a sure winner. By the end Newman has proudly taught Redford things "only five guys in the world know." At one point Redford asks Newman why he has gotten involved in this big con, a moment akin to the one in *Deliverance* when the issue of why the men take trips together is posed. "Seems worthwhile, doesn't it?" Newman says evasively. But what is it that appears so enticing? The action itself is pointless, a passing revenge which, given the power of Doyle, will have swift consequences. The real value resides in the mutual experience, the marriage of these two men in adventure.

Redford in *The Way We Were:* The sex object, all manicured and prettied up.

In the final scene, "the sting" brought off, Newman and Redford go off together, like hero and heroine. "Well, kid, you beat him," says Newman. And Redford replies, "You're right. It's not enough. But it's close." They are speaking ostensibly about having avenged the death of their comrade, Luther. But the words resonate beyond their literal meaning. The two men have found something together which does not promise perfect happiness; no seventies film, no post–*Pillow Talk* film, would dare promise unalloyed joy. But together Newman and Redford have achieved something "close." In homage to the purity of their friendship and the priceless love they have nurtured by participating together in "the sting," each refuses to accept his share of the stake. Money would cheapen the love that has grown out of the effort. Content to be together, they walk off to an iris-out, growing smaller and smaller until we lose sight of them altogether. We leave them to savor their union, perhaps in more such adventures, but always in the pleasure of each other's company.

In the mid-seventies, a lunatic asylum (*One Flew over the Cuckoo's Nest*, 1975) and the newsroom of a big city newspaper (*All the President's Men*, 1976) serve equally as congenial environments for buddy relationships to flourish. *Cuckoo's Nest* depicts the friendship and affection of Jack Nicholson as McMurphy and Will Sampson as the Chief. Nicholson may import a couple of obligatory whores into the insane asylum where all reside, but that he does not take women seriously is clear. *All the President's Men* chronicles how two bright young men, working as buddies side by side without any women in their lives, restore the Horatio Alger myth supposedly still accessible to young American men.

The buddy film can even come disguised as a heterosexual love story. In *Robin and Marian* (1976), an aging Robin Hood (Sean Connery) returns to Sherwood Forest after twenty years of adventure by the side of his buddy, Little John, and in the service of an even more formidable buddy, King Richard. Robin hasn't thought of Maid Marian (Audrey Hepburn) "for years." Richard the so-called Lion-Hearted is a disappointing, mad, sadistic old man who dies in Robin's arms with a question as explicit in its homosexual pleading as any: "You couldn't leave me . . . could you?" Robin is indeed unable to leave him, although he respects neither Richard's cause nor his person. But Robin is loyal both to the relationship and to the office. To serve a king or president, to fight for one's country, have been classic masculine pursuits; it is these which have occupied our hero. Such loyalty, director Richard Lester indicates, is inspired by the affection men have for each other and by their desire to spend their lives side by side with other men. Richard happens to be a tyrant, but that has little bearing on Robin's decisions. Lester remains basically uncritical of the buddy relationship, fondly chronicling Robin's continuing commitment to his dearest friend, Little John, over long years—until, in fact, his head has grown bald and his beard grey.

Robin's love affair with Maid Marian is temporarily rekindled. The scenes between them are delicate and tentative: "You never wrote"—"I didn't know how." It is as if we were witnessing a romance of middle-aged love. But a love affair with a woman is not enough for Robin, a real man, and never his first choice. Marian irrelevantly asks if there were many women on his great crusade; she is a small-minded woman with petty thoughts. Robin hears the warning horn and "must have a look at who's hunting me." Sean Connery's Robin of the 1970s, inhabiting a world grown stale, cares as little for women as for life itself. The exuberance and exhilaration of those earlier Robins, Fairbanks and Flynn, are gone, to be replaced by malaise and a revulsion from a decaying world recalcitrant to change. There will always be kings, sheriffs, and brigandage. The Robin of the seventies returns to combat entirely as a reflex, a subordination to an old mystique in lieu of belief that through bold adventure he can make the world a better place.

Little John and Marian thus inevitably become rivals, and she clearly perceives him as a sexual threat: "You've had years and I'll lose him." But after defeating sheriff Robert Shaw, Robin is depleted, both for sex and adventure. "I doubt I'll have a day like this again," he laments. All Marian can do in such final defeat is to poison them both as Little John, about to lose the person he loves best, cries, "No! No!"

Like Butch Cassidy and Sundance, Peckinpah's Billy the Kid, and their audience admirers, Robin lacks the means to realize his style of masculinity. All have outlived the time when they might live as adventuring men. Robin even asks his former Merry Men, "What do you do for a living?" What indeed can the male adventurer do when the times view adventure with alarm? To be reunited with a woman, particularly now that women like the middle-aged Marian are outspoken, perceptive, and wiser than before, is no longer possible for a man in a seventies film. Death, in fact, is preferable.

IV

When American films of the seventies do not issue calls to vigilante terrorism or paeans to the love between men, they champion male superiority and glorify the brutal domination of men over women. Such male heroes make the blunt and blustering John Wayne seem by comparison gentle and tender; they have even inspired a John Wayne cult among some feminists.

Bobby Dupea (Jack Nicholson) of *Five Easy Pieces* (1970) is made the natural superior in sheer vitality, wit, and intelligence of each of the "five easy pieces" of his acquaintance, despite the presence on the project of a woman screenwriter, Adrien Joyce. The women are either whiners or betrayers, and the worst may well be Bobby's emotionally retarded pianist sister, lusting after their father's brutish male nurse. She murmurs over her music, spoiling one recording session after another, and seems hardly worthy of her concert status. This professional woman is emotionally awry, so hysterical and repressed as to constitute a living refutation of the breed. But every woman in this film is denigrated, the better to elevate the *angst*-ridden hero. For whatever weaknesses the virile, masculine Bobby manifests, the callowness of the women fully vindicates his refusal to form a permanent attachment to any of them. When he skips out on his girlfriend Rayette (Karen Black), leaving her in a filling-station bathroom, we may be startled by his coldbloodedness, but we are unable to doubt the wisdom of this desperate move.

Our sympathies, then, are all entirely directed to Bobby, who has rejected an effete life of refinement epitomized by his musical family, but who has found no alternative life. He yearns for his father's approval, which he can never gain, least of all now that the father, a victim of two strokes, can no longer speak. Bobby's aimless violence and aggression are presented as the inevitable reaction of the man in the seventies who feels powerless to shape a life in keeping with his feelings. Intellectuality is once again the mark of the frigid, repressed, and ineffectual and must be shunned by any real male. But in the America of the closed frontier, Bobby can do nothing but roam the industrial wasteland, cut off from a vital past and unable to go home again. Catherine (Karen Anspach), his brother's mistress, accuses Bobby of having "no respect for himself, no love of himself," but the film sees this too as inevitable, given the times, and makes no criticism of its energetic hero. We are all, says *Five Easy Pieces*, like little children before our fathers. "I don't know if you'd be particularly interested in hearing anything about me," Bobby begins. Not able to be what his father wanted, a disciplined musician like all the repressed members of his family, Bobby cannot be anything. He breaks down and cries, an anti-hero to whom at this moment we feel close indeed.

Loving (1970) also demonstrated that a film could retain audience identification with its male character by making the women in the film so obnoxious that the anti-hero becomes heroic in spite of himself. However shabby a person husband George Segal may be, an artist who has sold his talent for money, a fool making love to a slovenly neighbor at a suburban party watched by all his friends via closed-circuit TV, he is still the intellectual and moral superior of every woman in the film. He is ironic toward himself, sophisticated and wry, an engaging, witty man for all his moral inadequacy. His wife (Eva Marie Saint) is greedy and a bore, lusting after a new house and wearing eyeglasses to bed. His mistress is unfaithful. He at least remains sensual and conscious of the values he finds so difficult to uphold in a corrupt commercial world. Like Bobby Dupea, he is the only person in his film with quick intelligence and ideas. If he is a failure in a world that allows only capitulation or martyrdom—the world of the seventies—he at least transcends its multiple indignities by knowing better.

The antiquated Gary Cooper myth of the male as silent rescuer was resurrected in *Klute* (1971), with call girl Jane Fonda saved from death at the hands of a maniac by an indomitable superman whose capacity for effective action once again makes language superfluous. Klute (Donald Sutherland) doesn't say much, but he is a marvelous lover ("like a tiger"), a considerable endorsement from so experienced a partner as call girl Bree (Fonda). "You remind me of my uncle," Bree tells Klute. This is no rejection. It flows from the best tradition of the American film where a male doggedly devoted to the quest for justice makes a cliff-hanging, last-minute rescue of the heroine. Klute is sure of himself and knows who he is; he calls the big city life of Bree "pathetic," and the film supports this assessment by putting Bree in constant danger. Klute is just there, coolly loyal and willing even to be domesticated. He might be the Virginian of 1929. And, once again in a seventies film, the hero is a cop. If Bree is shrewd and independent, she is also a whore whose emotional disarray reflects the price of autonomy for women. Despite all, what she really needs is a protective, powerful man. When men are with women in the seventies film, the women surrender all their hard-won gains.

Well into the seventies the male protagonist of films from *The Godfather* (I or II) to *Serpico* uses women solely to discard them. In *Serpico* our hero functions alone, a conventional male stereotype despite the rebellious veneer of his attack on the corruption inherent in police departments of our time. There is only one honest scene. In his hospital bed, having been betrayed and brutalized by fellow cops and finally shot through the face, Pacino as Serpico bursts into tears, overwhelmed by the sense of his utter isolation and loneliness. Any instant when a male in a Hollywood film is permitted to cry uninhibitedly and openly becomes transcendent, given the omnipresent emotional strictures to which men are subjected. But the moment is quickly snatched from us. Serpico remains that old-fashioned loner, if in hippie dress, a superman singlehandedly confronting the corruption of the very universe. Only his failure preserves him as a believable person. The extent to which such superhuman courage is needed to struggle at all deters us from following his example.

Women in the seventies film, when they are more than shadows, have things done to them by men, as when Jack Nicholson furiously slaps the ghoulish Faye Dunaway across the face in *Chinatown* (1974) until she admits to her demeaning "secret": that she bore a child through incest with her father. *Shampoo* (1975) was made solely as a narcissist exercise for Warren Beatty as the white Shaft, a superstud. The pretentious absurdity that the life of this Don Juan, who works as a hairdresser, forms some

Shampoo: Beatty plays the sexual gymnast who, like body builders and weight lifters, calls such attention to his body that it is reasonable to wonder what fuels his need of such display. Compulsive and exhibitionist heterosexuality finally appears to be a mask for the distaste for women.

parallel to the politics of the day, in particular to Nixon's election in 1968, is as fatuous as it is philistine. Nor do the self-serving announcements by the filmmakers that *Shampoo* is really critical of stud Beatty carry any conviction. Beatty plays the sexual gymnast who, like body builders and weight lifters, calls such attention to his body that it is reasonable to wonder what fuels his need of such display. Compulsive and exhibitionist heterosexuality finally appears to be a mask for the distaste for women. The women in *Shampoo* all behave like nymphomaniacs—mothers, daughters, and all the middle-aged clients of Beatty's establishment. Poor irresistible Beatty must answer their incessant calls, a weary bull servicing the insatiable herd. If the women are rendered absurd and forever in heat, the put-upon stud seems not to enjoy sex with them after all. He certainly finds no fulfillment in his compulsive sex, suggesting that women may not be the answer, sexual or otherwise, for this particular hairdresser. The film sympathizes with him by suggesting that no one "understands" him, but this pretext wears thin. Hairdresser Beatty even pretends to be searching, in the barren seventies, for a reason to be alive. When he is abandoned at the end by the woman he finally chooses (Julie Christie), we are meant to care about him as the moral superior of all the women in the film. *Shampoo* is far more hypocritical than *Carnal Knowledge* in its pretense of criticizing the stud hero it actually worships as desirable and appealing.

Women return to films in 1976 in such works as *Fun with Dick and Jane* and *A Star Is Born*, and in 1977 in *New York, New York* and Robert Altman's *Three Women*. The men in these films are far from being the moral or intellectual superiors of the women; in *A Star Is Born, New York, New York*, and *Three Women*, they are cads, incapable of giving solace, affection, or understanding. But none of these three films treats seriously the psychic or moral failure of the men. Rather, they are vehicles for female stars whose worth shines through as they bear their existence in a nihilist world where they must sustain themselves alone. As a variation on films about the superiority of men, these films propose a diametrical opposite: men are so lost, so selfish, and so disturbed that they are ir-redeemable, and women must go it alone in the harsh world of which men's cruelty is the emblem. Hardly, then, do these films revise the male image in film—or propose to men that many of their problems could be solved if they would only admit to themselves that brute force and invulnerability are not synonymous with masculinity.

V

The image of the black male had been, until the late sixties, that of an utterly sexless being, not a man at all. Eye-rolling, bowing, and shuffling train conductors, janitors, shoeshine "boys," and chauffeurs, infinitely obsequious to their white superiors, they were permitted on screen solely in an emasculated form. The black male was a manufactured dummy whose facial gestures, movements, and words were supplied by a white master pulling the strings and creating in his puppet the image he desired. Black men were thus dehumanized on screen.

The stereotype of the black male as a psychopath barely concealing vicious animal lusts had reached the screen in *The Birth of a Nation* (1915). This film's thesis was that under slavery the sexual violence of the black male was held in check. But after the Civil War and with freedom the black man—personified in Griffith's film by the renegade Gus—became an insatiable rapist, his aim in life being to overpower a white woman with his massive size, devouring the white flesh he had craved so long. Gus's rape attempt results in the woman's suicide.

But even more sinister than the pure black was the mulatto, as the film's anger over miscegenation symbolizes its over-all racism. Silas Lynch, a mulatto politician, is also at heart a rapist who covets a woman whom nature itself intended to be out of his reach. These black men with their unbridled sexuality wreak havoc on the community at large, and their lascivious behavior paves the way for the film's justification of the Ku Klux Klan as a necessary instrument of law and order in the chaotic South. As Donald Bogle points out in *Toms, Coons, Mulattoes, Mammies and Bucks* (1973), after the protests and bannings that greeted *The Birth of a Nation* the sensual black male would not reappear on the American screen until 1971 with Melvin Van Peebles's *Sweet Sweetback's Baadasssss Song.*

Since *The Birth of a Nation* was an overwhelming financial success despite the protests, the disappearance of the sensual black "buck" may in fact have been a result of the same racism that produced the image in the first place. For these buck heroes seemed to touch a chord of response in audiences, who were aroused by the very sensuality that the filmmakers feared and tried to condemn by portraying it in as distasteful a manner as possible. To see the black man as a sexual being is also to see him as a human being, transcending the dehumanization that would be his lot in the American film until the sixties and seventies. Thereafter, on screen the black male was emasculated in the hope that audiences, seeing him as something less than human, would not find it difficult to keep him in ghettos and deprive him of employment.

The enslaving image of the black as servant and comic buffoon was sustained through the fifties and early sixties, even in the films of Sidney Poitier, the first major black male star. The Poitier roles still deprived the black male of his sensuality and his body. Were a black male to be presented as an adult sexual being, Hollywood implied by these characterizations, his legendary attributes would at once provide an enticement to miscegenation, so feared was the sexuality of the victim by his oppressors. Even in *The Blackboard Jungle* (1955), a film crackling with violence and sensuality, Poitier played a tamed black who in his loyal decency saved the besieged white teacher. Tied to whites in *Edge of the City* (1957) and *The Defiant Ones* (1958), he was defined by his compliance. His presence was allowed as testimony to the possibility of assimilating blacks to the values of the white society from which they had been so long excluded. In a film as late as *Guess Who's Coming to Dinner?* (1967), Poitier as the groom to a white bride-to-be moves stiffly, a puppet purged of spontaneity and present only to act out the virtues of an integrationist marriage. In this film Poitier is once again the white black, permitted none of the particular elements of black culture, speech, gestures, and consciousness. He is made a doctor, a reminder to blacks, the majority of whom have lacked the opportunity of an undergraduate education, that they too could obtain the spoils of the society if only they would pull themselves up by their own bootstraps and thus join the professions. If it were not for his color, the figure played by Poitier in *Guess Who's Coming to Dinner?* might be perceived as an ordinary, upward-mobile, ambitious professional marrying a rich woman. Far worse of course than these Poitier films, which at least had a black figure at their center, were all those portraits of black men without lives of their own, mere appendages to whites, neoslaves and hence "good niggers," like the role given Woody Strode as John Wayne's faithful servant in *The Man Who Shot Liberty Valance.*

But in the late sixties the image of the black man in the American film began to change. These films appealed to a new black audience aware of black culture and "black power" and defiantly asserting an identity of which they had been taught to be ashamed. This politicized audience could never again acquiesce in the bleached-out image of the black perpetuated by Poitier. However, this figure was replaced by another white projection, the black stud. Not merely ungrateful to whites, he was violent and sadistic, an image projected by ex-football player Jim Brown, restoring to the black man on screen his sexual prowess. But this very assertiveness was made to seem as brutal, sexist, and insensitive as the worst excesses of sexist white males.

If black children are now permitted black heroes instead of white, most of these black supermales are sufficiently unreal that they do not finally inspire emulation of their superhuman feats. Their sadistic violence parallels that of Clint Eastwood as Josey Wales, who slaughters so many men under such incredible odds that his image remains on the level of fantasy. Often the black superman is safely returned to a slave context for the same reason, as in *Mandingo* (1975) or *Drum* (1976), implying that only the condition of slavery itself justifies the violence. Or he achieves the impossible, like the cocaine dealer of *Superfly*, who grows rich and quits, but not before accomplishing those sexual feats which pander to white myths of the stamina and virility of the black male. The old notion of the oversexed black, the ever-potential rapist, is now only slightly disguised in the image of the stud superblack. Yet even this viciously racist stereotype seems preferable to those continuing portraits of the black male as a person upon whom torture is heaped and who, like the husband played by Paul Winfield in *Sounder* (1972), suffers and endures in the manner of Faulkner's Dilsey. With the exception of a solitary brilliant characterization, that of the garbage man played by James Earl Jones in the black, independently produced *Claudine* (1974), the black male as a whole person has been thoroughly absent from the screen. Jones gave a powerful performance in *The Great White Hope* (1970), which chronicled the persecution of heavyweight champion Jack Johnson. But Johnson's cruelty to his devoted white wife, if explained by the terrible punishment he endured, still left black male sexuality only thinly removed from the stereotype.

Claudine must be contrasted with both *Shaft* and Melvin Van Peebles's *Sweet Sweetback's Baadasssss Song* (1971) for the black image they project. It is true that the heroes of *Shaft, Superfly,* and *Sweetback* are no longer the subordinates of whites nor feel inferior, yet they all remain content with the values of a culture that still reduces blacks to weakness and immobility. Shaft and Superfly, in particular, are selfish men, out for themselves without much regard for their fellow blacks. Each of these three films demonstrates inadvertently that to project an image of a strong black male requires more than transcending Stepin Fetchit; it is no longer enough not to be harmless.

Director Gordon Parks argues that *Shaft* offers a positive image of the black male because his hero is "free of racial torment." Previously, black characters contrived their identities in terms of acceptance by whites, whereas Shaft is a black man who belongs to himself. Parks has said that he even altered the original story to give Shaft a black rather than a white woman, in keeping with his black identity. But this misses the point. For the victim to emulate his oppressor is hardly liberating, for it merely strengthens the values that permitted blacks to be enslaved in the first place. If black counterparts of white oppressors are glorified on screen, all that this reveals is that white values have been assimilated in a different way. Before, they were internalized, and blacks felt like "niggers." Here also they are internalized, because blacks are shown as wanting to be like James Bond.

Finally Shaft, in his leather jacket worn open despite the cold, is little more than what the white commercial backers of the film had wanted all along: the black supermale. If Shaft is a positive figure, as some have argued, it is in the Bond manner, an anachronism ten years after the height of the Bond rage. The Shaft films are weakened because they appear in the seventies, at a time when film has recognized that the enemies of the hero are no longer individuals he can track down and knock out with bare fists. A Bond of the seventies would have to resemble Jack Nicholson's Giddis of *Chinatown*, a private eye facing a conglomerate enemy, huge power forces which he cannot see and which do what they will through government channels and with official sanction. Shaft's antics against the Mafia seem pathetically incredible in the seventies and finally rob him of the very supermale identity nominally conceded to the black man. He is given a false strength, since it is granted at a time when the audience knows that such strength is insufficient. He is awarded the male prowess hitherto considered a white prerogative, but placed in a setting where the audience knows it is irrelevant.

The same insidious undermining of the black hero occurs with respect to Shaft as a sex machine. White male values—that sex confers power, and brutality toward women is masculine—are offered as an aspect of a black

Richard Roundtree as Shaft: It is as if Stepin Fetchit were given the chance to be "Massa" himself, retaining the values of domination and submission, of master and slave. Throughout, Shaft remains little more than a black man's Bogart, less assured if more violent.

experience of which it may not have been a historical part. It is as if Stepin Fetchit were given the chance to be "Massa" himself, retaining the values of domination and submission, of master and slave, by grafting them onto black experience.

Throughout Shaft remains little more than a black man's Bogart, less assured if more violent. If his woman is black, she is also light-skinned, as *Shaft* reaffirms, this time with a black director, the notion that the attractive black woman is she who is closest to being white. And despite the sincerity of its black militants, *Shaft* sees revolution for the blacks as merely a vendetta against "whitey" rather than as a revolt against a dehumanizing society that inflicts unemployment on whites as well as blacks. Meanwhile, in his sexist virtuosity Shaft functions as a pacifier of black pride. The militants in *Shaft* are really advocates of black racism, and in this sense the film presents a justification for further repression of blacks by white society through the suggestion that black discontent is itself fundamentally racist and vengeful in motive, rather than based upon the urgent need to better the lives of the poor. *Shaft* recedes into its many fantasies: of white women lusting after the supercool Shaft, of Shaft as James Bond. Shaft does indeed win, taking on the entire Mafia with the aid of a handful of militants and the white police in an "integration" of forces. He is slick, clever, and physically strong. These paltry elements alone account for the success of the film among young blacks still anxious for a brief, vicarious release from their own frustration.

Melvin Van Peebles has asserted that his *Sweet Sweetback's Baadasssss Song* is "revolutionary." But when we examine this story of a black stud on the run after murdering two white detectives to avenge their killing of a brother, we find but another version of the same stereotype. At least Sweetback, more realistically, is a renegade, an enemy of the society that has brought his people so much pain. But as a man he is nothing more than an embodiment of how white society has fantasized black sexuality.

Sweetback is the "buck nigger" of inexhaustible sexual powers, with whose graphic sexuality blacks and whites in the audience can identify. In one scene he performs sexually to a white nightclub audience. Even before the credits we observe Sweetback as a child, working as an errand boy in a house of prostitution where he becomes adept at "humping." The remainder of the film has him improving on his style. On the run as he is, Sweetback is always capable of energetic sex. Frequently he is helped, fed, and nurtured by women, in another stereotype of black life.

Sweetback's survival through escape to Mexico is accomplished on his own, entirely through personal physical superiority to his enemies. His acrobatics anticipate those of Shaft. Each poses as a superman, yet each bespeaks an essential impotence of the black male precisely because his powers are clearly inaccessible to the ordinary man watching these films. One of the closing titles, after Sweetback has made it to Mexico, is "A baadasssss nigger is coming back to collect some dues," a promise as dubious as Sweetback's original solo escape was fantastic. The other blacks in the film are largely isolated, fearful, and vulnerable to violence. An ironic motif, a neon sign flashing "Jesus Saves," suggests their plight. The hero is superimposed on an environment that exudes hopelessness. All meaning dissolves until we are left with those titillating images of sexual orgies staged for slumming whites in which Sweetback re-earns the right to his name.

In contrast is the black male as human being of Third World Cinema Production's *Claudine*. Unlike Shaft's girlfriend, Claudine's man, Roop, (James Earl Jones) is dark-skinned, the black male as a black. He is no rich private eye like Shaft, no slick cocaine dealer like Superfly, no pimp, but rather a good-natured garbage collector. Yet he is as virile as any of these; he is no Sidney Poitier either. His life is dictated, not by James Bond fantasies, but by his own experience. The film was not made in Hollywood, and Hollywood's values are not superimposed upon James Earl Jones's skin.

Roop's muscles may be enormous, but he remains a garbage man, a credible occupation for a member of the black oppressed. He shares the vitality of the ghetto in his enthusiasm for Claudine (Diahann Carroll), but she is a maid on welfare, not the owner of a flashy boutique like the woman in *Shaft*. In nonworking hours Roop dresses elegantly and drives a convertible, defenses to shield him against his pain, of which the film is thoroughly conscious. No mindless darky of Stepin Fetchit days, yet not a man who controls his own destiny either, Roop likes—when he can afford them—chateaubriand and clams casino. He is a good lover, but no superstud. And as a divorced man with a low-paying job, he is being bled dry by child-support payments. Logically, he shuns remarriage, although he is a kindly surrogate father to Claudine's six children. Claudine accuses him of evading responsibility when she states, refreshingly, "You men have some crazy ideas about being a man," but in his case she is not entirely justified. Roop finally agrees to marry her, although he is besieged by debts, having been as a result accused of "willful neglect" for nonsupport of his own children; his salary has been attached. It is at once an acknowledgment of black male abandonment of families and a powerful account of what is responsible for it.

Faced by such insurmountable problems, Roop bursts into tears of frustration, his mouth open and full of scrambled eggs. He is man enough to reveal feelings of weakness and to cry in the face of a condition he has no means of changing. Crying does not make him any less a man nor any less desirable to a woman. *This* is perhaps the most emancipated view of a genuine black man we have had in film. One must, says *Claudine*, be a man true to the conditions of one's own life. In the ghetto as a garbage collector, one cannot be Shaft. One of Claudine's sons, aged eighteen, has a vasectomy because, as he acutely puts it, "manhood does not reside between your legs."

Many such insights emerge from this film. Roop laments that it takes a lot of money to be a daddy. One of Claudine's younger children writes to him, "I don't eat much." Roop is needed despite his lack of wealth and success, which, like crying or sexual prowess, have nothing to do with being a man. Roop can be a father without providing all the luxuries Spencer Tracy bestowed upon Elizabeth Taylor in *Father of the Bride* or those promised by Claudette Colbert's father in *It Happened One Night*. *Claudine* is a film of much honesty, with a portrait of a black man who is beautiful because he is real.

VI

Some films with alternative male images have managed to appear during the seventies. They recognize that to urge men to emulate Cooper, Brando, or Eastwood abets them in nothing so much as self-hatred for their failure sufficiently to conceal and repress weakness and vulnerability. Woody Allen's comedies about the puny neurotic male in glasses attempting to be a man in a culture glorifying John Wayne and Humphrey Bogart have honest moments despite Allen's failure to transcend the values of Wayne. He is the small man who, protestations and irony aside, aspires to be six feet tall and strong. Allen's films always culminate in a fantasy whereby the physically insignificant male becomes Brando or Bogart by accepting himself. But the nature of this acceptance is that it is not of the self but of the extent to which the slight male can still emulate more powerful men. Rather than recognize the damage done to males who cannot live up to destructive and impossible ideals, the Allen films, including *The Front* (1976), insist that the little guy *can* get the most beautiful women too if he learns to feel macho despite his size.

Play It Again, Sam (1972) is Allen's most direct treatment of what it means to be a man in a society glorifying the indomitable male. It poses the issue of how a small, rather unattractive male—by Hollywood's arbitrary standard—can even approach a woman in a culture where the romantic ideal assimilated through movies is Bogart's Rick of *Casablanca*. Yet *Play It Again, Sam*, far from reassessing Bogart's style of manliness, actually insists that a Woody Allen can do what Bogart did, if with his tutoring, and win the woman of his dreams before, in the heroic manner of *Casablanca*, sacrificing their love to a higher ideal. He can be Bogart, the man of his dreams, and duplicate the scene at the end of *Casablanca* in which Bogart says goodbye forever to Ingrid Bergman only to begin his "beautiful friendship" with Claude Rains.

If *Play It Again, Sam* demonstrates hilariously how the romantic notions of love and the sense of male identity derived from Hollywood are more real to us than the humdrum of our own lives and make our existence intolerable. He achieves this by re-enacting the airport scene in his own circumstances, as Allen further idealizes the old masculine mystique. *Play It Again, Sam* never rejects or betrays any irony toward the image of the suave, stoical, confident Bogart.

What is marvelous about *Play It Again, Sam* is its open acknowledgment that most men are secretly tortured by not being Bogart. If the film does not quite admit the harm engendered, it still shows how devastating the image has been. Men have been drilled in this culture to believe that one must be as self-assured as the hero of *Casablanca*. "Who am I kidding," mourns film buff Alan (Woody Allen) after yet one more screening of *Casablanca*, a film to which he is addicted. "I'm not like that and I never will be." Depressed, divorced, and a movie critic, hence even more a victim of Hollywood's values than most men, after watching the Bogart film once again he is overwhelmed by a sense of his own worthlessness. For the first time in American movies, Hollywood admits on screen to the psychological damage and suffering it has caused the American male in imposing so unreal a definition of masculinity.

Lonely and rejected, tormented by memories of a wife who told him he did nothing for her sexually, Alan is visited by the ghost of Humphrey Bogart. He provides Alan with advice on how *he* did it. "Women need a slap . . . all you gotta do is whistle," says Bogart, the latter line ironically having belonged to Bacall and not to him. In struggling to profit from this tutoring by Bogart himself, Alan is a flop. If the laughs mount at his expense, the film itself fails to notice the incongruity of an ugly little man who always wants women who fulfill Hollywood's ideal for their sex. His demands on women are the precise counterpart to his own dilemma and equally the result of the Bogart façade. His obsession with his own physical ordinariness does not lead Alan to the insight that, just as he would rather women did not judge him by the physical proportions of John Wayne, so he should not value them according to whether they look like Rita Hayworth or Raquel Welsh. This double standard is engrained in Alan, and he never questions it, for to do so would conflict with the film's acceptance of the Bogart mystique and its formula that if one is simply oneself, the ways of Bogart will become accessible, allowing success with women—beautiful ones only, of course. "Bogie is the perfect image," says Alan. "Who should I pick, my rabbi?" One of his anxieties is called "homosexual panic," a trepidation that could only be acknowledged in a non-buddy film.

Only with Linda (Diane Keaton), the wife of his best friend, can Alan be himself, if mainly because she seems inaccessible to him. The beautiful Linda responds by liking him for himself. They make love successfully,

Woody Allen with Diane Keaton in *Play It Again, Sam:* "Bogie is the perfect image. Who should I pick, my rabbi?"

the beast winning his beauty as in the fairy tale. Her husband has neglected her—a trite convenience. The significance of Alan's ability to make it only with the wife of his best friend goes unnoticed as the film fails to explore the vicarious relation between the men implicit in their sharing the same woman. It is aware, however, that the businessman male, the "strong" male by conventional standards, often does not bother with women at all.

That Alan becomes a good lover after all, "incredible" in bed, belongs to the Hollywood tradition of assuaging anxiety through identification with a fantasy come true. Alan gets the girl by being himself and not a "phony." He will now imitate Bogart in life by giving her back to her shallow husband who needs her more, as Victor Lazlo in *Casablanca* required Ilsa to accompany him to America.

"Everybody is Bogart at certain times," says *Play It Again, Sam* in what amounts to a ploy to get Hollywood off the hook. Such a statement suggests that even *Casablanca* did not demand that we be like Bogart all the time. "He did a right thing for a pal, there are other things besides dames in life," says the ghost of Bogart. And thus even *Play It Again, Sam*, despite its emphasis on heterosexual love, proves to be, like *Casablanca* in its closing moments, something of a buddy film. The real relationship has been between Bogart and Alan, with the older, experienced masculine male again initiating the awkward novice. The Woody Allen film insists finally that life can be as Hollywood has painted it. Alan is thus paid the tribute of the master himself: "That was great!" Only then does he gain enough confidence to joke at Bogart's expense: "The secret is not being you. It's being me. I'm short enough and ugly enough to succeed on my own." Bogart, after all, was not a handsome man. Style is more within our reach than conventional good looks. The erotic energy, caring, and love are all of Alan for Bogart, and through the fantasy, of Bogart himself for the hapless Alan, to whom, at the end of *Play It Again, Sam*, Bogart even directs the classic line once addressed to Ingrid Bergman: "Here's looking at you, kid!"

In *Buffalo Bill and the Indians*, his demolition of the myth of Buffalo Bill Cody, director Robert Altman deflates his sexuality as well. That paradigm male of American frontier mythology is exposed here, in the person of Paul Newman, as a self-centered, arrogant rooster with a penchant for Italian opera singers. Buffalo Bill fails to lure one such singer to his bedroom because she has found a male with more status than he —a general, and hence, because he is more powerful, a man of presumably greater sexuality. Myths of power have long been used by men to grant them an aura of sexual prowess, and Altman brilliantly refers this to our very creation of both the Buffalo Bill and the Paul Newman legends.

Cody is a poseur who conceals his grey hair beneath a blond wig, a greedy lout at the service of the highest bidder. The very barbarism of such men, like the genocide they enacted on the Indians, required the romantic lie, the male myth which so imprisons us that it impairs our ability to transcend this history. The accouterments of the "star" are used by men who fear that if seen as themselves, they will appear wholly inadequate, both personally and sexually. The subtlety of his insight, and the radical daring of his relating it to the past and present of American culture, place Altman's treatment of male sexuality in an entirely different category from the frivolous ambivalence of Woody Allen's farce with its adolescent notion that by "being oneself" one can become Humphrey Bogart. Altman reveals that the very elevation of the Buffalo Bills and of movie stars like Paul Newman, the creation of these legends of inexhaustible male prowess, has caused men to fear and deny their own sexuality. Men have finally been both denigrated and emasculated by the substitution screen experiences for real ones. Such myths—whether of a Buffalo Bill or a Newman—would disappear if we refused any longer to endorse the lie. If *Play It Again, Sam* had been a true alternative to the glorification in film of rampant male sexuality, it would have demythologized the Bogart mystique and deflated his image in the very manner in which Altman deflates not merely Buffalo Bill Cody but actor Paul Newman, who in playing a performer and star is also playing himself.

Cody, we are shown, is not merely incompetent but morally corrupt. His heroism is reduced to attempts to shoot his opera singer's canary. Time after time he misses, like his efforts at erection the night before, until the murder is consummated at last, a cruel act and an obvious attempt to exorcise the self-hatred brought on by impotence. This great male hero fawns upon authority and power in the person of a rotund, morally degenerate President Grover Cleveland, who refuses to allow Sitting Bull even to finish a sentence. Before he hears Sitting Bull's request, Cleveland intones, "It's out of the question." Only a fool like Cody could appreciate such unspeakable injustice; he compliments Cleveland for knowing how to retaliate "before it's his turn." The "stars" curry favor with those in power as they too use coercion to conceal their fraudulence. For what is Buffalo Bill but the creation of a down-and-out entrepreneur (Burt Lancaster), who through promotion of an entirely fabricated image made him a star? Beneath his paint and curly blond wig, Cody is a vainglorious tyrant who hates no one quite so much as the man who made him what he is. He refuses Lancaster even a handout, unable to bear the presence of a man who knew him when. Up to the last scene of *The Shootist,* John Wayne at sixty-nine is permitted to retain his toupée, to maintain his image. Mercilessly, Altman portrays a frantic Newman-Cody, hysterical when someone enters his tent at night before he has a chance to arrange that blond wig over his straggly grey hair.

In contrast to the callow, fake Buffalo Bill Cody, Altman offers the sweetness of Sitting Bull, a true and authentic male who "dreams out loud." Sitting Bull and his interpreter Halsey (Will Sampson in a brilliant performance) marry maleness and morality until the last sequence, when, after the death of Sitting Bull, Halsey suffers the horrendous fate of being reduced to performing in Buffalo Bill's circus. Altman was aware that he could not explore the deceit of his stars unless he also demonstrated what genuine males are like, men who see through the lies of people like Cody. In one sequence Buffalo Bill actually does battle with the ghost of Sitting Bull. The ghost is much younger than the old Indian had been, and Cody, superficial to the end, scoffs at his appearance: "You ain't even the right image." All is show, appearance and surface, beneath which the star is without inner substance. Cody's taunt to the ghost reveals that, notwithstanding his stupidity, he is aware that in a white supremacist society his legend will be sustained, no matter what he really is: "In a hundred years I'll still be Buffalo Bill—Star," he brags, "and you'll still be the Indian." If Altman's film failed commercially, inspiring its producer Dino de Laurentiis to repudiate it, the mood of resigned despair with which the film challenges the mythmaking lies churned out by Hollywood is fully warranted. *Buffalo Bill and the Indians* unveils all the shabby legends and the distortion of our actual history which the American film has perpetuated to foster its unwholesome definitions of masculinity.

An even more brilliant repudiation of Hollywood's conception of male identity came in *Dog Day Afternoon* (1975), a film which shatters the artificial sexual standard imposed upon men throughout the history of the American film. *Dog Day Afternoon* sweeps aside the prejudice that homosexual men are unmasculine and vile. Bank robber Sonny (Al Pacino), the film's protagonist, proves to be both bisexual and a capable, cogent male in every respect. In one of the only times on screen—the British film *Sunday, Bloody Sunday* was another exception—the homosexual male is presented as both manly and morally sympathetic. Moreover Sonny is allowed to be real. He is often confused, he admits to weakness, and he feels pain; at moments he is desperate. In short, he is a complex human being for whom the John Wayne mystique has neither relevance, value, nor appeal. Sonny is a Vietnam veteran, a person who has killed, yet he makes no association between asserting himself aggressively against others and being masculine. "I'm a Catholic, and I don't want to hurt anyone," he assures the hostages he holds as he robs a bank in order to finance a sex-change operation for his male wife, Leon.

It is a measure of Sonny's sweet humanity that the hostages themselves begin to root for him. Nor does director Sidney Lumet ridicule the formal open marriage ceremony, complete with male bridesmaids and the attendance of his mother, arranged by Sonny for himself and Leon. Sonny's extraordinary courage, robbing a bank apart, is that of a male too manly to deny his sexuality because it is scorned in the world. Whatever his weaknesses—and the film is careful not to present him without them

—he has accepted himself as he is without hesitation, something Woody Allen can never do in his films.

Unlike that collection in *The Boys in the Band,* Sonny is no freak. Nor is he the homosexual as victim, like the aging hustler beaten to a pulp by Jon Voigt at the close of *Midnight Cowboy.* A virile man who married and has children, Sonny has chosen to be homosexual. His preference for Leon enhances his character because it involves courage and moral choice. Sonny is noble under duress, for the pressures of his jobless existence have made him feel continually on the verge of death. Yet he has had the strength of character to accept his feelings for another man. In this image *Dog Day Afternoon,* a highly underrated film, achieves a significant breakthrough for the male image on screen.

The characterization of Sonny's bank robbery, based on a real-life episode, excludes the option of the male as superhero. The entire event proceeds without a plan, guided only by Sonny's improvisatory street-smartness. When a cop asks his name, he gives it. When he asserts, "We're Vietnam veterans, so killing doesn't mean anything to us," it is apparent to all that this is sheer bravado. Because he is an amateur, the crowd is with him, particularly when he responds to their own sense of victimization in the mid-seventies by crying out "Attica! Attica!" Unlike that of Little Caesar and his imitators, Sonny's sexuality remains independent of his "criminality." Sonny is simply a man who in the depression of the seventies could get neither a union card nor a job and is now outnumbered by a hoard of cops and FBI agents while the press watches in glee. "They're going to spill our brains out . . . instead of *As the World Turns,*" exclaims Sonny as he watches the event on the bank's TV set.

Sonny is a hero, a worthwhile man, if only because of his humanity. He checks out the air conditioner because one of the hostages is suffering from asthma, and he pays for the pizza he has ordered delivered for these hostages. Leon himself testifies to Sonny's being "a wonderful father . . . a wonderful son" who pays his parents' rent. "So how are you?" Leon asks Sonny over the police telephone. "I don't know, Leon, I'm dying," is Sonny's reply. Leon, the weaker, the stereotypic homosexual too pathetic to stand up to the police, replies, "You're killing the people around you." Leon's cowardice is a measure of Sonny's courage, just as Sitting Bull's dignity commented upon Buffalo Bill's moral paltriness in Altman's film.

The entire telephone scene, a lovers' quarrel in which Sonny goes unappreciated by this boy for whom he is risking all, is moving and sad. It is Sonny who cares deeply and who can't hang up the phone. He makes up a will in which he writes, "To my darling wife Leon, more than any man has loved another man in all eternity." Lumet restrains his direction at this point so that neither hostages nor audience dare snicker. There is no exploitation of the relationship by a prurient camera; a projected scene in which Sonny and Leon were to have been shown in bed together does not appear in the final cut of the film. Only some hostile camera angles of gay demonstrators crying "Out of the closet, into the street!" depict homosexuals as coarse and repulsive. But this adds only a fleeting dishonest moment to director Lumet's otherwise sympathetic and straightforward portrayal.

"I'm me and I'm different," Sonny had written. He requests the military funeral to which he is entitled as a veteran. At the end he is betrayed, having foolishly believed that he would be allowed a plane for escape. It is out of naïveté and innocence that he asks his partner, Sal, to show their "good faith" by putting down his gun. In a split second the FBI agent, until then covered by Sal, shoots him at point-blank range. Sonny is reduced to asking somberly, "Don't shoot me." His eyes move in his head as his rights are read out loud. When Sal's body is carried by, Sonny closes his eyes and cries. There is no indication, however, that his defeat by hostile authority is in any way a punishment for his being homosexual.

Hollywood has always remained recalcitrant to change, as its adamant refusal to alter in the slightest the deformed image of women in film amply illustrates. Independent productions cannot do this job because the distribution system is so tightly controlled by an interlocked handful. Thus, small independent films cannot be offered as evidence that the damaging distortion of sexuality in film is changing. One small study, however, is worthy of mention because it so directly attacks the issue of male identity and the masculine role in our society. *Men's Lives* (1975), by Josh Hanig and Will Roberts, is a documentary film which explores masculinity in America by tracing the male growing-up process from boy scout camp to factory. "I'm not going to work ten or twelve hours and come home and scrub floors," asserts a male factory worker, arguing that women should remain at home. But the consciousness of the young male filmmakers themselves offers the hope of change.

The narrator asks, "What choices are open to men growing up in America?" and undertakes to "re-examine the roots of our masculinity." The images to which we are introduced and which shape our sense of self from earliest childhood are delineated. A female teacher, internalizing these values, asserts that she expects more of boys than of girls. The film confronts us with a collage of those images most potent and formative for boys growing up in America fixated on male priority and prowess: Superman of the comic strip, Walt Frazier the basketball superstar, a growling Broderick Crawford bragging in a Western about who is fastest on the draw, Charles Atlas no longer a ninety-eight-pound weakling, and finally, John Wayne in a war film.

Any film honest about challenging the traditional male role must propose alternative images of masculinity. In *Men's Lives* we visit a ballet class in which a boy and a girl practice the same steps. They are equally graceful. The boy, about sixteen, admits that his friends call him a "sissy," and that even his parents are embarrassed by his dancing. The boy insists that a man is someone who stands up for what he thinks is right, regardless of what other people think. He has been accused of homosexuality because he is not physically large and does not play football, the continuing group standard for manhood in this culture.

The old stereotypes are with us in full force. A high school football player exclaims, "I like to kill. I like to kill opponents," echoing a conditioning order in army basic training. The film makes it clear that such impulses flow from the learning process and not from any aggressive instinct implanted in the male genes, as Lionel Tiger and Robert Ardrey would have us believe. One boy discloses that his car makes him feel nice and girls "think it gives you strength to handle a car like that." Sexual repression produces such projection and surrogate sexual gratification. A male teacher pompously asserts that those boys who are not enraged when they lose will be failures in life; and we perceive the origin of the football player's pleasure in physical combat. A boy confides that there are two kinds of girls, one's steady girlfriend and the quick pickup, as if he had formed his conceptions straight out of films like *My Darling Clementine*, which enshrines with rigid insistence the double standard and the dichotomy between "good," or passively dependent, and "bad," or autonomous and sexually free, women.

Men's Lives, in its mélange of *cinéma vérité* interviews with boys and men, recapitulates the history of the American film. Each dreadful cliche, from "without competition, there's nothing" to "a man needs to be in control," has been celebrated as a truth in decades of the popular arts from film and pulp novel to comic strip and television. All the while, filmmakers Hanig and Roberts discover that most men in our society see themselves as inadequate, not as supermen but as failures because supermen are the standard. The image of the invulnerable male perpetuates itself. It provides men with an outlet in fantasy through which they can feel briefly masculine, but as with a heroin high, when the narcotic of vicarious living and its exhilaration recede, the reality is all the more demoralizing. Thus even the masculine mystique perpetuates the sense of men's own unworthiness by its impossibility, requiring ever more intense fantasies of indomitable strength. Real-life men in this film lament that they can never allow other men to know them well for fear of appearing vulnerable. Hollywood in the seventies, responding to this crisis in the culture, consoles men with buddy films which aim to diminish real-life male anxieties, for by watching Newman and Redford men may vicariously feel close to other males without actually having to open up and expose weakness. The desire to have close male friends, thwarted in a culture that paranoically sees homosexuality everywhere, and as a diminution of one's humanity, is satisfied on screen only in asexual buddy relationships, increasing the alienation of the men in the audience from their own feelings. It is the very repression of the need for close male friends which magnifies that desire to the point that it does indeed approach homosexual longing.

Men's Lives suggests that so long as aggressiveness and competitiveness rule the economic life of our society, men will have to cultivate these tendencies in order to survive in it. And there is a backlash in Hollywood against the new male consciousness just as there is against the women's movement. *One on One* (1977) glorifies a young athlete who wins a liberated woman and puts down her obnoxious intellectual boyfriend, a psychology professor who relates athletics to the military and to male mindlessness. The films of the seventies, more than those of any preceding decade, demand an equation of masculinity with dominance, products as they are of those conglomerates like Gulf & Western and RCA which control the film industry in America. Dirty Harry, the belligerent John Wayne, the male as hunter in *Jeremiah Johnson* (1972), and the male as hunter of dissidents, like Bronson in *Death Wish* and Harry himself, all express their values. These vigilantes of male supremacy still rule the screen, their violence a threat to all our liberties in their ever more explicit attempt to purge our society of those who even articulate the need for change.

But it remains true that the more strident and hysterical the propaganda for this degenerate male ideal becomes, the more those .44 Magnums flash in the night as if they were the ultimate male organ, the more this definition of masculinity will be undermined, exposed as being unhinged. In the culture at large people have become wary of official deception, weary of social decay. Humane styles of masculinity are increasingly sought by young men. A growing movement of men's liberation is learning from the experience of the women's movement and identifying at last its own suffering, the real-life male's psychic burden in America. Their ideas and aspirations are surfacing in small independent films like *Men's Lives* and in major productions like *Dog Day Afternoon* and *Buffalo Bill and the Indians*. Each time we view in an American film the healing tears of a vulnerable male hero, from James Dean in *East of Eden* to even—in spite of his caustic macho self—Jack Nicholson in *Five Easy Pieces*, and are offered warm, loving, and powerful men like James Earl Jones in *Claudine* and Al Pacino in *Dog Day Afternoon*, one more blow has been struck on behalf of a civilized male image on screen. Such images prepare for that day of the liberation of men from the distorting and cruel masculine mystique in the name of which our movies, no less than our culture, have been demeaned.

INDEX

abortion, 72, 194–5
Across the Pacific, 145–6
Action in the North Atlantic, 142
action vs. thought, 5, 7, 9, 13–14;
   in counterculture era, 269;
   in Eastwood films, 268; in
   Virginian, 74. *See also*
   intellectualism
Adams, Nick, 273
Adam's Rib, 171–3, 191
Additional Dialogue (Trumbo), 190 *n*.,
   209
Admirable Crichton, The (Barrie), 32
Adventurer, The, 113
Adventures of Robin Hood, The, 65,
   124–5
African Queen, The, 15, 318; male
   image in, 161, 196; plot, 196–9
Agar, John, 182–3
aggressiveness, 71, 73, 75, 167; in
   Detective Story, 193–4; diminished
   in 30's, 98. *See also*
   competitiveness
Agnew, Spiro, 308
alienation, 190, 317, 344; in *Easy
   Rider*, 280–1; in *Graduate*, 275–8;
   in *Joe*, 283; of working men,
   25–6; of youth in 60's, 268–9
All Quiet on the Western Front, 92–4
All the President's Men, 12, 324
Allen, Woody, 336–40; cf. Sonny in
   Dog Day Afternoon, 342
Allnut, Charlie (character in *African
   Queen*), 196–9

Alpert, Jane, 269, 275
Altman, Robert, 250, 329; and male
   sexuality in *Buffalo Bill*, 41, 289,
   339–42; and *Mash* heroes, 313
American culture and society: and
   Bogart model, 337; competition
   and success, 25–6; conformity of
   50's, 186–8, 190, 192–3, 202, 226;
   during Depression, 72–3, 76,
   130–1; helplessness of average
   person, 11, 26; and homosexuality,
   312, 318; hostility to women, 20,
   87, 311, 315; masculine ideal, 7,
   217, 285, 311–12, 343–5; postwar,
   140, 155, 159, 164–6, 169;
   puritanism, 195; racism, 40, 261,
   334; in 60's, 246, 248–51, 258; and
   sports, 163–7; in 30's, 96–8, 100,
   117; in 20's, 27–8, 41, 45, 55–6;
   and Vietnam, 268–9; Wayne
   model, 260, 285. *See also*
   audiences; blacks; counterculture;
   frontier theme
"Americanism," 98–100, 104, 137,
   162–3
Anderson, Broncho Billy, 223
Anderson, Lindsay, 224
Andrews, Dana, 174
Anger, Kenneth, 281
Anglo-Saxon race, 9, 143; and film
   stars, 4
Ann-Margret, 317
Anspach, Karen, 326
anti-hero theme, 23, 326

About the Author

Joan Mellen is Professor of English at Temple University, where she teaches courses on American and Japanese film. She is the author of *The Waves at Genji's Door: Japan Through Its Cinema, Marilyn Monroe, Women and Their Sexuality in the New Film, A Film Guide to "The Battle of Algiers,"* and *Voices from the Japanese Cinema.*